ESSAYS ON
TWENTIETH-CENTURY
HISTORY

IN THE SERIES *Critical Perspectives on the Past,*

EDITED BY
SUSAN PORTER BENSON, STEPHEN BRIER, AND ROY ROSENZWEIG

ALSO IN THIS SERIES:

ESSAYS ON TWENTIETH-CENTURY HISTORY

Edited by MICHAEL ADAS

for the American Historical Association

TEMPLE UNIVERSITY PRESS
PHILADELPHIA

Temple University Press
1601 North Broad Street
Philadelphia, Pennsylvania 19122
www.temple.edu/tempress

Library of Congress Cataloging-in-Publication Data

Essays on twentieth century history / edited by Michael Adas for the American
Historical Association.
    p. cm.—(Critical perspectives on the past)
  Includes bibliographical references.
  ISBN 978-1-4399-0269-1 (cloth : alk. paper)—ISBN 978-1-4399-0270-7 (paper : alk.
paper)—ISBN 978-1-4399-0271-4 (electronic) 1. History, Modern—20th century.
2. Twentieth century. 3. Social history—20th century. 4. World politics—20th century.
I. Adas, Michael, 1943– II. American Historical Association.
  D421.E77 2010
  909.82—dc22
                                             2009052961

Printed in the United States of America

2 4 6 8 9 7 5 3 1

CONTENTS

INTRODUCTION

MICHAEL ADAS

By any of the customary measures we deploy to demarcate historical epochs, the twentieth century does not appear to be a very coherent unit. The beginnings and ends of what we choose to call centuries are almost invariably years of little significance. But there is little agreement over when the twentieth century C.E. arrived, and there were several points both before the year 2000 (the collapse of the Soviet Union, the reunification of Germany, the surge of globalization from the mid-1990s) and afterward (9/11, or the global recession of 2008) when one could quite plausibly argue that a new era had begun. A compelling case can be made for viewing the decades of the global scramble for colonies after 1870 as a predictable culmination of the long nineteenth century, which was ushered in by the industrial and political revolutions of the late 1700s. But at the same time, without serious attention to the processes and misguided policies that led to decades of agrarian and industrial depression from the late 1860s to the 1890s, as well as the social tensions and political rivalries that generated and were in turn fed by imperialist expansionism, one cannot begin to comprehend the causes and consequences of the Great War that began in 1914. That conflict determined the contours of the twentieth century in myriad ways. On the one hand, the war set in motion transformative processes that were clearly major departures from those that defined the nineteenth-century world order. On the other, it perversely unleashed forces that would undermine Western world dominance and greatly constrict the forces advancing globalization, both of which can be seen as hallmarks of the opening decades of the twentieth century. This intermingling of the forces and processes that were arguably essential components of two epochs we routinely set apart as centuries suggests the need for flexibility in demarcating phases of world history, and for determining beginnings and endings that accord with major shifts in political and socioeconomic circumstances and dynamics rather than standard but arbitrary chronological break points.

In the decades that followed the Great War, the victorious European powers appeared to have restored, even expanded, their global political and economic preeminence only to see it eclipsed by the emergence of the Soviet and U.S. superpowers on their periphery and a second round of even more devastating global conflict. The bifurcated international system that resulted from the cold war standoff extended the retreat of globalization, but nurtured the liberation of most of humanity from colonial rule. The collapse of the Soviet empire, and the freeing of its satellite states across Eastern Europe beginning in the late 1980s, marked another major watershed that further problematizes uncritical acceptance of the historical coherence of the chronological twentieth century. And the reunification of Germany and the reemergence of international terrorism, which were powerfully symptomatic of the unprecedented reach and intensity of the processes of globalization on either side of the otherwise unremarkable last and first years of the old and new millennia, represented both a return to trends reminiscent of the opening decades of the twentieth century and a major break from the prevailing dynamics of the cold war.

In addition to the problems posed for conceptualizing the twentieth century as a discrete era of world history due to overlap with the preceding period and disconcertingly radical shifts in the course of global development in the 1900s, contradictory forces and trends, which perhaps more than any other attribute distinguish this turbulent phase of the human experience, render it impervious to generalized pronouncements and difficult to conceptualize broadly. As the essays in this collection document in detail, paradox pervades the time span we call the twentieth century, no matter how it is temporally delineated. Never before in history, for example, had so many humans enjoyed such high standards of living, and never had so many been so impoverished or died of malnutrition and disease. If the period from the 1870s is included in a long twentieth century (and perhaps even if it is not), migration served as a mode of escape from oppression and poverty and, in many instances, as an avenue toward advancement for an unprecedented number of people that soared well into the hundreds of millions by century's end. But for a clear majority of these migrants, movement was coerced by flight from war and oppression or was enticed by labor recruiters who preyed on the desperately poor. The prospects for the great majority were almost invariably lives of drudge labor in urban sweatshops, on tropical plantations, or on the wharves of an expansive, global export economy.

Throughout the century, advances in human rights, which were spread ever more broadly among different social groups—including women, laborers, ethnic minorities, and gays—made strides that were perhaps greater than all of those achieved in previous history combined. During the same time span, however, state tyranny and brutal oppression reached once unimaginable levels—in large part due to the refinement or introduction of new technologies of repression and surveillance and modes of mass organization and control. Breakthroughs in the sciences that greatly enhanced our understandings of the natural world and made for major advances in medicine and health care were very often offset by the degradation of the global environment and massive spurts in excessive mortality brought on by warfare, famine, periodic genocidal onslaughts, and worldwide epidemics. In no previous epoch of history was war so vilified and peace so consciously pursued through the establishment of international organizations and diplomatic exchanges. Despite these endeavors, the levels of domestic and international violence within human populations and the ravages visited upon animals and the natural world by humans vastly exceeded that of any previous era in history. In a century where human communities globally and individuals locally had the potential to be much more intensely connected by new communications technologies, state-sponsored programs to achieve autarky, a global epidemic of ethnic strife, uncontrolled urban growth, and the dissolution of extended family ties in many societies divided nations and communities and isolated individuals to an extent unparalleled in recorded human history.

For teachers, in particular, the challenge of weaving together in meaningful ways the seemingly disparate strands of global history in the twentieth century has often led to its neglect. The fact that the most recent phase of the human experience is usually covered only at the end of a multiterm sequence of world history units has meant that it often ends up becoming a rushed add-on of rather random, abbreviated capsule summaries and general overviews. In view of the fact that no phase of history can begin to match the twentieth century in terms of the extent to which it has shaped the contemporary world, this marginalization is particularly pernicious and has been at times literally lethal. The unmatched abundance and accessibility of primary documents and secondary works on world history in the past 100–150 years, which are clearly evident in the citations that accompany the essays in this collection, makes this neglect all the more lamentable. Taken together, the key themes and processes that have been selected as the focus for each of the eight essays provide a way to conceptualize the twentieth century as a coherent unit for teaching, as well as for written narrative and analysis. Though they do not exhaust the crucial strands of historical development that tie the century together—one could add, for example, nationalism and decolonization—they cover in depth the defining phenomena of that epoch, which, as the essays demonstrate, very often connect in important ways with these and other major developments.

The opening essays of this collection underscore the importance of including the late 1800s in what is best conceived as a "long" twentieth century. The contributions by Jose Moya and Adam McKeown and Howard Spodek consider in nuanced detail key developments in transport and communication technologies, demographic trends, and socioeconomic shifts that represented watershed transformations in where humans lived, how they earned their livings, and their unprecedented ability to move about the globe. Moya and McKeown set the patterns of migration in the twentieth century against those extending back millennia, and they compare in imaginative ways the similarities and differences among diverse flows in different geographical areas and across ethnic communities and social strata. They consider not only the nature, volume, and direction of migrant movements motivated primarily by opportunities for economic advancement—including the massive movement of rural agriculturalists to rapidly growing urban areas—but also the often-neglected displacements of populations that resulted from the wars, revolutions, and natural and man-made disasters of the twentieth century.

Howard Spodek's essay charts the development of the urban areas that have been the destination for the great majority of both international and domestic immigrants in the modern era, and that in 2005 became the place of residence for the majority of the world's human population for the first time in history. He gives considerable attention to changes in city planning, patterns of urban growth, and important differences between industrialized Europe and North America and the developing world, as well as the contrasts in urban design and living conditions between different sorts of political regimes—communist, capitalist, colonial, and fascist. Particularly revealing are Spodek's discussions of the influence of prominent urban planners and architects—including Le Corbusier and the Chicago School—urban preservation and the city as the locus of global cultural development, and the ways in which slums and shanty towns have morphed into long-term homes and viable communities for perhaps a majority of urban dwellers worldwide in the last half of the twentieth century.

Broadly conceived and remarkably comprehensive, Bonnie Smith's essay provides an overview of the gendering of political and social transformations over the course of the twentieth century. Attentive to differences across cultures and regions and under varying political regimes, Smith chronicles the struggles of women to improve their situation within the domestic sphere and the conditions under which they labored to expand the career opportunities available to them at different times and in diverse settings. She places special emphasis on the important but often overlooked roles they played in politics, particularly those associated with resistance movements, and their contributions to arts and letters worldwide. Drawing on the essay collections and series on women in world history that she has edited over the past decade, Smith's fully global perspectives make clear that even though gender parity has rarely been attained in any society and there have been major setbacks or few advances in many countries, the position of women worldwide has improved dramatically and has very often empowered a substantial portion of humanity in ways that would have been unthinkable a century ago.

Jean Quataert's contribution to gender shifts in the twentieth century focuses more narrowly on the variable fortunes of human rights causes in an era marred by phases of totalitarian oppression and genocidal excesses that were far more severe and widely distributed throughout societies across the globe than at any other time in human history. She traces the ways in which humanitarian impulses—which were often linked to pacifist movements and largely confined to visionary leaders, social thinkers, and small groups of activists in the 1890s—were institutionalized on a global basis by the establishment of the League of Nations and its subsidiary agencies in the aftermath of the catastrophic war that engulfed much of the world between 1914 and 1918. Though the colonized peoples of Africa and Asia and the peasants and laborers that made up much of the world's population in the postwar decades derived little benefit from the interwar campaigns for human rights and dignity, principles were enunciated and precedents established that would form the basis for the more broadly based human rights struggles of the last half of the century. Due in large part, however, to the weaknesses of the League, resistance to the rise of internal repression and interstate aggression in the interwar years was feeble at best. Stalinist, fascist, and Japanese militarist contempt for civil rights, much less even peaceful protest, opened the way for brutally repressive regimes that actively promoted or systematically engineered the massive episodes of rape, oppression, and genocidal killing that were major offshoots of a second global conflict in the early 1940s. The barbarous treatment meted out to tens of millions of men, women, and children in a decade that marked the nadir of recorded human history provided much of the impetus for a worldwide resurgence of human rights activism, agitation, and legislation that came to be centered in the United Nations after 1945.

The two global wars that generated the myriad abuses of human rights, while also unleashing potent forces for the liberation of women and colonized peoples more generally, are analyzed in considerable detail in John Morrow's wide-ranging essay on the causes, experience, and impact of mechanized warfare in the twentieth century. Departing from a tendency among historians to specialize in one or the other of what have been viewed as very different wars, Morrow not only compares the two conflicts in detail, but also approaches each war and its linkages from a thoroughly global perspective. This combination of rigorous comparison and breadth allows him to repeatedly challenge long-established myths, provide alternatives to narrowly conceived interpretations, and offer quite an original take on the most extensively covered conflicts in human history and the decades of unprecedented global violence they framed. Morrow's contribution here, as in his recent research and scholarship as a whole, treats the two wars and their prehistory and aftermaths as genuinely global phenomena, not as conflicts among the great powers of Europe, the United States, and Japan, which has been the obsessive focus of most of the vast literature on this subject that defined much of twentieth-century history.

As Carl Guarneri argues cogently in his contribution to the collection, which provides the fullest bibliographic references, the emergence of the United States first as one of the world powers in the late 1800s and—however briefly—as a global hegemon in the second half of the twentieth century, comprised one of the more dramatic historical shifts in a century replete with transformative processes. One of the most articulate of a growing number of advocates of the full integration of American history into the broader global experience, Guarneri explores a whole range of ways that the United States has from the outset been connected to broader global developments and often a major contributor to those larger processes. Though he focuses on these linkages in the twentieth century, as his citations amply illustrate, many of them had their origins in the 1800s and even the colonial era. Guarneri argues that it is necessary to include the United States in world history surveys and give serious attention to global influences on American history. He traces the legacies of the various European powers that colonized different portions of North America; the impact of major migration flows from virtually all of the other continents; contacts and exchanges across the borderlands; patterns of expansionism and interaction with indigenous peoples that parallel those of other settler colonies; the direct cross-influences among the U.S. and various European nations in terms of political institutions, social movements, and economic systems; and the repercussions of transcontinental and overseas American interventions from the late 1800s.

The last two essays in this collection focus on vital themes that assumed growing importance in the last decades of the twentieth century, and will very likely be considered by subsequent generations to be among the processes that distinguish that era, not only from those proceeding it but from the rest of human history altogether. The essay by Gabrielle Hecht and Paul Edwards provides a nuanced interweaving of analyses of the nuclear arms race, debates over nuclear power as a major energy source, and the communications revolution made possible by computer technologies that did so much to shape the cold war standoff between the Soviet and American superpowers and the transition to a new century and millennium. Hecht and Edwards underscore the vital connections between the genesis of and incessant innovations in computer technologies and the development of both nuclear power generators and atomic weaponry, and they also examine the ways that advances in these enmeshed fields of scientific and technological endeavor became emblematic in the cold war decades of national power and prestige, as well as symbols of modernity itself. They go well beyond the usual focus on the two superpowers to look at "nuclear politics," which encompasses both state initiatives and popular dissent, in former but diminished national great powers such as France and Great Britain and in emerging and aspiring high-tech states of very different sorts in Israel, India, and China. Equally impressive in terms of the global range of questions they include, Hecht and Edwards look at the impact of the nuclear nations' quest for viable, stable sources of uranium and sites for testing nuclear devices in locales as disparate as French Polynesia, Niger, Gabon, and the Belgian Congo.

Having had the good fortune to escape the global nuclear holocaust that was once widely accepted as inevitable if not imminent, humanity came to recognize, albeit more gradually, a second threat to global survival in the last years of the century—accelerated climate change brought on by the release of ever-increasing, polluting emissions into the earth's atmosphere. But, as Richard Tucker shows, this ultimate peril comprises only one of the many strands of environmental degradation that have, in their intensity and cumulative repercussions, set the world history of the twentieth century off from all previous phases of the human experience. Though he takes into account natural planetary processes and the impact of human endeavors on the environment in previous epochs, Tucker focuses on how the exponential increase in human reliance on fossil fuel energy sources over the course of the long twentieth century has degraded the land, water, and air of the planetary environment. From multinational corporations to impoverished peasants burning away the rain forest for land to plant their crops or pasture their cattle, he seeks to identify the specific agents responsible for both pollution and ecological degradation. And he tracks underlying trends and factors—such as rapid population growth, rampant consumerism, and global warfare—that have contributed to global climate change. Tucker concludes his rather pessimistic assessment of these key dimensions of the twentieth-century experience with cautionary explorations of key sources of our increased recognition and understanding of these processes and their implications for life on the planet, as well as with an overview of some of the measures that have been proposed for bringing them under control.

Taken together, the thematic essays included in this collection provide the basis for fashioning a coherent, inclusive, and wide-ranging approach to teaching and thinking about the history of the long twentieth century. As that designation suggests, they surmount the problems involved in designating a starting point by including the last decades of the 1800s, which are critical for all of the key subjects and processes considered—from demographic and gender shifts to war, the rise and decline of the great powers, and environmental change. Each essay deals with an underlying and all-encompassing process that in its depth and magnitude is one of the more distinctive features that is definitive for the era as a whole—the advance and retreat of the process of globalization.

Exploring the forces that explain this dynamic not only helps to explain some of the apparent paradoxes that bedevil those who aspire to make sense of the history of planet Earth over a span of more than a hundred years but also provides the basis for maintaining a semblance of continuity despite the genuinely cataclysmic break points that obscure the century's fundamental unity.

CHAPTER 1

World Migration in
the Long Twentieth Century

JOSE C. MOYA AND ADAM MCKEOWN

Migration is a basic feature of the human species. Along with mutation and natural selection, it is one of the three basic mechanisms of human evolution. The movement of primates in central Africa gave birth to the first hominids some 5 million years ago. Movement made possible the appearance of every hominid species since then, including our own some 150,000 years ago, and the spread of Homo sapiens from our African cradle to every major area of the planet since 50,000 B.P.. These migratory currents have connected all the continents since 1500 C.E., helping create the political, social, and ethnic landscapes of the world today.

Premodern societies were far from static.[1] But we cannot project this fact into a history of mobility that is one of simple continuity or gradual change. The conceptual association of mobility and modernity is not just a teleological assumption. Moving may have been one of the elemental activities of our species, along with eating and reproducing, but mass movement was a new phenomenon—as was the related "massification" of reproduction, production, trade, and transportation, as well as communication, consumption, and culture. Mass migration is an integral part of these broader global processes that have shaped the modern world.

Dating the shift is—like the periodization of any social process—a slippery affair. But for mass migration, and for some of the other linked processes, the first half of the nineteenth century offers a more meaningful turning point than the beginning of the twentieth. The decades since 1840 have witnessed a striking and unprecedented increase in the human population, in industrial and agricultural production, in global trade and its shift to nonluxury commodities, in international capital flows, in transcontinental economic integration, in transportation and communication technology, and in the movement of people. These upsurges and their regional unevenness created unprecedented incentives for long-distance migrations, as well as the resources and technologies that made them possible. In turn, these migrations provided the labor and markets that made these upsurges in production, integration, and flows possible.

Modern migration is unprecedented in its volume and in its temporal concentration. Less than 3 million Europeans went to the New World during more than three centuries of colonial rule (1492 to the 1820s), while more than 55 million did so during the eight decades that spanned the middle of the nineteenth century and the Great Depression of 1930.[2] More immigrants entered the United States in a single year (1.3 million in 1907) than had done so in the 170 years between the English settlement of Jamestown in 1607 and the country's independence. More Europeans entered the port of Buenos Aires alone in the three years preceding World War I than had come to the entire Spanish Empire during three centuries of colonial rule. And in Asia, the nearly 2 million Chinese who arrived in Singapore from 1925 to 1930 (when it was the largest immigrant port in the world—and second largest after New York over the entire period from 1840 to 1940) equaled or exceeded the total number of Chinese who migrated to mainland Southeast Asia over the entire three centuries before 1820. While many of the most dramatic increases were in transoceanic migration, other kinds of migration grew as well. In Europe, total per capita migration—including emigration, movement to cities, colonization of empty lands, and seasonal migration—increased from 6.5 percent of the population from 1750 to 1800 (total migration divided by the average population during this period) to more than 30 percent from 1850 to 1900.[3]

Global migration increased dramatically from the 1840s to the 1870s; slowed a bit in the global depression from 1873 until the early 1890s; reached new peaks in the years up to 1914; shrank during World War I; revived during the 1920s; contracted again with the Great Depression of the 1930s and the Second World War, except for internal migrations and refugees; and rose after 1950, gaining momentum during the 1980s until the world recession of 2008–2009. Those who migrated during the second wave that began after World War II were about three times as numerous as those in the first wave, although in per capita terms, the peaks of international migration in the 1990s and 2000s were similar to those of the early 1910s and late 1920s. But if we look at all forms of mobility—domestic and short-term as well as long-term international mobility—other trends clearly surpass anything that has ever happened in the past. An extreme example of the recent volume and temporal concentration of modern flows would be the 130 million Chinese who have moved from the interior to the coastal provinces since 1990.[4] Even more significant are the 900 million people who, in the early twenty-first century, have left their homes every year for more than twenty-four hours and "not more than one consecutive year for leisure, business or other purposes," as tourists are described by the World Tourism Organization.[5]

Much of this mobility is a continuation and expansion of practices that have been going on for centuries: travel for trade and business, the colonization of agricultural lands, the movement of soldiers and sailors, and the constant ebb and flow of forced and free labor to plantations, mines, factories, and domestic service both far and near. But the explosion in quantity was also a transformation in quality. Migrations were inseparable from unprecedented urbanization and population growth, the expansion of industrial production and global markets, the spread of wage labor, the growth and extraction of food and resources to feed those workers, the revolution of transportation technologies, and the accompanying creation of an international system of nation states, borders, and population management techniques.

Cities were the epicenter of this world in transformation, and one of the main magnets for migrants. In 1800, 6 million people lived in the largest ten cities of the world. By 2000, this had grown to more than 200 million, increasing over five times more rapidly than the world population. In Europe, the number of town and city dwellers more than quintupled during the nineteenth century, from 19 million to 108 million or 12–38 percent of the total population, compared with an increase from 8 million to 19 million or 10–12 percent of the total population during the previous five centuries.[6] Globally, the proportion of humanity that resided in towns and cities rose from 3 percent in 1800 to 14 percent a century later, and to 30 percent in 1950. Currently, more than half of the people in the world live in cities.

The first wave of mass migration from the 1840s to the 1920s also filled the frontiers of the world, transforming remote plains, forests, and jungles into integral parts of the world's economic and political landscape. In part, this reflected an expanding world population, as residents of the highest-density regions of Europe, South Asia, and China moved into the relatively empty spaces of the Americas, Southeast Asia, and northern Asia. But migrants to these areas also mined, cultivated, or harvested the minerals, cotton, rubber, hides, and other resources that fed the urban factories, as well as the wheat, soybeans, sugar, rice, and other foodstuffs that fed the ever-increasing numbers of city dwellers and wage laborers. Other migrants were the traders and shopkeepers who moved and exchanged these resources and manufactured goods across the world. This growing web of mass production and markets shaped the likelihood and direction of migration in many forms. Labor demands and low frontier populations produced both higher wages and increased opportunities for employment and trade. At the same time, increased commercialization impacted rural relations around the world, creating both the need and the opportunities to spend money earned through the wages of migrants. The growth of commercial agriculture and rural industry also provided an impetus for seasonal rural-to-rural moves.[7] In Europe alone, this type of migration increased nearly ten times between 1800 and 1900, while the population as a whole only doubled, and at least 90 percent of the more than 50 million migrants into Southeast Asia before 1940 moved to rural areas.[8]

All of this was tied to the veritable revolution in mass transportation and communication that made the mass movement of people possible after the mid-nineteenth century.[9] Migrants (whether domestic or external) in turn built more railroad lines (which increased worldwide from 8,000 kilometers in the 1840s to more than a million by 1914) and steamers (whose tonnage increased twenty times over the same period). These transportation advances then made possible the movement of even more people and of the heavy or bulky commodities with low price per weight or mass that came to make up much of global trade. The trading, extraction, and processing of these commodities then required even more migrants. Both flows, of goods and people, have thus moved in tandem—although not always in the same direction. And both have relied on the proliferation of communication systems, including the postal system, telegraphs, telephones, photographs, and radios. These spread the information about markets, jobs, and opportunities that fueled both migration and trade.

As part of these transformations, the new migrations were notably freer than those of the previous three hundred years. This was especially the case in the Atlantic and western Eurasia. Two-thirds of the westward and eastward migrations out of Europe from 1500 to 1820 were coerced in some form (serfs, indentured servants, military conscripts, and convicts).[10] Coercion was more complete for the 1–3 million Poles, Ukrainians, and Russians traded in the Crimean Tartar slave traffic during the seventeenth century. The same was true in the largest migrations of any period before the mid-nineteenth century: the move of 10 million African slaves across the Atlantic and of a similar number across the Sahara Desert and the Indian Ocean.[11] The movement of Chinese and South Asians before 1820 was generally freer, dominated by traders and short-term debt arrangements. But slave raiding was still common in the waters of Southeast Asia and, like African slavery, grew increasingly common over the eighteenth and early nineteenth centuries along with the growth in global commerce.[12]

Long-distance migration after the middle of the nineteenth century, by contrast, was mostly free. The transatlantic African slave trade, which had been banned by the British Empire in 1807 with limited success (a third of all slaves taken to the New World arrived after the ban) had come to a virtual end by the 1850s.[13] The westward-bound movement of European indentured servants had ended decades earlier, and the eastward-bound movement declined to the point that only one in eight of the 6 million Russians who moved to northern Asia between 1850 and 1914 did so as serfs.[14] Within Europe, the proportion of all long-distance mobility made up by soldiers declined from more than half during 1500–1850 to less than a sixth during the second half of the nineteenth century.[15] After the 1840s, there was a small growth in the migration of Asians indentured to Europeans, but it amounted to less than 3 percent of Chinese emigrants and 10 percent of Indian overseas emigrants, and had largely peaked by the 1870s. Like European migrants, most Asian migrants were free or organized through debt obligations to other migrants (although most Indian migrants still worked on European-owned plantations, recruited, paid, and organized by Indian labor recruiters).[16]

The swell in free global mobility in the middle of the nineteenth century corresponded with a reduction of state controls over migration. However, by the end of the century, ever-growing numbers of migrants generated new efforts to control or restrict such mobility—this time in the form of national borders and immigration policy. Nation-states increased from a handful before the Napoleonic Wars to more than 190 by the early twenty-first century, emerging contemporaneously with increased integration and mobility. Delimiting physical space, turning it into "territory," and establishing institutions of population management have been constant objectives of these polities. The early days of this international system in the mid-nineteenth century, however, were a heyday of liberal and laissez-faire mobility marked by a decline of coerced labor and many mobility controls. By the 1860s, most European nations had dropped their exit, domestic movement, and passport controls.[17] Empires that still maintained controls, such as Russia, Japan, and China, were subject to relentless criticism. At the same time, the authority to manage mobility shifted away from localities to central governments as nation-states insisted on their power to register, count, deport, and monitor the peoples within their borders. Revolutionary France is an early and iconic example of this paradoxical shift. Its constitution of 1791 guaranteed the "natural and civic right" of freedom "to move about, remain and depart." At the same time, it is credited with the "invention of the passport," inasmuch as this new passport was a standardized identity document issued by a central government and required of all people moving within the nation.[18]

Trends toward liberal migration started to reverse with the exclusion of Asians from many white settler nations after the 1880s, the rise of medical inspections at about the same time, and the more general rise of passport and systematic immigration laws after World War I.[19] Restrictions on international migration in the 1920s heralded the retrenchment of economic liberalism into greater isolation and autarky that characterized the next two decades. And the later revival of global liberalism (after 1950 and more worldwide after 1990) did not stop the multiplication of migration controls, the proliferation of identity documents, and ever more complex laws to sift and select the optimal migrant. In this sense, neoliberalism has proved to be more "quasi" than "neo," promoting the free movement of goods, capital, technologies, information, and culture, but not of people.

At the most brutal level, the consolidation of borders and purification of national spaces has produced millions of refugees as one of the defining features of twentieth-century migration. At a more mundane level, migration itself has become inseparable from the daily machinery of migration control and evasion. Indeed, borders have shaped our knowledge of migration as deeply as the process of migration itself. The historiography of migration is built and fragmented around nation-centered themes such as assimilation, push-pull, national identity, debates over national legislation, and diasporas with their attachment to home nations. Enormous and inconclusive social science literatures have tried to gage the effect of immigration and emigration on national economies, political participation, social structures, and national demography. Recent work on "transnationalism," "diaspora," and migrant networks has tried to move beyond this kind of knowledge, but more often than not it presents itself as a depiction of a "new" kind of migration and does not challenge nation-centered depictions of migration history. Scholars have pointed out the numerous failures of borders and migration control, noting their many unintended consequences and great difficulty in counteracting the workings of migrant networks or the broad economic forces that generate migration. But at the same time, no migrant experience can be understood in isolation from the pervasive categories of migration control such as guest worker, permanent resident, family reunification, occupational preferences, asylum seeker, refugee, illegal, undocumented, and irregular.

A global perspective on twentieth-century migration history is grounded in two interlinked perspectives: (1) a broad picture of migrations around the world as embedded in shared global processes, and (2) more specific pictures that focus on ties between localities and people rather than on the imaginaries of nation-to-nation flows. Recent social science and historical scholarship has already produced much excellent work on the migration networks that make up perspective 2, but the implications and application of a historical global perspective are much less developed. The two perspectives, however, are deeply complementary. A global picture provides the demographic, economic, and political context for understanding migrant networks that transcend national borders, and the more particular histories of migrant flows help to flesh out the variations, contingencies, and basic mechanisms of those broad processes.[20]

FIRST WAVE OF MODERN MIGRATION, 1840s–1930s

Estimating migration numbers is a challenging task. Records of long-distance migration are much more readily available than of short-distance and domestic migrations. But even many long-distance moves—such as those by ship passengers not traveling in third class or steerage—were not categorized as migration. Others were not recorded at all. In some cases, authorities did not have the interest or capacity to keep semiaccurate records; in others, migrants purpose-

fully avoided being recorded, as in the case of draft dodgers or anyone traveling in spite of restrictions. Return migration often went unrecorded. Repeated
migration meant that the same individuals were counted more than once. And
numbers from ports of emigration and immigration could vary by 20 percent
or more.[21] The situation for overland migration is even worse. Such migrants
were rarely counted, and when we do have numbers, it is very difficult to distinguish between short-term travelers and migrants for work or resettlement.
Most estimates for overland and domestic migration are based on census data,
which means they are less likely to account for short-term travelers and those
who made multiple journeys. And the movement of nomadic, seminomadic, and
itinerant peoples, as well as others whose residences and jobs have not yet been
fixed within the matrices of property and tax laws that have spread around the
world are even more difficult to count and compare to other migrations.

Despite these limitations, the data that we present in table 1.1 show the
massive proportions of long-distance migration between 1840 and 1940 and
their many directions. Sections with subheadings and numbers that cover a relatively small range are more firmly based in port statistics, censuses, and research. The wider the range in the numbers, the more it is grounded in estimates
and educated guesses.

The most voluminous transoceanic and transcontinental flows came out
of Europe. The exodus of 73 million Europeans during this period amounts to
the largest global redistribution of human population of any time, and arguably
the most significant since the species' original exodus from Africa insofar as it
ushered the modern world and shaped its geography. Table 1.1 gives the destinations by country. But at a global ecological level, these polities seem irrelevant
and the transference could be better described as one from the most densely
populated region in the temperate belts of the planet to the most sparsely populated frontiers within those belts. Sixty-eight million Europeans, or 96 percent
of the total emigration, headed for those frontiers. Thirteen million did so
overland across the Urals into Siberia and 57 million across the oceans to temperate America (38 million and 12 million to the northern and southern thirds
of the hemisphere, respectively), Australia/New Zealand (4 million), and southern Africa (close to 1 million). Cuba was the only place within the tropics to
receive a significant European, mainly Spanish, inflow. The global population
transfer had been major: in 1800, less than 4 percent of all people of European
ethnic origin lived outside of Europe; by 1940, one-third of them did.[22]

More than 22 million Chinese also migrated abroad from the southern
provinces of Guangdong and Fujian. The vast majority went to destinations
throughout Southeast Asia. Up to 11 million traveled from China to Singapore
and Penang, from where more than a third of them transshipped to the Dutch
Indies, Borneo, Burma, and places farther west. Another 8 million to 10 million
traveled directly to other Southeast Asian destinations, especially Thailand,

TABLE 1.1: LONG-DISTANCE GLOBAL MIGRATION, 1840–1940		
	millions	*millions*
Out of Europe		60
United States	33	
Argentina	6.5	
Canada	5	
Brazil	4.5	
Other Americas	3	
Australia & New Zealand	4	
North Africa	3	
Elsewhere	1	
Russia to Siberia		13
Out of South China		21–23
Malaya and Singapore	7	
Dutch East Indies	4–5	
Thailand	4.5	
French Indochina	3–4	
Philippines	1	
Americas	1	
Other	0.5	
China to Manchuria		30–33
Northeast Asia		7
Koreans Abroad	4.5	
Japanese Abroad	2.5	
India		43–50
Burma	15	
Ceylon	8	
Malaya	5	
Emigration Elsewhere	2	
Assam	3–5	
Internal Migration	10–15	
Intra-China		20–40
Intra–Southeast Asia		4–8
Sub-Saharan Africa		6–10

	millions	millions
Eastern Mediterranean/ Western Asia		9–13
Europe–Turkey Refugees	7	
Other	2–4	
Intra-Europe		74
Russians	25	
Central Europe	14	
Italians	12	
UK (including Ireland)	12	
Iberia & France	4	
North Sea, Scandinavia, Baltic	3	
Southeast Europe	2	
Others	2	
Intra-Americas		35
U.S.–Canada Westward	13	
Intra-U.S.	11	
Canada to U.S.	3	
Mexico and Caribbean to U.S.	2	
Down from Andes	2	
Intra-Caribbean	1	
Southern Cone	1	
Other	2	

Sources: Imre Ferenczi and Walter Willcox, eds., *International Migrations*, vol. 1, *Statistics* (New York: National Bureau of Economic Research, 1929); Adam McKeown, "Global Migration, 1846–1940," *Journal of World History* 15 (2004): 155–189; Jose C. Moya, "Immigration, Development, and Assimilation in the United States in a Global Perspective, 1850–1930," *Studia Migracyjne* [Warsaw] 35, no. 3 (2009), 89–104.

Vietnam, Java, and the Philippines. One and a half million (about 7 percent) traveled far beyond Southeast Asia to the Americas, Australia, New Zealand, Hawaii, and other islands in the Pacific and Indian oceans. Only about 750,000 Chinese were ever indentured to Europeans—approximately 3 percent of the total—roughly a third of whom went to Cuba and Peru, a third to Sumatra, and another third to multiple locations in Malaya and the South Pacific. The great bulk of Chinese were free migrants, financed by family or Chinese merchants.[23]

More than 30 million Chinese also migrated to Manchuria, where they joined the Russians, 2 million Koreans, and 2 million Japanese in peopling the vast frontiers of northern Asia. Migrants had trickled into Manchuria and Siberia for hundreds of years before the Qing and Russian governments' gradually relaxed restrictions against movement into this region after the 1850s. But the inflow to both regions only acquired massive dimensions after 1900, and peaked in the 1930s when global migration had sharply declined. Another 2.5 million Koreans migrated to Japan, especially in the 1930s, and more than 2 million Japanese also moved to Korea and Manchuria, along with a half million who crossed the Pacific to Hawaii, California, Peru, and rounded Cape Horn to Brazil.[24]

Migration from India is more difficult to divide into domestic and overseas movement, given the closeness of important destinations like Ceylon and Burma, even with Burma having been officially under the rule of Indian colonial government for most of this period. Like the Chinese, the great majority of Indians ended up in tropical destinations, mostly around the Indian Ocean. Unlike the Chinese, these destinations were almost entirely part of the British Empire, with the great majority traveling to Malaya, Burma, and Ceylon. Only about a million Indians, mostly indentured laborers drawn equally from northern and southern India, traveled to lands beyond the eastern Indian Ocean, including Fiji, Mauritius, South Africa, the Caribbean, and Canada. More than a million merchants, including Gujaratis and Sindwerkies from the northwest and Chettiars from the south, also traveled to various places around the world. Within India, millions of migrants went to work on the tea plantations of Assam in the northwest, in the weaving districts of Bengal, and on the plantations of the south.[25]

Given current states of knowledge, other migrations within Asia and Africa are very difficult to estimate. Within China, migrants continued to move to the northwestern and southwestern frontiers, and continued in regular labor and artisanal migrations associated with markets, skilled trades, and transportation work. The mass military movements and devastation of the Yangtze Valley in the 1850s and 1860s, as well as the roving armies of the 1910s and 1920s, created mass mobility in their own right, not only in terms of the soldiers who were conscripted and then demobilized far from their homes (often draining areas of the young men who might otherwise have been potential migrants) but also in terms of the migration of millions into the depopulated Yangtze Valley areas and Shanghai after the mid-nineteenth-century rebellions were suppressed.[26]

Migrations within highland and maritime Southeast Asia, central Asia, Arabia, and Africa are especially difficult to get a handle on because much of the movement circulated according to patterns of nomadic and seminomadic mobility that followed very different trajectories than migration from more settled areas. In fact, it could be argued that the very infrastructures that helped facilitate much of the migration described above also helped to limit this kind of mobility, as these mobile peoples were increasingly subject to state expansion, taxes, property law, and commercial cropping.[27] Nonetheless, we can still speak of the millions of workers who moved to plantations and mines in southern and central Africa and to agricultural areas and coastal cities in western and eastern Africa. In the first half of the twentieth century, colonial governments also regularly mobilized African labor as soldiers and to work on public projects.[28] The building of the Suez Canal and the creation of new irrigation projects in Egypt also generated much migration. In Southeast Asia, up to 500,000 Javanese traveled to plantations in Sumatra and the Southeast Asian mainland. And, in what may have been some of the densest emigrations anywhere, more than 300,000 Pacific Islanders worked on plantations and as seamen throughout the region.[29]

Movement also continued in forms other than labor migrations. The millions of Christians who moved from the decaying Ottoman Empire into Greece and the Balkans, and Muslims who moved into Asia Minor were the precursors of the mass refugee movements of the twentieth century, as were the 1 million Armenians expelled from Turkey after 1915.[30] Merchant diasporas also continued to flourish, including Lebanese merchants, who spread throughout the world and became especially prominent in West Africa, and Hadramis and Omanis from the southern Arabian peninsula, who moved throughout the Indian Ocean regions from eastern Africa to Java.[31] In a different kind of movement, more than 20 million people also took part in the *hajj* (pilgrimage) to Mecca.[32]

Migrations within Europe and the Americas are better documented. Most of these moves, like everywhere, continued to be along short distances. But the most important change, and the one we recorded in table 1.1 in general, came in the tremendous increase in long-distance moves. Some of them were to new agricultural lands, particularly within European Russia, where Czarist and Soviet censuses showed significant movement.[33] But the bulk of these moves were to more urban, commercialized, or industrial regions than the ones the migrants left behind. Ten million Italians crossed the Alps—a number slightly higher than those who crossed the Atlantic—and 2 million more moved north from the peninsula's Mezzogiorno to the industrial Piedmont and Lombardy. Two million Irish moved to England, and another 10 million workers moved between the kingdoms and regions of the United Kingdom, many toward the industrial Midlands. Six million Poles moved westward. The *Ostflucht* (flight from the East) carried 3 million migrants of various ethnicities from Prussia to the Ruhr, the industrial powerhouse in North Rhine-Westphalia.[34] More than a million Spaniards moved to the industrial areas of Asturias, Catalonia, and the Basque country.[35]

The exodus from Europe also overlapped with massive migrations within North America. More than 13 million North Americans moved to the western frontiers of the United States and Canada. In some cases, these were the same folks who had crossed the Atlantic or their descendants, but they also included many Native Americans, often moving under conditions of forced relocation. At the same time, 3 million Canadians moved to the United States, along with some 2 million from Mexico and the Caribbean. Eight million Americans left the U.S. South (two-thirds of them white and one-third African American) for the industrial centers of the Northeast and Midwest.[36] Indeed, the United States had one of the most intense rates of mobility in the world. In every census year from 1850 to 1940, 20–25 percent of the native population had been born in a state other than the one where they resided. Within the Caribbean, a million West Indians moved to Cuba, the Atlantic coast of Panama and Costa Rica, and between other islands.[37] Many migrants also moved down from the Andes, to the pampas of Argentina, and within and between the other nations of the southern cone.

These data can be organized and interpreted in different ways. One approach is to arrange the information into the three main systems of migration, connecting major sending regions with major receiving frontiers: (1) 55–58 million European migrants to the Americas; (2) 48–52 million Indians and southern Chinese to Southeast Asia and the Indian Ocean; and (3) 46–51 million northern Chinese, Russians, Koreans, and Japanese into central and northern Asia.[38] This arrangement leaves out several significant areas, such as migrations within each of the sending and receiving regions, migrations in Africa, and movement in and out of the Middle East. But it highlights the role of migration in the major shift of world population toward frontier areas, as the populations of all three receiving frontiers grew at twice the rate of world population (Americas, 1.72 percent; North Asia, 1.57 percent; and Southeast Asia, 1.44 percent). Taken together, they accounted for 10 percent of the world's population in 1850 and 24 percent in 1950. Conversely, the population in all three major sending regions grew more slowly (China, 0.21 percent; South Asia, 0.66 percent; and Europe, 0.67 percent a year) than world population (0.74 percent a year). See figure 1.1.

This mode of organizing the data also highlights the global scope of migration. From 1870 to 1930, approximately 35 million migrants moved into the 4.08 million square kilometers of Southeast Asia, compared to the 39 million migrants who moved into the 9.8 million square kilometers of the United States. At first glance, 19 million overseas emigrants from China or 29 million from India seem like a drop in the bucket compared to the several millions from much smaller countries like Italy, Norway, Ireland, and England. But if we compare particular European nations with Chinese provinces of similar size and population, the rates are very similar. Peak annual emigration rates of around 10 per 1,000 population (averaged over a decade) were typical of Ireland and Norway in the 1880s, of Italy and Spain in the years before World War I, and of Guangdong, Hebei, and Shandong provinces (the latter being sources of migration to Manchuria) in the 1920s.[39] The timing of the Atlantic and Southeast Asian migrations also was not greatly different, although the migrations to Southeast Asia did not peak until the late 1920s, about fifteen years after the peak of the European emigrations. The North Asian migrations did not really get moving until the 1880s and 1890s, about four decades after the other two, but they are still contemporaneous enough to fit within an overall global wave.

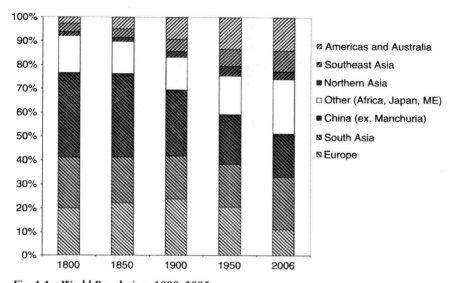

Fig. 1.1   World Population, 1800–2005

Source: Based on data in Colin McEvedy and Richard Jones, *Atlas of World Population History* (London: Penguin, 1978).

The nearly concurrent rise of overseas migration around the world was not coincidental. The increase of mass communication and rapid, inexpensive transportation, the growth of global markets and industrialization, the loosening of controls over internal migration, and the expansion into global frontiers all reinforced each other in a snowball effect. It was a world on the move, flowing into factories, construction projects, and trade entrepots, and into the mines, plantations, and agricultural frontiers to supply those centers of concentration. The development of mass communication only then made the mass movement of people possible. Inexpensive steamships crossed the oceans of the world after the 1860s, as railways crossed North America and North Asia. Where mass transport did not extend, its agents did, supplying information and access. Rice planters in Burma and Thailand helped feed the tin miners and rubber planters in Malaya, who provided the raw materials for factory workers in Manchester and Chicago. So, too, ranchers in the Great Plains of North America and pampas of Argentina, canal diggers in Egypt and Panama, railroad builders in East Africa and Siberia, gold miners in South Africa and Australia, soybean farmers in Manchuria, coffee growers in Brazil, and the millions of small merchants who collected raw materials and distributed manufactured goods, and credit from the Amazon jungles to the West African savannas to the slums of New York were all a part of this global economy. Their activities produced more goods that generated more trade, more movement, and more disruptive commercialization that generated yet more migration.

At the same time, it is clear that there was a North Atlantic core to global migration. The world was connected, but the connections came hand in hand with the emergence of inequalities and new differences. In terms of the migrations counted above, emigration from Europe (including to Siberia) amounted to at least 15 percent of the total population in 1900, whereas the Chinese (including Manchurian) and Indian outflows fell somewhere in the range of 7–13 percent. The difference becomes even more apparent when we compare migrations internal to the regions. When we estimate (based on table 1.1) all forms of migration within the North Atlantic core of central and western Europe and North America, where industrialization, massification, and communication technologies were most intense, we find that less than a quarter of the world's population produced from one-third to half of the migration. The gap was largest in the period from 1850 to 1910, after which migration rates around the world began to converge once again.

The variations in migration rates are significant, but still small in comparison to the enormous gaps in industrialization and urbanization that emerged in the same period. The 1851 U.K. census revealed a watershed demographic event: for the first time in the history of any large nation, more people lived in towns than in the countryside.[40] By the early 1900s, several other countries in Europe and in the European diaspora had reached that mark or were close to it. By comparison, the proportion of China's inhabitants living in cities was 5 percent in 1800 and 4 percent a century later, and India's was 11 percent in 1800 and still 11 percent in 1921.[41] In 1800, only three of the world's top ten cites were in the North Atlantic. By 1900, nine out of ten (Tokyo being the tenth) were in the North Atlantic. Some Asian cities like Shanghai, Tianjin, Rangoon, Hong Kong, Singapore, and Calcutta increased at phenomenal rates, but did not come close to the absolute size of megacities such as Chicago, New York, and London. More significantly, the size of many cities in Asia remained stagnant, and even declined over the nineteenth century.

The trend in manufacturing production is even more striking. In 1800, China and India had produced more than half (53 percent) of the world's manufacturing output and Europe less than a third (27 percent). By 1900, China and India's share had dropped precipitously to 8 percent, while Europe's had risen with equal speed to 60 percent.[42] By the early twentieth century, industry accounted for the bulk of the economy and employment in many European regions, while others remained rural for decades—an optimal condition to spur mobility. Such inducements barely existed in China and India. Nor did regional economic inequalities in general provide an important incentive for internal mobility. For example, real wages for unskilled workers in China declined during the nineteenth century and the gap between Beijing and its rural hinterland were minimal.[43] Both countries' gross domestic product

(GDP) as a share of the world's had dropped as precipitously as their share of manufacturing and had remained stagnant in absolute terms.

These trends in urbanization and industrialization and the greater development of communication and transportation infrastructures also produced more dynamic patterns of emigration in Europe, where sources of overseas migration disseminated across the continent in a kind of "contagion." It normally appeared first in a few specific spots along channels of communication and trade, such as ports and railroad connections, and diffused to hinterlands in a manner resembling an inkblot on a paper. However, rather than spreading evenly on the map, the spot would often leap to farther regions because people residing there had learned of opportunities overseas from relatives who lived in zones of emigration. This process formed new and seemingly isolated loci of overseas emigration from which the behavior then diffused, thus speeding the geographical diffusion of the behavior. Through this process, "emigration fever" spread from northwestern Europe and a few loci in northern Iberia and Italy to the rest of the continent and the Levant in less than half a century.[44]

In Asia, by contrast, emigration began and acquired high intensity in particular regions without spreading its origins geographically. The bulk of mass Indian emigration to destinations in Southeast Asia departed from southern areas with only small flows from the north. Similarly, most overseas migration from China departed from the same regions of the southern provinces of Guangdong and Fujian over the entire period from the 1840s to the 1930s. The specific villages of emigration may have shifted, but the basic regions remained the same as migration became a multigenerational economic strategy for many families. Mass Chinese migration to Manchuria started later, but Shandong and Hebei supplied almost the entire stream.

The most dramatic example of differences between European and other migrations can be seen in the long-term demographic effects of migration. As table 1.2 shows, in 1955, European emigrants and their descendants outnumbered Chinese and Indians more than four to one. Indian emigrants make up a mere 1.4 percent of the total counted in this table (migrants to Manchuria and Siberia are counted because they are the progeny of mass migrations, even if they did not strictly live outside of China and the Soviet Union). Whatever the differences or similarities in actual numbers of migrants, it was the European emigrants who left the strongest impact on the world.

Several factors have gone into the making of these numbers. These include differences in environments, occupations, and social structures at the destinations, different rates of return, female migration, and the general wealth and power of Europe. Nearly all Asian emigrants other than those to Manchuria moved into tropical areas with well-established native or colonial states. In contrast, Europeans tended to move into sparsely populated temperate areas where they became the majority and where they held the political power.

TABLE 1.2: DESCENDANTS OF EUROPEAN, CHINESE, AND INDIANS ABROAD, CIRCA 1955

Europeans and Euro-descendants Living Outside of Europe

Place of Residence	Thousands	% of Total Pop.
United States	134,942	89
Asian USSR	38,835	62
Brazil (mainly South)	29,393	52
Argentina	15,301	89
Canada	12,438	98
Australia	8,207	97
Chile	3,654	60
Cuba	3,239	55
Southern Africa	2,867	10
Uruguay	2,019	91
New Zealand	1,880	88
Algeria	1,050	9
Other Americas	9,800	10
Total	263,625	

Chinese and Sino-descendants Living Outside of China

Place of Residence	Thousands	% of Total Pop.
Manchuria	47,560	98
Thailand	3,690	16
Malaysia	2,452	34
Indonesia	2,000	2
Vietnam	1,000	4
Singapore	893	68
Burma	300	1
Cambodia	218	4
Philippines	149	1
United States	118	0
All Others	170	
Total	58,550	

Indians and Indo-descendants Residing Outside of India

Place of Residence	Thousands	% of Total Pop.
Ceylon	1,132	11
Burma	700	21
Malaysia	650	9
South Africa	404	3

Place of Residence	Thousands	% of Total Pop.
Mauritius	399	67
East Africa	352	1
Trinidad	302	37
Guyana	268	48
Fiji	198	49
Singapore	104	35
Surinam	94	8
Total	4,609	

Sources: Calculated from data in Galina V. Selegen, "The First Report on the Recent Population Census in the Soviet Union," *Population Studies* 14, no. 1 (1960): 17–27; L. T. Badenhorst, "The Future Growth of the Population of South Africa and Its Probable Age," *Population Studies* 4, no. 1 (1950): 3–46; Angus Maddison's data sets on world population, www.ggdc.net/maddison; U.S. historical statistics at www.census.gov; Kingsley Davis, "Recent Population Trends in the New World: An Over-All View," *Annals of the American Academy of Political and Social Science* 316 (March 1958): 1–10; Chandra Jayawardena, "Migration and Social Change: A Survey of Indian Communities Overseas," *Geographical Review* 58, no. 3 (1968): 426–449; Amarjit Kaur, "Indian Labour, Labour Standards, and Workers' Health in Burma and Malaya, 1900–1940," *Modern Asian Studies* 40, no. 2 (2006): 425–475; Dudley L. Poston Jr. and Mei-YuYu, "The Distribution of the Overseas Chinese in the Contemporary World," *International Migration Review* 24, no. 3 (1990): 480–508; and various other sources.

A majority of Asians also moved into rural wage labor, a fact that is even more the case for Indians than Chinese. Tropical plantations and mines were much less amenable to long-term settlement and families than were small farms on temperate frontiers, or even the new cities of the Americas.

Rates of female migration also tended to be much lower for Asians until the 1930s. They were as low as 5–10 percent for some destinations, with Europeans more likely to range from 25 percent to 50 percent female. This must have meant that Asians were more likely to return or to not have children. And Chinese and Indian migrants did indeed have higher return rates than Europeans before 1900—ranging from 60 percent to 70 percent, compared to a range of 20 percent to 60 percent for Europeans. These rates tended to converge for Asians and Europeans during the twentieth century, but the higher rates of settlement and female migration in earlier years were even more significant than later migrations in producing the descendants that filled up the population charts of 1955. A variety of factors caused the differences in rates of return and female migration: the poor conditions for settlement provided by wage labor on tropical frontiers, different family structures, larger numbers of native females in the destination areas, and shorter and lower-cost return voyages. The effects of this last factor can be seen in the distribution of descendants of Indian migration. More than fifty-five times as many Indians went to Southeast Asia as to the Caribbean, but by 1960, the Indian community in Southeast Asia was only four times larger than its counterpart in the Caribbean because returns from there were much lower and the female proportion among emigrants was much higher.

In this context, the comparison between Manchuria and the southern Chinese migrations is instructive. The Manchurian migrations are an example of migration to a temperate frontier with substantial urbanization, where the natives were almost entirely displaced and where, despite interludes of Russian and Japanese intervention, the Chinese ultimately maintained political control (not least because they overwhelmed the area with migrants). The results of this difference with the southern migration can be seen in the nearly 50 million Chinese who resided in Manchuria by 1953, nearly 4.5 times the number that could be found abroad. This is despite the fact that average rates of return and female migration were similar for the southern Chinese. Conversely, both the United States and Manchuria started with populations of about 6 million in 1800 and received similar numbers of migrants over the following 140 years, yet this produced a population of 134 million people of European descent in the United States by 1955. Lower return rates, higher rates of female migration, greater economic growth, and better conditions of settlement all conspired to produce this disparity.

We still have to ask the question of why Europeans managed to dominate the temperate frontiers. Here we must appeal to European wealth and power—their ability to travel more readily to such places and to exclude others from joining them. While the geographic scope of European migration may not have exceeded that of Chinese or Gujarati merchants, their ability to concentrate and reproduce themselves under favorable social and political conditions of their own choosing surely did surpass that of the Asian migrants.

GLOBAL MIGRATION AND GLOBAL INEQUALITIES

An increasingly connected world grew hand in hand with an increasingly unequal world. Indeed, global migration resulted from inequalities and, in turn, also reversed, produced, and diminished those inequalities. At the broadest level, differences in the patterns and effects of migration in the Atlantic world and Asia are linked to differences in the wage gaps and relationships between the movement of people, goods, and money. And when we break migration flows down to more specific destinations in the Americas and Asia, we can often (but not always) find a link to socioeconomic development, in which migration helped to reverse inequalities. All migrants were part of an industrializing and increasingly interconnected world, but they were incorporated into those processes to significantly different degrees and in different ways.

The effects of migration on socioeconomic development in the Western Hemisphere are especially clear. Before 1800, the colonial success stories had been based on the exploitation of indigenous labor and precious minerals in the highlands of the hemisphere, and of African slaves and cash crops in its tropical islands and coastal lowlands. Peru and Mexico were the jewels of the Spanish imperial crown. Saint-Domingue and Barbados were two of the richest spots on the planet, worth much more to their French and British colonial masters than the vast expanses of Louisiana, Anglo North America, and Quebec. But as the industrial revolution and urbanization in Europe shifted global trade from silver and luxury goods to foodstuffs, agropastoral commodities, and base minerals, what had been natural features in temperate America became some of the world's most important "natural" resources. The abundance of a black sedimentary rock turned the United States into the world's coal king. The most extensive—and emptiest—arable plains on the planet became its principal breadbasket. The European population and urbanization explosions created a demand for its fruits, trains and steamers provided a means of transporting them, and European immigrants provided a way to grow and harvest them. In 1800, the entire North and South American plains, which covered an area larger than European Russia, contained a smaller population than that of tiny and mountainous Switzerland and even the tinier city of London. A century later, they had become the site of the wealthiest countries on the globe.[45]

This trend manifested itself in the shift of the Americas' urban rank. In 1810, the ten largest cities in the Americas, and forty-five of the largest fifty, were in the colonial Indo- and Afro-American cores. Mexico City alone was larger than the five top U.S. cities combined. By 1910, the eleven largest cities in the Americas, and eighty-one of the top one hundred, were cities of immigrants in what had been the most marginal regions in the temperate northern and southern ends of the hemisphere; and its five most urbanized countries (Uruguay, Cuba, Argentina, the United States, and Canada, in that order) were the ones with the highest proportion of European immigrants in their populations.

Migration helped to create, rather than reverse, regional inequalities beyond the Western Hemisphere. In the eighteenth and early nineteenth centuries, China and India may not have been much richer than Western Europe, but they were not much poorer either. However, as figure 1.2 illustrates, a wide wealth gap developed between the three main global exporters of emigrants between the middle of the nineteenth century and 1930. By then, GDP per capita in Europe had become six times higher than India's and eight times higher than China's; the economies of India and China had stagnated while Europe's grew by a factor of 2.56. A similar gap opened up between the main receivers of immigrants. The Southeast Asian economies performed somewhat better than those of China and India, but still below the world's average, and way below those of the Anglo and Latin countries of European immigration.

Several factors explain such diverging results. Unlike previous transatlantic crossings, which had led to the decimation of the Amerindian population and to the mass enslavement of Africans, the nineteenth- and twentieth-century movements were mutually beneficial to a much higher degree than migrations elsewhere in the world. The mass migrations from Europe after the 1830s amounted to a huge transfer of labor—from an industrializing continent with a high ratio of population to resources, to fertile frontiers with the highest

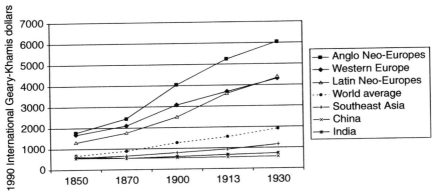

Fig. 1.2 Per Capita GDP in Regions of Emigration and Immigration

Note: Calculated from data on GDP available in Angus Maddison's www.ggdc.net/maddi-son. The category "Anglo Neo-Europes" represents the average for the United States, Canada, Australia, and New Zealand; "Latin Neo-Europes," the average of Argentina and Uruguay; and "Southeast Asia" that for Ceylon, Burma, Malaysia, Indonesia, and Thailand.

ratio of resources to population on earth. Land-to-labor ratios in American agriculture in 1900 were four to ten times higher than in European countries, and output per agricultural worker was twice that of Germany and four times that of Italy and Spain.[46] Such ratios and levels of productivity translated into high wages across the economy, empowering workers and making it easier to organize. Opportunities and actual levels of upward economic mobility were higher than in most other places in the world.[47] The fact that the export economies produced basic staples rather than crops such as tea, rubber, or cacao prevented a situation common in tropical export economies in which business boomed but the nutritional level of the population declined as cultivation in the best lands shifted from basic staples to cash crops. The abundant and inexpensive grains and beef produced in the prairies and the pampas had a visible effect: the children of immigrants became on average two inches taller than their parents, whatever their ethnicity. Home-ownership rates in the cities of immigrants in the New World were higher than elsewhere. So was per capita water usage and sewer infrastructure. Not surprisingly, mortality rates in places like Buenos Aires and New York were the lowest in the world outside of Scandinavian cities. And the high cost of labor and resulting high incomes increased popular purchasing power, fueling the economy further through the expansion of mass consumption and domestic markets.

Although the benefits of emigration were more dramatic in the receiving countries, in part because of their previous marginality, they also accrued to the sending continent. The transatlantic outflow diminished demographic, ecological, and social strain in Europe. New World foodstuffs may have undermined Old World farmers, but they increased the caloric intake and life expectancy of its expanding urban population. The intense circulation of goods, capital, technologies, information, institutional practices, and people created a holistic system and the first truly integrated zone of the world economy in the "immigrant Atlantic," where prices and wages tended to converge across the ocean. Indeed, this convergence was one factor in the spread of emigration across the continent. As wages and prices in northwestern Europe grew similar to the Americas, emigration declined. But the spread of commercialization and industrialization to the south and east continued to pick up the slack.

Some of the same correlations between heavy immigration and economic growth also can be found in Asia, but at a less-intense and more-localized level. Regions with small native populations, relatively egalitarian and fluid social structures, and high proportions of immigrants, such as Singapore, Malaya, Taiwan and Manchuria, transformed from Asian backwaters in 1800 to major economic centers of the second half of the twentieth century (although Manchuria is now reverting to a rust belt). Similarly, the immigrant heavy areas of the Mekong Delta in Vietnam and of southern and central Thailand are more developed than the rest of the country. But there are also exceptions to this pattern in Asia. Burma and Sri Lanka have experienced relatively little economic growth. And both Japan and South Korea have undergone extensive economic development in the second half of the twentieth century, despite relatively low rates of both immigration and emigration.

In comparison with the Atlantic, Asian migration was neither as dynamic nor as deeply linked to general economic growth. Wages were higher in the destination zones, but remained so until the 1930s without much significant convergence.[48] The main regions that sent migrants in the 1850s were the same regions that produced migrants in the 1930s. Most migrants continued to travel from rural areas to rural areas. Occupations abroad also remained relatively stagnant without the transition from agriculture to industry, finance, and urban sectors that was seen in the Atlantic. Despite a gradual concentration over time into retail and middleman activities in Southeast Asia, by and large the agricultural, mining, transportation, and artisanal jobs that occupied migrants in the 1850s still predominated in the 1920s.[49]

As in Europe, emigrant regions tended to be highly commercialized—probably a necessity for the establishment of long-lasting migrant networks—but they did not experience anything like an industrial revolution. This is not to say that the global economy did not penetrate the interior of India and China. By the 1910s in China, the Chinese used Swedish or Japanese matches to light cigarettes sold by the British American Tobacco Company and lamps filled with Standard Oil kerosene so that they could see more clearly while using their Singer sewing machines. The Indian countryside was also decisively transformed by colonialism and integration into global markets—albeit with policies that at times made Indians less mobile rather than more so. But the holistic relations of migration, goods, and money that characterized the Atlantic system were not present in Asia. Increasingly over the nineteenth century, capital from Europeans displaced Asian capital that came with the migrants to Southeast Asia. In turn, goods, foodstuffs, and profits were diverted away from the migrants' homes to Europe. Manchurian patterns conformed a bit more closely to Atlantic patterns, with capital traveling in with Russians and Japanese. But the overwhelming majority of migrants still came from China, and despite being a relatively open frontier like in the Americas, it still remained a colonial state torn between competing elites rather than a self-governing migrant polity.

MIGRANT NETWORKS

If global economic and political forces shaped the broad aggregate trends of global migration, migrants still moved through specific, personalized, and particularistic networks. Each flow has its own story of how it got started, where it went, how many people settled and returned, and what jobs the migrants took. At the same time, each of these unique stories was forged at a specific nexus of forces and patterns common to all migration. These forces included not only the broad global economic patterns and their local ramifications but also the fact that most migrations around the world were organized locally, through networks based on village, neighborhood, and particularly kinship relations. Migration decisions everywhere were taken mainly in the context of family rather than individual strategies. These strategies aimed to augment the family's resources through higher earnings at destination, remittances, assistance for other kin to migrate, and eventual return home. Since many ended up staying, tensions between the interests of emigrating individuals or nuclear families and relatives back home became a leitmotif everywhere. Nonetheless, transregional or transnational families provided the basic mechanisms that made global migration possible and reproducible. The kinship-based diffusion of information, behaviors, and habits that was carried through family letters and photographs, travel, local tales, and word of mouth had a multiplying effect. Links not only connected forward to younger relatives and new generations but also connected laterally, branching out to increasingly distant relatives, to "cousins of cousins of cousins," who would in turn become "trunks" and ramify even further.

It is true that many people migrated through nonprimary mechanisms of recruitment—such as military drafts, imperial bureaucracies, churches, political parties or groups, *padroni* (employment agents), and through labor recruiters for local governments, plantations, and businesses. But the vast majority moved through the sponsorship and assistance of family members, even when the flow had originated in more formal recruitments, such as the case of Italians in the coffee plantations of Sao Paulo.[50] Indeed, some of the movements that appear in the scholarly literature as examples of indentured servitude controlled by European planters or imperial governments—such as that of Indians in Mauritius or Burma—were actually organized by the *kangani* system in which individuals recruited among their own fellow villagers and kin group.[51] Mass migration thus came not from the actions of institutions at the national and colonial levels but from the interaction of macrostructural trends and microsocial—but eventually transnational or intercontinental—networks.

The family was the fundamental arena of decision making. Migrant families can be compared to an investment portfolio, sending children and spouses to a variety of diversified places and occupations in the hope that one would provide a return on the investment. The specifics of this family economy changed in accordance with local family structures, inheritance customs, patterns of land tenure, and changing opportunities to acquire property and status at home and abroad. The experience of migration might also alter the original intentions of the migrant and his family, creating new desires to relocate either all or a portion of the family abroad rather than merely to earn money to support the family in the old country. But few migrants ever made choices only as isolated individuals. Decisions were made in the context of information and assistance obtained from relatives and village members around the world.

These networks were often institutionalized as businesses, mutual aid organizations, and other associations that helped channel aid and exploit more migrants.[52] These institutions also helped bring disparate networks together in broader ethnic, national, and diasporic identities. At the same time, these institutions and the elites that often dominated them were the mediators that linked migrants up to outside officials, transportation companies, credit, and jobs. In other words, they were the interface that linked particularistic networks directly to the economic and political processes that produced mass migration around the globe. The basic structures of these networks and associations were remarkably similar around the world,[53] but the specifics were always unique, varying according to family structure, locality, occupation and the particular timing and history of a flow. Ultimately, through these networks and institutions, individual choices came together in aggregate global patterns shaped by processes far beyond the consciousness of most individual migrants. These geographically dispersed communities were the social space within which many migrant decisions and activities took place. They produced a social geography that was not congruent with physical geography. A migrant might have more knowledge of distant Bangkok, Durban, or Havana than the nearby market town because that was where all his uncles and cousins were.[54]

These networks both created and constrained opportunities. Migration would have been generally too expensive and risky without the information, assistance, and opportunities provided by friends, relatives, and other resources available through these networks. It also would have been a pointless endeavor without the links to home and family maintained within these networks, through which money, support, and the other fruits of migration could be channeled. But the very strength of these channels also restricted opportunities. It was difficult for an established network to access new job opportunities and new destinations, even if only rudimentary new skills were necessary and the economic benefits were high. Many migrant elites even had an interest in controlling and limiting information in order to further profit from their position at the nexus of opportunities.

Studies of aggregate nation-to-nation movements can be quite successful at explaining the ebbs and flows of large streams, but they provide few tools to understand the mechanisms of migration. For example, one village may have had a population so devoted to emigration that even the fields were left barren or leased to outsiders, while another village a few kilometers down the road with almost identical conditions may have produced no migrants at all. Aggregate models and economic approaches are also hard-pressed to explain why migrants chose to travel to one location when wages and opportunities were clearly superior elsewhere. Why did some Italians choose to work in Montreal when the local French Canadians were looking for better-paid work in New England?[55] Conversely, scholars who emphasize social networks over economics have difficulty explaining the decline of migration flows.

A map of the world drawn from these geographically dispersed spaces and networks would look much different than the familiar mosaic of geographically discrete territories. These networked spaces make up a world of complex and overlapping flows and nodes, none of which can be entirely captured within a single national or regional history.[56] Each network occupies a distinct niche that articulates with many local histories but has its own specific patterns. To be sure, states, international borders, and local social structures are important aspects of migration history, but they are just some of many interwoven factors. The means of recruitment, institutions established by previous migrants, and the ways that travel, information, money, and opportunities are channeled and controlled are all aspects of migration not reducible to a single location. These processes and institutions are also inseparable from regulation, legal rights, and boundaries. These boundaries erect potential barriers, but they are also a source of opportunity because many migrants make their living precisely by their skills in negotiating these boundaries, managing multiple regulatory regimes, crossing customs and migration obstacles, and operating in spaces that are ultimately subject to no single regulatory regime. Migration itself can become a source of sustenance and a self-reproducing goal, above and beyond the sending and receiving societies.

THE SECOND WAVE, 1950 TO THE PRESENT

International migration began to grow steadily again after World War II. The almost trebling of the global population from 2.5 billion in 1950 to 6.8 billion in 2009, looser migration controls in many favored destination countries since the 1960s, the end of the cold war and emigration restrictions in Socialist countries, continuing refugee flows, and the expansion of the global economy have all contributed to this trend. Especially since the 1970s, economic liberalization has created the kinds of disruptions and commercialization that have always produced migrants without necessarily erasing the international wage differences that are an important stimulus of migration at the other end.[57]

It is actually more difficult to get an accurate count of migration for the second half of the twentieth century than for the first half. This is due largely to the spread of laws and institutions to regulate migrants. These have not only created new incentives for migrants to avoid officials who might count them but have also generated a plethora of new categories for admissible migrants that can be unclear in their meaning and incomparable across nations for the purpose of statistical measurement. The United Nations prefers to define migrants as those who plan to stay abroad for a year or more. But counting such people at the border is often impossible because many migrants change their status after arrival or overstay their visas illegally. For example, the United States experienced a near doubling of immigrants in the single year of 1993 because of its amnesty law, in which migrants who might have been residing illegally for decades were finally counted as "immigrants."

Thus, international organizations have resorted to counting "migrant stock" rather than migration itself, basing their numbers on foreign-born peoples counted in national censuses. This, too, is an imperfect form of measurement because some censuses count foreign birth, while others only count foreign residents who have not become citizens and others merely note racial or ethnic distinctions. This measurement may also count people who did not move while international borders moved around them. The many nations that emerged from the breakup of the Soviet Union account for a good proportion of the increase from 1990 to 2000, when many people became foreigners without ever leaving their homes, as new international borders were created around them. Other events could have a disproportionately large effect on these numbers, such as the partition of South Asia in 1947 that created more than 20 million refugees. These people accounted for nearly 15–25 percent of the world's "migrant stock" through the 1970s, even though South Asia is more important as a migrant-producing than a migrant-receiving region (see table 1.3).

We can also attempt a crude estimate of annual migration flows in the 1990s.[58] As in the previous wave, the United States was still the largest single country of immigration, averaging 860,000 legal migrants a year, and more than 300,000 (some say up to a million) illegals. Annual migration to the European Union amounted to 1.2 million legal migrants and 400,000–500,000 illegals. Migration into Canada, Australia, and New Zealand accounted for another 300,000 each. More than a million migrants went each year to the Persian Gulf states and Israel. Other major destinations included Argentina, Venezuela, South Africa, Singapore, Malaysia, and Japan, as well as large flows between countries

TABLE 1.3: MIGRANT STOCK AS PORTION OF WORLD POPULATION

Year	Foreign-Born Population (mil.)	Percentage of World Population
1910	35.7	2.0
1930	42.9	2.1
1965	75.2	2.3
1975	84.5	2.1
1985	105.2	2.2
1990	155.5	2.9
2000	195.2	3.2
2010	213.9	3.1

Sources: For 1910 and 1930, International Labour Office, *World Statistics of Aliens: A Comparative Study of Census Returns, 1910–1920–1930* (Geneva, 1936), 56; for 1965 and 1975, Hania Zlotnik, "International Migration 1965–96: An Overview," *Population and Development Review* 24 (1998): 431; for 1990 to 2010 (using a revised methodology that produces higher estimates than for 1965–1985), United Nations Population Division estimates at http://esa.un.org/migration; and world population numbers are from United States Census Bureau, www.census.gov/ipc/www/idb/worldpop.php.

in Africa, Southeast Asia, and the ex-Soviet republics. A generous estimate of 3–4 million migrants seems appropriate for these other destinations. More than half a million asylum applications were also made each year around the world, often not counted in migration statistics. Added up, this produces an annual migration of 8–9 million a year. A return rate of about 40 percent correlates to the growth of 55 million migrants in migrant stock estimates from 1990 to 2000.

An attempt to compare this to earlier numbers brings more difficulties. Pre–World War II migrant stock numbers were based on fragmentary data beyond the Atlantic, and migrants to Manchuria, Siberia, and Burma would not even have been counted as international migrant stock. Also, most migrants who crossed land borders within Africa, Europe, and the Americas before the 1940s remained uncounted in migration statistics. But if we put these caveats aside and compare the transoceanic numbers of the first wave to these contemporary estimates, it appears that per capita global migration has approached levels roughly similar to earlier rates. Peak long-distance migration rates around 1912 and again in the late 1920s reached more than 3.3 million a year. Contemporary migration is double to triple that number, but a total of 85 million migrants in the 1990s would only account for 1.4 percent of the world population of 2000, as compared to the 1.7 percent of world population in the decade before 1915, or 1.5 percent of world population in the 1920s.

Contemporary migrations can be compared to earlier migrations in several other productive ways, all of which help understand continuities and changes in global migration. Some of these processes, such as closing of frontiers and the increases in refugees and migration control have their roots in the 1910s and

1920s or even earlier. For example, women have also come to make up nearly half of all international migrants, continuing trends that began in the 1920s and 1930s. Other processes, such as the shift in origins and destinations and the rise of professional migration have emerged later in the twentieth century.

One clear change since World War II is that sources have shifted and diversified. During the first wave, Europeans and their descendants, southeastern and northeastern Chinese, and southeastern Indians accounted for nine-tenths of all long-distance movements. After World War II, Western Europeans restarted their transoceanic crossings, but these lasted only two decades and by the 1980s, even the southern streams (out of Italy and Iberia) had thinned. Eastern Europe had a reverse experience. Emigration remained obstructed until the 1980s by the policies of communist regimes and became a rush in the following decades. The same was true of mainland China, where emigration also boomed after 1980, although absolute numbers have still not reached the levels of the 1920s. Emigration also spread to a more diverse range of sources in East Asia, of which emigration from South Korea (before the 1980s) the Philippines, Indonesia, and Vietnam (much in the form of refugees) is especially notable. Africa became an important exporter of people for the first time since the end of the slave trades with trans-Mediterranean crossings from its northern coast that were later joined by sub-Saharans. Others traversed the Atlantic and much larger numbers crossed international borders within Africa. Latin America shifted from a net receiver to a major sender of migrants and the outflow spread from northern Mexico and the Caribbean to the entire region. In terms of origins, therefore, the second wave is much more global than the previous one. By the early twenty-first century, only the main migrant destinations in North America, Western Europe, Australia, the oil kingdoms, and a few other countries were not furnishing significant numbers of emigrants.

Like the estimate of migrant flows above, table 1.4 shows the persistence of some destinations and drastic change in others. The United States continues to receive about one-fifth of all international migration.[59] Western Europe shifted from sender to receiver during the last third of the twentieth century so drastically that by the mid-1990s, it had slightly surpassed the United States. The other countries of European settlement (Canada, Australia/New Zealand, and Argentina) host about 7 percent giving Western Europe and its offshoots almost half of all the world's international migrants. Eastern Europe contains 12 percent of the world's immigrant stock, but that may be inflated by the presence of nonmigrant ethnic minorities following the breakdowns of the Soviet Union and Yugoslavia. The Persian Gulf kingdoms (Saudi Arabia, the United Arab Emirates or UAE, Kuwait, Qatar, Oman, and Bahrain, in order of importance) received 7 percent. The more-developed countries of Asia (Japan, Hong Kong, Singapore, and, in smaller numbers, South Korea and Taiwan) account for 4 percent and 6 percent if Israel is added. And so-called south-to-south migrations make up the remaining fourth (see table 1.4).

TABLE 1.4: PLACE OF RESIDENCE OF INTERNATIONAL MIGRANTS IN 2005

Region or Country	Number	% of Total
Northwestern & Southern Europe	41,737,698	22
United States	38,354,709	20
Other European "Offshoots" (Canada, Australia/New Zealand, Argentina/Uruguay)	12,429,346	7
Eastern Europe	22,378,152	12
Persian Gulf "Oil" Kingdoms	12,801,253	7
Developed Asia (Japan, Singapore, Hong Kong, Taiwan, South Korea, Israel)	10,519,200	6
Rest of World (South-to-South)	52,413,206	27
World	190,633,564	

Source: UN, World Migrant Stock: The 2006 Revision Population Database, esa.un.org/migration.

Some of the south-to-south migrations are made up of refugee flows between neighboring states, but the bulk consist of economically motivated moves to higher-income countries within regions in the less-developed world. Within Africa, Libya serves that function in the north, South Africa in the other extreme, and Cote d'Ivoire and Ghana in the west. Jordan and Iraq (before the first Gulf War) absorbed more than 4 million workers from Egypt and other poorer countries in the Middle East. Kazakhstan hosts 2.5 million workers from central Asia, which about replaced the number of Russians, Ukrainians, and Volga Germans who left after 1989. Malaysia and Thailand have 1.7 million and 1.1 million foreign residents officially and a much larger number of undocumented workers. Venezuela, Costa Rica, and Chile play a similar role in Latin America. These migrations at times form a set of steps along the national income rank. So, for example, Haitians move to Santo Domingo while Dominicans move to Puerto Rico and Puerto Rican professionals move to Florida.

Main contemporary destinations also tend not to be the frontiers of the past with their low but rapidly expanding populations. Where new frontiers have become occupied in the late twentieth century, such as the Brazilian, Peruvian, and Ecuadorian Amazon, new plantation areas in Malaysian and Indonesian rain forests, and the dry areas of Tibet and central Asia, family agriculture has been less productive and more difficult to sustain ecologically.[60] Almost three-quarters of international migration today flows to economically developed countries or regions in possession of excess wealth, such as the oil kingdoms. With the exception of the oil kingdoms, these are all places with populations that are steady or declining in proportion to world population, although much of the growth the Persian Gulf states is the result of immigrants outnumbering natives and it remains to be seen if this will amount to long-term population growth, as was the case in the frontiers of the first wave. But overall, rather than the global population redistribution of the past migrations, the current migrations seem only to be mitigating the effects of lower growth rates in the wealthier parts of the world and of higher growth rates in the poorer parts of the world.

These shifting migration patterns can also be seen in changing rates of urbanization. Only two of the ten most populous cities of 1900, New York and Tokyo, were still in the top ten of 2000. The rest are located in some of the major migrant-sending regions of the world, such as India, Mexico, Brazil, China, and Indonesia. International migration is clearly only part of the story of global migration since the 1950s. Massive waves of domestic migration have accompanied the population growth of the undeveloped world. Without the relatively liberal migration regimes and sparsely populated frontier destinations of the earlier waves, the effects of this new urbanization and population growth may be different than a hundred years ago, as immigrants are less able to leave the poverty of these overpopulated cities for better opportunities abroad.

Lachrymose visions of global migration, however, are not new and, as in the past, they may prove to be overly pessimistic. Indeed, the gap between the discursive association of migration with personal poverty and national failure and a reality of dynamism and social mobility has remained quite unchanged over time. Then and now, long-distance migration originated mainly in the most dynamic and connected regions of the world and among their better-off inhabitants. In the cases during the first wave where the areas of origin were not particularly rich, such as Ireland and southern India, they were at least closely linked to the world economy and transportation routes. In most other cases, like northwestern and coastal Europe and southeastern China, they were among the richer and more connected areas in their parts of the world.

The same is true of the first regions to join, or rejoin, the second wave: Japan and northwestern Europe in the late 1940s and 1950s; southern Europe, beginning at the same time, but continuing for two extra decades; northern Mexico, Puerto Rico, Cuba, Colombia, and Chile; Taiwan, Hong Kong, South Korea, and Thailand; Turkey; and Algeria and other northwestern African countries. From these pioneering regions, emigration later spread to poorer ones in southern Mexico, Central America, the Andean region, sub-Saharan Africa, the Philippines, Cambodia, Bangladesh, and so forth. Moreover, the poorer regions actually joined the flow when they were becoming less poor. Contrary to traditional narratives about migrants coming from the most impoverished areas, they actually are most likely to come from areas that are undergoing economic transformation and growth, are increasingly commercialized, are connected via transportation and preexisting networks, have a wage gap somewhere between two and six times more at the destination than at the origin, and have more access to resources to fund migration.

The argument that, unlike in the past, global migration today is not narrowing regional economic disparities also overlooks several factors. Wage gaps between northwestern Europe and its destinations were on the lower end of the spectrum because all of these places had relatively high wages, but these disparities nevertheless took more than seven decades to even out. The wage gap between southern and eastern Europe and the transoceanic destinations narrowed but did not close, and those between sending and receiving areas in Southeast Asia did not even narrow. In contrast, wage convergence and the resulting diminution and end of emigration actually happened in dozens of places during the second wave. War-devastated Germany and Japan had stopped exporting labor by the 1960s. Italy, Spain, Portugal, and Greece stopped sending workers to the north or across oceans by the 1980s, joining the group that imports labor and exports tourists. Taiwan, Hong Kong, South Korea, Chile, Costa Rica, and Puerto Rico have moved into that category, and Thailand, Turkey, northern Mexico, and Malaysia seem to be heading there. However, migration controls, variations in labor and wage laws, and the constantly shifting flows of trade and finance that often failed to reproduce the holistic cycles of goods, money, and people in the previous Atlantic migrations will drag the process out.

As in the past, migrant remittances have varied effects. Much of the money sent home then and now has gone toward conspicuous consumption, the support of family, and charity. But a great deal also goes into the purchase of land, small family businesses, the education of children, and other activities with clear connections to production. The economic impact of technological and entrepreneurial practices imported by returnees and of increased family consumption often goes unmentioned because it is difficult to measure. This impact of remittances changes hand in hand with the kinds of opportunities and the level of development at home. Few of the remittances back to Asia before the 1980s were used for productive investment, and those that attempted such investment often failed.[61] Since the 1980s, as home economies have boomed, remittances for the sake of investment have been much more successful, and many educated and successful migrants have taken a significantly greater interest in investment and return residence. What was once seen as brain drain has become the accumulation of new skills and wealth abroad that could be profitably utilized at home.

Some sociologists and economists also argue that deindustrialization and the mechanization of agriculture in the developed countries have forged a dual-labor market in which highly educated native workers are increasingly dependent on immigrant service labor—not to mention the manufactured goods produced by domestic migrant labor in other countries.[62] The existence of segregated occupational sectors, they argue, will impede social integration and upward mobility. But there is currently little evidence that jobs in factories or agribusiness in developed countries offer greater opportunity than service jobs. Involvement in commerce at any level has consistently provided one of the greatest platforms for immigrants' upward mobility.

Service jobs, moreover, include those of educated professionals, who have comprised up to 20 percent of the migrants to North America and Europe since the 1960s, as well as significant streams of professionals from the developed countries into the oil kingdoms. Several immigrant groups in the United States, from Indians and Filipinos to Argentines and Nigerians, have higher educational levels and family incomes than the native-born white population. Immigration law preferences for the wealthy and educated play an important role in this stream, as does the lack of intellectually and financially attractive jobs in many poorer countries. Over time, however, migrant flows once dominated by educated professionals open the door for a rise in less-skilled migrants who take advantage of family reunification opportunities. And shorter-distance, lower-cost, south-to-south international movements allow the poor to migrate, even if those moves have not been preceded by those of better-off and more-educated relatives. Indeed, in terms of alleviating extreme poverty, these may be the most important streams in the world.

Legal restrictions threaten to obstruct economic opportunities and convergence opportunities, even if they have mixed results in blocking migration. Restrictions raise the cost of movement, preventing many from relocating. They are probably most effective in stopping incipient streams. They are less effective in restraining well-established streams in which the economic incentives for migration are high and transportation costs are relatively low (the U.S.-Mexico border is the best-known example).[63] These restrictions also have a number of undesirable effects. Those who have to pay exorbitant amounts to traffickers start their lives abroad with heavy debts. Many nations have developed guest- and temporary-worker policies that perpetuate dual economies while insulating migrants from the broader society and retarding the broader development of skills and wealth that might have a positive development on economic development at home.[64] Legal restrictions also hinder circulatory movements that would make the system more adaptable and efficient. There are surely millions of undocumented immigrants who at one point in time or another would be better-off and more productive at home or in some other destination, but who remain where they are for fear of not being able to return. This is a different form of legally imposed immobility.

Proponents of modern immigration and border controls often depict it as an indivisible aspect of national sovereignty. In fact, it has its roots only in the late nineteenth century. Free mobility was often considered the hallmark of the modern nation in the middle of the nineteenth century. Many of the institutions and techniques of modern migration control were only developed after the 1870s, through increased medical inspections and attempts to keep Asians out of white settler nations around the Pacific. By the 1920s, these techniques had developed into widely accepted principles that migration control was the unilateral prerogative of receiving nations and should properly happen at borders. The modern passport system and common forms of legislation and documentation also began to circulate around the world at that time.[65] Since then, the most notable development of these laws has been the constant expansion of administrative categories to define migrants as students, asylum seekers, holiday workers, tourists, temporary residents, guest workers, family migrants, immigrants, business travelers, illegals, undocumented persons, and so forth. It is commonly argued that these categorization and surveillance measures help to protect both the human rights of migrants and the interests of the nation.[66] But they also generate the Byzantine red tape that so many observers complain about. In their preferences for wealthy and educated migrants, they also comprise one of the last and most significant institutions of systematic discrimination in the world today, defining by mere accident of birth those who are and are not free to move where they wish in the world.

The reinforcement of national borders and the management of population within those borders have not only hindered economic convergence between senders and receivers but have also helped produce what is perhaps the darkest side of global migration since World War II: the tremendous increase in refugee flows. These flows had surged in the past with the decline or disintegration of empires, which despite their negative image actually had a greater tolerance for ethnocultural pluralism than the nation-states that replaced them. The weakening of the Ottoman Empire within Europe had led to the first mass refugee movements of the modern period. Some 1.5 million Muslims, and a much smaller number of Christians, were forced out of their homes in the Caucasus and Balkans between 1864 and 1880.[67] The final collapse of the empire during and after World War I produced a much larger and even exchange of Muslim and Christian refugees (5 million to 6 million people). And the breakdown of the Austro-Hungarian and Russian empires during the same period ushered similar movements.

Several trends, however, have swelled these tragic flows since the 1940s. One is the increase in the number and intensity of wars, of civilian casualties, and of processes of ethnic cleansing in their aftermaths. During World War II, Germany and the USSR each deported more than 1.5 million Poles. The end of the war ushered the expulsion throughout Central and Eastern Europe of more than 12 million ethnic Germans and 10 million refugees of other ethnicities (mainly Poles, Czechs, Russians, Finns, and Baltic people). On the other side of the Eurasian landmass, 5 million Japanese fled or were deported from East Asian countries, and 60 million Chinese were left homeless. The 1948 Arab-Israeli war led to the expulsion or flight of some 600,000 Palestinians and to an equal inflow of Jews expelled or fleeing from Arab countries. The Chinese takeover of Tibet in 1950–1951 and their repression of the 1959 uprising pushed thousands across the border into India. The Lebanese civil war between 1975 and 1990 and Israeli military incursions displaced close to a million people. The Rwanda massacres of July 1994 led to the exodus of close to a million mostly Tutsi refugees. The victory of a Tutsi-led government led to a larger outflow of Hutus. Most recently, the U.S. invasion of Iraq generated an exodus of 2.2 million, according to the Office of the UN High Commissioner for Refugees, and a larger number of civilians have been displaced by the war in northwestern Pakistan between the government and Taliban militants since 2004.[68]

As in the past, the collapse of empires has fueled these movements. The end of British rule and partition in South Asia in 1947 pushed 7 million Muslims from India to Pakistan and an equal number of Hindus and Sikhs from Pakistan into India. The second chapter of this struggle, which produced the country of Bangladesh in 1971, drove 8–10 million Hindus into India. The process of ending French rule in Algeria (1954–1962) uprooted 2 million Algerians and pushed 1 million *Pied-Noirs* across the Mediterranean. Decolonization in sub-Saharan Africa was followed by the exodus of tens of thousands of French, English, and Portuguese residents, the expulsion of some 80,000 Indians, and the flight of millions of members of African ethnic groups from some of the new and arbitrarily delimited nations to others. The balkanization of the multiethnic state of Yugoslavia in the 1990s drove more than 3 million people from their places of birth and the fragmentation of the Soviet Empire produced much larger outflows.

The third main producer of refugees in the post–World War II period was the spread of communism and the cold war. Two and a half million East Germans fled to West Germany between 1946 and the erection of the Berlin Wall—and many other barriers—in 1961. Many other Eastern Europeans fled westward soon after the war. More than half a million were able to flee following the Warsaw Pact put-down of the Hungarian and Czechoslovakian rebellions of 1956 and 1968, respectively. The Korean War of 1950–1953 ushered the southward movement of 1 million people. A slightly smaller number left Cuba after what seemed a nationalist revolt turned into a communist revolution in the early 1960s. Over the next three decades, repression by anticommunist and U.S.-supported regimes in Chile, Argentina, Uruguay, Guatemala, and El Salvador created tens of thousands of exiles. The Soviet invasion of Afghanistan in the early 1980s, and the subsequent civil war and Taliban takeover, caused more than 6 million refugees to flee.

In some cases, cold war politics became entangled with ethnic animosities. More than half of the 1 million "boat people" who fled Vietnam in the aftermath of the communist victory of 1975 were ethnic Chinese. They were also highly overrepresented among those who were massacred or fled during the contemporaneous Khmer Rouge genocide in neighboring Cambodia. In Indonesia, Chinese residents have been persecuted and expelled for being, at different times, pro-Western imperialists, communists, and capitalist exploiters of the Indonesian masses. Tens of thousands of Hmongs who had been recruited by the Central Intelligence Agency (CIA) had to flee from Laos to Thailand, and eventually across the Pacific, after the American military withdrew from Southeast Asia. In a similar situation on the other side of that ocean and one decade later (in the 1980s), thousands of Miskito Indian "contras" were driven from their Nicaraguan homeland into Honduras by the Sandinista army. Further north, a larger number of "leftist" Guatemalan Mayans crossed the border into Mexico, fleeing the persecution of anticommunist, U.S.-backed governments.

The interest in purification and management of population that has generated many refugee flows also can be seen in the many discussions about assimilation and the effects of migrants. Will new migrants be able to integrate economically, politically, and socially like previous waves? Will they contribute to the national economy? Arguments that the new migrants are different and less able to assimilate than those in earlier waves often point to the rise in transnational connections and ease of return travel, the expansion of dual citizenship, the prevalence of home-language media, stronger ethnic and racial differences, the emergence of segregated labor markets that block advancement, and the illegal status of many migrants.[69]

Most of these arguments rest on weak historical foundations. In nations where assimilation is the norm, integration has generally taken two or more generations. Indeed, numerous studies have shown the continuing relevance of white ethnicity in the United States, not only regarding public activities like voting but also in terms of intimate behavior such as mores and manners, child-rearing practices, adolescent styles, and attitudes toward illness, psychiatric disorders, and authority, even in cases where the individuals examined were not particularly aware of their ethnicity.[70] The recent waves of migration are still too new to say anything definite based on the situations of existing migrant communities.

The idea of an unprecedented difference in race and culture also has weak historical foundations. In the past, Irish, Asians, Jews, Italians, and others were thought to be distinct and unassimilable races compared to Anglo-Protestants Americans, and Australians. The major immigration restriction legislation in the United States (the act of 1924) was intended to curtail the inflow of what were openly described as racially inferior Southern and Eastern Europeans and passed with overwhelming support in the U.S. Senate and Congress. Nevertheless, all of these people eventually became both white and fully "American." So, again, it is impossible to predict if, or to what degree, the complexion of the new immigrants will prevent them from becoming full members of the polities where they settle, as has happened to African descendants in many parts of the Americas. The situation of the latter, after all, arose from a history of slavery and cumulative exclusion rather than from some sort of permanent cultural "pigmentophobia." And the relevance of whiteness can decline as other social markers (e.g., education, occupation, income, place of residence, lifestyle, and status) gain importance in societies that are becoming more "racially" exogamous.

Many observers assert (but rarely demonstrate) that the unprecedented speeds and low costs of contemporary communication have created unparalleled new forms of transnationality.[71] To be sure, communication is easier and short-term movement is much more common, but it is far from clear what kind of effect this may have. Much of what has been described here as "migrant networks" are very similar to what appear in recent scholarship as "transnational" and "diasporic" spaces. Indeed, these forms of migrant organization, and the cheaper and faster communication technologies that have strengthened them, have been fundamental to the rise of mass migration over the last two hundred years. A vibrant home-language print media and involvement with home politics were also the norm in earlier migrations, as well as causes for great concern by observers worried about incorporation. Like transnational networks, political involvement of migrants and home states is not as new as is often claimed. Ties to the home village are probably as old as migration. Modern politicized diasporic identities have their roots in the nationalisms that covered the world after the late nineteenth century and had already become an important feature of migrant life around the world by the turn of the twentieth century.[72] This historical origin also gives diasporic identities a much shorter lineage than the timeless entities often claimed by their proponents. Indeed, rather than being subversive to the nation-state, diasporic identities have their origins in precisely the same forces that that built nationalism and the international system of nation-states.

The spread of dual citizenship and absentee voting in the present is new. But at the turn of the twentieth century, citizenship laws and democratic states were still few and far between. It was precisely this transnational activism and political involvement of migrants, and the difficulties that arose from them that helped create more detailed citizenship laws and participatory rule in the first place. Recent scholarship has demonstrated that political participation is not an either-or choice. Migrants involved in homeland politics are also more likely to be politically active in their new nation and look beyond their migrant networks. Much the same was true historically. For example, the Japanese government was strongly involved in the affairs of emigrant communities, but often used its influence to encourage migrants to build a positive image of Japan by assimilating to local norms.[73]

There are, however, some historical discontinuities with the past. The spread of migration controls is the most obvious. Many migrants increasingly reside as illegals, temporary workers, or with other statuses that do not allow for citizenship and political integration. This may hinder integration in the long run and create a subordinate laboring caste even more than the presence of a segregated labor market. Indeed, the fears of a segregated laboring class may create discrimination more than the actual fact. For example, it was precisely the fear that Asian immigrants would create a degraded working caste in white settler nations that helped create discriminatory migration laws. These laws themselves then helped produce Asian groups that were underprivileged and discriminated against.

But most discussions of assimilation assume the existence of a mainstream national culture (even if that culture is itself the product of migration) that is attractive and powerful enough to make incorporation desirable.[74] Given that the majority of migrants now travel to developed countries that have worked to forge a mainstream identity, this is not an unreasonable assumption. But the paradigm of assimilation may not be an appropriate lens through which to view migrant incorporation everywhere and at all times. Many other different examples can be seen around the world.

In many parts of Southeast Asia, Africa, and, to a lesser degree, Latin America, immigrant groups have persisted over generations as middleman minorities and merchant elites. In general, this is a consequence of moving to an area with a hierarchical or castelike social structure, whether as a result of colonial rule or well-entrenched patterns. In these conditions, migrants make a living by crossing the different social groups, or usually forging economic links between them, through financial and retail activities—in short, by adapting the institutions of a trade diaspora to a middleman situation. The long-term consequences may vary. Sometimes, these migrants may maintain their culture and language for generations, as has been the case for Chinese in many parts of maritime Southeast Asia since the 1500s.[75] Policies in newly independent nations such as Indonesia and the Philippines have attempted to suppress Chinese language and restrict their ability to hire other Chinese in their businesses. But the Chinese still remain identified with mercantile power, and have developed a symbiotic relationship with native elite. In the slightly more democratic nations of Latin America, the descendants of Lebanese, Japanese, and Chinese have become somewhat more integrated into elite political and social culture, even producing presidents in Ecuador and Peru. In both cases, however, it is clear that wealth and power are crucial to the ability to choose an ethnic identity over assimilation.

Malaysia presents one of the most interesting alternatives to immigration narratives. With a Chinese minority of about 35 percent and an Indian minority of about 8 percent, it falls between characterizations as being a country of immigrants or a country with an immigrant minority. The Chinese are clearly a powerful economic minority collaborating with a native political elite, although many Chinese are also working class. And more than anywhere else in Southeast Asia, including Singapore, the Chinese in Malaysia have maintained their dialects, as well as religious and cultural practices. In some parts of Malaysia, such as Penang, Chinese is clearly the mainstream culture. But the Chinese also are subject to discrimination in favor of Malays for certain political and educational opportunities, and Islam is often described as key to Malay identity (few Chinese have converted). In other words, very little assimilation toward a single national culture has taken place. Yet Malaysia is clearly a stable nation that is very self-consciously made of different groups with different statuses.[76]

The attractiveness of assimilation may also change over time. In the middle of the twentieth century, in the context of declining international migration, decolonization, cold war suspicions, and strong nationalisms, the pressure to integrate and assimilate was strong around the world. Since the 1970s, ethnic and multicultural identities have grown more attractive. For example, in Southeast Asia immediately after World War II, many Chinese tried to identify entirely as local nationals of Chinese descent, and social scientists predicted imminent assimilation. Since the 1970s, however, individuals of Chinese descent who once identified linguistically and culturally as Thai, Filipino, or some other nationality have increasingly emphasized their Chinese identity, joined Chinese cultural associations, and started to teach their children Mandarin. This has emerged as part of the expansion of regional Chinese business networks, the opening of China, and the identification of being Chinese with power and modernity. Many people of Chinese descent, especially those from relatively wealthy countries such as North America or Australia, resent attempts to pull them into an essentialized Chinese "diaspora." But this only emphasizes that the attractiveness and meaning of assimilation must always be understood in a specific historical context, not as a natural and inevitable process. In this case, it is a global historical context, in which the opening of China, the rise of neoliberal trade regimes, the ability to revitalize dormant networks, and the creation of global hometown and surname associations has opened a space for the production of new Chinese identities that float free from nation and place. Power and wealth often determine the attractiveness of assimilation, but they may reside somewhere other than the mainstream national community.[77]

Presenting perhaps the greatest challenge to historical precedent, however, are not the new forms of migration, but the new forms of mobility that are not usually counted as migration. In 2000, 700 million tourist entries were counted, up from 480 million in 1990 and 300 million in 1980. This kind of short-term movement is several magnitudes of order larger than in the previous migration waves. Many of these tourists overstay their visas and become migrants, contributing to the difficulty of counting contemporary migration. But perhaps of more significance is the growth in short-term contacts and tourism, for which there is no direct counterpart in the earlier waves of migration. Indeed, the line between migration and travel is increasingly blurred, as in the case of Hong Kong residents in the 1990s, who established households abroad but still commuted regularly back to Hong Kong for work. More than any changes in the nature or patterns of labor migration, this short-term mobility can best justify claims for an unprecedented new era of transnational ties and mobility.

NOTES

1. Dirk Hoerder, *Cultures in Contact: World Migrations in the Second Millennium* (Durham, NC: Duke University Press, 2002); Patrick Manning, *Migration in World History* (London: Routledge, 2005).

2. About 1 million Spaniards migrated to the Americas between 1492 and the mid-1820s, when the last colonies in the mainland empire became independent. The British began arriving about a century later, and about 800,000 of them (plus 250,000 immigrants from German states) had arrived by the 1820s. Estimates of Portuguese migration to colonial Brazil hover around half a million. Jose C. Moya, "Migration," in *Encyclopedia of Latin American History and Culture* (New York: Charles Scribner's Sons, 2008).

3. Jan Lucassen and Leo Lucassen, "The Mobility Transition Revisited: Migration Patterns in Europe, 1500–1900," unpublished article, forthcoming in *Journal of Global History*. The Lucassens also include soldiers in their calculations. This makes the increase less dramatic, growing from 15.7 percent in 1750–1800 to 35.3 percent in 1850–1900. But even with soldiers, the total number of migrants they count for 1850–1900 (118 million) is only slightly smaller than the total for the entire period of 1600–1850 (137.7 million).

4. Kate Merkel-Hess and Jeffrey Wasserstrom, "A Country on the Move: China Urbanizes," *Current History*, vol. 108 (April 2009), 167–172.

5. World Tourism Organization, *Collection of Tourism Expenditure Statistics* (Madrid: World Tourism Association, 1995), vi. For statistics, see the World Tourism Organization publications *World Tourism Barometer* and *Tourism Market Trends*.

6. Paul Bairoch, *Cities and Economic Development* (Chicago: Chicago University Press, 1988).

7. Historically, village exogamy has been an important cause of rural-to-rural migration, including some flows that appear as international movements, such as those from Nepal to India and vice versa. These "marriage" or "associational" movements explain in part the preponderance of women in short-distance migration globally. But although short-distance marriage migration is still important in absolute numbers, it has decreased in relative terms during the last two centuries, as rural populations have declined as a proportion of the world's inhabitants.

8. Lucassen and Lucassen, "The Mobility Transition Revisited," table 2, estimates the number of rural seasonal laborers in Europe at 610,000 from 1750 to 1800 and 5.8 million from 1850 to 1900.

9. For a discussion of the transportation and communication revolution as part of a broader process of "massification," see Jose C. Moya, "Modernization, Modernity, and the Transformation of the Atlantic World in the Nineteenth Century," in *The Atlantic in Global History, 1500–2000*, ed. Jorge Canizares-Esguerra and Erik Seeman (Upper Saddle River, NJ: Prentice Hall, 2007).

10. David Eltis, ed., *Coerced and Free Migration: Global Perspectives* (Stanford: Stanford University Press, 2002), 7.

11. Markus Vink, "'The World's Oldest Trade': Dutch Slavery and Slave Trade in the Indian Ocean in the Seventeenth Century," *Journal of World History* 14, no. 2 (June 2003): 131–177.

12. Anthony Reid, ed., *Sojourners and Settlers: Histories of Southeast Asia and the Chinese* (Honolulu: University of Hawai'i Press, 2001); Anthony Reid and Jennifer Brewster, eds., *Slavery, Bondage and Dependency in Southeast Asia* (New York: Palgrave McMillan, 1984); James Warren, *The Sulu Zone, 1768–1898: The Dynamics of External Trade, Slavery, and Ethnicity in the Transformation of a Southeast Asian Maritime State* (Quezon City, Philippines: New Day Publishers, 1985).

13. The trans-Saharan slave trade continued throughout the nineteenth century, with kidnapped Africans transported to North African ports and from there to the Ottoman Empire. But it was conducted in a clandestine form and it declined over time. John Wright, "Enforced Migration: The Black Slave Trade across the Mediterranean," *Maghreb Review* 31, nos. 1–2 (2006): 62–70.

14. David Moon, "Peasant Migration, the Abolition of Serfdom, and the Internal Passport System in the Russian Empire, c. 1800–1914," in *Coerced and Free Migration*, ed. David Eltis, 324–360.

15. Lucassen and Lucassen, "The Mobility Transition Revisited," figures 10 and 11.

16. Marina Carter, *Servants, Sirdars and Settlers: Indians in Mauritius, 1834–1874* (Delhi: Oxford University Press, 1995); Frank Heidemann, *Kanganies in Sri Lanka and Malaysia: Tamil Recruiter-cum-Foreman as a Sociological Category in the Nineteenth and Twentieth Centuries* (Munich: Anacon, 1992); Arnold Meagher, *The Coolie Trade: The Traffic in Chinese Laborers to Latin America* (Bloomington, IN: Xlibris, 2008); David Northrup, *Indentured Labor in the Age of Imperialism, 1834–1922* (Cambridge: Cambridge University Press, 1995); Wang Sing-wu, *The Organization of Chinese Emigration, 1848–1888: With Special Reference to Chinese Emigration to Australia* (San Francisco: Chinese Materials Center, 1978). On European migrants, see Gunther Peck, *Reinventing Free Labor: Padrones and Immigrant Workers in the North American West, 1880–1930* (Cambridge: Cambridge University Press, 2000).

17. That right to depart spread throughout Europe, mainly from the north and west to the south and east, as the nineteenth century matured: Britain (1820s); Sweden, the German states, Belgium, the Netherlands, and the Swiss Confederation (1840s); Spain and Portugal (1850s); and Russia (1890s). See Aristide Zolberg's suggestively titled "The Exit Revolution" and John Torpey, "Leaving: A Comparative View," in *Citizenship and Those Who Leave: The Politics of Emigration and Expatriation*, ed. Nancy L. Green and Francois Weil (Urbana: University of Illinois Press, 2007).

18. Andreas Fahrmeir, Olivier Faron, and Patrick Weil, eds., *Migration Control in the North Atlantic World: The Evolution of State Practices in Europe and the United States from the French Revolution to the Inter-War Period* (New York: Berghahn Books, 2003); John Torpey, *The Invention of the Passport: Surveillance, Citizenship and the State* (Cambridge: Cambridge University Press, 2000).

19. Adam McKeown, *Melancholy Order: Asian Migration and the Globalization of Borders* (New York: Columbia University Press, 2008); Carl Strikwerda, "Tides of Migration, Currents of History: The State, Economy, and the Transatlantic Movement of Labor in the Nineteenth and Twentieth Centuries," *International Review of Social History* 44 (1999): 367–394.

20. See Jose C. Moya, *Cousins and Strangers: Spanish Immigrants in Buenos Aires, 1850–1930* (Berkeley: University of California Press, 1998) for an effort to fuse these global and local perspectives on migration and adaptation.

21. Imre Ferenczi and Walter Willcox, eds., *International Migrations*, vol. 2, *Interpretations* (New York: National Bureau of Economic Research, 1929); J. D. Gould, "European Inter-Continental Emigration 1815–1914: Patterns and Causes," *European Journal of Economic History* 8 (1979): 593–679.

22. Timothy Hatton and Jeffrey Williamson, *The Age of Mass Migration: Causes and Economic Impact* (New York: Oxford University Press, 1998).

23. For sources on numbers, see Adam McKeown, "Global Migration 1846–1919," *Journal of World History* 15, no. 2 (2004): 188–189. More generally, see Philip Kuhn, *Chinese among Others: Emigration in Modern Times* (Lanham, MD: Rowman & Littlefield, 2008); Adam McKeown, "Conceptualizing Chinese Diasporas, 1842 to 1949," *Journal of Asian Studies* 58 (1999): 322–326, and "From Opium Farmer to Astronaut: A Global History of Diasporic Chinese Business," *Diaspora* 9 (2000): 317–360; Qiu Liben, *Cong shijie kan huaren* [*Looking at Chinese from a World Perspective*] (Hong Kong: Nandao Publisher, 2000).

24. Thomas Gottschang and Dana Lary, *Swallows and Settlers: The Great Migration from North China to Manchuria* (Ann Arbor: University of Michigan, Center for Chinese

Studies, 2000*)*; Robert H. G. Lee, *The Manchurian Frontier in Ch'ing History* (Cambridge, MA: Harvard University Press, 1970); Alan Moriyama, *Imingaisha: Japanese Emigration Companies and Hawaii 1894–1908* (Honolulu: University of Hawaii Press, 1985); James Reardon-Anderson, *Reluctant Pioneers: China's Expansion Northward, 1644–1937* (Stanford: Stanford University Press, 2005); Michael Weiner, *Race and Migration in Imperial Japan (*London: Routledge, 1994).

25. Kingsley Davis, *The Population of India and Pakistan* (New York: Russell and Russell, 1951), 99–100; J. C. Jha, *Aspects of Indentured Inland Emigration to North-East India 1859–1918* (New Delhi: Indus Publishing Company, 1996); Claude Markovits, *The Global World of Indian Merchants, 1750–1947* (Cambridge: Cambridge University Press, 2000), and "Indian Merchant Networks Outside India in the Nineteenth and Twentieth Centuries: A Preliminary Survey," *Modern Asian Studies* 33 (1999): 895; Kernial Singh Sandhu, *Indians in Malaya: Some Aspects of Their Immigration and Settlement (1786–1957)* (Cambridge: Cambridge University Press, 1969); Dharmapriya Wesumperuma, *Indian Immigrant Plantation Workers in Sri Lanka: A Historical Perspective, 1880–1910* (Colombo: Vidyalandara Press, 1986).

26. Ge Jianxiong, Cao Shuji, and Wu Songdi, *Jianming Zhongguo yimin [Concise History of Chinese Migration]* (Fuzhou: Fujian Renmin Chubanshe, 1993); G. William Skinner, "Mobility Strategies in Late Imperial China: A Regional Systems Analysis," in *Regional Analysis*, vol. 1, *Economic Systems*, ed. Carol A. Smith (New York: Academic Press, 1976), 327–364.

27. Eric Tagliacozzo, *Secret Trades, Porous Borders: Smuggling and States along a Southeast Asian Frontier, 1865–1915* (New Haven, CT: Yale University Press, 2005); Warren, *Sulu Zone*.

28. Dennis Cordell, Joel Gregory, and Victor Piché, *Hoe and Wage: A Social History of a Circular Migration System in West Africa* (Boulder, CO: Westview, 1996); Patrick Harries, *Work, Culture, and Identity: Migrant Laborers in Mozambique and South Africa, c. 1860–1910* (Portsmouth, NH: Heinemann, 1994); François Manchuelle, *Willing Migrants: Soninke Labor Diasporas, 1848–1960* (Athens: Ohio University Press, 1997); Patrick Manning, *Slavery and African Life: Occidental, Oriental and African Slave Trades* (Cambridge: Cambridge University Press, 1990).

29. Adrian Graves, "Colonialism and Indentured Labour Migration in the Western Pacific, 1840–1915," in *Colonialism and Migration: Indentured Labour before and after Slavery*, ed. Pieter Emmer (Dordrecht: Martinus Nijhoff, 1986), 237–259; Lydia Potts, *The World Labour Market: A History of Migration* (London: Zed Books, 1990).

30. Gülten Kazgan, "Migratory Movements in the Ottoman Empire and the Turkish Republic from the End of the 18th Century to the Present Day," in *Les Migrations Internationales: de la fin du XVIIIème siècle à nos jours*, ed. CIDMSS (Paris: Editions du CNS, 1980), 212–213; Roger Portal, "Phénomènes migratoires en Russe et à partir de Russie au XIXème siècle," in *Les Migrations Internationales*, 207–225.

31. Linda Boxberger, *On the Edge of Empire: Hadhramawt, Emigration, and the Indian Ocean, 1880s–1930s* (Albany: State University of New York Press, 2002); William Gervaise Clarence-Smith, "Middle-Eastern Entrepreneurs in Southeast Asia, c. 1750–c. 1940," in *Diaspora Entrepreneurial Networks: Four Centuries of History*, ed. Ina Baghdiantz McCabe, Gelina Harlaftis, and Ioanna Pepelasis Minoglou (Oxford: Berg, 2005), 217–244; Christine Dobbin, *Asian Entrepreneurial Minorities: Conjoint Communities in the Making of the World-Economy, 1570–1940* (Richmond, VA: Curzon, 1996); Enseng Ho, *Graves of Tarim: Genealogy and Mobility across the Indian Ocean* (Berkeley: University of California Press, 2006).

32. David Long, *The Hajj Today: A Survey of Contemporary Makkah Pilgrimage* (Albany: State University of New York Press, 1979), 127; Michael Christopher Low, "Empire of the Hajj: Pilgrims, Plagues, and Pan-Islam under British Surveillance, 1865–1926" (M.A. thesis, Georgia State University, 2007), 79.

33. J. William Leasure and Robert A. Lewis, "Internal Migration in Russia in the Late Nineteenth Century," *Slavic Review* 27, no. 3 (1968): 375–394; J. William Leasure and Rob-

ert A. Lewis, "Internal Migration in the USSR: 1897–1926," *Demography* 4, no. 2 (1967): 479–496.

34. Annemarie Steidl, Engelbert Stockhammer, and Hermann Zeitlhofer, "Relations among Internal, Continental, and Transatlantic Migration in Late Imperial Austria" *Social Science History* 31, no. 1 (2007): 61–92; Christoph Klessmann, "Comparative Immigrant History: Polish Workers in the Ruhr Area and the North of France," *Journal of Social History* 20, no. 2 (1986): 335–353; Timothy J. Hatton and Jeffrey G. Williamson, "After the Famine: Emigration from Ireland, 1850–1913," *Journal of Economic History* 53, no. 3 (1993): 575–600; Klaus J. Bade, "German Emigration to the United States and Continental Immigration to Germany in the Late Nineteenth and Early Twentieth Centuries," *Central European History* 13, no. 4 (1980): 348–377; James H. Jackson, *Migration and Urbanization in the Ruhr Valley, 1821–1914* (Atlantic Highlands, NJ: Humanities Press, 1997).

35. Javier Silvestre, "Internal Migrations in Spain, 1877–1930," *European Review of Economic History* 9, no. 2 (2005): 233–265.

36. James Gregory, *The Southern Diaspora: How the Great Migrations of Black and White Southerners Transformed America* (Chapel Hill: University of North Carolina Press, 2005).

37. Orlando Patterson, "Migration in Caribbean Societies: Socioeconomic and Symbolic Resource," in *Human Migration: Patterns and Policies*, ed. William McNeill and Ruth Adams (Bloomington: Indiana University Press, 1978), 106–145.

38. McKeown, "Global Migration."

39. Timothy J. Hatton and Jeffrey G. Williamson, "What Drove the Mass Migrations from Europe in the Late Nineteenth Century?" *Population and Development Review* 20, no. 3 (1994): 533–559, table 1; Walter Nugent, *Crossings: The Great Transatlantic Migrations, 1870–1914* (Bloomington: Indiana University Press, 1992), 43. Population data for China is from Thomas Gottschang and Dana Lary, *Swallows and Settlers: The Great Migration from North China to Manchuria* (Ann Arbor: University of Michigan, Center for Chinese Studies, 2000), 172–173, and Robert Marks, *Tigers, Rice, Silk, and Silt: Environment and Economy in Late Imperial South China* (Cambridge: Cambridge University Press, 1998), 280.

40. Jason Long, "Rural–Urban Migration and Socioeconomic Mobility in Victorian Britain," *Journal of Economic History* 65, no. 1 (2005): 1–35.

41. Gilbert Rozman, "East Asia Urbanization in the Nineteenth Century: Comparisons with Europe," in *Urbanization in History: A Process of Dynamic Interactions*, ed. Ad van der Woude, Akira Hayami, and Jan De Vries (New York: Oxford University Press, 1995), 61–73; Susan Mann, "Urbanization and Historical Change in China," *Modern China* 10 (1984): 79–113. Gavin W. Jones and Pravin M. Visaria, eds., *Urbanization in Large Developing Countries* (Oxford: Clarendon Press, 1997), 267.

42. Paul Kennedy, *The Rise and Fall of Great Powers* (New York: Vintage Press, 1989), 149.

43. Robert C. Allen, Jean-Pascal Bassino, Christine Moll-Murata, and Jan Luiten van Zanden, "Wages, Prices, and Living Standards in China, Japan, and Europe, 1738–1925" (Global Price and Income History [GPIH] working paper no. 1, University of California Davis, 2005).

44. Moya, *Cousins and Strangers*, 95–120; J. D. Gould, "European Inter-Continental Emigration: The Role of 'Diffusion' and 'Feedback,'" *European Journal of Economic History* 9 (1980): 267–316.

45. Jose C. Moya, "A Continent of Immigrants: Postcolonial Shifts in the Western Hemisphere," *Hispanic American Historical Review* 86, no. 1 (2006): 1–28.

46. Patrick K. O'Brien and Leandro Prados de la Escosura, "Agricultural Productivity and European Industrialization, 1890–1980," *Economic History Review* 45, no. 3 (1992): 514–536.

47. Moya, *Cousins and Strangers*, 150–153, 266–276. Joseph P. Ferrie, "History Lessons: The End of American Exceptionalism? Mobility in the United States since 1850," *Journal of Economic Perspectives* 19, no. 3 (2005): 199–215 also shows exceptionally high levels

of upward mobility in the United States compared to Western Europe, but the reversal of that gap in the second half of the twentieth century.

48. Timothy Hatton and Jeffrey Williamson, *Global Migration and the World Economy: Two Centuries of Policy and Performance* (Cambridge, MA: MIT Press, 2005), 146–147.

49. Anthony Reid, "South-East Asian Population History and the Colonial Impact," in *Asian Population History*, ed. Ts'ui-jung Liu (Oxford: Oxford University Press, 2001), 55–59.

50. Thomas H. Holloway, *Immigrants on the Land: Coffee and Society in Sao Paulo, 1886–1934* (Chapel Hill: University of North Carolina Press, 1980).

51. Carter, *Servants, Sirdars and Settlers*; Amarjit Kaur, "Indian Labour, Labour Standards, and Workers' Health in Burma and Malaya, 1900–1940," *Modern Asian Studies* 40, no. 2 (2006): 425–475.

52. Historical and theoretical works on migration networks around the world include: Teofilo Altamirano, *Presencia Andina en Lima Metropolitana* (Lima: Pontificía Universidad Católica del Perú, Fondo Editorial, 1984); Monica Boyd, "Family and Personal Networks in International Migration: Recent Developments and New Agendas," *International Migration Review* 23 (1989): 638–670; James H. Jackson and Leslie Page Moch, "Migration and the Social History of Modern Europe," *Historical Methods* 22 (1989): 27–36; Ivan Light and Parminder Bachu, eds., *Immigration and Entrepreneurship* (New Brunswick, NJ: Transaction Publishers, 1993), 25–49; Alejandro Portes and József Böröcz, "Contemporary Immigration: Theoretical Perspectives on Its Determinants and Modes of Incorporation," *International Migration Review* 23 (1989): 606–630; Oded Stark, *The Migration of Labor* (Cambridge: Basil Blackwell, 1992); Charles Tilly, "Migration in Modern European History," in *Human Migration*, 48–72, and "Transplanted Networks," in *Immigration Reconsidered: History, Sociology, and Politics*, ed. Virginia Yans-McLaughlin (New York: Oxford University Press, 1990), 79–95.

53. Jose C. Moya, "Immigrants and Associations: A Global and Historical Perspective," *Journal of Ethnic and Migration Studies* 31 (2005): 833–864.

54. Gould, "European Inter-Continental Emigration: The Role of 'Diffusion.'" 294–295; Moya, *Cousins and Strangers*, 114–116; Adam McKeown, *Chinese Migrant Networks: Chicago, Peru and Hawaii, 1900–1936* (Chicago: University of Chicago Press, 2001), 70–76.

55. Bruno Ramirez, "The Crossroad Province: Quebec's Place in International Migrations, 1870–1915," in *A Century of European Migrations, 1830–1930*, ed. Rudolph Vecoli and Suzanne Sinke (Urbana: University of Illinois Press, 1992), 243–260. See also Chen Ta, *Emigrant Communities in South China* (New York: Institute of Pacific Relations, 1940). It may also be noted that criticisms of economic models as based exclusively on wage differentials may be attacking straw men. Hatton and Williamson, *Age of Mass Migration*, for example, develops a complex model that takes networks, population, wage differentials, and commercialization into account. For an analysis of how the interaction of networks and macrostructural conditions shape migratory flows and shift destinations, see Moya, *Cousins and Strangers*, 80–88.

56. For critiques of national perspectives, see Hasia Diner, "History and the Study of Immigration: Narratives of the Particular," in *Migration Theory: Talking across Disciplines*, ed. Caroline Brettell and James Hollifield (New York: Routledge, 2000), 27–42; Donna Gabaccia, "Is Everywhere Nowhere? Nomads, Nations, and the Immigrant Paradigm of United States History," *Journal of American History* 86 (1999): 1115–1134; Nancy Green, "The Comparative Method and Poststructural Structuralism: New Perspectives for Migration Studies," in Lucassen and Lucassen, *Migration, Migration History, History*, 57–72.

57. For other comparisons of the first and second waves, see Nancy Foner, *From Ellis Island to JFK: New York's Two Great Waves of Immigration* (New Haven, CT: Yale University Press, 2002); Giovanni Gozzini, "The Global System of International Migrations, 1900 and 2000: A Comparative Approach," *Journal of Global History* 1 (2006): 321–341.

58. *World Migration Report 2000* (Geneva: United Nations and World Organization for Migration, 2000); Hania Zlotnik, "International Migration 1965–96: An Overview," *Population and Development Review* 24 (1998): 429–468.

59. Continuity is also noticeable in the proportion of the total population that immigrants represent in the United States and in the fact that this proportion has not been particularly high by international comparison. It was 15 percent in 1910, when it was twice as high in Argentina and Australia and 20 percent in Canada; and it was 13 percent in 2005, when more than forty countries surpassed that figure.

60. R. E. Bilsborrow, "Rural Poverty, Migration, and the Environment in Developing Countries," Policy Research Working Paper, World Development Report, WPS 1017 (Washington, DC: World Bank, 1992).

61. Madeline Hsu, *Dreaming of Gold, Dreaming of Home: Transnationalism and Migration between the United States and South China, 1882–1943* (Stanford: Stanford University Press, 2000); Kuah Khun Eng, *Rebuilding the Ancestral Village: Singaporeans in China* (Aldershot, England: Ashgate, 2000).

62. For a general review of migration theories, see Douglas Massey, Joaquín Arango, Grame Hugo, Ali Kouaouci, Adela Pellegrino, and J. Edward Taylor, "Theories of International Migration: A Review and Appraisal," *Population and Development Review* 19 (1993): 431–466.

63. Joseph Nevins, *Operation Gatekeeper: The Rise of the "Illegal Alien" and the Making of the U.S.-Mexico Boundary* (New York: Routledge, 2002).

64. Cindy Hahamovitch, "Creating Perfect Immigrants: Guest Workers of the World in Historical Perspective," *Labor History* 44 (2003): 70–94; Ulrich Herbert, *A History of Foreign Labor in Germany, 1880–1980: Seasonal Workers/Forced Laborers/Guest Workers*, trans. William Templer (Ann Arbor: University of Michigan Press, 1990); James Hollinger, *Immigrants, Markets, and States: The Political Economy of Postwar Europe* (Cambridge, MA: Harvard University Press, 1992).

65. McKeown, *Melancholy Order*; Torpey, *Invention of the Passport*.

66. Don Flynn, "New Borders, New Management: The Dilemmas of Modern Immigration Policies," *Ethnic and Racial Studies* 28 (2005): 463–490; International Organization of Migration, *World Migration Report 2003*; Lydia Morris, *Managing Migration: Civic Stratification and Migrants' Rights* (London, Routledge, 2002); Kathleen Newland and Demetrios Papademetriou, "Managing International Migration: Tracking the Emergence of a New International Regime," *UCLA Journal of International Law and Foreign Affairs* 3, no. 2 (1998–1999): 637–657.

67. Justin McCarthy, "Muslims in Ottoman Europe: Population from 1800 to 1912," *Nationalities Papers* 28, no. 1 (2002): 29–44.

68. Michael R. Marrus, *The Unwanted: European Refugees in the 20th Century* (New York: Oxford University Press, 1985); Aristide R. Zolberg and Peter Brenda, eds., *Global Migrants, Global Refugees: Problems and Solutions* (New York: Berghahn Books, 2001); Office of the United Nations High Commissioner for Refugees, *The State of the World's Refugees: Human Displacement in the New Millennium* (New York: Oxford University Press, 2006).

69. Virginie Guiraudon, and Christian Joppke, eds., *Controlling a New Migration World* (London: Routledge, 2001); Samuel Huntington, *Who Are We? The Challenges to America's National Identity* (New York: Simon and Schuster, 2004); David Jacobson, *Rights across Borders: Immigration and the Decline of Citizenship* (Baltimore, MD: Johns Hopkins University Press, 1996); Christopher Rudolph, "Globalization, Sovereignty, and Migration: A Conceptual Framework," *UCLA Journal of International Law and Foreign Affairs* 3 (1998–1999): 355.

70. Kathryn P. Alessandria, "Acknowledging White Ethnic Groups in Multicultural Counseling," *Family Journal* 10, no. 1 (January 2002): 57–60; Monica McGoldrick, Joe Giordano, and John K. Pearce, eds., *Ethnicity and Family Therapy* (New York: Guilford Press, 1996).

71. Linda Basch, Nina Glick Schiller, and Cristina Sztanton Blanc, *Nations Unbound: Transnational Projects, Postcolonial Predicaments, and Deterritorialized Nation-States* (New York: Routledge, 1993); Aihwa Ong, "Mutations in Citizenship," *Theory, Culture & Society* 23 (2006): 499–531; Alejandro Portes, Luis Guarnizo, and Patricia Landolt, "The Study of

Transnationalism: Pitfalls and Promise of an Emerging Research Field," *Ethnic and Racial Studies* 22 (1999): 217–237.

72. Nina Glick Schiller, "Transmigrants and Nation-States: Something Old and Something New in the U.S. Immigrant Experience," in *Handbook of International Migration: The American Experience*, ed. Charles Hirschman, Charles Philip Kasinitz, and Josh DeWind (New York: Russell Sage Foundation, 1999), 94–119.

73. Eiichiro Azuma, *Between Two Empires: Race, History and Transnationalism in Japanese America* (Oxford: Oxford University Press, 2005).

74. Richard Alba and Victor Nee, *Remaking the American Mainstream: Assimilation and Contemporary Immigration* (Cambridge, MA: Harvard University Press, 2005); Milton Gordon, *Assimilation in American Life: The Role of Race, Religion and National Origins* (New York: Oxford University Press, 1964).

75. G. William Skinner, "Creolized Chinese Societies in Southeast Asia," in *Sojourners and Settlers*, ed. Anthony Reid, 1–41.

76. Amy Freedman, *Political Participation and Ethnic Minorities: Chinese Overseas in Malaysia, Indonesia, and the United States* (London: Routledge, 2000); Edmund Terence Gomez, *Chinese Business in Malaysia: Accumulation, Ascendance, Accommodation* (Honolulu: University of Hawai'i Press, 1999). G. William Skinner, *Leadership and Power in the Chinese Community of Thailand* (Ithaca, NY: Cornell University Press, 1958) applied an American assimilation model to Thailand and has generated numerous refutations. See Chan Kwok Bun and Tong Chee Kiong, eds., *Alternate Identities: The Chinese in Contemporary Thailand* (Leiden, Netherlands: Brill, 2001).

77. Chang-yau Hoon, *Chinese Identity in Post-Suharto Indonesia: Culture, Politics and Identity* (Sussex, UK: Sussex Academic Press, 2008); Constance Lever-Tracy, David Ip, and Noel Tracy, *The Chinese Diaspora and Mainland China: An Emerging Economic Synergy* (New York: St. Martin's Press, 1996); Aihwa Ong, *Flexible Citizenship: The Cultural Logics of Transnationality* (Durham, NC: Duke University Press, 1999).

CHAPTER 2

Twentieth-Century Urbanization

In Search of an Urban Paradigm
for an Urban World

HOWARD SPODEK

In 2006, for the first time, more than half of the world's population lived in cities. In 1900, about one person in six lived in a city, a total of about 260 million people. By 2000, 47 percent were urban—about 3 billion people. According to United Nations estimates, the 50 percent mark was reached in 2006. Individual cities grew to enormous population size. By the end of the twentieth century, nineteen cities had become "megacities," holding populations of 10 million or more; they expanded geographically to breathtaking proportions. The Los Angeles metropolitan region, for example, held a population of 12 million, spanned a diameter of 120 miles, included five counties and 132 incorporated cities, and produced a gross annual economic output of nearly $250 billion.

Through the twentieth century, the location of cities also shifted dramatically and unexpectedly. The link between economic growth and urbanization, which had once seemed so logical and natural, was broken. In earlier times, cities had mostly arisen in wealthier regions, where their presence seemed to reflect the "pull" of urban economic growth and job opportunities. In the late twentieth century, they became more characteristic of poorer regions of the world, where their presence seemed to reflect the "push" from an overcrowded countryside with a scarcity of jobs. In 1900, cities in the "economically developed world" held about 163 million people; those in the "underdeveloped world" held about 97 million. By 2000, the developed world held 900 million urbanites and the underdeveloped world held 2,150 million.

The change in the key economic functions of cities was equally dramatic. Large-scale industrial manufacture of commodities, like steel in Pittsburgh, automobiles in Detroit, and textiles in Bombay, mostly closed down. This gave way to service industries, like the information technologies of California's Silicon Valley and India's Bangalore; the film industries of Hollywood and Bollywood (the Indian film industry); the pleasure palaces of Las Vegas and the somewhat more risqué Bangkok and Manila; the theme parks of the Disney empire in Florida, California, Paris, Tokyo, and, in 2005, Hong Kong; and such holiday destinations as Cancun, Rio de Janeiro, and Cape Town. China provided exceptions. In 1980, for example, the Chinese government established the new city of Shenzhen as a "special economic zone" to foster manufacturing. The new city, adjacent to Hong Kong, took root and flourished, expanding to some 3 million inhabitants by the end of the century. Outside China, however, such urban industrial growth had become the exception.

By the end of the twentieth century, two shifts in international politics allowed the cities of the world to be incorporated into a single global system, not for the first time, but with a density of interaction that was unprecedented. First, the two world wars and the cold war—which had interrupted earlier movements toward an integrated global system of cities—came to an end. Second, vast regions of Asia and Africa, which had been divided into separate spheres of colonial influence, became independent of colonial control. The countries of Latin America, under the quasi-colonial influence of the United States, also gained increasing power to chart their own paths. By century's end, the political forces that had carved up the world into the "first world" of capitalist democracy, the "second world" of Communist Party dominance, and the "third world" of mostly impoverished colonies had given way to a more thoroughly integrated global system of cities.

So extraordinary were the size, technological transformation, and global integration of twentieth-century cities, that many observers viewed this combination of urban developments as a fourth turning point in world history, equivalent in its impact to each of the three earlier urban revolutions: (1) the move from nomadic existence to settled village life, about fifteen thousand years ago; (2) the establishment of the first full-fledged cities, with their greater size and complexity, about five thousand years ago; and (3) the industrialization of cities, about two hundred years ago. Any paradigm seeking to comprehend the global evolution of twentieth-century urbanization must take into account all three factors—population, technology, and political systems—and their transformation throughout the century.

GLOBAL POLITICS COMPLICATE URBAN THEORY

Capitalism and Democracy in Western Europe and the United States

On the eve of the twentieth century, students of urbanization seemed to know what a city was and how to study it. In 1899, Adna Ferrin Weber completed, revised, and published his dissertation, *The Growth of Cities in the Nineteenth Century: A Study in Statistics.* Usually regarded as the first important American contribution to the study of urbanization, the monograph captured both the development of cities and methods of studying them in ways that still speak to us more than a century later. Weber saw the growth of cities—in number, territory, population, and proportion of total population—as one of the most striking features of the nineteenth century. Alert to the relationship of the urban to the rural, he devoted his seventh chapter to the physical and moral health of urban relative to rural dwellers. Weber attributed changes in the life of urban populations to technological changes, immigration—both within countries and across international and intercontinental borders—and to the sheer density and diversity of population. He analyzed this diversity in terms of sex, age, race, nationality, and occupation.

Unusual for his time, Weber studied urbanization worldwide and saw that it had certain common factors, whatever the country or geographical region. In particular, he saw that the rates of urbanization and of economic development were closely correlated. Countries with high rates of industrial and economic development had high rates of urbanization, and vice versa. In global terms, this correlation of urban economic development and urban population growth represented his principal theory, and his data supported it.

German social scientists, speaking in somewhat more philosophical terms, similarly equated the process of urban growth with the increasing quest for financial profit. Georg Simmel wrote, "The metropolis has always been the seat of the money economy" (Sennett 1969, 49). Simmel took for granted the growth of the metropolis as a consequence of the growth of the economy. Financial motives determined the lifestyle of urbanites, which was marked by "punctuality, calculability, exactness," but also by "a mutual strangeness and repulsion, which will break into hatred and fight at the moment of a closer contact, however caused. . . . One nowhere feels as lonely and lost as in the metropolitan crowd." City life "grants to the individual a kind and an amount of personal freedom which has no analogy whatsoever under other conditions. . . . stimulations, interests, uses of time and consciousness are offered to it from all sides." Simmel's view was widely shared: financial gain was the principal goal of metropolitan life; social isolation and individualism were its by-products.

In the 1920s, American cities grew by 19 percent, suburbs by 39 percent (Hall 2002, 297). Scholars sought to understand the causes and consequences.

Chicago, America's second largest city, after New York, emerged as both the fastest growing industrial metropolis of the time and the focus of the most important academic studies. By 1930, Chicago surpassed the 3 million mark in population. Industry, immigration from overseas, transportation hubs, a vast agricultural hinterland, and soaring skyscrapers inspired and marked this phenomenal growth. The poet Carl Sandburg famously captured the city's exuberance and might:

> *Come and show me another city with lifted head singing so proud*
> *to be alive and coarse and strong and cunning.*
> *Flinging magnetic curses amid the toil of piling job on job, here is a tall*
> *bold slugger set vivid against the little soft cities;*
> *Bragging and laughing that under his wrist is the pulse, and under*
> *his ribs the heart of the people,*
> *Laughing!*
> *Laughing the stormy husky, brawling laughter of Youth, half-naked,*
> *sweating, proud to be Hog Butcher, Tool Maker, Stacker of Wheat,*
> *Player with Railroads and Freight Handler to the Nation.*

In more scholarly form, the "Chicago School," a cluster of social scientists based at the University of Chicago, sought to understand this city both for itself and as an example of an evolving global process. Their 1925 collection of essays, *The City*, edited by Robert E. Park, Ernest W. Burgess, and Roderick McKenzie, laid out the basic contours of their inquiries.

Led by Ernest Burgess, the academics of the Chicago School proposed a model of urban expansion, driven by capitalistic economic competition, pushing outward in concentric circles from an original town center. The Chicago School argued that the economic competition spilled over into social competition, as people sorted themselves by class, race, and ethnicity into "natural" groupings that clustered together into "natural areas." As these "natural" groups became more numerous, more crowded, and better organized, they competed with each other for urban land in patterns of "invasion, succession, and segregation," consistent with Darwinian views of competition and survival of the fittest. The Chicago academics created and named their new field "human ecology," the study of human interaction within the confined geography of the modern city. This ecological competition expressed itself economically, in the capitalist competition for land.

Others in the Chicago School cited transportation systems as a principal source of new urban design patterns, but they agreed that people's ability to take advantage of the new train and automobile transportation was determined by class, and therefore by their financial capacity. Wealthier people tended to move outward to the suburbs, although some resolute urbanites—especially those without children—remained in the center cities.

For the most part, the Chicago School took for granted the political and economic environment of the United States, and especially Chicago, at that time. It took for granted that cities were capitalistic, enmeshed in an economy of competition, supply and demand, and free markets for land, labor, and commodities. It took for granted rapid industrialization and relatively open immigration (until 1924), especially from Europe. It took for granted democratic politics.

Cities under Communism: Eastern Europe and Central Asia

In Eastern Europe, after the Russian Revolution of 1917, a communist government rejected democratic politics, capitalism, and the free market. During a trip to Moscow in December 1926 and January 1927, the German-Jewish literary critic Walter Benjamin asked whether the communist system had produced a different and better kind of city. He concluded that communist cities were different—better in some important dimensions, but seriously flawed in others. He contrasted capitalist Berlin and communist Moscow in the late 1920s. Moscow had about 2 million residents, but tucked behind its main streets, Benjamin found vestiges of rural villages:

> In the streets of Moscow there is a curious state of affairs: the Russian village is playing hide-and-seek in them. If you step through one of the high gateways—they often have wrought-iron gates, but I never found them closed—you stand on the threshold of a spacious settlement. Opening before you, broad and expansive, is a farmyard or a village, the ground is uneven, children ride about in sleighs, sheds for wood and tools fill the corners, trees stand here and there, wooden staircases give the backs of houses, which look like city buildings from the front, the appearance of Russian farmhouses. (1978, 124–125)

This semirural city teems with life. Sounding like many subsequent visitors to the third world—who also came to appreciate the thriving, bustling life in its streets, and found Western cities comparatively bare, lonely, and sterile— Benjamin exclaims:

> [W]hat fullness has this [downtown Moscow] street that overflows not only with people, and how deserted and empty is Berlin! (98)

Workers and children seem to fare especially well in communist Moscow:

> The liberated pride of the proletariat is matched by the emancipated bearing of the children. Nothing is more pleasantly surprising on a visit to Moscow's museums than to see how, singly or in groups,

sometimes around a guide, children and workers move easily through these rooms. (104)

What Moscow, and Russia, had lost, however, was freedom. Working with newly opened archives and access to the city, Timothy J. Colton analyzed Moscow's development under communism more academically and formally:

> The socialist urban paradigm as exemplified in Moscow contained distinctive political-economic elements: governmental ownership of the factors and means of production, including land; superintendence of administrative agents and clients via directive planning and administrative hierarchy; direct public provision of most goods and services at politically determined prices; and the lordship of investment and production goals over consumer welfare. Comprehensive planning, the proudest badge of socialist urbanism, was inculcated in such instruments as police curbs on in-migration, uniform formulas for allocation of housing and installation of infrastructure, and Moscow master plans, the two most important promulgated in 1935 and 1971. . . . [Moscow's communist rulers] exalted representations of the secular, the statist, and the collectivist over the religious, the commercial, and the individualist. They annihilated cathedrals, abbeys, fortifications, and ceremonial gates and towers and did their utmost to erect idols to themselves and their creed (1995, 3–4).

In 1928, as Stalin introduced the first of his five-year plans for Russian economic development, primarily through industrialization, and began to do away with private farms by collectivizing agriculture in the 1930s, rural people fled the countryside and migrated into the cities. Within a decade, the urban percentage of the Soviet Union almost doubled to 32 percent. The government attempted to limit the growth of large cities by requiring all urban immigrants to have official documentation that showed they held urban employment and the housing that came with it. Without such documentation, immigration to the cities was illegal. Implementation of this restriction was erratic, however, as new industrial and service sector jobs and new amenities attracted new urban residents, with or without documentation. Moscow alone multiplied from about 1 million inhabitants in 1920 to 2 million in 1926 to 3 million in 1932 to 4 million in 1939 (Colton 1995, 757–758).

The center city retained the dominant institutions of social and political life, although it lacked commercial enterprise. Major cities across the USSR, like Moscow, had large public spaces near the center of town that could accommodate mass meetings and demonstrations (Bater article in Gugler 2004, 194). Unlike the United States, the Soviet central city retained its residential population (194). A high proportion of center city residential spaces—considerably larger and better appointed than those in the suburbs—went to managerial, technical, and Communist Party elites. Although conspicuous consumption by the wealthy was frowned upon, a new social stratification did emerge, based on party membership.

As industrialization expanded, the government often located industries in the ring outside the central city. It built high-rise housing for workers somewhat farther out from the center, at densities exceeding those of the center, reversing the usual pattern of the Western, capitalist city. These industrial suburbs were dominated by blue-collar workers, "a great many of whom were obliged to live in communal housing. Single persons and families alike who were assigned a communal apartment typically occupied just one room of a multiroom apartment, the toilet, bath, and kitchen facilities being shared by all occupants" (Bater in Gugler, 2004).

The party, the government, and the government-run industries controlled the overwhelming proportion of urban housing. Private ownership was minimal. Bureaucrats fought over location decisions. Economic planners sought the most rapid national growth regardless of location; spatial planners sought to disperse industrial and population growth more evenly across the country, even if the process of growth was slowed. The economic planners usually won out. Also, despite the intention to locate housing for workers adjacent to industrial plants, residence and occupation were frequently quite separate. Commuting times tended to be long, overtaxing the facilities of public transportation.

To implement its policies of rapid industrialization, the government built new cities, like Dnepropetrovsk, with its immense hydroelectrical capacities, and Magnitogorsk, with its gigantic steel mills. It could forcefully direct waves of new urban immigrants to these new cities, create massive new housing complexes, place them as it wished in proximity to the new industries, and provide them with the facilities and amenities that it thought desirable—usually at a very shabby level, since creating industry had a higher priority than providing consumer goods. The privation endured by workers was explained and applauded by the government as dedication to nation building, to securing the fatherland against the threats of Germany to the west and Japan to the east. With Western Europe and the United States in severe economic depression after 1929, the USSR proclaimed that it had achieved full employment as compared to the upwards of 25 percent unemployment in the West.

Even before the Depression, many aspects of the communist experiment challenged the bourgeois nations of Western Europe and the United States. In response, they created new policies to improve the lives of their own urban poor. In implementing a new urban housing program in Britain in 1919, a British parliamentary secretary said, "the money we are going to spend on housing is an insurance against Bolshevism and Revolution" (Hall 2002, 72). "The new houses built by the state—each with its own garden, surrounded by trees and hedges, and equipped internally with the amenities of a middle-class home—was to provide visible proof of the irrelevance of revolution" (72).

Russians also took control of the towns of their holdings in central Asia— today's Uzbekistan, Turkmenistan, Kyrgyzstan, Tajikistan, and Kazakhstan— where the people were largely Muslim speakers of Turkic languages. The Russian imperial armies began to conquer and annex these regions beginning in the mid-1850s, long before the revolution. They began to develop them in the classical dual form of colonial cities, leaving the existing indigenous cities more or less as they were, with mosques, bazaars, a citadel, town wall, and semisegregated neighborhoods of narrow, twisting, meandering streets, and mud-covered brick buildings constructed around courtyards. Contiguous to these existing urban features, they implanted military and administrative headquarters of their own, with military barracks and drill spaces for the soldiers and wide, clean streets—even grand boulevards—and European-style architecture, services, and amenities for the civilians. This dual-city pattern was similar to that of other imperial administrations, for example, the British in India, the French in Africa, and, later, the Chinese in cities like Kashgar in Xinjiang, East Turkestan, and Lhasa, Tibet. In areas that lacked cities to serve as points of administration and commerce, the Russians created them. Leading examples were Alma-Ata, Dushanbe, and Ashkhabad. By the 1880s, they introduced a railway to connect and open these central Asian cities. After the Russian Revolution and Civil War, the new communist government began to infiltrate Russians into the cities of central Asia to transform them demographically. By 1989, the largest of them, Tashkent, had a population that was 40 percent Russian.

Cities under European Colonial Rule

As the Russian Empire was transforming existing cities and constructing new ones in contiguous regions of central Asia, so Western European empires were establishing new urban patterns in their far-flung, overseas colonial possessions. In 1927, Chicago School geographer Roderick McKenzie visited briefly in Japan, China, and India and wrote "The Concept of Dominance and World Organization."[1] The short essay illuminated the global system of cities that had been emerging under colonialism for more than a century, and the turbulence that began to threaten it.

McKenzie also addressed the internal systems of the Asian cities, noting their differences from Western patterns. These historic cities had grown according to different principles than competitive capitalism, and prior to the technologies of the industrial revolution. They contained multiple centers, none of them dominant.

For instance, cities like Soochow, Hangchow, and Foochow, to mention only a few, have, generally speaking, no centers of dominance. The narrow winding streets are of almost uniform importance throughout. The gates which give ingress and egress to the important outlying regions are the spots of leading activity. (McKenzie 1927, 30–31)

McKenzie did not distinguish among the cities of Japan, China, and India. But they were not the same. Japanese cities adopted policies different from the others. Unlike the cities of China, Tokyo and Osaka had not been colonized; they could plan their development as they chose. McKenzie visited Tokyo after the 1923 earthquake and fires that killed 100,000 people and left 70 percent of the population homeless. Tokyo used the rebuilding process as an opportunity to restructure its neighborhoods and transportation systems. New railways built in the 1920s and 1930s facilitated the expansion of the city. The first subway line opened in 1927. Japan planned its rebuilt capital as a world city.

The purpose of the colonial city, in contrast, was to serve the economic and administrative needs of the colonial power rather than, or at least more than, those of the indigenous peoples. Thus, their railway transportation networks did not usually link the internal regions of the country with one another, but rather only with the port city, facilitating the export of raw materials, the import of foreign manufactures, and the dispatch of colonial troops. The British introduced into India more than forty thousand miles of railway network after fully constructing all of its components in Britain—engines, cars, and tracks—on payment from the colonial government of India of cost plus 5 percent, and then transporting them for installation in India. All the economic and technological benefits of the construction process went to England. Similarly, the modern industries that were built in these new cities were mostly—but not entirely—owned and controlled by Europeans. While apologists for the imperial system gave it credit for introducing industrialization where it had previously been unknown, more critical commentators called this a system of *dependency*, in which the colonial powers used their political and military authority to rig the economy for their own benefit—imports, exports, taxes, commercial agriculture, banking, and limited industrialization—leaving the colonized people dependent upon them (Gilbert and Gugler 1992).

At first, in the sixteenth and seventeenth centuries, the Europeans planted their new cities on seacoasts, especially in Africa and Asia, less so in Latin America, so that they could be supplied easily by ship from the mother country. Many of the colonial cities were built more or less from scratch, on locations where there had been no previous city of any substantial size. This was the pattern, from west to east, of Buenos Aires, Rio de Janeiro, Dakar, Lagos, Cape Town, Karachi, Bombay, Colombo, Madras, Calcutta, Kuala Lumpur,

Singapore, Hong Kong, Manila, and Batavia (Jakarta). Many others were built as dual cities; that is, they were built contiguous to already existing port cities—Casablanca, Algiers, Mombasa, and Shanghai's foreign concessions. Later, in the nineteenth and twentieth centuries, as Europeans penetrated ever deeper into their colonial realms, they built cities in the interior as well: New Delhi, Kandy, Harare (Salisbury), Lusaka, Nairobi, and Kampala.

The Spanish had built their cities in the Americas for permanent residence; the new cities in Africa and Asia were normally built for temporary residence by colonial officials and those working with them. They did not buy land and real estate locally. The residences were permanent, but the residents were not; they were transients in service, not settlers. At the end of their imperial service, these residents would normally return to their home countries.

The technology of the colonial city was usually European, and its town planning, although modified for the climate and political conditions of the colonial situation, was usually derived from European models.

By the twentieth century, most patterns of European colonial urbanization were in place. The dual-city pattern was the norm. The European enclaves were quite distinct from the indigenous city: They were more spacious (lower density) in overall design and located on wide, tree-lined roads—grand accommodations for the European administrators and officials who lived there. The architecture was built to European design, topped off with ornamental touches to acknowledge particular local styles. Spacious and impressive offices were equipped with modern machinery, shops had glass show windows, and consumer products of fine quality were often imported from Europe. In the larger cities, higher up the administrative ladder, and especially in colonial capital cities, the public buildings were often built to monumental scale. Churches, too, dotted the landscape. Great attention was devoted to cleanliness of both public and private spaces. The Europeans feared local diseases—and local culture—and did their best to keep them at a distance.

Residence in these enclaves was often restricted to Europeans and people who worked with them. Most local people lived in the indigenous city, which was built to very different specifications that often reflected quite different resources, social organization, institutional structures, and values. These indigenous cities were comparatively crowded, often built within long-standing protective walls that unfortunately reduced air flow, and with narrow, twisting streets in neighborhoods based on local kinship patterns. They had relatively little public greenery, although larger homes, which turned blank walls to the street, often had lovely gardens in interior courtyards. Shop fronts opened fully in the daytime but were completely shuttered at night. Artisans frequently practiced their crafts within their homes or on the street directly in front of them. Streets were crowded with people throughout the day and well into the night, especially after the arrival of electricity and street lighting, and many events that might have been considered private in the European enclave—

such as marriages and funerals—were celebrated publicly, out of doors, in the indigenous sections of town. Public streets were not usually as clean as in the enclaves, and animals often shared the narrow streets with humans, cleaning the streets by eating refuse and soiling the streets by producing refuse. Religious institutions—mosques, temples—were often the most imposing structures in the indigenous city, and small, neighborhood religious shrines dotted the urban landscape. Since private resources were often limited, public institutions, such as community baths and bakeries, were often provided throughout the city.

The colonial cities, despite their residential segregation, offered—and required—interaction between the colonial rulers and the local, colonized people in offices, shops, industries, and schools, although not as much in recreation. The results of this interaction were unpredictable. In addition to the social science literature, biographies, autobiographies, fiction, drama, and films are filled with the stories of indigenous people and colonial rulers who were transformed in one way or another through their interactions with the diverse residents and the institutions of the European colonial cities, often in quite complex and ambivalent ways. Perhaps the most famous example of this genre is Chinua Achebe's *Things Fall Apart*.[2]

The Martinique-born psychiatrist, Franz Fanon, represented the colonial city as a bitter contrast in white and black:

> The settlers' town is a well-fed town, an easygoing town; its belly is always full of good things. The settlers' town is a town of white people, of foreigners. . . . The native town is a hungry town, starved of bread, of meat, of shoes, of coal, of light.[3]

Fanon called for violent revolution; most found the situation more ambivalent.

MIDCENTURY CHANGES

The two world wars, global depression, the cold war, and decolonization affected cities everywhere, but in somewhat different ways. For the most part, trends already in place continued at an increased tempo.

The United States

The years of war and depression slowed the suburbanization of America, but after 1945, millions of soldiers returned from war ready to resume civilian life, marry, and begin families. A revived building industry provided them with relatively inexpensive, mass-produced, suburban homes. The government of their grateful nation provided them with easy access to mortgages with which to purchase homes and a magnificent road system by which to reach them. The automobile industry provided the vehicles for the trip. Consumerism reached previously unknown levels. Industry also helped spearhead the new centrifugal movement. Suburban industrial estates—footloose thanks to the new highway networks, trucking industries, and abundant electrical power—provided single-story buildings where production lines could spread out easily. Pleasant office parks sprang up, surrounded by greenery. Between 1950 and 1960, although some large, older cities lost population, America's cities collectively grew by 6 million people; suburbs grew by 19 million. By 1990, more than 50 percent of all Americans lived in suburbs.

The growth of the suburbs came at the expense of the older central business districts. These historic downtowns languished as they lost businesses, industries, jobs, population, and the tax bases necessary to support basic urban services. Filling in the deserted inner-city neighborhoods, a massive new wave of immigrants arrived. During the years of World War I, African Americans had already begun their migrations from the impoverished, rural, racist South to the industrialized, urbanized, racist North. During and immediately after World War II, the migration resumed in full force. Displaced by the new mechanical cotton pickers, invented in 1944, and in search of industrial jobs, 5 million African Americans moved north. Unfortunately, they were arriving just as opportunities were slipping away. In addition, government institutionalized the racial practices of the private real estate market, by redlining neighborhoods with a majority African American population, denying them access to the kinds of easy mortgages that were enabling the suburbs to flourish, and further isolating them economically and residentially. Public housing, built after World War II with the working classes in mind, soon became the haunt of the poor, and often the black, population of the inner cities. These high-rise apartment buildings, similar in appearance and quality to those built in Europe, deteriorated so badly, and were supervised so poorly, that all those who could manage to leave them did. By the 1970s, city governments across the United States began to tear down these largely empty, crime-ridden structures.

As the civil rights movement of the 1960s exposed the racial injustices of the United States, a series of riots swept across the black ghettos of more than twenty American cities. They reached a crescendo in 1968, following the assassination of the Nobel laureate civil rights leader Martin Luther King Jr. Dozens of people were killed, millions of dollars in property damage were inflicted, and army tanks patrolled the streets of many American cities. But the movement encouraged civil rights legislation and affirmative action programs, and some gates of opportunity edged open. To some degree, American racial attitudes became more tolerant, and some black Americans began to join their white compatriots in the suburbs. Ironically, this new freedom of movement rendered those left behind in the ghettos even more excluded than before. They had even fewer role models of neighborhood successes and even less access to connections that might help them improve their situations. They were, as William Julius Wilson called them in his eponymous book, *The Truly Disadvantaged*.[4]

Western Europe: Recovery and New Problems

At the end of World War II, Europe's first agenda was recovery, rebuilding, and restructuring. The urban population rose quickly, as large numbers of people left the countryside, especially in Mediterranean Europe. The number of Eastern and Western Europeans was 280 million in 1950; by 1975, it reached 446 million. The population living in cities rose from 51 percent to 66 percent (United Nations 2003, 7). Cities could not keep up with the demand. The upper and middle classes could not all fit in the center cities—which was usually their cultural preference—especially as many governments legislated greenbelts around them. In time, suburbanization leaped across those barriers, or penetrated them. With the "economic miracle" of the 1950s and 1960s, many Europeans acquired the automobile obsession of Americans and the accompanying desire for private homes and open spaces.

For the expanding middle classes who wished to move out of the city center, or could not afford to live there, many countries began to construct "New Towns," relatively self-contained towns that included industrial jobs, residences, shopping, and recreation for populations of approximately fifty thousand residents. Britain, where Ebenezer Howard had pioneered the "New Town" concept at the turn of the twentieth century, led the way, building some forty new towns at about an hour's commuting distance from London. France followed in the 1960s, initiating the construction of five new towns on the periphery of Paris, each of 300,000 to 500,000 inhabitants. The government provided major subsidies and all the new cities held both public and private construction. France, however, adopted the high-rise apartment model advocated by the Swiss-French architect Le Corbusier more than Ebenezer Howard's low-rise model. The two towns to the west of Paris extended the upper-middle-class patterns of that sector, producing suburban developments with both high-rise and low-rise accommodations. The three new towns to the east, however, attracted populations similar to those in the eastern sections of central Paris: working-class immigrants, some of whom had been living in *bidonvilles* (clusters of shacks often seized by squatters). In those three towns, the housing was uninspired, high-rise, cold, and impersonal—not so different in quality and ambience from high-rise public housing in the United States.[5] Many countries had experienced similar dichotomies: upscale mixtures of high-rise and low-rise buildings in suburban settings for those who could afford them; low-quality, drab, cement-block high-rises for working-class people on the edge of town, usually—but not always—adjacent to industries.

Eastern Europe: Central European Expansion, Suburbanization, and a Faltering Economy

Following World War II, the Soviet Union imposed over Central and Eastern Europe a governing style similar to its administration at home: state control of the means of production and of the means of collective consumption, of investment, incomes, and the media. Inequalities in housing and the provision of urban amenities did not favor the wealthy businessmen—who were dispossessed—but rather party officials, government administrators, and top-level managers and technocrats. Industrialization was emphasized and domestic consumption neglected. The rural sector remained large, and villages in proximity to industrializing cities served as bedroom communities for workers who were joining the industrial labor force. Ties between urban and rural people remained relatively strong.

Russia became one of the leaders in new town development, in part to keep up with its rising urban population, which passed 50 percent of the total in 1961. It tried both to disperse industry and to build residential developments with recreational facilities nearby, yet separated from the industrial units by a greenbelt. Russian planners also employed Le Corbusier's high-rise models, especially in the new industrial cities, such as Novosibirsk and Novokuznetsk, established to continue their long-standing commitment to the development of Siberia. The quality of construction and planning, however, was dismal.

Worker housing was built in vast estates, with five thousand to fifteen thousand units each, sometimes mass-produced in prefabricated high-rise units, usually of inferior quality. "The result in all these cities, from Berlin to Stalingrad, was the classic Soviet-era housing solution: mile upon mile of identical gray or brown cement blocks cheap, poorly-constructed, with no distinguishing architectural features and lacking any aesthetic indulgence (or public facilities)."[6] Since the party and the government usually allocated apartments in conjunction with workers' jobs in the factories, residents had little choice in their housing. Nevertheless, some people of higher social status also moved into these housing estates because their homes in the center of town, previously the most desirable area, were becoming dilapidated, the result of decades of warfare and minimal civilian investment.

In addition to enlarging existing cities and building new ones, the post-Stalin Soviet government under Nikita Khrushchev (1953–1964) expanded several hundred villages across the country by adding additional service capabilities and amenities to them. Some were transformed into industrial dormitories by a mass influx of workers in the nearby factories. Others became *agrogorods*, agricultural towns, surrounded by greenbelts and populated by the workers of the collective farms.

F. E. Ian Hamilton noted a common general pattern of spatial development in the communist-dominated cities of central Europe. Implicitly, he was drawing a contrast with the concentric geographical model created by the Chicago School:

> When travelling out from the city centre one can observe the following zones: (1) the historic medieval or renaissance core; (2) inner commercial, housing, and industrial areas from the capitalistic period; (3) a zone of socialist transition or renewal, where modern construction is partially and progressively replacing inherited urban or relict-village features; (4) socialist housing of the 1950s; (5) integrated socialist neighbourhoods and residential districts of the 1960s and 1970s; (6) open or planted "isolation belts"; (7) industrial or related zones; and (8) open countryside, forest, or hills, including tourist complexes. (French and Hamilton 1979, 227)

Central Europeans saw themselves caught between contesting architectural cultures. The Polish planners of Warsaw, for example, accepted Soviet monumental urban design in laying out Marzalkowska Avenue, with its wide, grand vistas appropriate to public parades, and in constructing the Palace of Culture, an enormous skyscraper designed to accommodate twelve thousand people, planned by the architects of the University of Moscow and modeled on it. At the same time, Polish architects had risked their lives during World War II to preserve the plans of Warsaw so that the city could be rebuilt after the Nazi devastation. After the war, they recreated Warsaw's downtown area as it had appeared historically, with a rebuilt Warsaw Castle as its anchor building. Throughout Soviet-dominated central Europe, a similar pattern arose: historic, central-city districts continued to give expression to indigenous, nationalistic, architectural, and cultural forms, while most new residential areas took on a uniform drabness and low quality of design, punctuated by some remarkable monumental architecture designed to glorify the communist state.

Because Eastern and Western Europe were divided by the cold war, comparisons abounded. In Western Europe, consumerism boomed; easterners experienced some rise in standards of living, but were faced with minimal availability of consumer goods, including apartments, telephones, and cars, as well as food and clothing; medical attention and education, however, were of good quality.

A single city, Berlin, came to represent and symbolize the cold war conflict. Situated within Soviet-controlled East Germany, Berlin was divided in the aftermath of World War II between the Americans, British, and French in the West and the Russians in the East. In 1948, the Americans thwarted a Russian attempt to blockade and take over West Berlin by successfully air-dropping food and supplies for a year and a half, until the Russians agreed to restore land access. The city lived on in its divided form. Thousands of East Germans used the Berlin crossing points as escape routes to the West until, in 1961, the

Russians built the Berlin Wall, establishing a complete physical division of the city. The destruction of the wall by the people of Berlin, in a spontaneous uprising in 1989, symbolized and prepared the way for the reunification of the city and the nation.

Europe's remarkable postwar recovery was marred, however, by the destruction of one of the continent's most prominent urban minority groups. Much of urban history focuses on minority-majority relationships, and the war and the Holocaust had destroyed almost the entire central and eastern European Jewish minority, an overwhelmingly urban group. In cities like Berlin, Budapest, and Warsaw, few remained. Jewish communities in the smaller towns ceased to exist entirely. Just a few years later, after the establishment of the state of Israel in 1948, almost all of the hundreds of thousands of Jews living in the cities of the Arab world, from Morocco to Iraq, pulled up roots and emigrated to Israel. Another regional branch of this urban ethnic/religious minority community that had flourished for centuries virtually ceased to exist.

THE POSTCOLONIAL WORLD: INDEPENDENCE, "OVERURBANIZATION," AND INDIGENOUS SOLUTIONS

In those largely impoverished nations that were just emerging from colonial rule, urban growth took on new force. The coming of independence brought great exhilaration, but also unprecedented new political problems. The rate of demographic growth was extraordinary, through both rural-to-urban immigration and natural increase. Total population in urban areas of "the less developed regions of the world" increased in 1950–1975 from 335 million to 875 million, 161 percent (United Nations 2003, 7).

This explosive growth was driven, in part, by massive growth in overall population. The total population of the less-developed regions in 1950 was 1,786 million; by 1975, it had reached 3,138, up 76 percent. In most regions, increasing population "pushed" villagers off the countryside as the overcrowding on farmland increased. Also, urban-manufactured products displaced rural craftspeople from their occupations. In addition, the "pull" of potential jobs, educational and cultural opportunities, and access to urban institutions like hospitals, law courts, and universities increased with the end of colonial control.

The end of colonial control over urban land removed some of the brakes on urban immigration. A few newly independent countries did attempt to impose their own limits on migration, but usually without much success. China, because of its powerful communist government, was a major exception. The Chinese government registered every family according to its residence and its occupations and forbade migration of any sort except to a known job already assigned to the migrant, validated by a permit issued by the government. These "internal passports" were difficult to obtain; even so, some illegal immigration did continue.[7]

The largest cities grew fastest—spectacularly and frighteningly. For example, between 1950 and 1975, moving in general from west to east, Mexico City grew from just under 3 million to 10.7 million; Buenos Aires from about 5 million to about 9 million; Sao Paulo from 2.5 million to more than 10 million; Lagos from 288,000 to almost 2 million; Teheran from 1 million to 4.3 million; Karachi from 1 million to 4 million; Mumbai (Bombay) from 3 million to 7.3 million; Bangkok from 1.3 million to 3.8 million; Shanghai from 5 million to 11 million; and Seoul from 1 million to almost 7 million.

These enormous population gains took place in countries with relatively few industrial jobs. Economists referred to this process as "overurbanization," meaning that there were more people than there were stable jobs, as compared to the processes that had taken place in the industrialized world a century earlier, in which expanding job markets had welcomed new workers. Moreover, these third world cities did not have the infrastructure—roads, water, sewerage, electricity, housing—needed to accommodate the population growth. Immigrants with education, skills, and connections could often overcome these challenges. For the majority of immigrants who had little education, few marketable skills, and fewer connections, the obstacles were formidable.

Some migrants came in annual, circular patterns. They worked the land during the agricultural season, but sought urban work during the agricultural off-season. Others came tentatively. If one member of a family—usually males in South Asia and Africa, more frequently females in Latin America—came to the city to seek work and succeeded, he or she provided an urban outpost for bringing in other members of the family and of the home village. Sometimes the single migrant remained in the city to work, leaving the family more or less permanently in the village. Remittances sent back home from often meager pay cemented the family bonds. In some cases, these remittances kept whole regions, as well as families, financially solvent. Many of the urban immigrants expressed wishes to return to their rural homes after their working lives were completed; it is not clear if they actually did, or could, act out these wishes.

The migrants found little support from the government or established institutions, and few jobs in the organized sector of the economy. (Manuel Castells compared their difficult condition to that of the "guest workers," who came from third world countries to seek work in European cities.) They created voluntary associations, "informal" labor markets, and "informal" housing. These associations provided information on urban institutions, jobs, training, and religious activities. They mediated disputes and family quarrels, which was especially important in urban settings where relationships between men and women, husband and wife, might be quite different than in the home village. They provided loans, often at low interest rates. Through voluntary institutions in the city, religious leaders could speak to each other across sectarian lines, and leaders of diverse tribal groups could negotiate rules of conduct in the new urban settings. Voluntary associations allowed new immigrants to remain in good standing with their families, religions, tribes, and villages of origin, while at the same time meeting on friendly terms with people of other, diverse backgrounds. (Immigrants to American and European cities in the age of high industrialization had created similar organizations.)

Unemployment, underemployment, and misemployment marked the labor markets of third world cities. Many able-bodied workers could not find jobs at all, or they could find only part-time employment or jobs not appropriate for their skill levels. Literate migrants with skills and connections might find better jobs with some levels of mobility. Those without literacy, job skills, or connections generally moved from the lowest economic levels of their villages to somewhat less-impoverished but still the lowest economic levels in the city. They found few opportunities for upward mobility.

Formal labor bureaus, newspaper ads, and employment agencies counted for little. Job seekers arriving in the city usually relied on relatives and friends to find jobs; sometimes they were on their own. For most, the search might result in "casual" or "informal" labor: waiting anxiously on street corners each morning hoping to be hired for construction projects or other manual labor; selling commodities door-to-door, or in the middle of the street at traffic lights; or working from home producing simple goods, from cigarettes to clothing, for piece rates.

In many third world regions, women became more economically independent and the range of their occupations more diversified. Young women in Latin America frequently sought employment as domestic workers in private homes, especially until they reached marriageable age. The new factories of East and Southeast Asia employed mostly women, creating new family dynamics in the process. As women entered the workforce, feminist planners, in particular, asked how systems of transportation, allocation of urban market spaces, provision of child care, and the design of residences might be differently configured to accommodate the needs of women, especially working mothers (Bhatt 2006).[8]

The migrant's first search was for a job. The second was for a home. Housing at affordable rents was virtually nonexistent, but villagers were accustomed to building their own housing and to improving and adding to it as their financial situation allowed. They adapted these practices to the city. They sought locations where water and perhaps electricity were available in the vicinity—toilets were often considered a luxury—and built their own shacks. Sometimes they paid rent to the owner of the land; sometimes they bribed policemen or intermediaries and stayed illegally; sometimes they managed to stay illegally without payoffs. Outsiders, viewing the squatters' shacks and their rural ways of life, often referred to these immigrants as "urban villagers."

Throughout Latin America, where large-scale urban migration began between the wars, *favelas* (self-built slum housing) arose wherever empty space was available, through legal purchase or rent, or through illegal squatting. Newcomers built their own housing and slowly improved it. A view of the favelas immediately revealed the contrast between older ones—where home improvements had been continuous over decades and shacks had been expanded into houses, albeit crammed into tiny spaces—and newer ones, just beginning as shacks. With the passing of years, the improvement in the shacks also reflected another political reality: Illegal squatter colonies were often given legal sanction. Once freed from the fear of eviction, the slum dwellers were willing to invest more time, energy, and capital into improving their homes.

The "informal" squatter colonies and slums multiplied throughout the third world: *favelas* in Brazil, *bustis* and *jhuggi-jhonpri* in India, *geçekondu* ("built overnight") in Turkey. In some areas of the world, like the large cities of Latin America, more than half of the residents lived in squatter settlements. John Turner led a new movement among planners in the 1960s and 1970s arguing that this self-built, "informal" housing offered the only feasible solution to the newcomers' need for shelter. Turner distinguished between "slums of despair," the usual view of the squatter slums, and "slums of hope," the designation he gave to this housing that new immigrants built for themselves as their toehold in urban society as they arrived, optimistically, in search of work. This view of the poor in urban society as hopeful and highly self-motivated rather than as parasitic, desperate, and destructive later led to many programs to aid rather than oppose them. Many upper-class members of the society rejected these favorable interpretations and strategies and continued to view the squatters as marginal and dangerous to health and safety. From the other side, more socialistically inclined critics, like Mike Davis, saw the self-help projects as last-ditch efforts by people whom government had failed.

For the few who were rich, housing was available: the now-deserted homes of the former colonial elites, most of whom left for "home." As the new elites took possession of this abandoned housing, they perpetuated the pattern of class segregation, although not of racial segregation.[9] These elites usually had little appreciation of the problems of slum dwellers and usually did not wish to encourage mass protest movements among the poor any more than had the European colonial rulers.

To get by—to survive—some slum dwellers turned to criminal behavior. In addition, many criminal businessmen, unethical politicians, and policemen on the take continued to exploit their poverty, instability, insecurity, and illegal status. Criminal activity sometimes spilled over the borders of the slum and threatened the welfare and health of the broader community. Biographies and autobiographies often reveal lives of theft, prostitution, murder, child abuse, family disorganization, and domestic violence, along with occasional examples of touching sympathy and kindness (Johnson and Bernstein 1982).

Groups that were not organized were at risk. In extreme cases—for example, the street children in Brazilian cities—the poor without homes and living by their wits were at risk for their lives in the face of vigilantes who hunted them down and shot them. Unorganized squatters easily could be evicted. The very difficulty of surviving in the city often led the poor, and especially the immigrant poor, to stronger organization and politicization. The new urban immigrants needed the services and protection that political legitimation could offer, and the politicians needed their votes.

To relieve the political and demographic pressures on existing cities, and to create nodes for further economic growth, many governments established new cities as "growth poles" or "development zones." Major examples included Ciudad Guyana in Venezuela's mineral- and oil-rich Orinoco River valley, and Shenzhen in China, adjacent to the port of Hong Kong. A "New Bombay," across the water from the existing Bombay, was built to relieve population pressures. New capitals were created as showcases, such as Islamabad, the new capital of Pakistan, and new state capitals in India: Chandigarh, designed by Corbu, in Punjab; Bhubaneshwar in Orissa; and Gandhinagar in Gujarat. Sometimes, new cities, especially capital cities like Yamoussoukro in Ivory Coast, seemed to have been created primarily to enhance the prestige of a powerful national ruler. The creation of Brasilia embodied several goals: to relieve population pressure on Rio de Janeiro; to help develop the Brazilian interior; and to create a spectacular new capital that symbolized Brazil's identification with the most modern urban design.

On a more modest level, perhaps modeling the *agrogorods* of Khrushchev's Russia, urban and regional planners sought to build up large villages into small towns and cities in order to provide market and administrative centers in remote regions and to link them to one another and to outside regions. They encouraged the creation of whole national systems of cities, completing the links between central metropolis and local small town. Advocates of these sorts of intermediate-scale cities focused on the interface where rural and urban facilities and ways of life met and hailed them as much-needed models of *agropolitan* regional development (E.A.J. Johnson 1970).

APPROACHING THE END OF THE CENTURY: CITIES AS LOCAL SYSTEMS WITHIN GLOBAL SYSTEMS OF CITIES

Systems of Cities

In the late twentieth century, the World Wide Web created an entirely new dimension in the historic networks of exchange of goods, people, and ideas. The Web, "the information superhighway"—created for military purposes in the 1970s and widely available to the general public beginning in the 1990s—transformed personal and institutional relationships as dramatically as the automobile had transformed them almost a century earlier. By reducing the cost of transmitting information anywhere in the world to virtually zero, the Web increased the density and the extent of communication and exchange of capital throughout the world system of cities. People understood the power of the Web immediately. By 1994, some 3 million had connected; by mid-1999, 200 million; and by the end of 2005, more than 1 billion.

The new technology of the Web and the new political economy of more open borders produced "globalization," the linking of cities and regions into global networks for the exchange of information, capital, commodities, and labor. The network was not entirely new, although its diversity and openness were. International competition and imperialism had forged an early model of globalization at the turn of the twentieth century, creating great wealth for some and extensive exploitation for others. Two world wars, a world depression, and a cold war had shattered that global system into noninteractive, often hostile blocs. Now it arose anew on the strength of the resurgent world economy, the new information technology, and dramatic changes in global politics.

Access to the Web was open to all, but some urban centers remained dominant and even increased their dominance. Economist Saskia Sassen emphasized the persistent power of New York, London, and Tokyo over the international economy, calling them—and only them—"Global Cities." At the other extreme, some areas were hardly touched by globalization. For example, only 13 million of sub-Saharan Africa's 765 million inhabitants, 1.7 percent, used the Internet in 2005. More typically, a tiny minority of a city in the developing world, or even an entire nation, might use the Internet extensively while the rest of the population remained completely out of touch. In India, for example, although computer centers of world importance were arising in cities like Bangalore and Hyderabad, the country as a whole remained predominantly agricultural, poor, and unconnected. While 51 million Indians were reported as users of the Internet, this was only 4.5 percent of India's total population of 1.1 billion. By contrast, in the United States, Japan, South Korea, Canada, Australia, and the Netherlands, about two of every three residents used an Internet connection.[10]

With the Web and e-mail providing instantaneous, virtually free communication everywhere in the world, it became easier for manufacturers to relocate their production facilities to poorer areas where wages were lower. The United States alone lost 35 million jobs between 1969 and 1976, one-half of them from its "rustbelt" industrial heartland.[11] Similar patterns appeared in Western Europe and Japan. The economies of these developed regions were shifting out of manufacturing into services. China was the great exception, demonstrating continuous growth in urban manufacturing. By 1980, the new post-Mao administration under Deng Xiaoping instituted new policies for economic development through urban growth. Boldly, Deng opened the country to foreign investment, much of it from Taiwan, Japan, and Chinese expatriates living overseas, and much of it invested in new industrialization and in new urban real estate ventures, both commercial and residential. Deng also began to modify the austerities of communist policy with an entirely new emphasis on bourgeois urban consumption and pleasure. "To be rich is glorious," he proclaimed.

China instituted four "special economic zones" to jump-start development. The largest, the city and region of Shenzhen, contiguous to Hong Kong, grew from virtually no population in 1980 to about 3 million in 2000 and 4 million in 2005. Manufacturing, trade, and services flourished. Directly across the Huangpu River from Shanghai, Deng designated Pudong a "national project" in 1991, also with the status of a special economic zone. By the early years of the twenty-first century, Pudong held some 10,000 financial, commercial, and trade institutions from more than sixty countries in more than one hundred high-rises, among them some of the world's tallest skyscrapers. China's urban population had risen from 16 percent in 1960 to only 19.6 percent in 1980; then it jumped sharply to 35.8 percent in 2000 (United Nations 2003, 21) and 40.5 percent in 2005. Similar policies of urban development through state-aided capitalist enterprise were also soon adopted in communist Vietnam, especially in Ho Chi Minh City in the south, but also in Hanoi in the north. Cities in communist countries, which had been cut off from the global economy for decades, were now joining it and adopting urban bourgeois consumer styles, although the Communist Party did not (yet) allow political democracy.

The Soviet Union remained committed to centralized state planning under a single-party state until 1989–1991, when the system imploded and the USSR dissolved as a political entity. At first, the shock led to a temporary economic depression, but by the end of the twentieth century, the region and its cities had mostly returned to at least the economic levels of 1989. New legal and regulatory systems began to emerge to support private rights in property, including urban land and real estate. Housing began to enter the private market, and mechanisms developed to allow this privatization after decades of control by the state.

Newly empowered city governments had to decide how much to keep some properties off the free market in order to preserve public housing for low-income and disadvantaged groups. The years of turmoil briefly reduced the population of Russia's capital, Moscow, from 9 million in 1991 to 8.5 million by the end of the decade. Then the trend reversed and Moscow revived; by 2005, it had expanded to 10.5 million, double the size of the next-largest Russian city, St. Petersburg. Russia's urban population reached 73 percent in 1990 and stabilized at that point. Ethnic diversity in the major cities, especially Moscow, also was increasing as Chechens and peoples from regions of the former Soviet Union, as well as immigrant Turks, Arabs, Chinese, and Vietnamese arrived in search of work. Ethnic competition sometimes broke out in violence. Russia's war against Chechen rebels spilled over into guerrilla warfare in the streets and cinema theaters of Russia.

In terms of business, Russian cities that had provided only minimal shopping facilities began, rather quickly, to see new shops open and private businesses flourish, giving the cities more life and color. Billboards proliferated. Business services, a sector of the economy virtually nonexistent under communist rule, employed almost 10 percent of Moscow's workforce by 2000. Many of the members of this new class were young, just beginning to master the language, computer, and business skills of their new tasks. Often they arose from among the former communist administrators of government enterprises, the people most experienced in administration and possessing the connections to buy the businesses from the state, which was now withering away at bargain-basement prices. Their prosperity inspired envy, as well as class and generational tensions—and new commercial outlets to attract their disposable income. By 2005, Moscow was estimated to have thirty-three billionaires, more than any other city in the world, and about thirty thousand millionaires.[12] They built some individual housing units, although virtually the entire population of Moscow, as of most large Russian cities, continued to live in apartments, mostly on the outskirts of the city.

Accountability was minimal as foreign investment poured in and businesses passed from state control to the hands of private businessmen. Corruption spread widely. Criminal organizations dominated much of public life, and began to deal in contraband goods, including nuclear weapons materials. As sociologist Ivan Szelenyi wrote of Eastern Europe generally, "The boredom of the socialist cities is gone, but so is their safety."[13]

Cities as Systems

As all cities gained access to the global system, albeit not on equal terms, to what degree did the internal structures of cities become more alike? To what degree did the global system of cities encourage similarities in the internal systems of cities everywhere?

One group of scholars claimed that Los Angeles was becoming the model of the emerging global city. A "Los Angeles School" of urban studies coalesced in the 1980s, a group of some twenty scholars joined loosely together at various universities and research institutes in Southern California. They identified Los Angeles as the new "shock city" of the United States. Los Angeles more than doubled in population between 1950 and 1975, from just over 4 million people to just under 9 million, easily leapfrogging Chicago to become America's second-largest city and, the scholars asserted, also surpassing Chicago as the scene of the newest trends in urban development. In addition to its world-famous film industry, Los Angeles became a major center in America for military contracting, especially in aeronautics, missiles, and electronics. It was also America's leading port city on the Pacific Rim.

Many of Los Angeles's "shock" characteristics set and reflected global trends: spatial and social fragmentation in a city with no geographical center, no central business district, no dominant social and economic group, and no normative cultural style; a vast hinterland of individual cities, each with its own personality; vast social divisions and inequities among its ethnically diverse residents; high levels of immigration, both high- and low-skilled, from several continents; a massive and lucrative film industry of illusion, fashion, and profit; high-tech industrialization, much of it based on industries for warfare, airplanes, missiles, and electronics; strong linkages to the global economy as America's leading port city on the Pacific Rim; a fast-growing economy with strong emphasis on consumption; challenging ecological problems (born of its semidesert location in a kind of topographical bowl); and reliance on privately owned cars running on endless miles of freeways as the principal means of transportation. In race riots, too, Los Angeles was a "shock" city. The riot in Los Angeles's Watts neighborhood in 1965 was one of the worst of America's many civil disturbances during that decade. In 1992, the most destructive urban rioting in the history of the United States erupted when a court exonerated white police officers, who had been captured on videotape beating Rodney King, an African American.

Many global megacities, like Los Angeles, had high rates of diverse immigration, fragmented social groups, and tense separations among classes. Third world megacities attracted migrants from all parts of their nation and beyond. For example, Abidjan drew from all of the West African Sahel, Mexico City from throughout Central America, and Shanghai from the entire Yangzi River basin. Oil-rich cities of the Persian Gulf attracted migrants from the surrounding Arabian Sea periphery in Africa and Asia. European cities received citizens from their former colonies: Paris, for example, from North and West Africa; London from India, Pakistan, and the West Indies. The immigrants did not always find the jobs they were seeking, and, as in Los Angeles, tensions came with the combination of diversity and inequality: "Large public housing projects in Paris and Amsterdam were increasingly populated by the structurally unemployed and their children, and—just as in their New York and London equivalents—violence was simmering just below the surface" (Hall 2002, 459). Not all violence was based on immigrant diversity. In many countries, electoral contests and sports competitions evoked periodic outbreaks of violence. Urban riots across India in the 1990s and early 2000s pitted Hindus and Muslims against one another, as social upheaval, religious tension, and political grandstanding combined to inflame both already-organized rioters and spontaneous mobs.[14] Violence among competing criminal gangs also flared up periodically in many cities around the world.

One group of scholars who carried out a comparative international study of the social structure of cities from across the United States and Australia and in individual studies of Kolkata (Calcutta), Rio de Janeiro, Singapore, Tokyo,

Brussels, and Frankfurt concluded that in the process of globalization, the spatial divisions among classes, ethnic groups, racial groups, and lifestyle groups within the city increased and "hardened, sometimes literally in the form of walls that function to protect the rich from the poor" (Marcuse and van Kempen 2000, 250). The specific social groups that were segregated, and segregated themselves, differed from city to city and nation to nation, but the patterns were common. They resembled Los Angeles. In all of the cities, people could live out their lives almost completely within geographically self-contained divisions, with residence, work, recreation, and socialization all included within their quarters of the city. These quarters were separated from one another also according to their political outlooks and self-interest. "Partially out of self-interest and partially simply because they do not see, meet and hear the others, decisions painful to others are easily made" (250). The spatial divisions were increasing, whether cities were industrializing or deindustrializing, whether they seemed to be on the leading edge of globalization or left out.

Nevertheless, integration also persisted. In the United States, racial segregation was banned by law. Housing covenants that fostered segregation were struck down and court orders attacked class-based segregation as well. In 1975 and 1983, the New Jersey Supreme Court ruled in the case of Mount Laurel that housing subdivisions for the upper middle classes also had to include housing for lower-income groups. The borough of Queens in New York City held immigrants and their descendents from one hundred different ethnic groups, people speaking some 138 languages. Researchers claimed that "Queens has the largest mix of immigrants and refugees in the world."[15] As one professional baseball player put it, hatefully, as he passed through Queens on his way to Shea Stadium, "The biggest thing I don't like . . . is the foreigners. . . . You can walk an entire block and not hear anybody speaking English. Asians and Koreans and Vietnamese and Indians and Russians and Spanish people and everything up there. How the hell did they get in this country?"[16] Yet, even within the polyglot diversity of Queens, there were semigated communities like Forest Hills Village, developed in the 1910s with an integrative design to the homes and the streets, on which only residents and their guests were permitted to park.

Socially, the segregation of Asian and African immigrants in Europe had similarities to racial segregation in the United States. As African Americans migrated from the rural South to the urban North in the United States, so migrants from poorer regions and nations came to the now-booming cities of Europe in search of jobs. Some came from the former imperial colonies: Indians, Pakistanis, and West Indians to London, Birmingham, Leeds, and other British cities; Algerians, Tunisians, Moroccans, Senegalese, and Malians to Paris. Millions of others came without imperial connections, especially from Yugoslavia, Turkey, and southern Italy. Millions of the migrants came from Islamic countries, introducing a new religious element into many European cities. By the year 2000, 15 percent of Paris's population was made up of international migrants; 15–25 percent of the population of Frankfurt, Stuttgart, and Munich; and 50 percent of Amsterdam. But their segregations were not nearly as intense as the racial segregation of the United States. A survey of immigrant communities in Dutch cities in 1998 showed that the highest index of segregation was of Turks in The Hague, at 53 on a scale from 1 (lowest) to 100 (highest). A similar study of Indians in London in 1991 showed 51, although Bangladeshis were at 75. Indices of African American segregation in the United States registered 85 in Detroit, 82 in New York City, and 81 in Chicago.[17]

Political parties, like that of Jacques Le Pen in France, ran on platforms urging bans on immigration and the expulsion of those immigrants already present. At the street level, fights between immigrant and native youths became frequent, sometimes leading to fire bombings. In many European cities, nativist youths shaved their skulls and, as "skinheads," went out seeking "foreigners," even those who had been in place for a generation and more. In England, the phenomenon earned its own name: "Paki[stani]-bashing." In France, as the Muslim population coming from the former colonies in North Africa increased, cultural conflict took on additional religious overtones. In 2005, rioting shook the immigrant, relatively poor, suburbs of Paris and spilled over into other cities in France and even into the Netherlands and Belgium. Beyond the immediate need to restore law and order, local and national political leaders appeared stymied as to what course to take economically, culturally, and politically. Anti-Semitism, too, began to reappear, reviving memories of the Holocaust, only a half century previous, in which 6 million Jews had been murdered, almost destroying one of the continent's most prominent urban minority communities. No one feared violence of that magnitude in the early 2000s but Europe still lived with a history that included radical intolerance of ethnic minorities. Also reviving those memories, continuing warfare throughout the 1990s between ethnic and religious groups in the Balkans brought a new term to Europe's vocabulary: "ethnic cleansing."

In the poorer countries of Asia, Africa, and South America, urban slums continued to expand in size and numbers. An estimated "924 million people lived in slums worldwide in 2001, or about 32 percent of the global urban population . . . with higher concentration in the developing world cities" (United Nations 2003, 2). Cities and nations experimented with diverse strategies for coping with their slums. Until the 1960s, most government plans in the developing world advocated the construction of public housing to accommodate new urban immigrants. The cost, however, was prohibitive. By the 1980s, programs of "sites and services" won favor. Governments would provide slum dwellers with space—a site marked off with individual plinths, or floors, often about two hundred square feet—and the basic services of water, sewerage, and electricity, which householders could not provide on an individual basis. The recipients of the plots would then construct their own housing from their own resources. Even this strategy proved expensive, and it was difficult to decide which of the slum dwellers should receive the plots. In addition, after construction, the owner-builders often sold their new homes to more middle-class buyers and returned to the slums, preferring the money to the home.

By the 1990s, a new strategy of upgrading the existing slums gained acceptance. Governments would retrofit slums with water and sewage lines and electric connections, and often create or reposition their street plans. Frequently, they also provided deeds or security of tenure. These improvements increased the physical quality of life of the residents while maintaining the basic social structure and organization of the slum. In some cities, these structural improvements were supplemented with social, health, and educational services. As governments and nongovernmental organizations (NGOs) gained years of experience, they created a wide array of successful partnership programs to work with—rather than just for—the slum dwellers.[18]

Despite Mike Davis's (2006) pessimistic account in *Planet of Slums*, not all situations were dismal. By the turn of the millennium, differences among the regions of the world were clearly emerging. Cities showed progress, especially those whose economies were generally improving, as in much of East and Southeast Asia, and those that implemented specific policies to improve the lives of slum dwellers, as in much of Latin America. In Africa, however, the proportion of slum dwellers continued to rise rapidly (United Nations 2003, 2). Especially in Latin America, the squatters had become more organized, more secure, and more professionalized. Investigative reporter Robert Neuwirth writes of Rio de Janeiro's Rocinha, the largest slum in Latin America:

> Most current construction in Rocinha is done by wage laborers who congregate at various locations on the hill, looking to be hired by professional contractors. And, to address community-wide issues, each favela has a residents' association, with an elected leadership. Large favelas may have several residents' associations. . . . The issues the residents' associations face are not all that different from those any block or community association would take on in an American town or city. (2005, 40)

To protect their illegal settlements, slum organizers negotiated with the police and the politicians. Neuwirth concluded that squatters could maintain their toeholds in the city only through collective organization, just as Peter Marcuse, John Turner, Charles Abrams, and others had been arguing for decades. The organizations included gangs of street toughs to enforce their negotiated settlements, however, and periodically battles broke out among them, leaving the dead in their wake.

Global Research and Planning

With half of the world's population urban, with metropolises sprawling for miles in all directions, and with the accessibility of the World Wide Web, the historic city with its legally delineated boundaries had become less distinct as a unit for study and action. In addition, the end of the cold war broke down many regional boundaries. In 1976, the United Nations sponsored the first Conference on Human Settlements, called Habitat I, in Vancouver, Canada, followed by Habitat II in Istanbul in 1996 and Habitat III, again in Vancouver in 2006. Urban research and study centers multiplied around the globe, some linked to government planning offices, some to universities, and some to NGOs. They addressed a wide spectrum of concerns that included physical planning, ecology, group relations, women's issues, youth organization, slum improvement, neighborhood planning, and the historic preservation of symbolically significant structures from the past. Cities were now firmly embedded in regional systems and global networks of communication, trade, and migration. Urban research and urban planning attempted to keep pace.

NOTES

Acknowledgments: Special thanks to Michael Adas for his editorial comments and for hosting a very helpful seminar on this paper at Rutgers (New Brunswick). Thanks also for similarly helpful seminars at Rutgers (Camden) and at Temple University, and to Lynn Lees for her comments.

1. Roderick McKenzie, "The Concept of Dominance and World Organization," *American Journal of Sociology* 33, no. 1 (July 1927): 28–42.

2. Chinua Achebe, *Things Fall Apart* (New York: Astor-Honor, c. 1959).

3. Frantz Fanon, *The Wretched of the Earth* (New York: Grove Press, 1968), 39.

4. William Julius Wilson, *The Truly Disadvantaged* (Chicago: University of Chicago Press, 1987).

5. Norma Evenson, *Paris: A Century of Change, 1878–1978* (New Haven, CT: Yale University Press, 1979) and James M. Rubenstein, *The French New Towns* (Baltimore, MD: Johns Hopkins University Press, 1978).

6. Tony Judt, *Postwar: A History of Europe since 1945* (New York: Penguin Press, 2005), 385.

7. Kam Wing Chang, *Cities with Invisible Walls: Reinterpreting Urbanization in Post-1949 China* (Hong Kong: Oxford University Press, 1994).

8. See also the Web site for Women in Informal Employment Globalizing and Organizing: www.wiego.org.

9. Akin Mabogunje, *Urbanization in Nigeria* (New York: Africana Publishing, 1968), 298–301.

10. Statistics on usage available at www.internetworldstats.com.

11. Barry Bluestone and Bennett Harrison, *The Deindustrialization of America* (New York: Basic Books, 1982).

12. *Times of London*, October 20, 2005, available from www.timesonline.co.uk/article/ 0,,13509-1833619,00.html.

13. Gregory Andrusz, Michael Harloe, and Ivan Szelenyi, eds. *Cities after Socialism: Urban and Regional Change and Conflict in Post-Socialist Societies* (Oxford: Blackwell, 1996), 314.

14. Paul Brass, *The Production of Hindu-Muslim Violence in Contemporary India* (Seattle: University of Washington Press, 2003).

15. Warren Lehrer and Judith Sloan, *Crossing the Blvd: Strangers, Neighbors, Aliens in a New America* (New York: Norton, 2003), 17.

16. Ibid., 10.

17. Sako Musterd and Wim Ostendorf, "Social Exclusion, Segregation, and Neighbourhood Effects," in *Cities of Europe: Changing Contexts, Local Arrangements, and the Challenge to Urban Cohesion*, ed. Yuri Kazepov (Malden, MA: Blackwell, 2004), 176, 179.

18. Janelle Plummer, *Focusing Partnerships: A Sourcebook for Municipal Capacity Building in Public-Private Partnerships* (London: Earthscan Publications, 2002).

ESSENTIAL BIBLIOGRAPHY

Abrams, Charles. 1964. *Man's Struggle for Shelter in an Urbanizing World* (Cambridge, MA: MIT Press).

Benjamin, Walter. 1978. *Reflections*, ed. Peter Demetz, trans. Edmund Jephcott (New York: Harcourt Brace Jovanovich).

Berry, Brian. 1981. *Comparative Urbanization: Divergent Paths in the Twentieth Century*, 2nd ed. (New York: St. Martin's Press).

Bhatt, Ela R. 2006. *We Are Poor, But So Many: The Story of Self-Employed Women in India* (New York: Oxford University Press).

Calthorpe, Peter, and William Fulton. 2001. *The Regional City: Planning for the End of Sprawl* (Washington, DC: Island Press).

Castells, Manuel. 1996. *The Rise of the Network Society*, vol. 1 in *The Information Age: Economy, Society, and Culture* (Oxford: Blackwell).

———. 1997. *The Power of Identity*, vol. 2 in *The Information Age: Economy, Society, and Culture* (Oxford: Blackwell).

———. 1997. *End of Millennium*, vol. 3 in *The Information Age: Economy, Society, and Culture* (Oxford: Blackwell).

Colton, Timothy J. 1995. *Moscow: Governing the Socialist Metropolis* (Cambridge, MA: Harvard University Press).

Davis, Mike. 2006. *Planet of Slums* (New York: Verso).

French, R. A., and F. E. Ian Hamilton, eds. 1979. *The Socialist City: Spatial Structure and Urban Policy* (New York: John Wiley).

Gilbert, Alan, and Josef Gugler. 1992. *Cities, Poverty, and Development*, 2nd ed. (New York: Oxford University Press).

Gugler, Josef, ed. 2004. *World Cities beyond the West* (Cambridge: Cambridge University Press).

Hall, Peter. 2002. *Cities of Tomorrow*, 3rd ed. (Malden, MA: Blackwell).

Harvey, David. 1990. *The Condition of Post-Modernity* (Cambridge, MA: Blackwell).

Jackson, Kenneth. 1985. *Crabgrass Frontier: The Suburbanization of the United States* (New York: Oxford University Press).

Johnson, E.A.J. 1970. *The Organization of Space in Developing Countries* (Cambridge, MA: Harvard University Press).

Johnson, Hazel, and Henry Bernstein with Raul Hernan Ampuero and Ben Crow, eds. 1982. *Third World Lives of Struggle* (London: Heinemann Educational Books in association with the Open University).

King, Anthony D. 1976. *Colonial Urban Development: Culture, Social Power and Environment* (London: Routledge and Kegan Paul).

Lees, Andrew. 1985. *Cities Perceived: Urban Society in European and American Thought, 1820–1940* (New York: Columbia University Press).

Le Galès, Patrick. 2002. *European Cities: Social Conflicts and Governance* (New York: Oxford University Press).

Mangin, William, ed. 1970. *Peasants in Cities: Readings in the Anthropology of Urbanization* (Boston: Houghton Mifflin).

Marcuse, Peter, and Ronald van Kempen, eds. 2000. *Globalizing Cities: A New Spatial Order* (Malden: MA: Blackwell).

McKenzie, Roderick. 1927. "The Concept of Dominance and World Organization," *American Journal of Sociology* 33, no. 1 (July): 28–42.

Mumford, Lewis. 1961. *The City in History* (New York: Harcourt, Brace & World).

Neuwirth, Robert. 2005. *Shadow Cities: A Billion Squatters, A New Urban World* (New York: Routledge).

Park, Robert E., Ernest W. Burgess, and Roderick McKenzie, eds. 1967. *The City*, introduction by Morris Janowitz (Chicago: University of Chicago Press, originally 1925).

Patel, Sujata, and Alice Thorner, eds. 1996a. *Bombay: Metaphor for Modern India* (New Delhi: Oxford University Press).

————. 1996b. *Bombay: Mosaic of Modern Culture* (New Delhi: Oxford University Press).

Rybczynski, Witold. 1995. *City Life: Urban Expectations in a New World* (New York: Scribner).

Scott, Allen J., and Edward W. Soja, eds. 1996. *The City: Los Angeles and Urban Theory at the End of the Twentieth Century* (Berkeley: University of California).

Turner, John. 1976. *Housing by People: Towards Autonomy in Building Environments* (London: Marion Boyars).

United Nations. 2003. *United Nations Human Settlements Programme (Habitat). The Challenge of Slums: Global Report on Human Settlements 2003* (London: Earthscan).

Weber, Adna Ferrin. 1963. *The Growth of Cities in the Nineteenth Century: A Study in Statistics* (Ithaca, NY: Cornell University Press; originally Macmillan, 1899).

Zukin, Sharon. 1995. *The Culture of Cities* (Oxford: Blackwell).

READERS

Fyfe, Nicholas R., and Judith T. Kenny, eds. 2005. *The Urban Geography Reader* (New York: Routledge).

Graham, Stephen, ed. 2004. *The Cybercities Reader* (New York: Routledge).

LeGates, Richard, and Frederic Stout, eds. 2003. *The City Reader*, 3rd ed. (New York: Routledge).

Miles, Malcolm, and Tim Hall, with Iain Borden. 2004. *The City Cultures Reader*, 2nd ed. (New York: Routledge).

Sennett, Richard, ed. 1969. *Classic Essays on the Culture of Cities* (New York: Appleton-Century-Crofts).

Wheeler, Stephen, and Timothy Beatley, eds. 2004. *The Sustainable Urban Development Reader* (New York: Routledge).

Williams, Norman, Jr., Edmund H. Kellogg, and Frank B. Gilbert. 1983. *Readings in Historic Preservation: Why? What? How?* (New Brunswick, NJ: Center for Urban Policy Research).

CHAPTER 3

Women in the Twentieth-Century World

BONNIE G. SMITH

In 1905 an Indian journal published the fanciful story of a nation called Ladyland, where men were secluded in the *zenana*—the portion of the home reserved for women—while women ran the economy and political affairs. "The Sultana's Dream" showed women using their brains to harness the sun's energy to repel invaders, for example, and to engineer all sorts of feats to make public life easier and pleasant. The author of "The Sultana's Dream," Rokeya Sakhawat Hosain (1880–1932), was a self-educated Bengali woman who, as part of her patriotism, advocated the education of women and a more scientific mind-set for all of her contemporaries. Hosain supported the wearing of the burka and veiling when among friends, while simultaneously working tirelessly as the founder of a school for young women and as a reformer more generally. As such, she was part of the activist spirit that has inspired women down through the twentieth century to the present day. She foresaw women in power and hard at work, using their brains for technological progress and the public good. She also envisioned a day when men might be helpful in the household, although she actually had them confined to the zenanas in Ladyland—mostly so that public life would be more peaceful.

Hosain wrote at the dawn of the twentieth century, when the world's women participated in feminist and other political movements that shaped the course of history, even as they held jobs, cared for their households, and participated in cultural movements of the day. These activities only increased across the course of the century, despite devastating wars, global depression, rising conflicts for independence from colonialism, and a deepening interconnectedness—both for good and for ill—of the world's peoples. In fact, historians have remarked on the coming to the forefront of women, self-consciously as women, across the globe during the twentieth century. Additionally, from the twentieth century on, there was regular global commentary about women instead of the sporadic eruption of debates that alternately denigrated or defended them that cropped up from time to time—in fourteenth-century Europe or eighteenth-century China, for example. Nor was this eruption of awareness about womanhood confined to the elites. Although workingwomen had been active in previous centuries on behalf of themselves and their families, such advocacy became more consistent and widespread than ever before, leaving historians today still charting the course of women's recent, consequential past.

WORK AND POLITICS AS THE CENTURY OPENS

As the twentieth century opened, few women led the privileged and secure life of Rokeya Sakhawat Hosain, and most lacked the wherewithal to give their efforts over to helping others. In contrast to her wealth and literacy, they eked out a living as unschooled peasants, domestic workers, craftswomen, and factory hands. Some performed their work as slaves. In addition to earning a living, they cared for children and aged parents and maintained their households. By far the greatest work responsibilities in the first decades of the twentieth century occurred on farms and in households. Women tended crops such as rice, manioc, and cotton, oversaw the production of milk, cheese, and other dairy products, and did the onerous work of preparing food in days before there were many modern household appliances. They also gathered wood, peat, dung, and other materials for heating homes and cooking in them. Additionally, the women and their children had to fetch water in the days before widespread public systems provided utilities to individual homes. Production of textiles still occurred in the home in many areas in 1900, and the household was also the site of health care, which included gathering herbs, tending the sick and dying, and birthing infants. Midwifery was a central women's job. At that time, especially where there was no formal schooling for working people (the case in most societies), both men and women raised children, educating them to fulfill their respective adult roles. Women often helped arrange marriages for their children and monitored their sexuality until these partnerships were formed. Sometimes, the responsibilities of powerful women for generating wealth were so vast that they took "wives" themselves, as happened among Africans. In Africa, agricultural production meant prosperity, so that men and women alike would want many wives to help produce riches through their work on farms.

Worldwide, the majority of work thus took place in families and echoed the legal and traditional hierarchies in family life. For instance, in Latin American countries, a gendered culture is said to have prescribed "machismo" as a goal for men, by which they would exhibit hypermasculine virility and military prowess. The counterpart was said to be "marianismo" for women, who were to be self-sacrificing and devoted mothers, though they might also be assertive if they were obedient as well. In East Asian cultures, strongly influenced by Confucian currents, wives owed obedience to husbands, children to parents, and younger siblings to the oldest male sibling. Daughters-in-law, trained in domestic and even money-earning skills by their mothers, worked hard at the direction of their mothers-in-law, who themselves obeyed husbands and oldest sons. Virtually all of the world—with exceptions, of course—was dominated by men, who shaped laws and customs to give men privileges over women, whether this involved political rule, the right of citizenship, religious power, or even the legal right in Western societies to appropriate women's wages and, in other societies, to sell their daughters into slavery. Simply put, men were considered better than women, valued far more than women, and were thus granted the economic and social goods to maintain that higher position.

Amid the general inferiority in women's social, economic, and political positions, they had distinct rituals accompanying stages in life, such as initiation and confirmation. In some societies, genital cutting marked a certain age (or stage) in life, while women at marriage and childbirth were surrounded by customs that often centered on female solidarity and ceremonies. At work, in religious observances, and in social rituals, women usually followed a female hierarchy by which older, wealthier, or more aristocratic women took precedence and were obeyed. Despite the deference that women could receive as mothers, in most societies, mothers favored their sons over their daughters. They naturally valued their sons' lives more than they did the lives of their daughters because of the higher value of men in the society at large. Many treated their daughters severely so that they could withstand the difficult condition of being an adult woman. Infanticide of infant girls was not uncommon, and needy parents sold daughters into slavery and prostitution. All of these behaviors were marked by a strong sense of social order, by which families and communities regulated such intimate events as marriage, property allocation, and livelihoods for their children so that the community as a whole would survive.

Despite the prevalence of agricultural life, distinct regions of the world— not just individual countries but also coastal cities—were drawing closer together in a global economy because of improved communications and the interconnections forged by trade and by European, Japanese, and U.S. imperialism. In earning their livelihoods and carrying out their family roles, many women and their families participated in a vast migration of peoples at the turn of the century. This migration to cities and to distant parts of the world—sometimes temporary, often permanent—formed diasporas and created diasporic cultures as economies globalized and as urban areas and accessible farmland came to offer the most opportunity. The rise and spread of industry over the course of the nineteenth century and into the twentieth created new jobs and continues to do so today.

After the death of her husband in 1910, the widow Marcela Bernal del viuda de Torres left her young sons to live with relatives and took her two daughters to Mexico City to find work in its thriving factories. Seeking opportunity, Marcela explained the move to her daughters: "I'm sure not going to let you end up as maids" (Porter 2003, 3–4). Word of factory openings traveled quickly to rural areas: "As far away as [Guanajuato, their village], news arrived that in Mexico City there was a factory where women worked." Early in the twentieth century, women around the world heard the news that there was opportunity for industrial work in the cities, causing them to leave their rural areas for factory life. As an example, the jute and textile mills of Bengal attracted widows in particular, for they lacked familial support in maintaining farms once their husbands were gone. In contrast, the opening of diamond and gold mines in Africa and the creation of vast plantations for the production of agricultural commodities led to male migration, partly to pay the taxes that imperial occupiers imposed. In some cases, women worked with their husbands or families on plantations, but in others, women were left in charge not only of family life but also of all economic pursuits necessary to sustain themselves and their children.

From Europe, where massive out-migration in the millions occurred, emigrant women moved to Australia, New Zealand, Latin America, and North America for opportunities. Although the vast majority of women worked on farms or as domestic servants, industrial work was often the most remunerative and industrial jobs for women grew throughout the century. Alongside these, white-collar jobs were also being created as industries grew more complex, developing a managerial sector that employed secretaries, typists, bookkeepers, and receptionists. Stores, especially large department stores that thrived in Tokyo, Buenos Aires, and other cities around the world, increasingly employed women as clerks, while the telephone and telegraph industries were often almost exclusively staffed by women at the lower levels.

Simultaneously, urbanization and industrialization around the world opened opportunities for women to extend their household tasks outward, making them available to those who worked long hours in industry and to newcomers who lacked families to provide domestic services. Women took in laundry or did sewing, they took in boarders, and they cooked tasty foods and opened cantinas. In Chile, they made empanadas and sold them outside factories and workshops; they brewed drinks to sell on the streets. Like Chilean women, many did an array of market work, selling charcoal, consumer items, and food. They often served as the primary local traders in Africa and throughout Southeast Asia, selling not only their own produce but also craft and imported goods.

Additionally, women did a variety of jobs at home, whether rural or urban. They made baskets, toys, artificial flowers, and boxes on an artisanal basis, but also worked at home for nearby factories, polishing metal, painting objects such as buttons, and finishing an array of products. Today, working at home remains an important source of funds for women, who have enlisted children and old people in their families as unpaid workers, despite the myths about global industrialization destroying work at home. Finally, in difficult times, such as during the Mexican Revolution (1910–1920), women pawned domestic items such as tableware and clothing—and in truly desperate situations, their sewing machines—to raise money for emergencies.

Another source of work, which rose with urbanization and migration, was sexual. Because women's pay was low, some newcomers to the city turned to casual prostitution to supplement craft income. But the growth of cities often led to high demand for sex from young single males who migrated without families. In Africa, sex work was often accompanied by domestic work, such as mending clothes or providing a meal for migrants living without family support. Under colonialism, women who turned to prostitution were often subject to gynecological inspection and other types of enforced medical inspection and treatment, said to protect men from syphilis. Other women were higher-class courtesans, whose skills in conversation, music, and poetry earned them substantial sums. They might even live together in all-female households with large fortunes. "Industrialists, government officers, other businessmen come here now; they have lots of black money [undeclared cash] that they bring with them," explained one member of a wealthy courtesan family dating back to nineteenth-century India. "We make sure that they leave with very little, if any" (Oldenburg 1992, 44). The more usual cases of prostitution were often desperate or at least associated with low incomes and higher risks of contracting sexual diseases, which rose with the globalization and urbanization of the modern period.

Even with the opportunities that accompanied the global spread of industry early in the twentieth century, a sexual division of labor (persisting to the present) reduced women's chances to earn a decent living or one equal to men of their own class. A sexual division of labor means that some jobs are called women's jobs and others are called men's jobs, even though this division is arbitrary and variable. For instance, weaving was labeled a man's job in some factories, but a woman's job in others. The designation of jobs as belonging to one sex or the other allowed ideas of gender to determine pay. Women's jobs were generally said to take less skill than men's jobs. When the International Labor Organization of the League of Nations did a study of skills needed for jobs early in the 1920s, however, it determined that a secretary needed more skills than almost any other kind of worker. Nonetheless, the public viewed secretarial work as women's work and secretaries thus received less pay. Women's labor outside the home gradually came to be "protected" by labor legislation, removing females from jobs that were said to be "dangerous" to women only, even though men in these jobs were often more susceptible to diseases and injuries than women. Denying women jobs in British potteries, for instance, did not take them out of the workforce but rather pushed them out of well-paid work into lower-paying jobs. In passing a 1920 law that banned women from working in establishments serving liquor because it exposed them to immorality, the Mexican government blocked women from the solid job of waitressing, while actually making them more apt to resort to prostitution. Finally, women faced sexual harassment, whether in getting and keeping factory work or service work. As a Russian woman commented in the early twentieth century: "Even the decent and well-paying jobs, for example, those in banks, are rarely available unless one first grants favors to the director, the manager, or some other individual" (Bonnell 1983, 197).

Racism and ethnic difference also shaped women's work lives. Imperial leaders and theorists justified their domination with increasingly complex notions of racial and ethnic superiority, most notably those based on Charles Darwin's ideas of evolution and natural selection. Although the Christian religion was believed to be a sign of civilizational advance, the "scientific" statements of Darwin that darker races and women were less highly evolved determined both attitudes and policy. These beliefs justified sexual aggression and other abuses of all women, and women of color and those in the colonies were especially exploited. The plight of ordinary women of color under colonialism was generally forced labor, prostitution, and relegation to demeaning jobs. Children of mixed race, fathered by men from imperial countries, often faced a bleak future, and were considered the dregs of society, for instance, in India and Indonesia. Japanese imperialists held Koreans and many other Asians in equal contempt, citing their non-Japanese ethnicity as indicating depravity and low intelligence. Women in Korea and Taiwan, in the case of Japanese imperialism, felt the same degradation in their work, sexual, and social lives. A premium on whiteness developed from the end of the nineteenth century on, shaping immigration and marital policies in countries such as Brazil, Argentina, and Cuba. Indigenous women in Latin America and the United States suffered under these and other even worse policies, such as the enforced sterilization of African American women, that aimed to stop darker-skinned, "genetically inferior" women from bearing children.

Harassment, low pay, and the lack of gender and racial equality led to a wide range of activism around issues of work and equity more generally. Where industry was concentrated in urban areas, women joined unions—often socialist ones—though not in the proportion that men did. In the cigarette and cigar industries of Mexico City, for example, women workers organized and protested pay cuts, hazards on the job, and speedups. In the Shanghai cotton mills, girls formed sisterhoods: "We would go to work together and leave work together because then it was not good to walk alone." After a while, groups of these girls would pledge loyalty to one another, vowing to protect one another from the gangs who stole paychecks or street women who seized these young girls and sold them to brothels (Honig 1985, 704). In Italy and Spain, rural women joined anarchist groups opposing the increasing immiseration of day laborers and sharecroppers. Similarly, white-collar workers started unions or joined those led by men. In the Orange Free State in South Africa, women who worked outside the home protested the "pass system" that forced them to gain permission from employers to move about the countryside. That is, in order to get a pass from an employer and thus be mobile, they could no longer conduct their own businesses such as laundering and brewing at home. The restrictions on their movement and on their choice of work caused them to march by the hundreds in protest. Their slogan was: "We have done with pleading, we now demand" (Wells 1993, 42).

Work activism thus shaded over into direct political activism. In addition to joining unions, many women around the world were members of socialist political parties, which generally espoused the ideas of Karl Marx and Friedrich Engels. Socialist thought explained that in very ancient times there was no such thing as private property. With all goods held in common, there was accordingly a rough equality between men and women. Once private property came into being, men began controlling women's sexuality and general conduct in order to assure that property was passed down to legitimate heirs. In his influential book, *Origin of the Family, Private Property, and the State* (1884), Friedrich Engels contended that the coming of socialism, whose goal was to eliminate private property, would automatically restore women's rights. Socialists contended, therefore, that there was no need for a women's movement. Women became socialists, though as in the case of trade unions, they were often so ill-paid and so occupied—not only with work outside the home but with child care and housekeeping—that they had no time for activism. Union and party dues simply took too big a bite out of paychecks that were already lower than men's. Moreover, many men did not want women's participation in the workplace, preferring instead that working-class women stay at home because they could possibly compete for men's jobs and drag down wages. Additionally, union leaders endorsed the middle-class ideology that men should be the sole breadwinners, with women dependent on them.

Famed socialist leaders Clara Zetkin and Rosa Luxemburg scorned middle-class feminists as activists only interested in getting power for themselves to the detriment of workers. Nonetheless, a feminist movement that in fact crossed class lines had developed around the world after the late nineteenth century. In England, women in textile factories joined in feminist marches for women's rights and feminists organized employment bureaus and wellness centers for poor and working women. In the United States, middle-class African American women were particularly concerned to "lift up" lower-class blacks as a way of promoting civil rights as a whole. In India, feminists published journals, set up schools, did philanthropic work to improve poorer women's conditions, and participated in political parties such as the Indian Congress in its work to achieve independence or at least to provide better opportunities for local people to serve in government and to lead society. Feminism flourished around the world.

In the first decades of the twentieth century, Latin American women's groups met to promote women's voting rights, their access to good jobs, and their welfare and housing in general. These feminists were especially concerned about the well-being of children, particularly the "warehousing" of those who were poor, orphaned, abused, or otherwise underprivileged. Providing education for girls and women was another major concern, as well as giving women access to teaching positions. Reformers in China helped the country gain some 134,000 schools for girls, instructing 4.5 million students before World War I. Indian and Egyptian women alike wrote for periodicals, participating in the growing mass media and proclaiming not only women's right to determine more of their own destiny but also the nation's right to do so. The feminist press reached a peak of first-wave development around the world with such publications as the Japanese feminist periodical *Seito*, founded in 1911. Men in most emerging countries were active in debating the question of women's rights to education, good jobs, property ownership, and the vote, and many sought to bring women into the fight against colonialism on behalf of national independence. Some colonial officials used what they perceived as the degraded position of colonized women to question the capacity of Indian, Egyptian, or African men to assume positions of leadership in the postcolonial nations they sought to create.

International feminism also developed, with women engaging in a growing array of international contacts. International congresses met regularly to discuss issues of reform. In the nineteenth century, Susan B. Anthony of the United States had launched the International Council of Women (1988), and this had expanded to the International Women's Suffrage Alliance, founded in 1902. By the end of the 1930s, the alliance had met in a range of countries, including Turkey in 1939. Other international efforts included the Pan American International Women's Committee, founded in 1916. Most of these groups included well-established women who worked within the political systems and social networks of their individual countries, many of whom became diplomats and government officials in subsequent decades.

Women's activism on behalf of their rights occurred despite the fact that women in some corners of the world held significant power. In Qing China, the most powerful person between 1861 and 1908 was Empress Dowager Cixi, who was poorly instructed but expert in manipulating factions within the government so that Chinese policies seemed paralyzed between advancing toward reform (which, in private, she uniformly opposed) and moving backward in its policies, thus causing China to lose ever more of its autonomy to the imperial powers. As the century opened, she had executed and otherwise stamped out reform movements that called for the relaxed grip of fathers and elder brothers on women in the family. Simultaneously, in 1900, she supported the Boxer movement, which saw the elimination of foreigners as a critical step in restoring Chinese prosperity and China's former grandeur. This movement included women who were attracted not only to the patriotic goals of the Boxers to free China from foreigners but also to its relatively advanced position of respect for women. Although their separate units, called "Red Lanterns," performed auxiliary services rather than actual combat and have been seen as adding little to the movement, they served some six decades later as one source of inspiration for women committed to the development of communism in China.

In Africa, "queen mothers" also exercised considerable political power. Queen mothers were not necessarily the mothers of kings, though they might be. In some regions of Africa, they were the most distinguished women from elite or ancient clans, and in many regions they chose the king—perhaps a nephew or son—and served the new king or chief as principal advisor. Because they were knowledgeable and highly competent, they were powerful in making a regime function and even in preserving it. By rallying clans to back the ruler in times of trouble, they kept the king in power. Under colonialism, officials from the European powers, who generally believed that women were inferior and should be kept out of politics, worked to undermine the position of the queen mothers in differing regions by eliminating them from circles of power and encouraging local chiefs to ignore or dismiss them. Additionally, as Islam spread and consolidated politically, the Caliphs at Istanbul also advised the diminution of queen mothers' roles in favor of exclusively male leadership. Given the tradition of powerful and respected women advisors among non-Westerners, it is not surprising that the first woman elected prime minister received that distinction in Sri Lanka in 1960—not in a Western country.

From War to Greater Activism

As a result of their activism, women gained more rights as the twentieth century opened and thus became the topic of public debate. The impetus for change also came from intellectuals and nationalist politicians who said that women's ignorance and oppression would keep a society mired in backwardness. Education and greater autonomy, in contrast, helped enlist women to follow the path of economic, political, and social progress. Toward the end of the nineteenth century, activists achieved reforms in some countries. The right to guardianship of one's own children, the right to divorce, and opportunities for education were hard-fought victories, seeming to culminate in the right to vote that women in New Zealand won in 1893—the first parliamentary government to grant women's suffrage. The campaign, led by Kate Sheppard of the Women's Christian Temperance Union, was opposed by many, including the entire liquor industry, which feared for its business. Women in Finland achieved the vote in 1908. Just before World War I, women won the vote in the Netherlands, followed by Norway, Denmark, Iceland, and Russia (during the revolution in 1917), which became the first major power to give women the vote. The professions opened up marginally, with teaching, librarianship, nursing, and medicine being the most accommodating, though even in those occupations, women were never on an equal footing with men. All of these jobs operated according to the lower value placed on women generally by paying them low wages, no matter what level of skill was involved in the job. By the early twentieth century, advances in the education of girls provided careers for tens of thousands of women teachers. These changes made women increasingly seem modern and independent, instead of bound entirely to the traditional ways of the home and child rearing.

Another event alleged to have advanced women's modernity was the demand for labor created by the century's wars, beginning with World War I, though there is much debate around this idea. Wars such as the Mexican Revolution that broke out in 1910 featured some swashbuckling men and others who led armies and kept the country terrorized even as they pursued reform and a new kind of government. In 1914, competition for a global empire, ethnic tensions, military buildup, and the force of near-hysterical nationalism led to the outbreak of a disastrous war directly affecting Europe, Africa, and the Middle East, though Europe was the main battleground and Europeans the main combatants. Nonetheless, the war drew in many of the world's peoples, especially those in Asia, Africa, and the Middle East, where battles were fought and from which soldiers were also mobilized. Women in Europe were recruited into factory, agricultural, and military jobs when it soon became apparent that World War I would be a prolonged struggle demanding enormous production of weaponry and other military supplies. Although many disapproved of women holding well-paid, often very dangerous jobs in munitions and other essential war work, women themselves enjoyed having financial and other independence as a result of weakening social rules during the conflict.

Visual propaganda for wartime patriotism and mobilizing civilian society used women as emblematic of a nation needing protection. Images of gentle, middle-class women with children on their laps sitting at home, of women who had been violated by the enemy, and of nurses heroically serving on the battlefront invoked those whom virile and courageous men would protect. Emphasizing the weakness of women was part of regendering the twentieth-century Western nation in the face of women's strength in taking the place of men as breadwinners and family caretakers. Men's role as soldiers was simultaneously made sacred, and those who died were sanctified as holy warriors. Whereas men had been virtuous citizen-soldiers during the Enlightenment and the founding period of modern nation-states in the eighteenth and nineteenth centuries, World War I sanctified the nation's wars as well as those who fought in them, making masculinity sacred too (Mosse 1990). At the same time, the contribution of colonized soldiers was converted from a sacred contribution to a menace when, with the coming of peace, the presence of soldiers of color either as still-active veterans or as part of occupying armies were said to threaten white women with rape. Thus, the combatant European nations remained in need of white male saviors.

In reality, World War I built women's fortitude while depriving many of financial resources, food, sleep, and health as they sacrificed for the well-being of their men on the front and for their nations more generally. During the Mexican Revolution, women had done no less and had been more brutalized and in most cases more deprived, as armies on all sides swept through areas, pillaging food and other supplies. Wartime inflation and scarcity led many in Europe and Russia during the Great War to conduct rent strikes and to riot for food. In the Middle East, men left home to fight in the war and women were left to deal with shortages, including the famines induced by the Allied armies to provoke civilian unrest against the Ottoman Empire and to destroy its citizens. Women across Germany and the Austro-Hungarian monarchy protested, even as they scraped together meager rations for their children and endured the outbreak of a deadly flu epidemic. In Russia a demonstration by factory women on International Women's Day in 1917—protesting high prices, scarcity, and overwork—led to the overthrow of the Romanov Dynasty and months later the Bolshevik Revolution, as soldiers and male factory workers joined the women's cause. Hard-pressed women in rural areas also joined in peasant confiscations of land in the Russian countryside.

Even before World War I, the military buildup and the horrific legacy of colonial and nationalist wars had led to activism on behalf of peace. The German pacifist, Bertha von Suttner, for example, persuaded Alfred Nobel to found a peace prize for outstanding efforts to prevent or end conflict. It was first awarded in 1901. During World War I, a group of women from twelve countries met in The Hague in 1915 and established the Women's International League for Peace and Freedom (WILPF). They also agreed to visit the heads of states of a number of countries—most of them combatants—and lobby them to negotiate peace. The effort was unsuccessful, but the declaration of principles these women drew up and circulated to heads of state was remarkably similar to President Woodrow Wilson's Fourteen Points, issued some two years later. WILPF continued to be active in the 1920s, the U.S. branch protesting the U.S. occupation of Haiti in 1926 and its invasions in Latin America and Asia in the interwar period. In the 1930s, pacifism was more muted in some parts of the industrial world because of the militarization of the masses and the simultaneous desire on the part of the democracies and threatened societies to fight the fascist form of this militarization. After World War II, WILPF received the United Nations' official approval as a nongovernmental organization (NGO).

Women in colonized countries moved onto the political stage with force in the context of early twentieth-century wars, revolutions, and the ensuing perilous conditions. Though China was not formally a colony, Chinese women had been active in resistance to foreign inroads into the country in 1900–1901, and for several decades they had participated in a movement to end foot binding, to provide women with education, and to modernize conditions of marriage. In 1911–1912, China underwent a revolution that overthrew the Qing Dynasty, in large part on the grounds of modernizing the country politically and economically. The leader of this movement, Sun-Yat-Sen, was married to Song Qingling, the daughter of a wealthy industrialist and herself a more up-to-date woman, whose sister, Song Meiling, had actually studied in the United States. These two women became emblematic of change. In 1919, women took part in the May 4th movement that aimed to reduce Japanese power after it was awarded territorial rights to Germany's sphere of influence in China at the Paris Peace Conference following World War I. The May 4th movement, like similar nationalist movements seeking independence, claimed that patriarchal control of women had to be reduced in order for the country to become free and modern to the same degree as countries in the West. In 1930, a new code of laws allowed women free choice of marriage partners and the right to equal inheritance. Conditions did not change for most women, however, for despite growing urbanization, the vast majority lived in rural areas where patriarchal customs remained in force. Ba Chin's *Family*, a novel written in the late 1920s and published in 1931, was a powerful indictment of the ways in which women in typical Chinese households—young women in particular—were harassed, even to the point of gruesomely taking their lives.

African women were similarly active under colonialism, and many had been further politicized by the war, as forced recruitment upset family life and caused hardship, especially where fighting brought seizure of goods and destruction of property. Drawn into global economic and cultural networks, some African women maintained ties with activists or religious and family networks in Latin America, the Caribbean, Europe, and the United States. On a local level, beer brewing was a traditional women's occupation and they continued to produce and market it, even when it was forbidden by colonial governments, eager to control and tax alcohol sales. Women in many areas resisted other forms of government encroachment on their livelihoods. In 1929, Igbo women in British-run Nigeria, for example, rebelled against new taxation that the colonial officials imposed on them by employing kin networks and mobilizing their associations. Painting their bodies and shaming the government, the women were attacked, arrested, abused, and killed by the army in order to put down this "Women's War" against colonial rule. Also in the 1919 uprising against the British, which persisted in some areas into the early 1920s, Egyptian feminists emerged from the sex segregation of the harem and joined men in seeking national independence from Britain. Women of all classes, ages, and religions engaged in the uprising; Muslim women took off their veils in public demonstrations, showing themselves to be modern and their country thus worthy of self-rule. Despite the male-female alliance, once Egypt gained its nominal independence in 1923, the males who dominated the anticolonial resistance refused to give women the vote and other rights. Huda Shaarawi, a pioneer in the movement, analyzed the situation in her memoirs: "In moments of danger, when women emerge by their side, men utter no protest. Yet women's great acts and endless sacrifices do not change men's views of women. . . . Men have singled out women of outstanding merit and put them on a pedestal to avoid recognizing the capabilities of all women" (Shaarawi 1987, 131).

In India a mass movement for independence developed after World War I, increasingly led by the single figure of Mohandas Gandhi. This movement marked a shift from the traditional strategies of the Indian Congress of which Gandhi was a member and which for much of its existence aimed for reforms in British policy in South Asia. After the war, the movement came to include millions of former servicemen and ordinary people alongside the upper- and middle-class men who had dominated the party and struggled for independence to that point. Additionally, women were well-represented among Gandhi's followers and they aided him in a variety of ways, not least of which included personal service of his daily needs. For decades under colonialism, Indian women had advocated for themselves, but this advocacy was joined by Gandhi and other leaders of the Congress Party in the 1920s, including Jawaharlal Nehru. In 1925, famed poet Sarojini Naidu became the first Indian woman president of the Congress Party, though she had long campaigned for women's rights. Educated at Girton College, Cambridge University, she joined Gandhi in many civil disobedience demonstrations and was arrested and jailed along with him, as were many other men and women. Women supporters of Gandhi such as Naidu were prominent and bold in their activism, with powerful groups, such as the Ladies' Picketing Board, organizing boycotts of British goods and picketing voting places. Tens of thousands of people were arrested. Moreover, quite different from activists in the civil disobedience movement, more-violent women used bombs and assassinations as a means of ending repressive British rule. One of these women, Bina Das, who attempted to kill the governor of Bengal, professed to have done so because he upheld "a system of repression that has kept enslaved three million of my countrymen and country women" (Kumar 1993, 86).

Women's activism thus had an international component in that colonized women mobilized against foreign oppressors, even as they cited ideas about the improvement of women's conditions from theorists in oppressor countries. This trend is called "colonial modernity" insofar as it relies on the progressive notion of women's improvement that spread worldwide from the time of the European Enlightenment in the eighteenth century. The impulse to improve women's lot—and indeed to recognize women as a category—only came to the fore, in this view, because of colonialism (Barlow 2004, passim).

Women also continued to mobilize internationally, but ironically, if the idea of "colonial modernity" holds, with an increasing distrust on the part of women from the colonized "south" toward those coming from the imperialist nations, armed with a firm belief in their racial superiority. When German activists at an international meeting of WILPF sponsored a resolution condemning the presence of black troops in their country after World War I on the grounds that blacks would rape white women, African American women had to lobby hard to block the motion even though they could not stop the pernicious racist speeches. Indeed, social movements in these decades, including those launched by women, were fractious because of racism and ethnic antagonisms. Local women in India, for example, did not want British women with their claims to superiority and omniscience arriving in their country to set up an Indian branch of WILPF; they insisted on doing the organizing themselves. Thus although women might seem to have been puppets of modernizing men, another interpretation is that, rejected by these same modernizing men as equal citizens or individuals whose opinions should be valued, women learned organizing and other political skills outside mainstream politics.

WOMEN AND POST–WORLD WAR I MODERNITY

All of these pursuits in the public sphere and politics may be seen as part of a modernizing trend that in many cases affected the outlook and behavior of women—a trend that is, like global feminism, said to arise from colonialism and its homogenizing force. When the Ottoman Empire fell at the end of World War I and lost what remained of its empire to the Allied powers, Turkey subsequently emerged as a modernizing state in 1923. Its leader, Mustafa Kemal or Atatürk, determined that the country had to become more secular and more modern. Influenced by a close woman confidante—the author and educator Halide Edib Adivar—Atatürk implemented a program calling for education for women and secular, Western clothing for women and men alike. Visual signs of change such as banning traditional clothing and adopting more streamlined styles were important in the postwar world on a national level.

However, on their own from the 1890s forward, women in general as well as those in colonial contexts began behaving differently and adopting novel fashions, making their appearances sleeker, and adopting lifestyles at odds with older norms. The women of Egypt who unveiled themselves on behalf of independence and modern nationhood were just one example of this global phenomenon; Atatürk's laws relating to attire provided another. Women in China went to Japan for an education and to find new role models. One prominent example of this search for modernity abroad was provided by Qiu Jin, who went to Japan at the end of the nineteenth century for an education, began dressing as a man, and took up radical political causes. She was arrested and executed. Following Qiu Jin's example, by the 1920s, many Chinese women had unbound their feet, adopted Chinese versions of what was said to be Western dress, put on makeup, and taken jobs. Makeup allowed them to transform their appearances, giving rise to a worldwide cosmetics industry that helped women appear more prosperous. Women in the West began having plastic surgery before World War I, and this behavior only increased after World War I, when great improvements in corrective surgery took place to help remedy soldiers' disfigured bodies.

Other young women moved away from their families and took jobs far from home, living in boardinghouses and going out on their own. This was different from housing associated with turn-of-the-century industrialization, where women were jammed into dormitories and treated abominably. The housing provided by Japanese textile mills was a prime example. These "new women" might have children out of wedlock and have no interest in marrying—ever. Often from the middle class, these rebels were called "new women" or, after World War I, the "modern girl" (in Japan, *mogas*). The "modern girl" jettisoned traditional garb from a past rural life, while modern Western women in cities eliminated the corsets and garlands of fabric, and put on clothing that was slimmed down and some said made them look androgynous. Chinese, Japanese, South African, and Western modern women also cut their hair short, while those in the West might have a permanent wave so that their hair looked more like that of African or African American women, who in contrast often sought to straighten theirs. The "modern girl" was a truly transnational phenomenon, put together from ingredients around the world.

The modern girl of the 1920s and 1930s came from all ethnic and racial groups and she flourished in Africa, Asia, Europe, North America, and South America. Novels such as *Naomi*, serialized in the mid-1920s by Japanese author Tanizaki Junichiro, portrayed these modern women as not only complicated in themselves but also complicating the social order as a whole. Tanizaki's heroine in this work is a seductive young woman, entirely taken up with modern Western culture. The film industry also portrayed modern women as vamps, screwballs, and earnest forces for good, thus introducing this new incarnation of women via multiple interpretations of their modernity. The stars of this period—such as Butterfly Hu in Shanghai and Louise Brooks in Hollywood—were adept at creating these many incarnations of the modern woman, from heartbreaker to heart of gold. Other modern girls became sports stars, aviators, or filmmakers themselves, like former star Leni Riefenstahl of Germany. Around the world in the 1920s and 1930s, films became a prime form of entertainment for women, who in many places constituted the majority of the cinemagoing audience.

In this and other ways, women participated in the modernity disseminated by mass culture, which included not only cinema but also magazines, the popular press, pulp fiction, and the radio. The visual media carried advertisements for clothing and cosmetics that promised to make women modern, and these ads influenced women's consumerism, even when the stars whose images shaped choices were male actors performing women's parts—as in the case of India in the interwar years. Given the feminist afterglow of voting and the immediacy of women's activism, there were also articles about strong and heroic women, even historic figures from the past, in addition to more light protagonists. Women were also prime purchasers from department store catalogs that were widely available, as well as from the new institution of book-of-the-month clubs, which cropped up in many regions of the world. Many of these clubs carried global literature that made for a more uniform modernity centered on a burgeoning cosmopolitanism. When radio came to rival cinema for popular attention, women had access not only to a variety of music and news but also to soap operas, which grew in popularity over much of the world.

Turkish women performers sang in cafes and private clubs, making records for still another media device—the phonograph, which was fast becoming the basis for a thriving industry. African American women performed jazz and the blues both in clubs and on records. Now considered a kind of classic, their artistry rivaled that of women painters and sculptors. Frieda Kalho, a Mexican painter, mingled the imagery of native peoples, Catholicism, and Mexican forms in her stirring, sometimes grim and lush portraits of herself as the Virgin Mary, a wheelchair victim, or a tortured woman wrapped in chains while garbed in vividly colored clothing. In the Soviet Union, women were pioneers in the coming of modern art that was abstract. Olga Rozanova, who died in the 1918–1919 influenza epidemic, had painted shimmering lines of color on a white background, hoping to make color and form—not "accurate" representations of people and nature—count as capturing a deeper reality. In Japan, Uemura Schoen, though following many of the conventions of Japanese print making that focused on women's sensuality, broke with those conventions by showing women hard at work both inside and outside the home.

It was not the high arts, however, but rather the mass media that dictators became expert at using to preach the importance of women's domestic roles, especially their childbearing potential. Their aim to boost the population was sparked by the drop in fertility and by the global birth control movement that also arose in the 1920s and 1930s, making knowledge of fertility limitation more widely available. Knowledge of women's ovulatory cycles and the vulcanization of rubber—both in the 1840s—and the development of the diaphragm between the 1860s and 1880s made fertility control more reliable and led women in Europe and the United States to cut fertility by almost half before the 1930s. A number of women became prominent in the twentieth-century birth control movement, foremost among them the American Margaret Sanger, who made world tours in 1922 and 1935, influencing such rising leaders as Shizue Kato of Japan to become activists as well. Kato and Sanger, like most advocates, were concerned with the welfare of poorer women, but also wanted all women to have access to family limitation. Governments were often hostile to family-planning efforts, as the century was one of rising militarism and politicians made their name with militaristic statements that promoted virility, measured not only in martial but also sexual prowess. The growing war machines of the interwar years in Italy, Japan, and Germany needed more population, not less.

Despite much activism against contraception, it continued to spread, bringing the birthrate in 1930s Europe, for example, below replacement rate. People, including those in rural areas, widely used abortion as well as infanticide— mostly of girl babies—to control families. Other conditions also affected access to birth control: In the Soviet Union, the severe population loss caused by World War I, the Bolshevik Revolution, the civil war, and famines following the destruction of the kulaks and the introduction of collective farming caused the Communist Party to reverse its liberal reproductive policies. In the 1930s, the Soviet government outlawed abortions, homosexuality, and divorces.

From Global Economic Depression to Global Warfare

The modern girl, who might have used cosmetics and been sexually aware, was a global but far from universal phenomenon, as the majority of women still led peasant lives on the land and did arduous work, often suffering from natural disasters and man-made catastrophes. From the outbreak of World War I, women of Asia and Africa had participated in a drastic expansion of agricultural productivity to compensate for the downturn in European agricultural and industrial capacity. In the 1920s, this expansion had run its course and agricultural prices collapsed. Many had flocked to factories during the war, again to supply the European war machine and to replace lost production of consumer goods. But in manufacturing, too, hard times struck. Dramatic political changes were taking place, most notably the strengthening of anticolonial movements, the birth of fascism and totalitarianism, and the struggle for national reform in countries like China and several on the South American continent. At the same time, the collapse of the U.S. stock market combined with the agricultural crisis to bring on the Great Depression of the late 1920s and 1930s that hit factory and farm alike. Women's employment in the service sector, however, continued to rise in those years and they were often adept at maintaining their low-tech artisanal work such as sewing, stone polishing, knife grinding, and the like. They took in laundry and did domestic service for white settlers in the colonies. But the hardship on families around the world during those years led to greater exploitation of young women in prostitution and semislavery to keep the family economy going.

Economic catastrophe empowered dictators and authoritarian rulers who promised recovery in exchange for obedience. Germany, Italy, and Japan rushed the world to war on a program to revive militarism, expand their country's borders, and thus gain resources to heal economic wounds. All of these regimes promoted a muscular masculinity based on conquest, increased virility, and the submission of women to men's will. In the 1920s and 1930s, the leaders of these states eliminated any vestiges of democracy, claiming that constitutions and consensus building were effeminate and backward, while military rule was modern and efficient. Riding on gender privilege for men, this drive for power had special consequences for women. In 1937, Japan invaded China from Shanghai and then moved to take Nanjing, raping, mutilating, and killing tens of thousands of women—thus the name "Rape of Nanjing." As the Japanese moved through the Pacific region, they persisted in their brutalization of women, and this continued to be a widespread behavior of all the armies involved in World War II and in the postwar occupation.

In Europe, where World War II (1939–1945) also took a ghastly toll, men were conscripted into armies, while civilians felt the increasing threat from bombs and from invading armies. The Soviet Union made the most extensive use of women in combat, as ace aviators and as soldiers. U.S. women also served in the armed forces but, unlike Soviet women, not in combat positions but in dangerous service near the front. Imperial governments enlisted women from the colonies even though racism plagued their service. Women from the British Caribbean provide a complex picture of imperial patriotism despite growing oppression during the economic slump. "We were taught that England was our mother country," said one, allowing that she felt herself to be fully British. "And if your mother had a problem you had to help her" (Bousquet and Douglas 1991, 47). The feelings were not reciprocated, however, and even though military leaders desperately needed help, throughout 1941, government officials at the highest levels did not want "coloured" women to enter the country. Ultimately, military needs trumped racism, and women from the Caribbean served as secretaries and hospital workers, among other jobs. One interesting fact is that Jamaican and other Caribbean women often refused to do cleaning for officers. "I'm not going to anybody's house to clean," one reported, especially, she added, because she was far more educated than the officers who believed that she—as a black woman—was first and foremost a servant. Nonetheless, the feeling among many of these servicewomen was, "Go ahead Britain. Barbados is behind you" (Bousquet and Douglas 1991, 115, 109).

However, women faced the greatest threats on the home front, because World War II was a war against civilians, and civilian casualties far outnumbered those of military personnel. Bombings destroyed homes and killed inhabitants from London and Dresden to Tokyo and the islands of Micronesia. With men away for wartime service, women were often the victims of bomb and firebomb attacks. As the Holocaust unfolded, women stood in the greatest danger, as young men were often the most able to emigrate, while women and old people stayed behind. In the death camps, women and children were the first to be killed—which is hardly to say that men were immune from death—and those women not killed immediately could be selected to serve as victims of reproductive and other experiments. Chinese, Filipino, and Korean women were made prostitutes for the Japanese army, and while these women were shunned and rejected by their families and communities at the end of the war, there were individual instances where these so-called "comfort women" had warm personal relations with the men who kept them in sexual slavery. Japanese women at war's end became the prostitutes for the occupying U.S. army, and many of the comfort women were also held by the American army to serve GIs well into the postwar period.

Both women and men were active in the global resistance to fascism and militarism, with women especially adept at a variety of tactics such as organizing housewives' resistance and luring Germans, Italians, and Japanese military to their deaths through sexual advances. Women also used gender stereotypes to plant bombs and carry weapons, as few thought to suspect pathetic women who purposely behaved timidly in public. Moreover, with the war taking up men as combatants, the peacetime gender order gave way to arrangements that were more subversive. Female-headed households were more common than not, and women came to live together in the absence of men. They developed survival skills, especially foraging for food and other tasks that would have been unthinkable for many outside the context of horrific wartime conditions.

In some countries, male deaths in the war—or their continued active service, in the case of the superpowers that conducted a series of proxy wars in the postwar period—meant that mature and married women, not just young unmarried ones, remained active both in the workforce and more generally in the public sphere. In fact, many parts of the world were so devastated that they needed all hands busy at rebuilding. A more consequential aspect of war that shaped the postwar period was the loosening of empire, which meant continuing brutality, devastation, and death for people in the colonized world and in emerging nations. Across the globe, the Allied powers of France, Britain, and the United States joined with the Dutch and Belgians to try to preserve at least parts of their empire—usually by inflicting additional violence on male and female nationalist leaders and activists alike. In some instances, using Japanese troops, these powers continued combat operations in north and sub-Saharan Africa, the Middle East, and Southeast and East Asia.

DECOLONIZATION AND POSTWAR LIFE

During and after the war, women engaged in labor activism that laid the groundwork for wider activism to come. In the 1940s, Nigerian women who had used the founding of the Abeokuta Ladies' Club to promote philanthropy used their organization to protect the livelihoods of market women who were susceptible to seizures of their produce by officials and strongmen. When this club became the Abeokuta's Women's Union in 1946, it broadened its campaigns to take on government corruption and the disproportionate taxation of local women entrepreneurs. Union women also were active in many parts of the world. During the war, when female civil service workers in England asked that they receive pay equal to men in the same jobs, Prime Minister Winston Churchill wanted to have them all arrested on charges of treason. Women workers' activism persisted into the postwar period with wide-ranging consequences. Other union women agitated in factories for better work conditions and equal pay, further stoking the coals of feminism.

Women also lobbied at the new United Nations (UN) for a commitment to equal citizenship for them and for basic human rights. They were particularly concerned because they were being kept from most meetings of the Allies and especially those laying the groundwork for the establishment of the United Nations at Dumbarton Oaks in 1944. Diplomats Minerva Bernardino of the Dominican Republic and Bertha Lutz of Brazil led a successful drive for an expression of gender equality in the UN charter, but only obtained—with great difficulty—a guarantee of equal employment opportunities at the new international institution. They and women diplomats from around the world failed to get an independent commission "of women" to monitor the status of women because of opposition from the United States. Eventually, a Commission on the Status of Women was subsumed under the Commission on Human Rights, where a strong group of activists began working on a wide range of pro-women issues (Hawkesworth 2006, 88–89).

Women joined the momentous Communist Revolution in China as it developed before, during, and immediately after the war because of the Communist Party's stand on women's work and equality. The movement ended with the triumph of communism in 1949, and the flight of nationalist forces under Jiang Jieshi to Taiwan. Once in power, the communists expanded the reforms that the nationalist government had made in the 1930s legal code, especially giving women the right to own property in their own names. With collectivization and the assignment of plots by the communist government, women's inequality resurfaced because the male officials making the assignments valued men more than they did women. Moreover, even though women were encouraged to work, the officials assigned them to the worst and lowest-paying jobs. Nonetheless, the trend toward women's parity in education that had begun early in the twentieth century continued. Although girls were just 28 percent of students in primary schools in 1950, they constituted 44.8 percent in 1985. While women composed only 22 percent of students in universities in 1951, by the twenty-first century, they made up 44 percent of the tertiary student body.

Alongside those gains came setbacks, as women communist leaders, who had joined the revolutionary movement because of the promises of women's equality, found themselves classified as enemies to Chinese development for expressing their continued concerns about the absence of that equality after the revolution. During the Cultural Revolution of the 1960s, many were singled out for punishment as counterrevolutionaries, even as Mao's wife, Jiang Qing, rose to power in part by forcing the theme of women's activism and parity with men under communism. An actress by profession, Jiang Qing's opera, *Hongdeng ji*, showed the heroism of a young woman taking up the Red Lantern of justice and resistance—a reference to the women's group of Red Lanterns affiliated with the Boxers in 1900. Jiang's power rose with the Cultural Revolution and for a brief time after the death of Mao in 1976. But the modernizing leaders, who wanted to end the ideological turmoil in favor of economic and technological development, arrested her. At her trial in 1980–1981, Jiang actually helped undo the Mao myth by her defense, which focused on Mao's arbitrariness and use of brute power: "I was Mao's dog," she proclaimed. "What he said to bite, I bit" (Terrill in Smith 2008, II:652).

Elsewhere, women participated in the resurgence of the nationalist independence movements that had already existed before the war, and some of these movements, such as communist groups in Southeast Asia, preached the equality of women. In most nationalist movements, women have historically been treated as "auxiliary" to the more intelligent and active men. Yet it is important to consider the wide-ranging and consistent activism of women. In Africa, there was virtually no independence activism that did not include women from the outset. For example, in the Ivory Coast, a French colonial holding, women began a hunger strike in 1949 to protest the arrest and incarceration of nationalist leaders. Even as the French shot and wounded some forty strikers, it gradually became clear that colonialism would not hold, and the French negotiated independence there and in many other countries thereafter.

Funmilayo Ransome-Kuti, president of the Nigerian Women's Union, followed the lead of the Abeokuta Ladies' Club by broadening her group's activism to confront British imperialism, taking strong action that ultimately brought Nigerian independence. One way of accomplishing this involved Ransome-Kuti pushing women to readopt Yoruba clothing and to reestablish local traditions, thus delegitimizing British culture as a whole. In the independence organization, which the British labeled the Mau Mau in present-day Kenya, women served as suppliers of weapons, food, and communications for fighters, and they were also dispossessed of their land, thrown into the British concentration camps, and tortured just as men were. In the war for Algerian independence in the 1950s, women freedom fighters, once again disguised as "women," worked for the independence forces in a variety of ways that included intelligence gathering and terrorism. As Algerian resistance fighter Jamillah Buhrayd put it, there were thousands of women who "moved, just like me, from the Qasbah to the French Quarter. Carrying bombs in their handbags and throwing them into cafés" (DeGroot and Peniston-Bird 2000, 227). In both the Chinese and Vietnamese revolutions, women served in combat, manufacturing, and transport to help the cause of revolution and independence from Western powers. Some 1 million Vietnamese women were active soldiers in the struggle against the French and then the United States.

Participants in decolonization, women were also its victims in special ways. When the independence of India was declared in 1947 and the area was partitioned into India and Pakistan, the migration of peoples into the new countries that supported their particular religion led to murder and other violence—notably the rape of hundreds of thousands of women. South Vietnam became a slaughterhouse of women, who, when captured with their children, were treated as enemy combatants and mutilated and raped before being killed. With conditions so dangerous in rural areas, through which armies on both sides passed regularly, young women often migrated to cities simply to save themselves and there turned to prostitution to stay alive.

Decolonization and nation building had other consequences, once achieved, and the aftermath of decolonization often dashed the hopes of those women who had helped forge independence. The women of North Vietnam had served as equal carriers of weapons, factory workers, and fighters, and in a remarkable number of instances, officers in the Viet Cong and People's Army of Vietnam (PAVN), in the unification and independence struggle between 1945 and 1975. "Women are half the people," leader Ho Chi Minh often said in common with Mao Zedong. "If women are not free then the people are not free." Once the U.S. and South Vietnamese governments had been defeated, however, women lost leadership and managerial positions, though a woman did head Vietnam's delegation to the United Nations in the 1980s. In South Africa, where the struggle to end white minority rule lasted longer than anywhere else on the continent, the fall of the apartheid government in the 1990s was interlaced with movements for women's equality. Even during the anti-apartheid agitations, they lobbied for representation and leadership positions. The new constitution, adopted in 1994, guaranteed that women would be equal citizens, just as they had shown themselves equal partners in the struggle to end apartheid. This, in fact, did not fully materialize, but having witnessed the failure of women's rights in other nationalist movements, women lobbied hard to be 30 percent of the candidates on any political party's slate. Indeed, despite this more promising situation, as newly independent countries became mired in debt by attempting to build national institutions such as schools and hospitals—not to mention developing the economy—social services such as clinics for mothers and children and educational institutions for girls were increasingly viewed as a dispensable luxury as the century came to a close. Moreover, the militarization of government that accompanied independence in Africa engulfed politics and often made it a masculine preserve. The superpowers that were eager to gain allies loaded new nations with weapons, thereby helping rule by male violence to become a norm. Development initiatives sponsored by the superpowers and those wanting to do business with the newly independent nations were almost always oriented to men, often depriving women of their livelihoods and independence.

Another, very different contribution to nation building in the postwar period came in the world of film, music, song, and culture generally. Umm Kulthuum, for example, began her career singing passages from the Koran, but then expanded her repertoire to include traditional desert songs, religious verses, and romantic ballads. Traffic came to a stop in Cairo on the first Thursday of every month in the 1950s when Umm Kulthuum's radio program was broadcast. She was a nationalist, traveling the Arab world on behalf of anti-Westernism and the integrity of Arab culture. Others revived and perpetuated the cultural canons of their newly independent countries. Suchitra Mitra, for instance, used her musical talent to spread the song of Rabindranath Tagore, as well as to popularize a range of Indian musical culture. Cultural nationalism fortified political independence.

In the aftermath of horrific loss of life in World War II and in the climate of cold war that threatened global annihilation, Gandhian tactics of civil disobedience gained resonance even in the industrial West (they had already been internationalized in numerous decolonization struggles—and they would be taken up in the late 1980s by the peoples of Eastern Europe and the former Soviet Union). On December 1, 1955, in Montgomery, Alabama, Rosa Parks, a part-time secretary for the local branch of the National Association for the Advancement of Colored People (NAACP), boarded a bus and took the first available seat. When a white man found himself without a seat, the driver screamed at Parks, "Nigger, move back." Parks confronted that system through the studied practice of civil disobedience. She refused to move back, and her action led to a community-wide, yearlong boycott, much of it directed by women, of public transportation in Montgomery by African Americans. Dolores Huerta, who cofounded the Farm Workers Association, also participated in boycotts and peaceful demonstrations for farmworkers' rights. She was severely beaten by police for demonstrating against U.S. presidential candidate George H. W. Bush in 1988. Women's pacifist organizations became more vocal and more publicly visible, staging widely covered sit-ins and other demonstrations. After the war, it was also hard in the decolonizing world for those wanting freedom to reject the violence that was often necessary to accomplish it. Nonetheless, the cold war roused women's activism in organizations such as the "Ban the Bomb" movement and demonstrations such as the Greenham Commons sit-ins at nuclear facilities—practices again copied from those of the British suffragists and Gandhi after them.

CONSUMERISM, POSTINDUSTRIALIZATION, AND ECONOMIC CHANGE

Within two decades, a good deal of the world had materially recovered from World War II, and countries like Japan and Germany were growing at a rate that outpaced that of many Western powers. The cold war between the United States and the Soviet Union fostered productivity around the world, as the superpowers concentrated on weaponry and other countries picked up the slack in nonmilitary production. So the industrial growth of Japan and Germany thrived on making consumer goods demanded globally, such as electronic equipment and automobiles. Agriculture gave way as a major occupation, leading women to work in manufacturing and service jobs. Underemployed women in rural areas began making craft goods at home for large export firms; in some Middle Eastern countries, for example, they produced hand-loomed rugs. Beginning in the 1960s, countries hoping to advance their economies made attractive offers to multinational corporations so that they would locate their new electronics and other factories there. Leaders promised a docile and inexpensive female labor force, which materialized in countries such as South Korea. Women flocked to these factories despite long hours, sexual harassment, and even physical abuse because the jobs meant a higher standard of living. Studies showed that South Korean women working in multinational firms raised their own and their family's educational levels and also cut their birthrate by learning practices of fertility control and using them.

Across the post–World War II globe, work became even more service-oriented, coming to surpass manufacturing as the main employer of the world's people in some of the more prosperous countries. Service-oriented jobs dominated women's work in the industrialized countries of the world's "north" in the twentieth century. This work included jobs in health care (such as reproductive counselors, technicians, or laboratory assistants), computing and other office services, and hospitality services (such as tourism, restaurants, and hotels). Women's service jobs often demanded a high level of psychological work, such as that expected of flight attendants, who were responsible for the safety of passengers as well as insuring their happiness and satisfaction. Social work, family counseling, and tutoring were all seen as extensions of women's domestic roles, which they continued to maintain while working full-time. To convert to service jobs based on knowledge rather than physical labor, societies expanded their university and technical educational systems, allowing more women to attend. Women became doctors, lawyers, and teachers to a greater extent than before—in the case of gender-segregated Islamic societies, they catered to the needs of other women.

In the second half of the twentieth century, then, women's lives increasingly differed from one another. Women in pastoral societies continued to care for animals, making cheese and other products that could be marketed for necessary cash. They still spun thread and wove cloth for family needs. In contrast, middle-class women in urbanized Japan kept all the family finances, arranged social networking, and in a status-conscious society did other tasks that would advance the family's standing—whether political, economic, or social activities. In countries under the Soviet system, a working woman's day might involve technical work, standing in line for food and other commodities, attending political education meetings, and doing such household tasks as laundry by hand. In these conditions, the workday for a woman in Eastern Europe in the 1960s ran to approximately eighteen hours.

Agriculture declined to the lowest level of employment than ever before because of modernizing forces that spread machine technology, hybrid seeds, and chemical use around the world. Further, communal land was being privatized, eliminating women's traditional access to resources; the planting of export crops such as soybeans on consolidated farms also eliminated a division of labor in which women played a strong part. This consolidation produced gigantic agribusinesses that employed fewer people working vast tracts of land, often for banks, multinational corporations, and other distant owners. Yet, because agribusinesses could pay women less, some women actually found jobs offered by thrifty managers—although these were not jobs with the independence of decision making and skill development that they had held before. Agribusiness drove many workers generally from the land. Women in Latin America, for example, gave up agriculture for work at home or in sweatshops making sneakers, clothing, and other products for multinationals, often under abusive conditions. Yet there was much global variety in women's relationship to the land and to manufacturing. From the 1990s on, young girls in China answered the call to leave the countryside and work in factories until, roughly, their midtwenties. They then returned to the countryside to marry and participate in village farming, which the post-Mao government had returned to individual families.

ACTIVISM AND GLOBALIZATION

As technology affected both daily life and their livelihoods on the land, women became active in a range of causes, among them organizing on behalf of the environment and often on behalf of ecofeminism. In some respects, the activism was a response as well to the increased agribusiness around the planet and the green revolution that involved the special breeding of seeds according to natural hazards such as for drought or disease. Deforestation also accompanied the rapid globalization of agribusiness. Beginning in 1977, Wangari Maathai organized women to plant trees to create greenbelts around Kenya's capital city of Nairobi. In creating this citizens' movement, Maathai fought the deforestation of her own local area. "It's important for people to see that they are part of the environment and that they take responsibility for it," she explained. Powerful politicians and businesspeople resented this grassroots activism and had her beaten up and run out of the country. Maathai, backed by world opinion, returned and in 2004 won the Nobel Peace Prize for her efforts to improve the environment and livelihoods of Africans ("Nobel Peace Prize for Woman of 30m Trees," *The Guardian*, October 9, 2004).

In India, activists fought multinational corporations that took farmers' seeds, sterilized and patented them, and then sued the farmers who originally developed them for infringing on the patent. As Vandana Shiva and Radha Holla-Bhar put it: "Whether it was seeds of the farm or plants of the forest, all were clearly understood to be part of the cultural, spiritual, and biological commons." Now, these scientists explained, there was an assertion of "plant breeder's rights," which "allowed commercial plant breeders to take traditional indigenous varieties of seed, 'improve' them (often by very minor alterations of genetic structure)" and then sell them back to the original farmers without paying royalties (Shiva and Holla-Bhar 1996, 146–147).

Theories surrounding ecofeminism varied. Some held that women had greater concern for the well-being and future of the earth because they gave birth to children and had to be alert to dangers, such as those posed by the degradation of the environment. Maathai saw her own ecological activities as empowering women to care for their surroundings; by receiving pay for the trees planted, the women planters also improved their own lives. For her, the movement "educates participants about the linkages between degradation of the environment and development policies. It encourages women to create jobs, prevent soil loss, slow the processes of desertification, loss of bio-diversity and plant and to eat indigenous foods. The organization tries to empower women in particular and the civil society in general so that individuals can take action and break the vicious circle of poverty and under-development" (Maathai 1995). Still other activists took their cues from Asian philosophies positing the oneness of humans and nature, where harmony had been upset, causing not only diseases such as cancer but emotional ill health.

Some of the most important activism came at the grassroots level in urban areas and involved operating outside the arena of national party politics or international organizations. Latin American women, for example, often formed some 80 percent of any demonstration for improved conditions of life in cities. In the *favelas* or slums of Rio de Janiero, Brazil, women on their own organized the services that the state effectively denied them. They collected garbage and cleared streets, they organized self-help groups where they taught themselves to read or to do math, and others taught what they knew about the political system as a whole. Leadership came from within their groups. In other cities, women set up shelters and soup kitchens for the hungry. It was this activism outside the political system that focused attention on issues like hunger and helped expand the definition of human rights toward issues of basic human needs such as food, shelter, and employment. The focus, in their case, came from being "outsiders" to the normal stream of party politics.

Latin American women also faced decades of repression under a series of dictatorships across the region, and they became notable in fighting them. These dictatorships used especially vicious tactics, rounding up critics or those even suspected of criticism and making them "disappear." Seized individuals were often tortured, incarcerated, and murdered, with little news of their fate being conveyed to families. In Argentina, for example, this repression was known as "the dirty war," and women became celebrated for opposing it. Beginning in April 1977, a group of women whose relatives were among those who "disappeared" began meeting at 3:30 in the afternoon in the plaza that fronted important government buildings. Walking in silent protest around the bustling center where Argentines gathered to chat or conduct business, the "Mothers"— women from all livelihoods and conditions—wordlessly demanded an account of their missing brothers, husbands, and children. Hebe de Bonafini explained the change from a traditional livelihood to activism: "My life had been the life of a housewife—washing, ironing, cooking and bringing up my children, just like you're always taught to do, believing that everything else was nothing . . . Then I realized that that wasn't everything, that I had another world too. You realize that you're in a world where you have to do a lot of things" (Kaplan 2004, 113).

The Mothers of the Plaza de Mayo, as the group was called, drew such national and international attention to the unspeakable state of affairs in Argentina that in 1983, a president was elected who set the country on a new course, especially renouncing the use of terrorism against citizens, and this was a major victory. "There's no more official torture here; there are no more 'disappeared,'" one journalist exclaimed of the more open political climate. "Whatever else may be happening, this is terribly terribly important." Repeated by housewives and mothers across the Latin American and Central American dictatorships, women's civil disobedience—conducted despite their own imprisonment and torture—changed the course of politics in the 1980s and 1990s.

At the same time, middle-class women around the world also took up gender issues with a ferocity hardly seen before, launching what is sometimes called a "second-wave" feminism. These activists had the benefit of decolonization and civil rights ideas, and some of them actually knew about the longer traditions of women's leadership in their countries. However, others came from pacifist organizations and had been participants in early civil rights struggles. Activists around the world also had experience organizing boycotts, but it was also the cultural activism and the attention paid to issues of reproduction and sexuality that captured media attention. From the 1960s to the present, feminists in a large number of countries lobbied (often successfully) for the right to equal pay, birth control, and abortion; rights in marriage and rape prevention; the decriminalization of same-sex relationships; and civil unions/marriage for same-sex couples. The Stonewall riots of 1969 in New York galvanized gays, which led to a wide range of activism and, indeed, the celebration of gay sexuality in such events as Gay Pride parades, which came to take place in many cities around the world.

Global feminism thrived in the last third of the century, as international meetings brought activists together to share political experiences, exchange ideas, and forge a common platform for change. International meetings in Nairobi, Houston, and finally in Beijing in 1995 brought together tens of thousands of feminists in talks that were both exhilarating and fraught with tensions over goals and strategies. The Beijing meeting was a much publicized forum for sharing points of view and developing consensus, and it yielded many new insights. African American women, for example, found that they were not considered women of color as much as representatives of the privileged and even oppressor nations of the world. Other women from the West, believing themselves to be expert organizers and activists, were overshadowed by the greater expertise and unity of women from Africa, Asia, and Latin America. Despite these revelations, the idea that "women's rights are human rights" inspired many to work for consensus. From Beijing, an impressive statement emerged focusing on specific areas for action by individuals, organizations, and national governments. The major areas of concern were: the physical safety of women and the girl child, the right to education, eradication of poverty, empowerment of women, and their full employment and participation in economic development. Among the areas of disagreement were reproductive rights, leading many countries to append statements indicating that their governments did not approve.

Across Asia, women became heads of state in the second half of the twentieth century: Golda Meir headed Israel; Indira Gandhi, India; Corazon Aquino and Gloria Arroyo, the Philippines; and Megawati Sukarnoputri, Indonesia. In the early twenty-first century, women became heads of state in Germany, Finland, Ireland, Iceland, Ukraine, Mozambique, Bangladesh, Liberia, Chile, and Argentina—to name a few—showing that feminism had affected human consciousness about issues of equality, fairness, and women's capacity for leadership. Women also became vigorous opposition leaders, Aung Saul Sun Kyi most notably in the contemporary world, for leading the struggle against the military dictatorship of Burma. The rising strength of women in local politics that has resulted from the achievement of women's suffrage in many countries in the twentieth century is also a sign that political conditions have evolved since the beginning of modern history in the eighteenth century. Increased political strength is a sign of the global evolution taking place—though not uniformly—in the lives of women in the contemporary world.

THE BIOLOGICAL REVOLUTION, REPRODUCTION, AND MOTHERHOOD

Among the most drastic changes in the twentieth century is that of fertility control, now estimated to be used by some two-thirds of couples around the world. While the reproductive span of women as a group has increased over the course of the twentieth century, their fertility has dropped. This has occurred because of the rubber condom and diaphragm that were perfected in Europe in the nineteenth century; the pill, which was developed in Mexico and the United States and tested on Puerto Rican women late in the 1950s, followed by the birth control patch; and a variety of surgical procedures for sterilization. Women in Mexico who heard of the pill often rushed to obtain it. In addition, the knowledge of a woman's ovulatory cycle, discovered in the middle of the nineteenth century, led to the rhythm method of birth control. Clinics developed around the world to provide information on birth control. By the twenty-first century, women in almost every part of the world severely limited their fertility through surgical, mechanical, or chemical methods.

Women's fertility was reduced in other ways by the twenty-first century. Although women continued voluntarily to use abortion, abandonment, and infanticide to limit the size of their families or to practice sex selection of their children, the state also intervened to force women to be sterilized in countries like India in the 1970s. Local officials were given bonuses dependent on the number of women they had sterilized, leading to coercion and abuse. After Mao Zedong's promotion of fertility produced an additional hundreds of millions of children, China's "one-child" policy, instituted after his death in 1978, similarly compelled women not to have children. With new testing for an array of diseases and disabilities, women also chose to abort potentially disabled fetuses, a practice condemned by disability activists as genocide. To the argument made by reluctant parents that they wanted to save fetuses from having a poor quality of life, disability activists proclaimed that the children themselves led rich, productive lives and that parents were simply thinking of themselves when they murdered fetuses. There were exceptions to the tendency toward the use of birth control: in order boost the workforce, Romania under Nicolae Ceaucescu banned all contraception and abortion, leaving tens of thousands of unwanted children without adequate care and even parentless.

The conditions of reproduction changed dramatically in the modern world due to the spreading influence of professional medicine and technology. At the other end of the spectrum from curtailing fertility, advances in science and technology addressed infertility, which was disabling for many women around the world. Fertility drugs and in vitro fertilization were among the new therapies available to infertile couples, especially in wealthy countries. In 1978,

Louise Brown became the first among many "test tube" babies born of the postwar revolution in biology and technology. Infertile couples also used surrogates to bear children for them, and the majority of women gave birth in hospitals, although home births were more common in poorer, less-industrialized countries. Finally, the introduction of new vaccines dramatically lessened childhood mortality, cutting the emotional costs of parenting. In sum, the medicalization of conception, pregnancy, and childbirth was one of the striking changes in women's lives in the modern world.

WOMEN IN GLOBAL CULTURE

Religious observance became more complex and global. Women were important to some Afro-Latin American religions such as Candomble and Santeria, portrayed as deities and spirits and also serving as priestesses and leaders. These practices often took faithful women on pilgrimages to distant places— from the Caribbean to Africa, for example. The Muslim faithful became more numerous in Europe and the United States, changing the outward appearance of millions of women in the West and leading them also on pilgrimages to the holy sites. Secularization receded in many Muslim countries and this too reversed such aspects of life as schooling for girls and dress for mature women. Simultaneously, Christianity advanced in Africa and Asia, offering outlets in the ministry and in religious orders. Asian religions expanded their appeal, especially the many forms of Buddhism, and women became some of the main practitioners and teachers of yoga. New sects developed, however, that exploited women and girls and led them to desperate lives and even death.

African authors Mariama Ba and Bessie Head became internationally celebrated in the 1960s and 1970s for their explorations of family, race, and religion in the postcolonial world. Ba's *So Long a Letter* (1979) describes a Muslim woman who, on her husband's death, reconsiders the tenor of her life as the neglected first wife. The heroine's thoughts are not centered on the problem of polygamy itself, but on the flaws in men like her husband who cannot live up to Islam's precepts about caring for a family. Ba also considered the difficulties in interracial marriages. Nawal el Saadawi, an Egyptian physician, wrote novels about the perils that women and girls faced in her society. Celebrated in many countries, El Saadawi was threatened in her own country for heresy. But these were only two of the many women authors whose works flourished after World War II. In 1945, Chilean Gabriela Mistral became the first Latin American Nobel laureate in literature for her moving poetry of war, death, the female body, and children. Mistral came too early for the "boom" in Latin American literature, but other women authors flourished in a style that was often called "magical realism," which featured outsized characters and passions, as well as violence. Isabel Allende was already a writer when her uncle, Salvador Allende, president of Chile, was murdered in 1973 and her family had to flee to safety abroad. In 1985, her novel, *House of the Spirits*, captured not only the titanic struggles of Chilean politics but also the activism of generations of titanic women, who are, among other fantastic qualities, clairvoyant. Laura Esquivel's *Like Water for Chocolate* (1989) was translated into two dozen languages and became a hit film because of its setting in a Mexican kitchen during the revolution of 1910, where cooking, sexuality, and brutality are intertwined. In 1993, U.S. author Toni Morrison became the first African American woman to win the Nobel Prize in Literature for her portrayals of African American life in the past and present.

The works of many women authors were adapted for the big screen by women directors and screenwriters across the world. Bapsi Sidhwa's *Cracking India* (1991), the story of the 1947 partition whose violence is seen through the eyes of a seven-year-old, became Deepa Mehta's film *Earth* (1998). Most of Mehta's films about women and India brought attacks on her sets, rioting, and death threats to Mehta herself. Women have participated individually and in groups in the visual arts, with African women stitching vivid banners and painting canvasses. Japanese women artists have worked making woodcuts, icons, and oil paintings, while pre–World War I women painters in imperial Russia were leaders of the worldwide modernist movement in the arts. A notable contemporary woman composer in the modernist tradition is Sofia Gubaidulina, originally from the Tatar Republic of the former USSR, who blends Eastern and Western musical traditions in her work. Similarly, women have pioneered in the creation of modern dance by borrowing traditions from around the world. In all of these ways, they have changed the face of the visual and musical arts and added to the diversity of the cultural world as they have to the politics, society, and economic development of the recent past.

BIBLIOGRAPHY

Allman, Jean, Susan Geiger, and Nakanyike Musisi, eds. 2002. *Women in African Colonial Histories*. Bloomington: Indiana University Press.

Barlow, Tani E. 2004. *The Question of Women in Chinese Feminism*. Durham, NC: Duke University Press.

Berger, Iris, and E. Frances White. 1999. *Women in Sub-Saharan Africa: Restoring Women to History*. Bloomington: Indiana University Press.

Bonnell, Victoria E. 1983. *The Russian Worker: Life and Labor under the Tsarist Regime*. Berkeley: University of California Press.

Bousquet, Ben, and Colin Douglas. 1991. *West Indian Women at War: British Racism in World War II*. London: Lawrence and Wishart.

Caulfield, Sueann. 2000. *In Defense of Honor: Sexual Morality, Modernity, and Nation in Early Twentieth-Century Brazil*. Durham, NC: Duke University Press.

Cooper, Barbara MacGowan. 1997. *Marriage in Maradi: Gender and Culture in a Hausa Society in Niger, 1900–1989*. Portsmouth, NH: Heinemann.

DeGroot, Gerard J., and Corinna Peniston-Bird, eds. 2000. *A Soldier and a Woman: Sexual Integration in the Military*. Harlow: Longman.

Farnsworth-Alvear, Ann. 2000. *Dulcinea in the Factory: Myths, Morals, Men, and Women in Colombia's Industrial Experiment, 1905–1960*. Durham, NC: Duke University Press.

Fassin, Didier. 2007. *When Bodies Remember: Experiences and Politics of AIDS in South Africa*. Berkeley: University of California Press.

Francois, Marie Eileen. 2006. *A Culture of Everyday Credit: Housekeeping, Pawnbroking, and Governance in Mexico City, 1950–1920*. Lincoln: University of Nebraska Press.

Gouda, Frances. 1996. *Dutch Culture Overseas: Colonial Practice in the Netherlands-Indies, 1900–1942*. Amsterdam: University of Amsterdam Press.

Grossman, Atina. 2007. *Jews, Germans, and Allies: Close Encounters in Occupied Germany, 1945–1949*. Princeton, NJ: Princeton University Press.

Guy, Donna. 2009. *Women Build the Welfare State: Performing Charity and Creating Rights in Argentina, 1880–1955*. Durham, NC: Duke University Press.

Hasan, Zoya, and Rita Menon. 2005. *Educating Muslim Girls: A Comparison of Five Indian Cities*. New Delhi: Women Unlimited.

Hawkesworth, Mary E. 2006. *Globalization and Feminist Activism*. New York: Rowman and Littlefield.

Hershatter, Gail. 2007. *Women in China's Long Twentieth Century*. Berkeley: University of California Press.

Honig, Emily. 1985. "Burning Incense, Pledging Sisterhood: Communities of Women Workers in the Shanghai Cotton Mills, 1919–1949," *Signs* 10, no. 4 (Spring).

Kaplan, Temma. 2004. *Taking Back the Streets: Women, Youth, and Direct Democracy*. Berkeley: University of California Press.

Kumar, Radha. 1993. *The History of Doing: An Illustrated Account of Movements for Women's Rights and Feminism in India, 1800–1990*. London: Verso.

Lavrin, Asuncion. 1995. *Women, Feminism, and Social Change in Argentina, Chile, and Uruguay, 1890–1940*. Lincoln: University of Nebraska Press.

Leutner, Mechthild, and Nikola Spakowski, eds. 2005. *Women in China: The Republican Period in Historical Perspective*. Berlin: LIT Verlag.

Loos, Tamara. 2006. *Subject Siam: Family, Law, and Colonial Modernity in Thailand*. Ithaca, NY: Cornell University Press.

Lowy, Dina. 2008. *The Japanese "New Woman": Contending Images of Gender and Modernity, 1910–1920*. New Brunswick, NJ: Rutgers University Press.

Maathai, Wangari. 1995. "Bottlenecks of Development in Africa." Available from http://gos.sbc.edu/m/maathai.html.

Mackie, Vera. 2003. *Feminism in Modern Japan: Citizenship, Embodiment, and Sexuality*. Cambridge: Cambridge University Press.

Malone, Carolyn. 2003. *Women's Bodies and Dangerous Trades in England, 1880–1914*. Rochester, NY: Boydell and Brewer.

Mosse, George. 1990. *Fallen Soldiers: Reshaping the Memory of the World Wars*. New York: Oxford University Press.

Nashat, Guity, and Judith E. Tucker. 1998. *Women in the Middle East and North Africa: Restoring Women to History*. Bloomington: Indiana University Press.

Navarro, Marysa, and Virginia Sánchez Korrol. 1999. *Women in Latin America and the Caribbean: Restoring Women to History*. Bloomington: Indiana University Press.

Oldenburg, Veena Talwar. 1992. "Lifestyle as Resistance: The Courtesans of Lucknow," in *Contesting Power: Resistance and Everyday Social Relations in South Asia*, ed. Douglas Haynes and Gyan Prakash. Berkeley: University of California Press.

Pollard, Lisa. 2005. *Nurturing the Nation: The Family Politics of Modernizing, Colonizing, and Liberating Egypt, 1805–1923*. Berkeley: University of California Press.

Porter, Susie. 2003. *Working Women in Mexico City: Public Discourse and Material Conditions, 1879–1931*. Tucson: University of Arizona Press.

Ramusack, Barbara N., and Sharon Sievers. 1999. *Women in Asia: Restoring Women to History*. Bloomington: Indiana University Press.

Shaarawi, Huda. 1987. *Harem Years: The Memoirs of an Egyptian Feminist*, ed. and trans. Margot Badran. New York: Feminist Press.

Shiva, Vandana, and Radha Holla-Bhar. 1996. "Piracy by Patent: The Case of the Neem Tres," in *The Case against the Global Economy and for a Turn toward the Local*, ed. Jerry Mander and Edward Goldsmith. San Francisco: Sierra Club Books.

Sinha, Mrinalini. 2006. *Specters of Mother India: The Global Restructuring of an Empire*. Durham, NC: Duke University Press.

Smith, Bonnie G., ed. 2000. *Global Feminisms since 1945*. New York: Routledge.

———. 2008. *Oxford Encyclopedia of Women in World History*. 4 vols. New York: Oxford University Press.

Tanaka, Toshiyuki. 2002. *Japan's Comfort Women: Sexual Slavery and Prostitution during World War II and the U.S. Occupation*. London: Routledge.

Tinsman, Heidi. 2002. *Partners in Conflict: The Politics of Gender, Sexuality, and Labor in the Chilean Agrarian Reform, 1950–1973*. Durham, NC: Duke University Press.

Weinbaum, Alys Eve, et al., eds. 2008. *The Modern Girl around the World: Consumption, Modernity, and Globalization*. Durham, NC: Duke University Press.

Wells, Julia. 1993. *We Now Demand! The History of Women's Resistance to Pass Laws in South Africa*. Johannesburg: Witwatersrand University Press.

White, Deborah Gray. 1999. *Too Heavy a Load: Black Women in Defense of Themselves, 1894–1994*. New York: W. W. Norton.

CHAPTER 4

The Gendering of Human Rights in the International Systems of Law in the Twentieth Century

JEAN H. QUATAERT

The twentieth century has been marked by an intensification of rights claims and struggles in the face of egregious rights violations and abuses. This tragic coincidence has been an inescapable part of the historic development of human rights norms, strategies, and institutions. It puts in bold relief the glaring tensions between an increasingly universal moral code and the daily practices of political and military power.

From multiple perspectives, the century offered its own disturbing record of horrors—brutal colonial wars, cataclysmic eruptions of civic violence in the aftermath of the cold war, genocides, ethnic cleansings, mass rapes, and countless numbers of destitute, displaced, and "disappeared" persons. Paradoxically, however, a public dedicated to humanitarian aid and rights values also emerged on the international scene at nearly the same time. This public has supported universal principles of rights ever more broadly conceived and established a wide range of legal and institutional mechanisms for their implementation at the local, national, and international levels. The creation of the United Nations (UN) in 1945 set the foundations for the first full-blown human rights system in world history and the General Assembly's Universal Declaration of Human Rights in 1948 heralded this new era. By the last third of the century, human rights rhetoric became the widely shared language of the global age, a seemingly commonsense affirmation of global interconnections, with its universal promises of equality, dignity, and security for all human beings, everywhere.

The continuing gaps between norm and reality remain a stark challenge to the proclaimed value of universality. In part, the tension is inherent in the cumulative effects of rights activities of any kind, which expand the bases of claims and simultaneously expose new forms of abuse. What constitutes a right in one historic context may not have been understood in the same way in an earlier time or a different place. However, this quality of malleability is also the key to the difficulties that surround the political movements to extend rights principles and laws. Rights are neither self-evident nor are they ethically monolithic; they are historical constructs, rooted in struggle and—despite the pervasive rhetoric of universality—partial and gendered. Continuously contested by calculations of power and self-interest, the cause of rights alone cannot assure a fair and equitable outcome.

Much of the recent literature on the history of human rights reproduces one or the other of two fallacies. The first regards all historical expressions of rights and moral principles as forerunners of human rights and, in fact, elides them altogether. Typical of this approach is the collection of documents entitled *The Human Rights Reader,* which, in tracing the origins of human rights, includes biblical principles and texts drawn from Buddhism and the Koran, as well as the Magna Carta. Undeniably, it is important to acknowledge the multiple moral traditions that have established ethical principles around justice and right. However, to claim that these precepts are equivalent expressions of human rights in any operative or legal sense is ahistorical. Such a claim fails to differentiate the subtle complexities as well as the specific historical and cultural meanings around the praxis of freedom, rights, liberties, privileges, and power in time and space.[1] Importantly, as well, rights are not the sum total of morality; they neither exhaust nor supplant moral systems that are rooted in religion, the charitable imperative, or powerful ideas of the common good. Rights coexist—and at times even compete—with other moral systems.

The second fallacy understands human rights to be a "revival" of the philosophical movement of natural rights, which sustained liberal revolutionary politics and nation building in the West, starting with the North American and French revolutions of the late eighteenth century. It is as if mid-twentieth-century human rights principles were a logical and inevitable rebirth of natural rights philosophy, with its premium on liberty and civil equality as well as rights of property.[2] There are problems with this interpretation. It essentially leaves out the whole post-Enlightenment history of radical, socialist, feminist, and colonial critiques over a century and a half that rested on alternative visions and strategies to achieve justice, dignity, and equality in society. Moreover, natural rights and human rights principles impose very different understandings of duties and obligations on the bearers. Natural rights contracts are, in effect, civic affairs among citizens, which are seen to constitute legitimate government; they require no further obligations to those outside the particular political society. Human rights, by contrast, are individual and collective rights that are applied to all human beings. They make clear that abuses elsewhere are of common concern.

This chapter builds on my critiques of the prevailing human rights literature and shows that the human rights system of international laws and institutions developed out of a concrete set of historical struggles. Indeed, there was nothing inevitable about its emergence and evolution. The system was a product of the reciprocities between legal changes and institution building from above and the continuous interventions of transnational groups and organizations, reflecting grassroots mobilizations from below. The human rights structure fed on growing linkages between understandings of rights norms at the local and state levels and their proclamation and defense by international institutions and agencies. Indeed, negotiations over rights became so prominent a fixture of international relations that the twentieth century was a watershed era in the evolution of international rights laws.[3]

Although insufficiently credited in the literature, women's organizations and international networks were essential components of the societal linkages across frontiers that helped build international institutions and laws. They were, however, a constant reminder that the presumed language of universality underpinning the effort to establish an international community rooted in law contained glaring gender and cultural biases. From their base of operations in the nation-states in the early twentieth century, many of these transnational feminist organizations worked for sex equality (between men and women) in international law, demonstrating, indeed, that the so-called "rights of man" were for men alone. By the 1970s, feminist and women's groups across the globe included gender (that is, the social construction of sexual differences) as a new lawmaking category. This shift turned attention to gender-specific discriminations and vulnerabilities on the basis of human sexual identities. Writing at the end of the century, human rights activist Jessica Neuwirth reminded readers of the important place of women's perspectives in the crucial connection between norms, activism, and legal change:

> I don't like the idea of human rights of women as a new wave or a new generation. The rights of women are set forth in the Universal Declaration of Human Rights, and *they have been there all along in international law*. It's the human rights movement that has neglected them.[4]

Whose voices are heard in the debates over rights? When did the older rights traditions, which structured the early international agreements binding states, transmute to *human* rights? Is the global human rights system simply a mask for ongoing Western imperialism and control, as some critics in the third world (which is, of course, the two-thirds world) maintain?[5] Can a gendering of rights be reconciled with its universal claims? Is universalism a viable project in a global age that simultaneously values diversity?

INTERNATIONAL HUMANITARIAN LAW
AND ITS LIMITATIONS

The late twentieth-century human rights regime grew out of the historic era of European, U.S., and Japanese Great Power domination. Early in the century, the world's political imbalances had reached an extreme. Formal European colonial empires stretched across most of Africa, large parts of South and East Asia, and many islands of the Pacific. The government of Meiji Japan established rule over Formosa in 1894 and annexed Korea in 1910, and Americans—through their gains in Hawaii, the Philippines, Puerto Rico, and Cuba in 1898—extended their power and influence more purposefully throughout Asia, the Pacific, and Latin America. Roughly half a billion people fell under the formal control of foreign colonial administrators.[6] Imperial rule had been imposed through deadly cycles of conquest and resistance. Colonial rhetoric, however, defined rule with reference to universalist principles that promised to abolish abuses (such as slavery, for example, or presumed aristo-cratic tribal misrule) and bring the technological and other cultural fruits of "civilization" to subject peoples. At the same time, this vocabulary justified growing multilateral ties between European sovereign states and the laws and customs of war that bound "civilized" nations. In the name of "progress," too, transnational organizations sought international labor protection, as well as an end to forced prostitution and sex trafficking across frontiers. Furthermore, inclusive assumptions of sisterhood brought Western feminists (both bour-geois and socialist) into international groups and alliances.

An international community of contracting states bound by law emerged at the dawn of the twentieth century. An unlikely source set this "wheel of progress" in motion, as one contemporary European author put it, placing the movement to codify international law among the defining hallmarks of the age. In 1898, at the request of the autocratic czar, the Russian foreign minister called for a select conference of state officials from around the world to work together to reduce the mounting budgetary expenditures for armaments, which so negatively "affect[ed] public prosperity," and to enhance the prospects for peace.[7] After a cool reception, a second circular expanded the topics to include arms control; revision of the laws and customs of war safeguarding the rights of soldiers, neutrals, and noncombatants; and proposals for international arbi-tration to prevent armed conflicts among nations. The Dutch government agreed to host the meeting, and on May 20, 1899, the first Hague Congress opened. Twenty-six states sent delegations comprised of officials and lawyers, mostly from the European nations, although representatives from North America and Mexico also attended. Working for two straight months, the del-egates drew up three conventions (a form of international treaty binding on the contracting powers), three declarations prohibiting the use of certain types of weapons and poisonous gasses in warfare, and "six wishes" for future deliberation.

A flurry of coordinated activities across national borders coincided with the government-sponsored international congress in the Netherlands. Many of these activists were members of women's reform organizations in national societies, who had established institutional ties abroad. From Germany, leaders of a women's transnational alliance put out a call for a large "international demonstration of women" to support the critical work of "peace" going on at The Hague. The appeal found a receptive audience. In response, 565 nearly simultaneous public meetings of women's groups involved in a wide range of causes from suffrage to trade unionism to temperance and other religious and moral crusades took place on and around May 15, 1899, in the "three divisions of the world," as a contemporary report described the breadth of contacts: from Europe to the Americas to Asia. Japan, however, was the lone participant from Asia and, despite efforts to reach Brazilian women's groups, only Americans and Canadians joined the publicized gatherings in the Western Hemisphere. Overwhelmingly European (mirroring the Hague delegations of all-male officials), organized women's groups nonetheless inserted their voices into the important questions of war and peace that affected the "common welfare of humanity."[8]

From the start of the efforts to codify international law, these negotiations among territorial states in the international arena found an echo in the transnational work of groups in society (in the language of human rights, what are called the nongovernmental organizations or NGOs). Furthermore, these vocal feminist groups were part of an expanding humanitarian public that was continuously shaped and reinvigorated by advances in photojournalism and a cheap mass press. Graphic visual images of the plight of fellow human beings helped to sustain humanitarian sentiments. The deliberations at The Hague were followed avidly by a growing reading public, which included many individuals and groups beyond the feminists who also were committed to arms limitations and the reduction of military burdens. Public expectations turned the Hague Congress (on armaments and war) into the Peace Conference.

To set the origins of the international rights community so neatly in 1899 is not fully accurate. The deliberations at The Hague both drew on and, in turn, nurtured growing "internationalist" sentiments that can be traced back far into the nineteenth century. The antislavery movements of the 1830s and 1840s throughout the Atlantic world had been a great international humanitarian crusade, although the powerful mobilizing sentiments behind a "brotherhood of man" did not sustain an image of human equality in the new age of European imperialism; some brothers seemed destined indeed to instruct others.[9] So, too, by midcentury, disillusionment with the pronounced male biases of abolitionism encouraged separate women's rights movements in England and America, paralleled by similar organizing efforts on the European continent and, later in the century, in Central and South America as well. Women's rights causes, as well as those of the working classes, contained a logic that pushed beyond state borders. Tested in a series of coordinated campaigns, which initially challenged state-sanctioned prostitution and then championed temperance and female suffrage, an International Council of Women emerged in 1888, open to all women's organizations across the globe, at least in principle. The next year, the Second International was founded and headquartered in Amsterdam to coordinate workers' common struggles and causes across the national divides. Both large social movements worked to expand political and social rights within state borders as part, however, of a wider internationalist identity. For many feminists, women's suffrage became the precondition for a fundamentally more peaceful international world; for many workers, too, success of their cause meant a radically new international community based on equality and justice. If constrained by their own cultural and social biases because of limited contacts outside of the West, these early movements nonetheless demonstrated the potential for expansive visions that are inherent in rights vocabulary. They confronted, however, the equally powerful strain of identities that drew on notions of exclusivity, hierarchy, and national uniqueness.

The deliberations at the Hague Conference, nourished by reform groups of various types within the nation-states, represented a movement of cooperation among states, which coexisted with a set of competing assumptions about the inviolability of national strength and military autonomy. Significantly, too, the socialist Second International stood aloof from these early efforts at "liberal" lawmaking at The Hague. The work of codification nonetheless capped a full half century of previous efforts to "humanize" warfare through multilateral agreements, initially among a Concert of Europe. Most significant had been passage of the Geneva Conventions in 1864, establishing the rights of wounded soldiers and the simultaneous creation of the International Red Cross and, after negotiation with the Ottoman Empire in 1877, Red Crescent societies, headquartered in Geneva. Organized in national branches, which extended down to local communities, these relief organizations promised impartial humanitarian aid to wounded soldiers of any nationality under a new, internationally sanctioned status of "neutrality." Multilateral cooperation had coalesced around the midcentury symbol of "suffering humanity"—the wounded enemy soldier. The duties and obligations to soldiers and civilians alike required interstate cooperation, even between belligerents. Subsequent agreements extended the provisions to maritime warfare.

The Hague Final Acts of 1899 (and a subsequent conference on the same topics, which met in 1907) codified nineteenth-century international law around the customs and practices of war on land and sea (including, eventually, aerial bombardments). They reinforced the principle of international arbitration, made it compulsory in restricted cases (initially involving contract debts alone), and established a permanent Court of Arbitration seated at The Hague.

Legal codification was matched by new institutions, which gave concrete forms to this arena of international norms. In 1907, the number of state delegations to the conference had risen to forty-four (including fourteen states from Central and Latin America and the nominally independent Asian countries of China and Siam [Thailand]), and provisions were made for nonsignatory powers to accede to the conventions. In the internationalist logic, as more states signed on, the codes, which became known as international humanitarian law, would be transformed into universal law.

The two Hague conferences of 1899 and 1907 could not escape the contradictions inherent in their own international project. In 1899, in deference to Great Power and imperialist interests, Britain kept the representatives from the Transvaal and Orange republics of southern Africa out of the deliberations (at the time, the countries were at war in the region) and Bulgaria appeared only as a subsidiary of the Ottoman Empire. In 1907, Japan prevented a Korean delegation from attending. More significantly, the international reach was purposefully limited. Deference to territorial sovereignty and military autonomy was the precondition for international cooperation in the first place. Similar constraints were shaping the International Red Cross, which allowed each national organization to operate independently, working out the specifics of role, place, and purpose within the military and political culture of its own state. The contracting parties well understood the limits; they were built into the legal language itself, which explicitly exempted the internal "political relations of states" and the "orders of things established by treaties" from the force of humanitarian law. The agreement also acknowledged the exigencies of "military necessity"; despite all the concrete provisions to protect humanity in warfare, the aim of the military still remained to win wars, at all costs if necessary. In addition, there were no effective international mechanisms set up to enforce compliance. Given these limitations, the workings of a humanitarian public took on added meaning. A poor substitute for obligatory international sanctions, public opinion nonetheless was a potentially powerful—if not fickle—participant, helping to define and address what were understood as humanitarian crises. In short, state governments increasingly have had to deal with their own domestic groups, as well as with the pressures of international opinion in wartime.

The limited scope of international cooperation belied any real notion of universality. In practical terms, the conventions were binding on the contracting parties alone. Those who had not signed on were under no formal obligation to the international community, although the normative powers of the rules and principles of warfare were assumed to hold sway in all cases of armed conflict between nations. Indeed, these very norms of humane warfare were seen to mark the "civilized" nations off against "savage" peoples. In circular fashion, the Hague conventions were open only to the so-called "civilized" states, which affirmed their status by adhering to this growing body of law. Formal membership in the international community was seen to diminish "the evils of war" as part of a broader quest for peace and, thus, "serve the interests of humanity and the ever progressive needs of civilization," to quote the 1899 language of the Hague Convention on the Laws and Customs of War on Land. But a Japanese diplomat captured well the subtle complexities of this embrace of a language of civilized warfare, which set the parameters for the international community to recognize war and work for peace. "We show ourselves at least your equals in scientific butchery and, at once, we are admitted to your council tables as 'civilized' men."[10] His justifiable sarcasm acknowledged that it was Japanese strength and not its civilization that had brought the country into the community of nations and now enmeshed it in the rules of war. But the tragedy was that the Peace Conference had defined warfare so narrowly as to exclude most types of armed struggle from the jurisdictions of international law.

The deliberations at both Hague congresses took place against the backdrop of wars that were placed squarely outside the legal reach of the new international community. From 1899 until 1902, Britain and the Boer republics were locked in a deadly combat over territory and empire in southern Africa. Similarly, while diplomats were arranging to meet at The Hague in 1907, the German government was concluding a brutal war of pacification against the Herero and Nama peoples in its main settlement colony of Southwest Africa (Namibia). As in other colonial empires on the African continent and in Asia and the Caribbean, resistance to colonial rule had been fierce and protracted. In the majority opinion of member states of the international community, however, these struggles over land and resources were internal matters of empire, rebellions of "uncivilized" peoples who would not follow the canons of accepted military behavior in any case. A memorandum in the Imperial German Colonial Office minced no words: "We are not fighting against an enemy respecting the rules of fairness but against savages."[11] These wars of empire at the dawn of the twentieth century, therefore, were "total wars," unrestrained by law and custom. They were grim examples—and tragically repeated in the century to come—of wars undertaken with no sense of any common human bond with the enemy. They demonstrate what happens when the laws of war, however limited and partial, are abridged at nearly every point.[12]

Both wars were pursued with extraordinary ruthlessness and involved gross violations of the codes and customs of civilized warfare that just had been reaffirmed at The Hague. The calculations of "military necessity" and the drive toward unconditional victory worked to blur the distinction between soldiers and civilians, which had been enshrined as the centerpiece of the new international laws of war. British and German colonial troops faced an unfamiliar world of mobile guerrilla warfare, intensified by a vigorous arms trade in the area; in response, both militaries resorted to scorched-earth policies of burning farmsteads and destroying crops. To clear the land and deprive the enemy of sustenance, they "concentrated" the remaining populations into fortified camps, a tactic that had been used by the Spanish general Valeriano Weyler to counter the Cuban insurrection of 1896.[13] Targeting the civilian populations was a deliberate military policy designed to force capitulation.

At times, colonial violence was tempered by public opinion. Early on at home, these wars became the terrains of heated domestic controversy and widespread concern abroad among the newspaper-reading public. The published lists of casualties in the daily press, the accounts of atrocities (as well as defeats and victories) by returning wounded soldiers, and—with the growing prominence of photojournalism—the sensational pictures of life in the concentration camps brought the wars to the heart of the imperial centers, weakening insular perspectives and values even though cultural stereotypes continued unchecked.[14] Indeed, it was partly vociferous international criticism—and calculations of political capital—that encouraged the German kaiser to halt the brutal military practices of his colonial troops. It helped, too, that the general staff had come to regard the military policy as basically unenforceable and counterproductive to the colony's long-term need for labor.

The British government also had to field domestic and international criticism for its conduct of the war. New forms of relief organizations that offered humanitarian aid—even to enemy noncombatants—mushroomed in British civil society and sponsored their own inquiries into war atrocities. Opposition was fueled by the extraordinary journey of Emily Hobhouse, a prominent member of the South African Conciliation Committee, who was convinced that women had a special role to play in mediation efforts among the warring parties. On behalf of the committee, she toured the Transvaal and Orange republics in 1900–1901 and wrote a scathing critique. Her exposé, intended to "shock the world," vividly caught the plight of women and children who bore *The Brunt of the War*, the title of her famous book that inserted gender imagery into the symbolism of human suffering. Drawing on a deep bedrock of customary assumptions about the need to protect women and children from combat, she called attention to the hypocrisy behind the law safeguarding civilians on the one hand and a military strategy of unconditional surrender on the other.[15] The cumulative picture drawn from hundreds of firsthand accounts provided chilling details of the flagrant violations of the law, the inhumane treatment of the inhabitants, and the destruction of the land, which had been turned into a war zone. The book also linked the issue of women's rights more closely with the cause of peace.

Public outcry about military policy forced the British government to establish an official "commission of inquiry," headed by the well-known moderate suffragist Millicent Garrett Fawcett, whose findings led to significant administrative reforms in the camps. In this example, the suffering and deaths of women and children seemed to fly in the face of all moral codes—let alone recently enacted legal codes. But public pressure was highly selective. The Fawcett

Commission did not examine the camps that had been set up for the native black populations. Furthermore, there was no public outcry over the terms of the peace, which postponed indefinitely the promise of black enfranchisement in South Africa even though, ostensibly (and for public consumption), the war had been waged to safeguard the political *rights* of "Utlanders" (British foreigners) and others in the Boer republics.[16]

Codification of the international laws of war had created a set of paradoxes. On the one hand, by limiting the formal rules and regulations to war between "civilized" states, it left those deemed "uncivilized" vulnerable to legally unrestrained military abuses. On the other hand, growing publicity about the norms of war served to make the public more critical of military actions outside the formal codes of warfare. In the early twentieth century, these sensitivities were more easily mobilized in defense of the dignity of women and children than of racial equality.

In the first two decades of the twentieth century, new forms of international humanitarian relief proliferated amid growing internationalist sentiments. The International Red Cross coordinated disaster relief efforts for victims at home and abroad. For example, in 1902, its local branch societies in many communities throughout Europe were mobilized simultaneously to raise money and supplies for the victims of a devastating flood in the French colony of Martinique, while similar coordination of groups across national borders took place in 1911 during a natural disaster in the Tyrol area of Austria. The peace movement, too, spawned new institutions and practices. Under sponsorship of the Carnegie Endowment for International Peace, founded in 1910, an international commission was sent to inquire into wartime atrocities during the Balkan Wars of 1912–1913. Such inquiries testified to the growing public commitment to the rules of fair play in war, as well as to the importance of truthful claims in crisis situations—that is, in the words of the commission's 1914 report, to a modernist faith in an "impartial and exhaustive" examination of the facts.[17]

In World War I, however, humanitarian relief showed its Janus face. The Red Cross societies of the belligerent nations saw their work as patriotic defense and wholeheartedly joined the war effort, contributing to its propaganda campaigns. Nonetheless, significant parts of the international machinery were indeed maintained on the western front in the war: oversight of the prisoner of war camps, protection of frontline medical services under the Red Cross and Crescent insignias, and coordination of vital information regarding the fate of individual soldiers.[18] On balance, the war experiences revealed crucial and previously unacknowledged gaps between individuals and groups committed to the principles of wartime relief and those fundamentally opposed to war.

The outbreak of hostilities in 1914 temporarily shattered the disparate movements for peace. By 1915, however, they had regrouped again, under two broad and increasingly hostile ideological camps. With great hardship, peace advocates from the neutral and belligerent nations who were members of the bourgeois women's international organizations met that year at a Congress of Women organized at The Hague (the location was chosen purposefully for its symbolism). In the midst of a cataclysmic war, they formulated a new vision for a world of permanent peace, which included the establishment of an international organization (a Society of Nations) and the passage of women's suffrage in the nation-states around the globe. In the view of this congress, women's political rights would bring maternalist sentiments favorable to peace directly into the domestic and international public arenas. These liberal feminist voices were part of wider debates among the entente powers that helped establish the League of Nations in 1919 as part of the peace process. The year 1915 also brought international socialists clandestinely together in neutral Switzerland. In Berne, representatives of socialist women's organizations met to condemn all wars unequivocally, and in Zimmerwald, the delegates of international socialism called for the transformation of the imperialist war into social revolution, a slogan that took on added clout with the 1917 Bolshevik Revolution in Russia. Indeed, in the postwar climate that added sharp ideological conflicts to older animosities among nation-states, humanitarian aid efforts easily became embroiled in political calculations of national self-interest and military security.[19]

THE LEAGUE OF NATIONS AND INTERNATIONAL RIGHTS

The League of Nations set a number of precedents in international institution building. Headquartered in Geneva, it was a permanent international structure, open to all sovereign states, and governed by an assembly of these states and a more select Council of the Great Powers.[20] A secretariat coordinated the league's business, while the Permanent Court of International Justice handled disputes involving international law. Significantly, the league was joined in Geneva by the International Labor Office (ILO), the first of numerous formal affiliations between international bodies around problems and issues that were seen to require transnational cooperation. The ILO, too, had been part of the peace treaties, a move by the victorious powers to stave off labor unrest and the socialist revolutions that had engulfed Europe at the end of the war. In a new departure, the ILO was able to set international work standards and living conditions for labor, which applied to each contracting state. In general, however, as in the past, the League Covenant exempted the "internal affairs" of the member states and imperial powers from international interference. The league's structure accommodated colonial rule, and even built on it through the mandates given to the victorious states to administer "the peoples not yet able to stand by themselves under the strenuous conditions of the modern world." These were the populations in the colonial territories of the defeated German and Ottoman empires.[21]

On one level, establishment of the league and the ILO drew public attention to Geneva, creating a new "center" of international activity. Geneva served as a magnet for many nongovernmental organizations with a multiplicity of causes to define and defend. Some groups shifted their headquarters to Geneva to be able to lobby assembly delegates more effectively; others set up bureaus and consultative committees that paralleled the work of the league (for example, on disarmament and nationality), while still others formed new supraorganizations, such as the Liaison Committee of Women's International Organizations, which was established in 1931 to coordinate the international work of a wide range of women's reform groups.[22] At another level, a perspective from the center also reflected the continuous efforts of intraregional cooperation and local mobilizations, which channeled and challenged the work from above. This bottom-up view permits new narratives that move beyond Eurocentric analyses. Rights debates under the auspices of the league mirrored these circular flows of influence.

Formed to insure the peace, international security, and disarmament in the aftermath of war, the League Covenant defended rights in limited contexts only: to "fair and humane conditions of labor for men, women, and children in their own countries and in all countries" and to "just" treatment of native populations in the territories under its control. It also called for an end to the trafficking of women and children and sought to curb the "dangerous" drug and arms trades. Other postwar international instruments protected the rights of minorities in the states of Europe that had been newly created out of the territories of the former Russian, Austro-Hungarian, and Ottoman empires. In an effort to harness the logic of self-determination, these Minorities Treaties (as they were known) insured all inhabitants of the new multiethnic states in Europe the full protection of life, liberty, and law "without distinction of birth, nationality, language, race or religion." They also guaranteed minority groups inside the sovereign nation a certain measure of cultural autonomy. Compliance became a condition of the states' full membership in the "Family of Nations," while, reciprocally, protection of these political and civil rights was made a new obligation of the international community, guaranteed by the league. While limited to Europe, these minority clauses broadened the debates beyond the stark civilized/savage dichotomy of the Hague precedent. Alas, the league proved to be ineffectual and weak, unable to safeguard the peace or the principles of rights. "The trouble with the League is not the League, it is the Nations," wrote the Brazilian feminist Bertha Lutz bitterly to her American colleague, Carrie Chapman Catt, in April 1936.[23]

The limited scope of formal protections did not go unchallenged. Pan-American cooperation and contacts, as well as renewed pressure by women's international NGOs, pushed for changes in two directions. The first sought to extend the minority protection principles to the internal organization of all member states in the league, not just to the few European nation-states created after the war; the second challenged the long-held international principle that the status of women was a matter of domestic jurisdiction alone.

The first proposal, in effect, expanded the foundation of international law according to a new formulation, which asserted the "international rights of individuals." It was put before the assembly by a delegate for the Republic of Haiti, then occupied by the United States in 1933 and 1934—both times unsuccessfully. The resolution nonetheless testified to new thinking about international law among Chilean and Parisian jurists, as well as to considerable Pan-American collaborative work and networking on issues of shared interest, such as security and arbitration, despite intense state rivalries and tensions.[24] Besides, it spoke to wider intellectual contacts across the Atlantic world around questions of democracy and social justice. It is especially fitting that the Caribbean nation of Haiti sponsored the resolution. During the turmoil of the French Revolution, the slaves in the former French sugar colony rose up to proclaim their own freedom and established in 1804 the world's first sovereign black nation-state. The Haitian case is a forceful reminder that notions of freedom and dignity come from multiple sources around the globe, even if these complex origins too often are lost in the standard compendia of rights histories.[25]

Latin American women's movements also had emerged early in the twentieth century and, with feminists from Uruguay and Argentina in the lead, the activists became well practiced in the politics of lobbying the Inter-American Conferences of States on their own issues of mutual concern, such as the family, public health, child welfare, and, in time, women's suffrage. In the case of Latin American women, it appears that the wider hemispheric contacts were the impetus for parallel work on the national level; similar ties among women's groups also sustained horizontal Pan-Pacific identities distinct from Europe and America in the interwar years. Furthermore, if the efforts to build on international contacts "screeched to a halt in 1939" in a Europe once again engulfed in war, internationalist feminists in Latin America continued their recruiting and organizing efforts for democratic and social causes throughout the 1930s and 1940s. World War II served as the "catalyst" for their intensified struggles on behalf of democracy.[26]

The strength of these regional ties and contacts also reinforced the work of lobbying for women's causes in Geneva between the world wars. The heads of women's international organizations were appalled at the absence of women in official administrative and leadership posts at the league itself despite Article 7, which had opened up all positions to women, and also among the state delegations to the assembly. After 1929, they became increasingly alarmed at the consequences of the world economic depression for women's right to work in many nation-states. The rise of fascism was also seen as a serious threat to women's position in society. Ten Latin American delegations, responding to concerns back home, took the lead in calling for a forceful response to the "encroachments upon the rights and liberties of women," and the women's international Liaison Council mobilized its affiliated organizations for this public relations campaign waged at the center. Bowing to considerable international pressure, the League of Nations Assembly in 1937 agreed to sponsor a "comprehensive and scientific inquiry" into the status of women worldwide, the first such broad investigation into the domestic life situations of women around the globe.[27] Women's organizations had come together and turned a gender-specific issue into a matter of grave international urgency. This marked a new step in public awareness of the international implications of sex discrimination for economic and social development, let alone for the cause of equality. However, it is important to recognize that these interwar efforts to expand and defend rights were not yet framed in the explicit language of *human* rights.

THE INTERNATIONALIZATION OF HUMAN RIGHTS

The human rights system emerged out of a precise historical "moment"—the Second World War and the collective efforts by the victorious powers to restructure a future world at peace (1937–1949). Its authority was directly linked to the Charter of the United Nations, the cornerstone of the postwar international order, originally signed by fifty-one states in June 1945 in San Francisco. Speaking for the *peoples* of the United Nations, the charter "reaffirmed faith in fundamental human rights, in the dignity and worth of the human person, in the equal rights of men and women."[28] This process of internationalizing human rights principles and instruments occurred before cold war hostilities between communism and democracy had settled in, which arguably would have made international agreements on fundamental rights all but impossible. The momentous anti-imperialist struggles for national liberation were also in the future and these anticolonial movements would not only draw on the existing norms and rights (to self-determination and dignity) but also push hard and successfully for inclusion of new rights into the mix (the right to economic development, for example). In 1945, the international community of "united nations" was therefore much simpler than would be true in later decades.

Importantly, the new human rights principles were fed by many different sources of state and nonstate agencies and organizations around the world. An explicit commitment to the protection of human rights had been part of the Allied war aims against the Axis powers of Germany, Italy, and Japan in the struggle for world public opinion. In January 1942, for example, twenty-six Allied nations proclaimed that "complete victory over their enemies is essential to defend life, liberty, independence and religious freedom, and to preserve human rights and justice in their own lands as well as in other lands."[29] René Brunet, a French official with the League of Nations, graphically caught the mounting pressures at the level of transnational contacts and commitments as well. Writing in 1947, he reminisced about the flows of exchange as the war progressed:

> Hundreds of political, scholarly and religious organizations have, by their publications, appeals, manifestations and interventions, spread and impressed the idea that the protection of human rights should be part of the war aims of the Allied Powers, and that the future peace would not be complete if it would not consecrate the principle of international protection of human rights in all States and if it would not guarantee this protection in an effective manner.[30]

Brunet was on the mark, but the final outcome still required dramatic interventions of transnational and regional voices, as well as an international public opinion visibly shaken by the first horrifying pictures coming out of Europe from the Nazi death camps.

Significantly, the 1944 Dumbarton Oaks proposals by the Allied great powers (the United States, Great Britain, the Soviet Union, and China), which set the blueprint for what became the United Nations, downplayed concrete references to human rights principles, despite their high visibility in the propaganda campaigns of the war. Leaders of the United Kingdom and the Soviet Union had been hostile, while the Chinese representatives wanted to include explicit mention of the "equality of the races." Publication of the weak draft proposals, therefore, led to a storm of protest and action. In Mexico City in February–March 1945, for example, the Chapultepec Conference (on the problems of war and peace) came out decisively for the international protection of fundamental rights to insure the peace and called for an inter-American human rights convention. In an effort to prevent a repeat of isolationist sentiments that had kept the United States out of the League of Nations in 1919, the U.S. government invited members of forty-two powerful NGOs to travel to San Francisco as official consultants to the state delegations. These included representatives of labor, women's, and church groups as well as lawyers, and they helped overcome the opposition to amending the Dumbarton Oaks plan that divided the U.S. delegation.

The final language of the United Nations Charter reflected the intersecting pressures of these disparate agents who jockeyed for influence in San Francisco. Respect for human rights and fundamental freedoms "without distinctions as to race, sex, language, or religion" became one explicit purpose of the United Nations. The founding conference called for the establishment of a Human Rights Commission, placed under the Economic and Social Council, the administrative body responsible for coordinating economic, cultural, and humanitarian matters of international scope. The shocking revelations about wartime atrocities and genocides, as well as plans for war crimes tribunals, also worked to reinforce international resolve in the immediate postwar era.

Similar organizational and diplomatic pressures led to the inclusion of the women's equality clause in the UN Charter. The explicit commitment to women's rights reflected the substantial presence of organized women's groups, which had been pressuring all along for legal changes favorable to women in the national and international arenas. Of the seven official delegations to San Francisco that included women members, five were from Latin and Central America; indeed, the efforts of prominent activists Bertha Lutz (Brazil), Minerva Bernardino (Dominican Republic), and Amalia Ledón (Mexico) helped garner sufficient support for insertion of the sex equality clause into the charter. They had worked tirelessly all through the war years and argued that a precedent already had been set in international law in 1938 at the Eighth Conference of American States in Lima, Peru, which "resolved that women have the right to the equal enjoyment of civil status."[31] Despite concerns about a separate women's commission in light of the newly formed Human Rights Commission (as if women's rights were somehow not the same as human rights), the United Nations General Assembly established a Commission on Women's Status in 1946, and also placed it under the Economic and Social Council. The pattern was set for ongoing postwar negotiations to give concrete legal and institutional expressions to the abstract commitment to human rights.

Important first steps in developing the international legal system of human rights were taken between 1946 and 1949, under the shadow of the traumas of World War II. In an unprecedented move, the victor powers established two International Military Tribunals (popularly known as the Nuremberg and Tokyo trials) to try high Nazi and imperial Japanese leaders as war criminals for "crimes against the peace" and "war crimes"—activating the precedents of international law established by the Geneva and Hague conventions—as well as for "crimes against humanity," a radically new conception of abuses of sovereign power in wartime by an agent or soldier of the state, irrespective of geographical location. The new category held key individuals responsible for gross crimes of exterminations, murder, and deportations of civilian populations, whether of one's own citizens and nationals or those in occupied territories. For the first time ever, it made state-directed violations of the rights of its citizens an international crime, even if there were no specific domestic laws at the time that protected those same citizens from the loss of their elementary rights to life, corporal integrity, and health. Human rights were seen to transcend the borders of the positive codes of law.

Similar changes in the bases of the laws and customs of war were taking place under the auspices of the International Committee of the Red Cross, which sponsored meetings and conferences in the late 1940s to revise the Geneva Conventions in light of the atrocities committed in the world war. Passed on August 12, 1949, the new conventions were a significant revision of the laws of war modified already in 1929; they included a civilian convention (Protection of the Civilian Persons in Wartime), the first time in international law that civilians were singled out by a separate convention, outlawing, among other actions, hostage taking, collective reprisals, violence to life and person, outrages upon personal dignity, intimidation, and terror. Significantly, the provisions broke new ground by extending these protections to armed conflicts that were not solely of an international character, which had been the Hague precedent. If the definition of these types of internal struggles was left somewhat vague, it was meant to include civil wars and other significant armed struggles within the territorial borders of each signatory power that was bound by the convention. The historian Geoffrey Best correctly called this new extension "a landmark in the law of human rights," acknowledging the increasing interpenetration of international humanitarian law and human rights laws after 1945. Best put his case well: "The principle involved was of momentous importance. It was being agreed by governments, on behalf of the whole communities they represented . . . that no matter what pitch of armed violence their internal disputes might attain, certain fundamental inhumanities would be banned."[32] Of course, as we have seen, binding international agreements repeatedly were abridged in practice, although their precepts feed into a parallel system of rules and regulations that is normative and also has the potential to affect individual and state actions. It took, however, the murderous wars in Yugoslavia in the early 1990s and the genocide in Rwanda in 1994 to resurrect the international institution of the war crimes tribunals, which had languished as a mode of international punishment since 1948.[33]

Human rights principles also were being codified in declarations, covenants, and treaties, setting a second legal pillar for the new human rights structure. On two consecutive days, December 9–10, 1948, the General Assembly of the United Nations unanimously passed the Convention on the Prevention and Punishment of the Crime of Genocide (which went into effect in 1951) and, with some abstentions, the Universal Declaration of Human Rights, the first substantive effort to catalog the specific rights and freedoms that had been promised in the UN Charter. The former declared genocide, whether committed in war or peacetime, to be a crime under international law, which the contracting parties pledged to "prevent" and "punish." But use of language itself is political. While the convention sought to unambiguously define the acts of genocide ("committed with intent to destroy, in whole or in part, a national, ethnical, racial or religious group as such"), application of the term in specific instances remains a continuous source of international and interstate controversy. For example, whether or not the Ottoman state committed genocide against its Armenian peoples in 1915 is causing grave frictions between the Republic of Turkey and the European states as Turkey seeks membership in the European Union. Furthermore, during the genocide in Rwanda in 1994, the international community avoided using the term "genocide" because by law it would have required that the member states take immediate and effective measures to halt the killings.[34]

The Universal Declaration of Human Rights was very much a product of its time and place. Drafted by the members of the newly established Human Rights Commission in the aftermath of wars and other vast human traumas, it rested on the belief that promotion of "inalienable" and "equal" human rights was the prerequisite for peace, freedom, and justice in the world and was necessary to assure the inherent dignity and worth of all members of the human family. The preamble called for a "common standard of achievement for all peoples and all nations" and, in contrast to earlier international documents, was addressed not only to the leaders of the sovereign states but also to "every individual and every organ of society." Achievement of universality was seen to require the continuous collaboration among and between the actors in transnational society and the states.

The document was a statement of rights that embraced the principles of political and civil equality and also declared social security and health, the right to work and equal pay necessary for human dignity. It gave men and women "of full age" the right to marry and found a family "without any limitation due to race, nationality, or religion" and made free, equal, elementary education an obligation of each and every community.

Significantly, it tackled neither the metaphysics of origins (such as the derivation of human rights) nor any of the philosophical principles that might ground rights (i.e., in human nature or universal reason). As a historical product, it drew on the traditions and achievements of rights struggles that had been most prominently enshrined in state constitutions to date—juxtaposing into twenty-eight articles the historical expressions of liberalism, liberal feminism, and socialism, most notably, but also precepts from international assemblies, including the Catholic Church, and visions in the anticolonial struggles for self-determination—positions themselves that were not easily reconcilable nor free of gender, social, and cultural biases. Indeed, in the final vote, eight of fifty-six states abstained because they opposed specific articles as an infringement on their sovereignty and cultural integrity.[35]

As a proclamation alone, the document had no binding legal authority. It was not until 1971 that the declaration was ruled an authoritative interpretation of the charter, incumbent on all UN member states. By then, the Human Rights Commission, as planned, had transformed the document's principles into two international conventions, the UN Covenants on Civil and Political Rights and on Economic, Social, and Cultural Rights (1966). These covenants went into effect in 1976, after the minimum of thirty-five states had ratified them. It had taken nearly three decades for the ideals in the Universal Declaration to become a binding fixture of international law.

The covenants were hardly the last word. The formation of so many new states out of the territories of Europe's colonial empires brought additional, insistent voices onto the international stage, beginning in the 1960s. Formal membership in the United Nations served to legitimize each state's sovereign status and the leaders could use the international platforms to highlight specific principles and values or add new ones to the list. Impelled by a bloc of new African and Asian nations, for example, the General Assembly adopted the International Convention on the Elimination of All Forms of Racial Discrimination in January 1966. In 1968, an International Conference on Human Rights met in Teheran, Iran. Holding conferences in sites across the globe beyond Europe's borders brought many new voices to the international debates.

Regional instruments, affirming rights and obligations, also became parts of the human rights system. Entering into force in 1953 was the European Convention for the Protection of Human Rights and Fundamental Freedoms. At that time a tool of cold war politics, after the demise of the Soviet bloc, this and other conventions became enforceable criteria for membership in the new European Union and fundamental to the construction of European identity. In 1969, the American Convention on Human Rights was adopted in San José, Costa Rica, and, a decade later, state representatives of the Organization of African Unity gathered in Monrovia, Liberia, to prepare a preliminary draft for what became the African (Banjul) Charter on Human and Peoples' Rights (1986). Defined with reference to the "values of African civilization" and to the "virtues of their historical traditions," this charter linked the international and national protection of fundamental human rights to the reality and respect of peoples' rights. The spread of an increasingly common vocabulary of rights in laws and treaties across broad geographic areas was, in practice, still refracted through distinct regional and local traditions and customs. Despite these regional principles, the local African states have not acted to protect their own citizens who have been at risk. Through an accumulating set of crises at the end of the twentieth century, including genocides, famines induced by foreign and civil wars, and massive displacements, the number of these endangered people has steadily mounted. But most of the states—sensitive to the abuses of historical colonialism—have clung to absolute principles of sovereignty and failed to initiate or facilitate remedial actions.

Important revisions to the Geneva Conventions in Protocols I and II, completed in 1977, also reflected the concerns and influences of states in the developing world. These protocols revealed the unanticipated challenges and ambiguities that were opened up for all actors by international and regional agreements. Protocol I explicitly extended the protections of the Geneva Conventions and the Nuremberg/Tokyo principles of individual responsibility for human rights abuses to colonial conflicts and struggles against racist regimes. For the first time, this protocol covered the victims of armed struggles against colonialism and racism by appealing to the rights of self-determination in the UN Charter. The International Red Cross, the United States, and some European imperial powers had sought in vain to oppose inclusion of these new clauses. Protocol II defined more carefully the types of "internal" armed struggles that would activate the Geneva Convention protections into these deadly civil conflicts. The protocol contained a presumption in favor of the territorial status quo against ongoing fragmentations along ethnic or religious lines of succession. Nonetheless, by acknowledging armed internal struggles on the ground, it continuously problematized the existing definitions of sovereignty. It also made possible an international (or regional) "humanitarian" mobilization into sovereign territories in cases of sustained intrastate violence that puts people at serious risk.[36]

The multiple contradictions inherent in the human rights instruments became more apparent in the 1970s, as the cause of human rights increasingly was intertwined with the institutions and practices of the emerging global world. During the first three decades after World War II, cold war tensions had served to limit recourse to human rights covenants and treaties as a shared foundation of international diplomacy. The complicated processes of globalization and, since 1989, the end of the cold war, have changed the rules of the game. Human rights activities around the globe have been increasingly mobilized by grave challenges that are transnational in character, including famine and poverty; an unprecedented scale of labor migrations; the need to safeguard the environment; and state, civil, and domestic violence; as well as flagrant state disregard of human rights norms and principles. In a tragic paradox, the failure to meaningfully resolve these same problems of poverty and state abuses has spawned networks of terror, which also have become global. These threats add more urgency to the work of human rights activists, whose agendas address the root causes of social injustice and unrest. Their efforts in the international arena challenge state governments to recognize that implementation of human rights principles has become an essential component of national security concerns.

Global tensions over rights have generated other fault lines in international relations. Rights treaties and covenants, as well as the international meetings called to hammer out the agreements, form one of the bases of global interconnections. However, the rights vocabulary of universal guarantees has had a contradictory effect. On the one hand, the insufficiencies of the laws in practice angered diverse groups of women and other constituencies who pressed for wider applicability. Starting in the 1970s, these groups began to employ gender as a new category to rethink the foundations of human rights principles. On the other hand, human rights norms and structures emerged as lightning rods for anger over the erosion of elements of national sovereignty. The growing prominence of human rights standards in international relations and trade negotiations rallied regional blocs of power in opposition. These tensions are seen vividly in the intersection of gender and culture, which has emerged forcefully to vex the global human rights community.

GLOBAL PERSPECTIVES ON
THE GENDERING OF RIGHTS

Gender as a legally protected category appeared nowhere in the early language of human rights. Due in good measure to the timely interventions of transnational women's movements and key women activists, the principle of women's equality with men was included in the first international and regional human rights documents after midcentury. The norm of equality appeared in two distinct forms, and both measured "female" lives by comparing them to and against putative "male" opportunities and experiences. One came out of the international labor movement and sought equality in work partly through "protective" labor legislation, which was believed to accommodate women's dual roles as mothers and as workers. Special labor protection for women workers was designed to level the playing field with men in the workplace. The second was elaborated as formal nondiscrimination; there could be no discrimination on the basis of sex, which was a distinct legal category mandating equal treatment of men and women in all walks of life, nationally and internationally. This equality clause in effect enjoined the contracting parties to revise their domestic laws to eliminate discriminations on the basis of sex from political, economic, and social life. In the main, these norms reflected the assumptions of the privileged leadership groups of the early transnational feminist movements, which had been the most vocal in the international arena to date. These human rights formulas were gender neutral and it was understood that women were covered, as were men, in all the gross violations of rights that might occur in times of national crises or war (in the conventions against genocide, torture, and slavery, for example), as well as in the guarantees of political and civil rights. Formal legal equality, too, would level the playing field for women and men.

Importantly, these norms were institutionalized in international commissions and agencies and defended by a wide array of nongovernmental women's organizations as well. In the early decades after World War II, the UN Commission on the Status of Women, comprised originally of fifteen members, worked tirelessly to keep women's issues on the international agenda. It collaborated with the Commission on Human Rights and other UN agencies such as the ILO and the United Nations Education, Scientific, and Cultural Organization (UNESCO) to update information on women's status around the globe; supported regional rights organizations and agencies; and helped write a number of specific conventions pertaining to women's political rights (1952), to the nationality of married women (1957), and to consent and the minimum age of marriage (1962). The Women's Commission prodded the General Assembly to proclaim 1975 as the International Women's Year and to convene a conference of UN member states, specialized agencies, and NGOs to address the pressing global issues of discriminations against women. The World Conference of the

International Women's Year was held in Mexico City in 1975 and, later that year, the General Assembly declared 1976 to 1985 as the UN Decade for Women, linking equality with development and peace.[37] By 1980, women's groups had learned to use the UN system to place women's issues on the agenda of every world meeting.

This work from above was matched and sustained by organization and mobilization below. As part of human rights monitoring, the gathering of statistics by grassroots groups was revealing disquieting patterns on the ground. The reports of UN agencies and affiliates issued during the Decade of Women captured conditions of poverty, violence, and systematic discrimination that affected women disproportionately. By the mid-1980s, the number of "economically active women" worldwide had reached 700 million and was estimated to rise to 900 million by the year 2000. Women typically were segregated in low-pay, low-skill, and low-status jobs, yet one-third of the world's families depended on the sole income of women. Simultaneously, poverty was being feminized. A representative of the ILO, noting its tradition of protecting women workers since 1919, wrote dishearteningly in 1985: "Never in the history of the ILO had women represented such a formidable challenge to the world of labor as now."[38] There also was a startling rise in the number of cases of violence against women.

But rights abuses and challenges are never mere statistics; they are lived tragedies that embody the horrifying realities and courageous activism of rights struggles on the ground. It is out of these concrete worlds of crises—and the collective voices of protest, which are broadcast well beyond distinct locales—that definitions of rights claims and causes are broadened and transformed.

A powerful local force for such change was Las Madres de Plaza de Mayo, an association of mothers that emerged on the public scene in Argentina to rail against the disappearance of loved ones during the brutal military dictatorship and the so-called "dirty war" of 1976–1982. At this height of the cold war, the Argentine military saw itself engaged in a "total war" against communism to safeguard the benefits of Christian civilization, which, in its eyes, were embodied by the state. The cause of human rights, however, had just taken an important step toward greater uniformity in practice. In 1975, under the Helsinki Agreement, the Soviet Union and its socialist allies in Eastern Europe had pledged to respect human rights and fundamental political and religious freedoms in return for international guarantees insuring the territorial integrity of the socialist bloc. The Helsinki accord also gave rise to several prominent Western rights-monitoring groups, among them the Human Rights Watch.

It is not surprising, then, that the mothers' voices were heard in this case, which fit the model of what at the time were the classic expressions of rights violations: kidnapping, torture, and mass murder of men and women by a dictatorial regime. By bringing their private pain into the public arena, however, the mothers—perhaps more surprisingly—inspired new definitions of women's human rights. Their actions helped erode one of the fundamental assumptions of international rights norms and institutions to date: the separation between the public sphere (subject to international monitoring for violations of rights) and the private realm (off-limits to the international community as a terrain of abuse).

The Argentine military regime had proclaimed the inviolability of the home and the traditional patriarchal family as the bedrock principles of society. The mothers revealed the extent to which the regime constantly violated the home, making their roles as mothers and nurturers impossible. Empowered by a maternalist ideology, these women courageously took the lead in defending human rights and, in the process, mobilized motherhood, the family, and the home for oppositional politics.[39] Just as important, these mothers also came to represent the inadequacies of any so-called transitional process from dictatorship to democracy that failed to provide for women's full participation in the political life of the newly constituted democratic state. Their example has encouraged redefinitions of the bases of citizenship to highlight social rights and, specifically, widespread health and reproductive protections for women. Under an unfolding human tragedy from below, women from a developing country played a decisive role in shaping the international discourses on rights.[40]

Shrouded in secrecy, enforced disappearance left little evidence of the crime and no body at hand. This technique of terror allowed authoritarian leaders to preserve a façade of respectability to the outside world, ever more aware of the growing power of human rights norms and obligations to draw international attention to violence within states. The hidden nature of the crimes limited the possibility of international sanctions. In the struggles against communists and other so-called urban terrorists of the cold war era, military governments could even find support for their basic principles (and money and training for the armed forces), if not for the specific tactics. The Argentine "dirty war" turned the word *disappear* into a transitive verb. However, it was one of many such brutal internal wars. In the mid-1970s, an array of repressive regimes used the tactic so widely that the General Assembly took up the problem in 1978, turning it over to the Commission on Human Rights, which established a Working Group on Enforced or Involuntary Disappearances. While the group continues to offer intensified focus on the national cases of state-sanctioned terror, it also sees these violations as global phenomena and works with individual families from all geographic areas to help uncover the fate of relatives. Unable to intervene domestically, its clout is limited to the powers of publicity.

The new communication networks assured Las Madres high global visibility and, therefore, protection at home. In 1980, the mothers formed a delegation to the UN World Conference on Women in Copenhagen, testifying to women's intense political activism in the name of human rights and dignity. Indeed, their example has fed a global movement to define women's rights more explicitly as human rights. They showed unmistakably the growing power of the language of human rights to mobilize a large, vocal, and diverse constituency across the globe in defense of rights causes. Their actions have served as inspiration for lesser-known counterparts in Chile, Uruguay, Nicaragua, and Honduras, for example, as well as in Sri Lanka in South Asia, locked since the 1980s in a murderous struggle between the majority Sinhalese peoples and the minority ethnic Tamils. As the lawyer Radhika Coomaraswamy noted persuasively:

> In Sri Lanka the ideology of motherhood has been appropriated for political action, symbolizing the widows and mothers who have lost their husbands and children in the recent violence. The Mothers for Peace or the Mothers of the Disappeared, precisely because of their appropriation of the mother ideology, have found a great deal of political maneuverability which even politicians, caught within the same ideological construct, are hardpressed to overcome.[41]

Born out of tragic experiences, these political movements on the ground combine a family-centered ideology with the demands for the right to security and life, as well as to freedom from arbitrary arrest. In a similar exchange, the experiences that went into the writing of the inter-American human rights conventions contributed to many of the parallel formulations found later in the African Charter. These patterns of influence speak to and shape new global interactions that move along horizontal lines within the southern regions.

These new geographic axes of influence forced a reexamination of basic assumptions behind the concept of universal rights at the international level. On the one hand, ongoing globalization has created structural commonalities that continue to sustain a transnational political identity of "woman" with shared claims and rights in the face of systematic gender discriminations. This identity, therefore, promotes the coordination of women's human rights activities across the regions of the world and encourages at times its alliance with other groups of advocates for racial and gender equality, as well as for indigenous peoples' rights. On the other hand, globalization indeed has opened new fault lines both within and outside the women's rights communities around complicated issues of cultural integrity and diversity. These competing pressures of commonality and diversity dramatically affected the tenor of negotiations at world meetings in the last third of the twentieth century.

Undeniably, the need to confront the corrosive forces of globalization has encouraged an increasingly coordinated response by grassroots women's rights groups. The common denominators in the structural disruptions caused, for example, by global economic changes or the violent struggles for resources and power are readily apparent to groups in close and easy communication with one another. The global perspective demonstrates, furthermore, how intertwined and complex the disparate problem areas are in practice.

Since the 1980s, market liberalization has had a devastating impact on standards of living in general, eroding fundamental economic and social rights long enshrined in the international charters. In the industrialized world, these policies have threatened welfare and social services and created wide pockets of poverty (measured by hard data on health, longevity, and infant mortality) that resemble the conditions of life in lesser-developed countries. For the developing world, the effects of Structural Adjustment Programs imposed on debtor nations by the International Monetary Fund and the World Bank have had an uneven impact, making a coordinated response at international meetings more difficult. These policies "from above" have drawn renewed attention to the links on the ground between women's status and rights, on the one hand, and sustained development, with its premium on an equitable distribution of resources in a context of growth, on the other. They have shown that economic growth is unrealizable if development plans fail to address women's economic, social, and reproductive needs.

Globalization has increased the economic vulnerability of female and male workers and it has done so in gendered forms. As global capital moves production to venues it can control, it has created new, partly denationalized "industrial zones" and "global factories" in poorer countries outside the protection of labor laws and rights. As cheap labor, young female migrants typically are drawn to these manufacturing jobs in foreign-owned factories. At the turn of the twenty-first century, women comprised about 80 to 90 percent of the labor force in the new global factories. The resulting patterns of internal migration have spawned large squalid settlements, lacking the most basic social and health services, including sewage, water, and electricity. Inside the factory, conditions are unregulated and harsh—long hours and low pay in unhealthy, crowded venues. These kinds of conditions have promoted a new consciousness of rights at the local level. A concrete example taken from life in the global factory demonstrates the point. It was poverty that drew the Kim family to the Masan Free Export Zone in South Korea. Eun-ja Kim began to work in a garment factory there in 1984. "I am the oldest of four children," she told an investigator,

> My family was so poor working as tenant farmers that my parents decided to move to Masan, where they thought they would be able to get jobs. . . . Even though four members of my family work hard, we are still poor. Not being able to get out of poverty made me think that something was wrong. Logically, if four of us are working, we should not be so poor, but we are. I did not know how to fight for our rights until I started to go to . . . meetings.[42]

Eun-ja joined a local union and, as she put it, "learned that workers have the right to receive enough wages to support themselves."

In the new global economy, other patterns of labor migrations also involve unprotected forms of labor. For example, high proportions of women workers take part in the long-distance treks from poorer to industrialized nations for service jobs that are not exportable "offshore." In the developed world, pools of immigrant women work as maids in individual households or in manual jobs in hospitals. These seemingly different types of migrations for work—within and across borders—are but two manifestations of similar processes restructuring women's work globally. In still other cases, young men and some women from poor regions desperate for jobs have gone to all lengths to smuggle themselves into Western nations, where they work illegally. A sizable number of them have died in transit. The human costs of global inequality have reinforced horizontal linkages among organized groups committed to universalizing work and other social rights.

Globalization also has supported a new focus on the problems of violence against women. The global communications networks have made activists see the commonalities behind what were once regarded as grave but unrelated instances of violence: domestic abuse and sexual harassment, genital mutilation of girls, sexual slavery in wartime, forced trafficking across borders, rape, and torture. Local activists, who increasingly linked their struggles with those of others abroad, confronted the limits of both national and international law. Their day-to-day work made it glaringly apparent that human rights laws and implementation did not provide adequate protection for these types of gender-specific abuses. The omissions, then, became the impetus for sustained critiques of the gaps between the alleged universality of human rights protections and whole categories of human experiences left ignored. As the Argentine mothers so pointedly showed, the original human rights formulations exempted domestic family relations from the reach of international scrutiny and protection. In this way, from the bottom up, organized women's groups began to think about gender-specific violence. The same perspective has fed the parallel movement for gay and lesbian rights, as well as campaigns to end the sexual exploitation of boys.

The proliferation of local initiatives with transnational links can be measured by a rise in the numbers of female delegates and grassroots NGOs attending the UN-sponsored world conferences on women's status and rights. These international meetings became one of the hallmarks of the late twentieth century. The constituencies brought their new understandings to the international debates. In 1975, at the International Women's Year (IWY) Conference in Mexico City, 125 of the 133 member states of the United Nations sent delegates, more than 70 percent of whom were female. However, the potential for transformative struggle and negotiation lay elsewhere. Responding to growing transnational networks of private organizations, the IWY Conference sponsored an independent NGO tribune, a new international mechanism designed to both tap and create public interest in problems requiring global cooperation. It was the third such forum of this type since a 1972 global conference on the environment in Stockholm and has since become a fixture on the international scene. More decentralized and democratic than the official multistate conferences, these NGO fora contain a mix of workshops, seminars, audiovisual presentations, and entertainment, as well as speeches by prominent international figures designed to draw the attention of the global media to their many causes. For example, the NGO forum on women in Beijing in 1995 opened its plenary session with a videotaped message from the captive human rights activist and Nobel Prize laureate from Myanmar, Aung San Suu Kyi. The international gatherings of states and NGOs typically are preceded by regional preparatory conferences that help to facilitate wide participation and input, as well as publicity. Regional meetings in 1984 in Tokyo, Japan; Arusha, Tanzania; Vienna, Austria; Havana, Cuba; and Baghdad, Iraq, paved the way for the Nairobi world conference, which met July 15–26, 1985, to "review and appraise" the achievements of the UN Decade on Women. With changes in technology, delegates also are linked through preparatory "satellite" meetings. The numbers of women and men who attend these international NGO open fora on women's rights have risen dramatically, from 6,000 in Mexico City to 8,000 in Copenhagen to 13,504 in Nairobi (when 60 percent came from the developing world) to 30,000 in Beijing.[43] It is no wonder that such a movement toward inclusion also brought serious ideological and cultural tensions to the forefront.

Disagreements had already surfaced dramatically in Mexico City, particularly at the NGO open forum, which replicated, in feminist idioms, much of the anger, frustration, and competition surrounding world integration in the face of profoundly different historic experiences and memories, as well as unequal levels of wealth and power. The divisions mirrored cold war tensions and the gaps between industrialized and developing countries and regions. They reflected divergent understandings of women's needs, experiences, and rights, exploding any claim to a universal feminist discourse based on a single hierarchy of feminist reforms and strategies. In 1975, participants fought furiously over end goals, as well as the preconditions for change. Some groups, mostly Western and energized at the time by women's liberation movements, stressed women's oppression and thus the need for legal equality. Others, energized by the heady successes of national liberation movements, turned to the place of women and children in economic development, decrying development strategies that neglected women. In their analysis, social and economic changes (not political and legal rights) were the necessary first steps in the struggle for equality. In the heated debates, which participants themselves experienced as "chaotic," the groups learned about each other's organizations, differences, and commonalities. Ten years later in Nairobi, there was no consensus either, but none had been expected. By then, the global women's rights movements had been forced to accept diversity and "agreed to disagree." The symbol of this position of tolerance was a "peace tent," a safe haven set up to facilitate contact and dialogue.[44]

In the legal arena, the basis for common action had been established by passage of the Convention on the Elimination of All Forms of Discrimination against Women, the most important women's rights treaty in international law in the second half of the twentieth century. Drafted by the Commission on the Status of Women and endorsed by the IWY Conference in Mexico City, it was adopted by the UN General Assembly in 1979 and made the centerpiece of a signing ceremony at Copenhagen in 1980. By 1999, 161 member states had ratified the agreement, which called for changing domestic laws and policies to conform to its principles. Under prodding by human rights groups and organizations, international covenants and treaties have come to require substantive changes in domestic laws and administrative practices. The convention also dovetailed with global strategies for social change. The Copenhagen world plan, for example, singled out the key roles of nongovernmental and grassroots groups in the efforts to promote and defend equality: "Such organizations will serve as forums for women to develop self-reliance and enable them to access resources and power and shoulder greater socio-economic and political responsibilities within their communities and societies."[45] Eliminating "all forms" of discrimination against women was seen as one crucial step toward these important end goals.

The Women's Convention (as it is known) has two distinct parts. The first sixteen articles defined the conditions that were hampering women's full achievement of "human rights and fundamental freedoms in the political, economic, social, cultural, civil, or any other field." The second part established a Committee on the Elimination of Discrimination against Women (CEDAW), a monitoring group formed to oversee compliance by the ratifying states. In calling for an end to discrimination in domestic laws, policies, and customs, the convention established women's rights to property, financial credit, choice of marriage, education, and work, as well as to full participation in all aspects of political life. Significantly, it expanded the scope of accountability, holding states responsible for discrimination against women by "any person, organization or enterprise" (Article 2, Section f). In a new departure in international law, behavior in the so-called private arenas of economic and family life now became subject to international jurisdiction, as did the actions of private individuals and organizations—that is, nonstate actors. The Women's Convention bound state authorities to take effective measures to prevent abuses by private persons; in effect, it blurred the constructed divides between the public and private spheres of human life.

In an equally unprecedented step, Article 4 introduced a new vocabulary into rights language, moving beyond the principle of formal equality to an acceptance of corrective provisions deemed necessary to handle discriminatory practices specific to women's life situations. While phrased cautiously, the pathbreaking article supported passage of "temporary special measures aimed at accelerating *de facto* equality between men and women." Given the different life conditions of women and men, even when class, racial, ethnic, or religious contexts were taken into account, formal equality had failed to address the patterns of discrimination adversely affecting women as women. The article declared that passage of such affirmative legislation "shall not be considered discrimination." The Vienna Declaration, proclaimed by the World Conference on Human Rights in 1993, took the argument to the logical next step. It used *gender-specific* language in its efforts to establish equitable human rights standards. Effective lobbying efforts by transnational grassroots groups had assured the outcome. The Vienna Declaration addressed head-on "gender-based violence and all forms of sexual harassment and exploitation, including those resulting from cultural prejudice and international trafficking, [which] are incompatible with the dignity and worth of the human person."[46] It called unequivocally for their elimination.

These shifts in definitions of gender abuse have not remained solely matters of language. In the 1990s, for example, they appeared in rights claims before the International War Crimes Tribunals. For the first time ever, a tribunal adjudicating crimes in the Bosnian Wars (1992–1993) focused in one of its trials solely on sexual violence. In February 2001, it prosecuted three former Bosnian Serb soldiers for "sexual slavery"—the rape and torture of Muslim women and girls—and declared rape in wartime a crime against humanity. In earlier international law, rape was punishable as a crime against family honor and dignity, but it was not considered to be under the category of violence. Furthermore, these new conceptions have intensified struggles for memory and accountability, as witnessed by renewed international attention to the "rape of Nanking" by the invading Japanese army in China in 1937, and to the ongoing revelations about that army's widespread (ab)use of "comfort women" during the wars in Asia between 1937 and 1945.[47]

REGIONAL CULTURES AND HUMAN RIGHTS

The gaps remain wide between the presumption of universal gender equality and the call for its implementation and enforcement through changes in domestic laws and administrative policies. Under the Women's Convention, each state is required to submit a full report to the CEDAW within one year of ratifying the treaty and every four years thereafter. The committee analyzes the data and makes recommendations for greater compliance to the General Assembly.

This intrusion into the sovereignty of the nation-state through lawmaking powers has been met by vocal opposition from numerous sides. In postcolonial states, it has mobilized powerful memories of colonial domination, when foreign administrators used the powers of the law to abolish cultural practices they deemed "uncivilized" and "savage" (e.g., female circumcision). In the age of Great Power imperialism, colonial officials had stood behind the inherent justice of law. The South Asian jurist and human rights critic Ashis Nandy reflected sentiments among many scholars, officials, and publicists in former colonial territories, who are suspicious of legal traditions: "The law is the central instrument in the colonial process that aims at erasing traditions and plurality and restructuring civil society along modern lines."[48] The problem lies in the disjuncture between the customs and values in indigenous cultures and the colonial inheritances of the modern nation-states. With legal homogenization, reinforced by international law, Nandy feared for the survival of distinct local cultures. Furthermore, historically, notions of culture often provided an effective source of local authority and strength. For example, during the protracted struggles for national liberation against colonial rule after 1960, a defense of culture mobilized resistance and underpinned "new" political identities. Reconstructing so-called authentic cultural traditions helped to define the very groups fighting against colonial domination. In both examples, appeals to "culture" have served as a valid and viable source of political and national identity.

Neither "culture" nor the presumed impartiality of the law has been unambiguous for women's position in social and political life. Feminist scholarship has shown, for example, that British colonial inheritance laws in South Asia deprived rural ethnic Tamil women of customary rights to land and resources, and the process is duplicated elsewhere. Similarly, nationalist movements against colonialism in the name of culture—notably in the cases of India and Korea—turned against indigenous middle-class women's movements as "inauthentic" and "diversionary." In these liberation contexts, the struggles for women's rights often were dismissed derisively as Western imperialist importations. However, this polarized position failed to credit women's own experiences or incorporate their voices into the search for a new identity. In the case of Korea, ironically, nationalist movements against Japanese colonial domination and imperial Japanese administrators colluded in opposing middle-class and literary women's efforts at female emancipation.[49]

The tension between universal human rights norms and distinctive cultural practices becomes exacerbated when antagonists see the customary roles of women as integral to their own sense of national, religious, or ethnic identities. Efforts to change women's status are seen to threaten the national culture. Perhaps not surprisingly, the Women's Convention has the largest number of reservations attached to it of any international human rights treaty—reservations that in good measure undercut the letter of the law. Most are raised in defense of family (the personal status codes) and religious laws at the heart of assumptions about the specific cultural identity of a particular state. Bangladesh, for example, made the following reservation against Article 2, which calls for national legislation to insure the principle of equality between men and women: "The government . . . does not consider as binding upon itself the provisions of [the article and others] as they conflict with Shari'a law based on Holy

Qur'an and Sunna." Bangladesh was hardly alone. Various Islamic nations offered similar qualifications, while still other sovereign states—among them Brazil, Canada, and Jamaica—sought to deny women specific safeguards, for example, to equal rights in divorce, choosing a profession, or acquiring and disposing of property. By the early 1990s, forty states had offered more than one hundred substantive reservations.[50] By then, the debates had transcended the immediate context of the Women's Convention.

Since the end of the cold war, international human rights norms and practices have served as catalysts for interregional tensions over authority and sovereignty. Often framed in starkly polarized terms, these debates mirrored the tensions in the relationships between the Western world and other parts of the globe and, in particular, the historic legacies of colonialism.[51] The arguments mainly have taken two forms, both of which are dismissive of the existing human rights system as being Western, biased, and therefore particularist (i.e., not universally applicable). One is more easily identifiable in regional terms, pitting so-called "Asian values" of community against what was labeled an inappropriate Western model of individual rights backed up by force and arbitrary use of international sanctions. For some of the critics, human rights norms were tools used by Western powers to destroy the regimes opposed by the West. This position was fed by the reality of Asian economic dynamism in the global economy in the late 1980s. Articulated most clearly by the leaders of Singapore, China, and Malaysia, by the early 1990s, it was a force to be reckoned with at human rights and other world conferences.

The second strand of opposition has centered on Islamic contributions to rights traditions and the role of religion in rights discourses. It represents less of a coherent regional identity since Islam embraces such widely dispersed geographic areas in Asia, the Middle East, and Africa, as well as old and new immigrant communities in Europe and North America. But it, too, spoke for an "impulse" toward regional integration in, for example, the Arab Middle East.[52] Notably, the debates in Asia and the Middle East were from two areas of the globe outside the regional human rights communities formally chartered under the United Nations.

Mapping these arguments is extremely complicated. They involve multiple positions and complex, often contradictory motives. Thus, for example, Asian values have been used to defend authoritarian political regimes that promised economic growth because of social control and discipline at the expense of political and civil rights, as well as worker rights to bargain. Ironically, this position drew on a line of Western conservative thinking that, since the 1960s, has favored a "soft" authoritarianism for capitalist developments. Defenders of Asian values argued that international human rights standards—as Western creations—had no place in Asian societies. For their side, Islamic scholars claimed that Islamic laws formulated fourteen centuries ago were the true foundations of human rights norms, not Western legal codes. Both positions failed to adequately acknowledge the significant contributions of perspectives from the non-Western world in the evolution of international rights since 1945.

While running parallel, the arguments surrounding Asian values or Islamic laws contributed to what arguably are serious discussions about the nature and breadth of current human rights standards within distinct cultural traditions. The simplified and highly stereotyped terms of the original debate elicited considerable internal self-reflection and discussion, revealing a multitude of understandings about culture, religious traditions, and history. While, for example, spokesmen for authoritarian regimes in Singapore and Malaysia equated Confucian (Asian) values with statist authority and power, their critics argued that dignity, self-empowerment, and the collective rites sustaining civility and morality were central to the Asian traditions of good governance. The Western Confucian scholar William Theodore De Bary summed up the arguments well. Drawing on the writings of two important Chinese thinkers (the communist Lio Shaogi and the Confucian communitarian Lian Shuming), De Bary came to the following conclusion:

> Together, these values bespeak a Confucian tradition that shared with the West a respect of the person that is in no way incompatible with human rights. . . . Together these complementary values belie any claim that modern human rights conceptions are exclusively Western, culture-bound, and inapplicable to China or the rest of Asia. They also belie any claim that communitarianism in China (or Asia) can be identified with the authoritarian state.[53]

Who, then, *is* authorized to speak for a particular culture? What is the status of the speaker? These questions reverberate in the work of grassroots women's groups that also raise queries about who in the culture determined the cultural practices that were seen to require exemption from universal standards.

A similarly complex debate is taking place within Islam among scholars and activists committed to human rights principles and opposed to any form of religious fundamentalism, which, by nature, is exclusionist and dogmatic. If the debates over Asian values have complicated the seemingly simplistic divides between universalism and cultural relativism, some Islamic thinkers have challenged the secular assumptions behind the dominant formulations of international human rights laws. Nikhil Aziz argued that secularism itself can be intolerant and serve to obliterate the liberal aspects of religious systems. He also made the point that for many cultures, the idea that only human beings in the living planet have particular claims to rights and protections is threatening. Bassam Tibi had pragmatic considerations in mind in entering the debate. Committed deeply to human rights principles, Tibi recognized that they "still lack cultural legitimacy in most third world societies, including Islamic societies." He therefore advocated learning to "speak one's own language in a new way" to reinvigorate Islam with its own inclusive visions of dignity and consultative democracy. These shifts in emphasis, he argued, promote change within religions as cultural systems and work to break free from the limitations of exclusivity. "We are," he wrote, speaking for a larger group, "in search of something quite different from an intensified process of global secularization."[54] Within Islam, considerable debate also centers on the connection between religion and women's rights. In many places in the Islamic global community, women activists are asserting the compatibility of changes in women's status and family law with faith.[55] These intracultural struggles speak to the nature and extent of state control, to freedoms for women and men, and to competing understandings of the concepts of liberty, dignity, democracy, and community. As such, they testify to the dynamic and evolving quality of cultures embedded in the day-to-day aspirations, behaviors, and struggles of individuals and local communities.

REFORMULATIONS OF WOMEN'S HUMAN RIGHTS

The heightened climate of debate and critique peaking in the 1990s reflected regional challenges to universal rights standards. Equally concerned, women's transnational organizations began to see existing human rights *practices* in a more critical light. Partly due to women's constant international lobbying, human rights laws enshrined the principle of nondiscrimination on the basis of sex. Implementation, however, remained biased. The mainstream human rights monitoring bodies—Human Rights Watch and Amnesty International, among the most prominent—failed to address the specificities of women's experiences in the tragedies of rights abuses. The limited interpretation of human rights laws characterized the period from the beginnings of the human rights system after World War II until the conclusion of the Decade of Women in 1985. The large NGOs have since acknowledged these omissions, which had become increasingly clear to the grassroots women's groups in closer contact with one another from the mid-1970s on. Kenneth Roth, executive director of Human Rights Watch, New York, assessed the early implementation of the Covenant on Civil and Political Rights, which guaranteed every human being freedom from arbitrary loss of life and protection from torture or inhuman or degrading treatment. Arguably, domestic violence should have been covered. Writing in 1994, Roth admitted that:

> Despite the broad potential reach of the Covenant's guarantees, international human rights organizations . . . treated these provisions as if they applied only to the victims of politically motivated abuse (and even then only if the abuse was at the hands of a government agent). It was as if the sweeping language of these provisions—"Every

human being," "Everyone"—were replaced by the narrower phrase, "every dissident."[56]

Although disturbed by the possible dilution of the distinctive human rights causes into common crime issues, Roth has come to believe that international human rights monitoring must serve to protect women from the dangers and degradations of domestic abuses.

Since the mid-1980s, the reformulations encouraged by gender as a perspective have raised women's rights to new prominence in the legal structures of human rights protections and practices. Nahid Toubia, the first woman surgeon in the Sudan, captured a sense of new beginnings when she noted how "the language of women's rights as human rights moved very quickly into the national and regional levels at a pace that far exceeded that of any previous movement on behalf of women internationally."[57] This long-present but newly crystallized focus on women's lives gave rise to what some advocates call a fourth generation of universal rights (to be added to the political, social, and economic rights, as well as the collective rights to development and self-determination). These are the sexual rights to health care, reproductive choice, the integrity of the body, and sexual preferences, as well as to freedom from sexual violence—for women and men, girls and boys. The Sri Lankan lawyer Radhika Coomaraswamy made the case carefully in light of the nearly century-long work of advocacy on which these rights rest. "It may be argued," she wrote from the perspective of women's activism alone, "that women's rights are the fourth generation, radically challenging the private-public distinction in international human rights law and pushing for the rights of sexual autonomy."[58] Under magnification, this new rubric of sexual freedoms is comprised of distinct lobbying efforts from below. Coomaraswamy identified four separate regional networks in operation, although the division of tasks is more fluid in practice. In her schema, African and South Asian women's organizations are concentrating on women's health issues, including dowry deaths and the practices of female genital mutilation, while North American, Latin American, and European women's organizations tend to highlight the issues of domestic rape and sexual harassment in spheres of public life. The international group Women Living under Muslim Laws is confronting the power of religious extremism, which deprives women of fundamental rights in public and private life, and Southeast and East Asian women's groups grapple with the problems of sex trafficking and forced prostitution. Violence against women in armed conflicts knows no geographic borders.

Globalization is forged not only from above but also from below, as Coomaraswamy and others understand clearly. The cumulative effects of local initiatives shape international advocacy and the evolving face of the law. Still, they have their most dramatic impact on the life chances of individuals caught in the tragic nexus of poverty and exploitation. The case of sex trafficking and prostitution clearly demonstrates the multiple levels of operation and coordination that go into successful international advocacy in the global age—and the tensions that also exist over strategies and goals.

Sex trafficking was one of the earliest of the "social wrongs" that galvanized transnational women's networks, beginning in Europe already at the end of the nineteenth century. Agreements under the League of Nations made it an international criminal activity, but the practice continues to thrive in the face of individual and family need for work and cash, as well as ongoing demand for sex. The example of Alexia, born in Venezuela, stands for countless other women driven to prostitution by isolation, poverty, and the desperate need to feed her children. She tells a story filled with danger, deceit, and brutality:

> When I was a child, I didn't have a family. . . . I started to be used in prostitution when I was still a girl. The first time, a man raped me. When I was fourteen, I escaped prostitution when a man married me. I had a son with him, and I divorced him two years later. I had no other choices, so I returned to prostitution to get money to support my son. . . .
>
> I also was trafficked, too. . . . We were transported by sea in a little boat to Trinidad under very dangerous conditions. There was always the risk that the boat would capsize. We went without legal documents. We were allowed to take only our handbags. If we were caught by immigration, we would be taken to prison and remain there for five, six months. When we arrived, we were taken to an apartment, which belonged to the man who did the negotiation. We were forced to work everyday whether we were ill or not, whether we had our menstrual periods or not.[59]

After twenty years in prostitution, with the help of others—in her case, the Sisters of Good Shepherd Community—Alexia was able to find other means to support herself and her children.

Globalization has expanded the scope of trafficking and simultaneously returned it to international feminist scrutiny. Wide disparities of wealth have encouraged a new form of consumption in "sex tourism," involving wealthy men traveling in groups to poorer countries for sex. These tours, openly advertised in the global media, play on racial and sexual stereotypes of "exotic" and "docile" sexual playthings and sell sex like any other commodity. From these sex markets, traffickers have organized intricate networks of exploitation, luring desperately poor women and girls with promises of work to leave their villages, only to ship them to brothels abroad where, as illegal migrants, many are virtually enslaved. Alexia was one of the fortunate ones to have returned to her children at home.

The phenomenon of sex tourism came to the attention of several key women who were instrumental in the first grassroots efforts to organize opposition in the 1970s. This movement was rooted in Asia. Yayori Matusui, a Japanese journalist who spoke on the global media culture at the NGO forum on women in Beijing, offered this historical assessment:

> Another issue that made me aware of Japanese-Asian and North-South relations was the sex tours taken by Japanese men in the early 1970s. A small demonstration at the Seoul airport by young Korean women opened my eyes to a problem Japanese women knew nothing about in those days. Many hundreds of Japanese men were traveling to Korea in groups for sex.[60]

Investigating the tours, Matusui wrote an article, but the editor published only "some twenty lines." Even this abbreviated exposé mobilized women readers. Matusui then founded a small organization, the Asian Women's Association (AWA), which published a newsletter detailing the patterns of sexual exploitation. The newsletter circulated also in other Asian countries. The problem has continued, Matusui noted:

> Trafficking in Thai women is now an especially serious human rights issue in Japan. They are treated as sex slaves, confined, beaten up, threatened, and forced into prostitution. Some have been killed by customers, and some have murdered their exploiters in an attempt to escape and are now in prison.

The tour and trafficking networks extended well beyond East and Southeast Asia. For example, Dutch tours to Thailand in the early 1980s encouraged Thai-Dutch collaboration through an organization called the Foundation against Trafficking in Women. News of an organized sex tour leaving Amsterdam galvanized action on both geographic ends. Women's groups led protests as the tour left Amsterdam, synchronized by demonstrations in Bangkok when the tour arrived. Thai women, too, were ending up in brothels in Amsterdam. The new collaborative organization quickly became a force to be reckoned with in national and international politics. The Amsterdam group offers social and legal services to the young women who, if their cases became known to the authorities, had faced immediate deportation before any legal action could be taken against the traffickers. Its members arrange counseling and safe shelters; provide free health care, day care, substance abuse programs, and job training; and set up witness protection programs. At the same time, the group lobbies for changes in national legislation that would broaden social welfare policies, safeguard migrant rights to asylum and refugee status, and punish pimps and traffickers. The foundation is active in international advocacy and, notably, helped insure that explicit mention of sex trafficking was included in the 1993 Vienna Declaration of Human Rights. It also was a driving force in the establishment of the Global Alliance against Traffic in Women (GAATW), headquartered in Chiangmai, Thailand. GAATW works closely with other international agencies and NGOs on matters of common concern. Its own allies include the UN Working Group on Contemporary Forms of Slavery, the International Movement against Discrimination and Racism, and the International Human Rights Law Group. Their overlapping agendas make clear the difficulty of separating sex trafficking from prostitution and other forms of forced labor and, in the age of the AIDS pandemic, from sexually transmitted diseases and vital public health crises.[61]

As an international practice, sex trafficking poses a challenge to rights principles, specifically freedom from sexual exploitation. It involves migrant issues and, on the state, regional, and international levels, the need for policy changes in welfare, immigration, and criminal justice laws. In short, the magnitude of the problem is not amenable to easy solutions; success in one arena may spell setbacks in others. These contradictions have emerged in Europe. Growing publicity about the vulnerable victims has aroused public anger at immigrant access to welfare provisions, increased police surveillance of neighborhoods, and limited the opportunities for labor migration among, for example, Philippinas and, since the 1990s, destitute Eastern European and Russian women seeking work. Due to the fear that the women will be drawn to prostitution, it has become more difficult for women outside the European Union to obtain legal work and residency permits, thereby limiting their opportunities to migrate for jobs. Furthermore, the move to decriminalize prostitution in the European Union at the end of the twentieth century affected only prostitutes who were European-born or naturalized, in essence leaving non-European women even more vulnerable to black market exploitation. Decriminalization raised the stakes for women's groups like the foundation, which oppose all prostitution as inherently exploitative and degrading to women. For others, prostitution is a job just like any other form of work. These contradictory and diverse responses to prostitution, whether voluntary or forced, are an inescapable part of the ongoing struggles around human rights norms, legislative changes, and grassroots organizing in the global age.

Given the profound disagreements over issues such as prostitution among the many problems involving rights principles, how can there possibly be the basis for a *universal* set of rights? Throughout the century, women's organizations and groups continuously raised disquieting questions about the reality of universal rights in law and in practice. Increasingly, their struggles opened up spaces for international negotiations, arenas for multiple voices with distinct perspectives to be raised. They made feasible, perhaps, the very cross-cultural dialogues that the rights philosopher Bhikhu Parekh argued are necessary to realize a "non-ethnocentric universalism"—in his view the only valid basis for universal claims in the global age. The contentious nature of the debates, Parekh wrote in his assessment of the fifty-year life of the human rights system, demonstrates unmistakably that human rights are not simply "discovered" as universal expressions of what it is to be human (as attributes, for example, of a putative human nature).[62] Rather, they must be debated in "open and uncoerced" dialogue and, significantly, incorporated into international practice—they must become part of the daily calculations that inform the behavior of state and non-state participants at various levels of interaction. The turn to gender in rights issues is part of this evolutionary process.

CONCLUSION

The twentieth century represented a milestone era in the movement to internationalize rights norms and legal safeguards. Rooted in collective state efforts to proscribe *inhumane* behavior in wartime as well as to protect soldiers and civilians, the human rights structure after mid-century emerged piecemeal, as an ongoing response to a multitude of ills, crises, and brutalities continuously plaguing the international system, which remained unjust in its allocation of resources and power. It reflected the transnational scope of the challenges of poverty and uneven development, of civil and state violence and terror, of an unprecedented scale of labor migrations and of changing understandings of domestic and communal abuses. The new technologies and modes of communication developed in the century insured both broad horizontal contacts and effective vertical linkages. They helped sustain networks of transnational organizations, increasingly linked by a shared language of rights, which also operated in local and state settings. These responses from below directly impacted the work of codification at the international level, imparting a dynamic quality to the international system of human rights. By the end of the century, through membership in the United Nations and acceptance of its charter, most states across the globe ascribed (with reservations) to the principles and priorities embodied in international human rights laws and their institutional structures. Human rights had become one way to express—and also to resist—the integrative forces of globalization.

Critics have pointed to the limitations of both the laws and the legal discourses of rights for a majority of the world's population. Most people pursue their daily routines and collective ideals with little reference to legal traditions or recourse to legal institutions. For some opponents, embittered by the colonial legacy, prescriptive law itself is suspect, an alien Western imposition at odds with the diversity and vitality of local traditions. Others take a more philosophical stand, as do those neo-Confucians who stress rites over rights—the practices of integrity, respect, and mutual aid that are necessary to sustain social interdependency and collective identity. Elaine Scarry has pinpointed the explosive potential of rights discourses. Human rights language, she noted, "has legitimized individual self-hood." As a powerful force working to constitute identity, it has "not only protected but produced modern individuality."[63] The ferocity of the current debates about human rights standards in the global context reflects the diverse responses to the many claims concerning individual, family, and community needs. Human rights standards challenge the sanctity of the principle of national sovereignty.

Throughout the century, women's organizations across the globe worked as both critics of the limitation of the law and defenders of its potential to remedy the specific gender vulnerabilities of women. The Nigerian NGO activist Adetoun Ilumoka, overviewing women's contributions to rights activities, incorporated both a critical and an acclamatory perspective in her analysis. As she noted in the Nigerian case, it is the "language of freedom, justice and fair play," not simply the rhetoric of rights, that has nurtured women's grassroots movements for social and customary changes in local communities. She acknowledged in addition that the discourse of rights can be "a mode of naming a local claim and acquiring political space to advance certain goals and so be empowering in the struggle for social justice."[64] As social ideals and legal claims, human rights principles work in tandem with local understandings of justice, equity, and fair play. The historic record demonstrates, indeed, that human rights laws, institutions, and advocacy realize their protective and transformative potential only when sustained by a dynamic and popular culture from below.

NOTES

1. *The Human Rights Reader: Major Political Essays, Speeches, and Documents from the Bible to the Present*, part 1, "Religious Humanism and Stoicism," ed. Micheline R. Ishay (New York: Routledge, 1997). For the multiple meanings of such terms as liberty, privilege, and freedom over time, see Orlando Patterson, "Freedom, Slavery, and the Modern Construction of Rights," in *Historical Change and Human Rights: The Oxford Amnesty Lectures, 1994*, ed. Olwen Huften (New York: Basic Books, 1995), 132–178.

2. Jan Herman Burgers, "The Road to San Francisco: The Revival of the Human Rights Idea in the Twentieth Century," *Human Rights Quarterly* 14, no. 4 (November 1992): 447–477. See also Peter Jones, *Rights* (New York: Palgrave Macmillan, 1995), 96. For an assessment of the multiple political and cultural traditions that shaped the writing of the Universal Declaration of Human Rights, see Johannes Morsink, *The Universal Declaration of Human Rights: Origins, Drafting, and Intent* (Philadelphia: University of Pennsylvania Press, 1999).

3. Rights are, however, constantly challenged. For many human rights analysts and activists, the international crises in the aftermath of the attack on the United States on September 11, 2001, are about the place of international law and cooperation as principles governing the relations among sovereign states. Combating terror has raised the stakes about domestic civil rights and liberties as well. In 2003, most state members of the United Nations Security Council opposed the U.S. move to invade Iraq. The war, which began March 19, 2003, and the unilateral plans to rebuild the country are profound challenges to the UN principles of peace, international cooperation, and law. The twenty-first century, therefore, has opened with major contestations over international law and human and civil rights.

4. "'Jessica Speaks,' Jessica Neuwirth and Equality Now" in *Women Reshaping Human Rights: How Extraordinary Activists Are Changing the World*, ed. Marguerite Guzman Bouvard (Wilmington, DE: SR Books, 1996), 239 (italics added).

5. A truly global perspective deals with each geographical subset of the globe as equally provincial and does not privilege one particular fraction. For new thinking on this important discussion, see *History after the Three Worlds: Post-Eurocentric Historiographies*, ed. Arif Dirlik, Vinay Bahl, and Peter Gran (Lanham, MD: Rowman & Littlefield, 2000). Typically, I will use developed and developing worlds, recognizing, of course, that in a number of social arenas (standards of health and social provisions, for example), some so-called developing nations are ahead of some so-called developed countries.

6. Marilyn J. Boxer and Jean H. Quataert, *Connecting Spheres: European Women in a Globalizing World, 1500 to the Present*, 2nd ed. (New York: Oxford University Press, 2000), 215.

7. A. Pearce Higgins, *The Hague Peace Conferences and Other International Conferences concerning the Laws and Usages of War: Texts of Conventions with Commentaries* (Cambridge: Cambridge University Press, 1909), quotes on 51 and 75.

8. *The International Demonstration of Women for the Peace-Conference of May 15, 1899*, ed. Margarethe Leonore Selenka, trans. Emily Darby, vol. I (Munich: August Schapp, 1900), 17–29.

9. Catherine Hall, "'From Greenland's Icy Mountains ... to Africa's Golden Sand': Ethnicity, Race and Nation in Mid-Nineteenth Century England," *Gender and History* 5, no. 2 (summer 1993), 221–230, traces the evolution of an antislavery society in Birmingham into the age of imperialism.

10. Higgins, *The Hague Peace Conferences*, 209. The Japanese quote is found in Geoffrey Best, *Humanity in Warfare: The Modern History of the International Law of Armed Conflicts* (London: Weidenfeld and Nicolson, 1980), 141.

11. In Horst Drechsler, *"Let Us Die Fighting": The Struggle of the Herero and Nama against German Imperialism (1884–1915)*, trans. Bernd Zöllner (London: Zed Press, 1980), 147.

12. The discussion of total war typically is written from the European perspective and downplays colonial wars. For a different perspective, see Trutz von Trotha, "'The Fellows Can Just Starve': On Wars of 'Pacification' in the African Colonies of Imperial Germany and the Concept of 'Total War,'" in *Anticipating Total War: The German and American Experiences, 1871–1914*, ed. Manfried F. Boemeke, Roger Chickering, and Stig Förster (Cambridge: Cambridge University Press, 1999), 415–435.

13. Hugh Thomas, *Cuba or the Pursuit of Freedom* (1971; updated ed., New York: Da Capo Press, 1998), 328–338. At the end of the Boer War, for example, 3,700 miles of barbed wire fences enclosed forty camps for the white civilians and sixty for the black populations. In the German case, a retrospective study estimated that around 80 percent of the Herero and 50 percent of the Nama peoples died in the German military's move to conquer the territory. For Britain, see S. B. Spies, "Women and the War," in *The South African War: The Anglo-Boer War 1899–1902*, ed. Peter Warwick (Essex: Longman, 1980), 165–166, 174. For Germany, see Drechsler, *"Let Us Die Fighting,"* 151–160, 213.

14. A new literature on colonialism links the colony and the metropole as one analytic whole. See particularly Antoinette Burton, *At the Heart of Empire: Indians and the Colonial Encounter in Late-Victorian Britain* (Berkeley: University of California Press, 1998) and Frederick Cooper and Ann Laura Stoler, eds., *Tensions of Empire: Colonial Cultures in a Bourgeois World* (Berkeley: University of California Press, 1997).

15. Emily Hobhouse, *The Brunt of the War and Where It Fell* (London: Methuen & Co., 1902).

16. *Report on the Concentration Camps in South Africa, by the Committee of Ladies Appointed by the Secretary of State for War; Containing Reports on the Camps in Natal, the Orange River Colony, and the Transvaal* (London: Eyre and Spottiswoode, 1902). Interestingly, the fate of these two distinct colonial territories became intertwined in the world war that followed in 1914. At the request of the British government, South African forces invaded German Southwest Africa and ran the territory under martial law. In 1920, the new League of Nations turned Namibia over to South Africa, acting on behalf of Britain, as a mandate and "sacred trust of civilization," in the language of the day. In 1945, Namibia was placed

under the trusteeship of the United Nations but illegally annexed by South Africa. The racist policies in southern Africa became one of the first causes that gave rise to new transnational advocacy networks in the human rights era after 1945. I develop the patterns of transnational advocacy in my forthcoming book, Jean H. Quataert, *Advocating Dignity: Historical Perspectives on Human Rights Struggles and Global Politics, 1945–2005*.

17. *Report of the International Commission to Inquire into the Causes and Conduct of the Balkan Wars*, Carnegie Endowment for International Peace, Publication No. 4, Washington, DC, 1914. While called international, it was an all-male committee of Great Power delegates from the United States, Russia, Great Britain, France, and Austria.

18. I deal with the involvement of Red Cross national organizations in civilian war preparation through the case of Germany in *Staging Philanthropy: Patriotic Women and the National Imagination in Dynastic Germany, 1813–1916* (Ann Arbor: University of Michigan Press, 2001).

19. For an excellent collection of primary materials on the women's peace movements in World War I, see *Social Justice Feminists in the United States and Germany: A Dialogue in Documents, 1885–1933*, ed. Kathryn Kish Sklar, Anja Schueler, and Susan Strasser (Ithaca, NY: Cornell University Press, 1998), part III in particular. Also, Leila J. Rupp, *Worlds of Women: The Making of an International Women's Movement* (Princeton, NJ: Princeton University Press, 1997). A study that recognizes the politics and interests behind charitable actions is Eric A. Belgrade and Nitza Nachmias, eds., *The Politics of International Humanitarian Aid Operations* (Westport, CT: Praeger, 1997).

20. Despite Woodrow Wilson's key role in shaping the principles of the League of Nations, the U.S. Congress refused to ratify the covenant. Nonetheless, from 1921, the United States actively participated in much of the day-to-day work of the league.

21. Article XXII of the Covenant of the League of Nations establishing mandates is in *The Human Rights Reader*, ed. Ishay, 305. In the interwar years, colonial powers such as France with its universalist rhetoric spoke of the progressive role of labor in colonial settings, seen to teach the modern values of hard work. At the same time, French authorities refused to sign the ILO's covenant condemning forced labor. It is difficult to square imperialist rule with any genuine tradition of human rights. For such an effort nonetheless, see Alice L. Conklin, "Colonialism and Human Rights: A Contradiction in Terms? The Case of France and West Africa, 1895–1914," *American Historical Review* 103, no. 2 (April 1998): 419–442.

22. Carol Miller, "Geneva—the Key to Equality: Inter-war Feminists and the League of Nations," *Women's History Review* 3 (1994): 219–245 and Rupp, *Worlds of Women*, 36–37.

23. Covenant articles are in *Human Rights Reader*, ed. Ishay, 304–306, as is the Polish Minority Treaty of 1919, ibid., 307–311. Lutz's critique is found in Rupp, *Worlds of Women*, 213.

24. Among the important figures were the Chilean jurist Alejandro Alverez, cofounder of the American Institute of International Law; the Russian émigré A. N. Mandelstam, who settled in Paris after the Bolshevik Revolution; and the Greek expatriot A. F. Frangulis, founder of the International Diplomatic Academy in Paris. See Burgers, "The Road to San Francisco," 450–451.

25. Burgers, "The Road to San Francisco," 455–459. I want to thank Tiffany Patterson, an influential theorist on the African diaspora, for helping me sort out the transatlantic linkages.

26. This new chronology challenges the history written from the European perspective. See, for example, Francesca Miller, *Latin American Women and the Search for Social Justice* (Hanover, NH: University Press of New England, 1991) and, for the Pan-Pacific case, Angela Woollacott, "Inventing Commonwealth and Pan-Pacific Feminisms: Australian Women's Internationalist Activism in the 1920s–30s," *Gender and History* 10, no. 3 (November 1998): 325–348. Of interest in the same volume are the introduction, 351, and "Forum," 520–521.

27. Miller, "Geneva—the Key to Equality," 236; Rupp, *Worlds of Women*, 215.

28. United Nations Charter, in *Human Rights Reader*, ed. Ishay, 406–407.

29. In Helle Kanger, *Human Rights in the U.N. Declaration* (Uppsala, Sweden: Academia Ubsaliensis, 1984), 12–13. Different motives led to the joint proclamation. U.S. Presi-

dent Franklin Roosevelt proclaimed the "four human freedoms" as key wartime principles to mobilize American public opinion in favor of the Allied cause before the U.S. involvement in the war. For Roosevelt, human rights principles were used to oppose all forms of totalitarianism, whether of the Right (fascism) or of the Left (communism).

30. Found in Burgers, "The Road to San Francisco," 474.

31. Miller, *Latin American Women*, 198, and her essay, "Feminisms and Transnationalisms," *Gender and History* 10, no. 3 (November 1998): 571. Latin American political elites at the time were Iberians (and, hence, Western) and did not incorporate indigenous values in their policies and perspectives. This changed in the last two decades of the twentieth century, when complex issues of racial equality and indigenous cultural politics intruded into women's organizing and party politics. For these observations, see David P. Forsythe, *Human Rights in International Relations* (Cambridge: Cambridge University Press, 2000): 39, and Asuncion Lavrin, "International Feminisms: Latin American Alternatives," in *Gender and History* 10, no. 3 (November 1998): 519–534.

32. Best, *Humanity in Warfare*, 300–301. Significantly, the *Human Rights Reader*, ed. Ishay, completely neglects the role of the international laws of war in shaping the legal foundations of modern human rights.

33. For a detailed account of international criminal law from Nuremberg to the emergence of the permanent International Criminal Court, which was officially established in July 2002, see Steven R. Ratner and Jason S. Abrams, *Accountability for Human Rights Atrocities in International Law: Beyond the Nuremberg Legacy*, 2nd ed. (Oxford: Oxford University Press, 2001).

34. The full text of the Genocide Convention is found in *Human Rights Reader*, ed. Ishay, 421–423. An international panel, sponsored by the Organization of African Unity, blamed the UN Security Council, the United States, France, and the Catholic Church for failing to prevent the slaughter of 800,000 Rwandans; in 1999, United Nations Secretary General Kofi Annan apologized to the Rwandans for the tragic inaction of the international community. In the case of present-day Turkey, these debates over the Ottoman past are also highly contentious within Turkish domestic politics. Among other sources, see the exchanges between Armenian and Turkish scholars in *Armenian Forum* 1, no. 2 (Summer 1998), 17–137.

35. Saudi Arabia, for example, opposed the article that permitted marriage without religious restrictions; South Africa feared the implications of political and economic equality for the rule of whites while the Soviet and Eastern European bloc countries felt the declaration did not go far enough in safeguarding social rights. Kanger, *Human Rights*, 20, and Morsink, *Universal Declaration*, 21–28.

36. Best, *Humanity in Warfare*, 322–323. Humanitarianism is a complicated concept, which, as we have seen, has not worked against war per se but, rather, sought to "humanize" war by imposing rules on military combat. Humanitarian appeals, however, can authorize military interventions, as in the case of the joint military missions of the North Atlantic Treaty Organization (NATO) and the United States against Serbia in 1999 to prevent a humanitarian crisis in the Serbian province of Kosovo. They also can become pretexts for aggressive preemptive armed interventions, as seen in some of the justifications for the U.S-led invasion and occupation of Iraq in March 2003. There are no internationally agreed-on criteria for a consistent and impartial application of humanitarian action, either by the UN or authorized states. It thus has emerged as one of the most contentious—yet potentially promising—aspects of human rights protections in international law in the twenty-first century. For a good summary of what is at stake, see Richard A. Falk, *Human Rights Horizons: The Pursuit of Justice in a Globalizing World* (New York: Routledge, 2000).

37. Laura Reanda, "The Commission on the Status of Women," in *The United Nations and Human Rights: A Critical Appraisal*, ed. Philip Alston (Oxford: Oxford University Press, 1992), 265–303; and Avronne S. Fraser, *The U.N. Decade for Women: Documents and Dialogue* (Boulder, CO: Westview Press, 1987). The commission had forty-five members (as of 2000) and increasingly has specialized in women and development issues.

38. *Report of the World Conference to Review and Appraise the Achievements of the United Nations Decade for Women: Equality, Development, and Peace, Nairobi, 15–26 July 1985* (New York: United Nations, 1985), 125.

39. The literature is vast and excellent on these Argentine activists, including many first-hand accounts. See, particularly, *I Remember Julia: Voices of the Disappeared*, compiled by Eric Stener Carlson (Philadelphia: Temple University Press, 1996) and also Jo Fisher, *Mothers of the Disappeared* (London: South End Press, 1990). The mothers are not without their detractors. Some feminist activists argue that their maternalist ideology is necessarily limited and fails to address domestic abuses and violence against women. However, reports from international women's meetings since the late 1970s make clear just how powerful a voice Las Madres has been in establishing women's perspectives in rights struggles and in turning attention to the home as an object of critical internationalist feminist scrutiny. For these debates, see Lavrin, "International Feminisms," 524–527. See also Naomi Roht-Arriaza, "The Need for Moral Reconstruction in the Wake of Past Human Rights Violations: An Interview with José Zalaquett," in *Human Rights in Political Transitions: Gettysburg to Bosnia*, ed. Carla Hesse and Robert Post (New York: Zone Books, 1999), 240–245.

40. Long after the end of the dictatorship, Las Madres continued to hold its weekly vigils. Keeping memory alive is highly political and continuing to speak remains a way to confront the past and demand public accountability and truth in the difficult transition periods to democratic rule. As seen in the many painful debates over amnesty or punishment in countries confronting past human rights violations, memory also can help sustain a public culture that will not tolerate repetition of such flagrant abuses of power.

41. Radhika Coomaraswamy, "To Bellow Like a Cow: Women, Ethnicity, and the Discourse of Rights," in *Human Rights of Women: National and International Perspectives*, ed. Rebecca J. Cook (Philadelphia: University of Pennsylvania Press, 1994), 46.

42. Quoted by Seung-kyung Kim, "Women Workers and the Labor Movement in South Korea," in *Anthropology and the Global Factory: Studies of the New Industrialization in the Late Twentieth Century*, ed. Frances Abrahamer Rothstein and Michael L. Blim (New York: Bergin & Garvey, 1991), 230–231. For similar personal narratives of life and work in the global factories on the U.S.-Mexican border, see Norma Iglesias Preito, *Beautiful Flowers of the Maquiladora: Life History of the Women Workers in Tijuana*, trans. Michael Stone (Austin: University of Texas Press, 1997). These factories are known in Spanish as *maquiladoras* for the fee that the millers charged to grind corn into meal in colonial times.

43. Fraser, *U.N. Decade for Women*, 17, 58, 78, and 147; *Report of the World Conference*, 93–94; *Look at the World through Women's Eyes: Plenary Speeches from the NGO Forum on Women, Beijing '95*, ed. Eva Friedlander (New York: NGO Forum, 1996), xvii, 3–6; Manisha Desai, "From Vienna to Beijing: Women's Human Rights Activism and the Human Rights Community," in *Debating Human Rights: Critical Essays from the United States and Asia*, ed. Peter Van Ness (New York: Routledge, 1999), 187.

44. Fraser, *U.N. Decade for Women*, 210.

45. Ibid., 104–105.

46. *Human Rights Reader*, ed. Ishay, 461–468 for the Women's Convention and 484–485 for the relevant sections of the Vienna Declaration.

47. For the trial, see *New York Times*, February 23, 2001. Also Iris Chang, *The Rape of Nanking: The Forgotten Holocaust of World War II* (New York: Penguin, 1997). Not all victims can speak out. Chang shows how the cold war silenced voices in communist China, in Taiwan, and in Japan itself. It is only in the post-Tiananmen era (after the government massacre of student protesters in 1989) that Chinese immigrant communities all over the globe were mobilized to protest the actions of the government; gradually, they developed grassroots organizations and Internet connections and began to coordinate efforts to fill the gaps in the historical record.

48. As found in the essay by Coomaraswamy, "To Bellow Like a Cow," 43–45.

49. Insook Kwon, "'The New Women's Movement' in 1920s Korea: Rethinking the Relationship between Imperialism and Women," *Gender and History* 10, no. 3 (November

1998): 381–405; Mary E. John, "Feminisms and Internationalisms: A Response from India," in ibid., 539–548; Florence Butegwa, "Using the African Charter on Human and People's Rights to Secure Women's Access to Land in Africa," in *Human Rights of Women*, ed. Cook, 495–514.

50. Anne F. Bayefsky, "General Approaches to the Domestic Application of Women's International Human Rights Law," in *Human Rights of Women*, ed. Cook, 352. Also Rebecca J. Cook, "State Accountability under the Convention on the Elimination of All Forms of Discrimination against Women," in ibid., 228–256.

51. Not all opposition in the name of national sovereignty is rooted in culture. Indeed, despite taking the lead on many aspects of human rights, the U.S. government has refused to adopt important human rights treaties that it sees as an infringement on American sovereignty. At the turn of the twenty-first century, the United States stood alone in the West in favor of capital punishment, opposed the Kyoto Treaty on the environment, and unsigned the covenant creating a permanent International Criminal Court. Worldwide anger mounted, and in spring 2001, the U.S. representative was voted off the UN Commission on Human Rights. This confrontation between law and power was repeated in the Security Council in the months before the U.S. invasion of Iraq in March 2003.

52. Kevin Dwyer, *Arab Voices: The Human Rights Debate in the Middle East* (Berkeley: University of California Press, 1991), 12. Several distinct Declarations of Human Rights have been passed under Islamic auspices: the Universal Islamic Declaration of Human Rights (September 1981) and the Cairo Declaration of Human Rights (1990) adopted by the Organization of the Islamic Conference, which formulated the rights found in the Shari'a. However, these rights are for Muslims alone; although they acknowledge minority communities such as Christians and Jews, they do not give them equal rights and they do not recognize any other groups. These limitations to universalism are pointed out by Bassam Tibi, "The European Tradition of Human Rights and the Culture of Islam," in *Human Rights in Africa: Cross-Cultural Perspectives*, ed. Abdullahi Ahmed An-Na'Im and Francis M. Deng (Washington, DC: Brookings Institution Press, 1990), 104–132.

53. William Theodore de Bary, *Asian Values and Human Rights: A Confucian Communitarian Perspective* (Cambridge, MA: Harvard University Press, 1998), 146–147.

54. Tibi, "The European Tradition," 106, and Nikhil Aziz, "The Human Rights Debate in an Era of Globalization," in *Debating Human Rights*, ed. Van Ness, 42–44.

55. See the following two collections: Nikki Keddie and Beth Baron, eds., *Women in Middle Eastern History: Shifting Boundaries of Sex and Gender* (New Haven, CT: Yale University Press, 1992); and Deniz Kandiyoti, ed., *Gendering the Middle East: Emerging Perspectives* (Syracuse, NY: Syracuse University Press, 1996).

56. Kenneth Roth, "Domestic Violence as an International Human Rights Issue," in *Human Rights of Women*, ed. Cook, 327–328.

57. Found in Elisabeth Friedman, "Women's Human Rights: The Emergence of a Movement," in *Women's Rights Human Rights: International Feminist Perspectives*, ed. Julie Peters and Andrea Wolper (New York: Routledge, 1995), 31.

58. Radhika Coomaraswamy, "Reinventing International Law: Women's Rights as Human Rights in the International Community," in *Debating Human Rights*, ed. Van Ness, 178. At the time of publication (1999), Coomarawamy was serving as special rapporteur in violence against women for the UN Human Rights Commission.

59. Alexia, "My Experience, I Don't Want for Anyone," in *Making the Harm Visible: Global Sexual Exploitation of Women and Girls, Speaking Out and Providing Services*, ed. Donna M. Hughes and Claire M. Roche (Kingston, RI: Coalition against Trafficking in Women, 1999), 327–329.

60. *Look at the World through Women's Eyes*, ed. Friedlander, 91.

61. Siriporn Skrobanek, "Trafficking in Women: A Regional Perspective," in *Asia-Pacific Post-Beijing Implementation Monitor* (Kuala Lumpur, Malaysia: Asian and Pacific Development Centre, 1998); see also Lawrence O. Gostin and Zita Lazzarini, *Human Rights and Public Health in the AIDS Pandemic* (New York: Oxford University Press, 1997).

62. Bhikhu Parekh, "Non-Ethnocentric Universalism," in *Human Rights in Global Politics*, ed. Tim Dunne and Nicholas J. Wheeler (Cambridge: Cambridge University Press, 1999), 139–140.

63. Elaine Scarry, "The Difficulty of Imagining Other Persons," in *Human Rights in Political Transitions*, ed. Hesse and Post, 323.

64. Adetoun O. Ilumoka, "African Women's Economic, Social, and Cultural Rights: Towards a Relevant Theory and Practice," in *Human Rights of Women*, ed. Cook, 319–320.

CHAPTER 5

The Impact of the Two World Wars
in a Century of Violence

JOHN H. MORROW JR.

This study of the First and Second World Wars represents part of the constantly ongoing efforts of historians to understand and interpret the most destructive wars in human history. The re-examination of the origins of these conflicts and of the wars themselves stems from prior revisions of the perceptions of both and suggests that historians in the long run will need to examine and understand them as an interconnected whole, though not necessarily in terms of current conceptualizations of the world wars as another Thirty Years' War.

The major difficulty with the traditional dating of the two wars—the first from 1914 to 1918 and the second between 1939 and 1945—is the Eurocentric nature of this periodization. Prior to the 1990s, historians of the First World War neglected the global and imperial nature of that conflict, with its origins in the collapse of the Ottoman Empire and the consequences of that process in North Africa and in the Balkans. Their Eurocentric perspective prompted them to concentrate on Britain, France, Germany, Russia, and Austria-Hungary as the locus of the origins of the conflict, often demonizing the German Kaiser as the major precipitant of the war, as western cartoonists had done during the war. American historians tended to confine themselves to the wartime experience of the United States and its critical contribution to the Entente war effort, but without regard for or attention to the rest of the war.

This Eurocentric approach extended to treatments of the course of the First World War as well. The British and Germans have received the bulk of the attention of Western historians writing in English, with the French, Russian, Austro-Hungarian, Italian, and American combatants receiving a lot less attention beyond the works of the national historians of each power. American historians have concentrated on the military exploits of the American Expeditionary Forces, but this leaves the continental powers at a disadvantage because of language deficiencies, and often occasions the denigration of their roles in the war. Naval studies of the war concentrate on its sole major naval battle, between the British and German fleets at Jutland in 1916, and on the struggle between the German submarine force and the Entente and American navies waged in the north Atlantic during the war. Finally, in most accounts, the First World War ends with the armistice of November 11, 1918, and then the Paris Peace Conference, in particular the Versailles Treaty with Germany, in June 1919.

The earlier studies of the origins of the First World War have also influenced approaches to the more extensive and costlier Second. If one could get away with demonizing the Kaiser, then Adolf Hitler rendered the task of assigning major responsibility for starting the war in 1939 ridiculously easy. Or did he? The study of the origins of the later conflict has occasioned at least one fascinating volte-face. In 1961, the celebrated British historian A.J.P. Taylor published *The Origins of the Second World War*.[1] Taylor shifted the responsibility for the outbreak of the war from Adolf Hitler, whom Taylor termed a "typical German statesman," to the leaders of Great Britain and France, who, he argued, after wretchedly appeasing their German counterpart in 1938, had declared war on Hitler in 1939. In this view, Hitler was merely a supreme opportunist, who presumed that the cowardly Anglo-French western statesmen had practically encouraged him to dismember Czechoslovakia in 1938 and would surely not fight over the lesser military prize of Poland.

Historians often still feel obligated to discuss *Origins*, perhaps because of the influence, or notoriety, of the interpretation. The book undoubtedly left many a reader who lacked the necessary historical background and capacity for critical assessment convinced that Britain and France were the culprits who had done Hitler wrong. Yet anyone aware of previous German history, as the notoriously anti-German Taylor certainly was, knew that Hitler was not a "typical" German statesman. In fact, the word "typical" seldom appears in reference to Hitler in the still proliferating multitude of biographies of *der Führer*. His limitless aims of world conquest differentiated him from the greatest of his German predecessors, Otto von Bismarck, who upon creation of the north German empire spent his remaining two decades as chancellor seeking to preserve the peace in Europe. And if Hitler's goal of conquest of world empire ranks him with Alexander the Great or Napoleon, his demonic visions of annihilation and enslavement differentiate him from his Macedonian and French predecessors.

Taylor's book demonstrates the glaring shortcomings of histories that fail to contextualize diplomatic events in the domestic developments of the countries under study. In particular, Taylor omitted entirely the overweening significance of Hitler's motivating ideological demons of rabid anti-Semitism and *Lebensraum* in his determination to launch first a European and then world war to achieve his goal of world empire. Nevertheless, Taylor's work offers two caveats: first, knowledge of imperial Germany and the world before the First World War was essential to discredit his outlandish statements; and second, study of war and its origins, especially in the case of "total" war, requires a balanced approach inclusive of international *and* domestic factors.

American and British historians once tended to concentrate on their joint conventional and ultimately victorious war in the Atlantic, North African, and Western European theaters. Then Americans would turn to naval war and a brutal island-hopping campaign waged against the Japanese that ended in outright victory for the United States over Japan. Until recently, both have largely ignored the complex, often irregular and unconventional war fought in the steaming jungles and paddies, and mountain forests of Southeast Asia and the great expanse of East Asia that may have resulted in Japanese defeat but not necessarily in Allied victory.

Finally, Anglo-American historians initially tended to denigrate and misinterpret the significance of the war in Eastern Europe, the Nazi-Soviet clash, a conflict far more monstrous and bloodier than anything the western powers encountered. For decades after 1945, historical and popular opinion, in the grip of the Cold War by 1947, contended that the United States and Great Britain had played the major role in defeating Nazi Germany through victory in the Atlantic, the strategic bombing campaign against Germany, and the invasions of North Africa, Sicily, Italy, and ultimately Normandy and Southern France. Western histories of the war on the Eastern Front initially rested on the uncritical use of written and oral sources from the German generals, who exonerated themselves and their soldiers of the war crimes committed on the Eastern Front and blamed the widespread criminality on Hitler and the Nazis, specifically the SS.

Western historians often seemed determined to reduce the Russian contribution to the Allied war effort to a bloody footnote to their "Crusade in Europe." Of course the Russians suffered enormous casualties, but that was due to their mistakes and a "Russian way of war" that devalued the individual in particular and human life in general. In any case, without the invaluable contribution of the U.S. Lend-Lease to the Russian war, which included the provision of motor vehicles and other supplies, the Russians would never have succeeded in recovering from the German onslaught, recouping their territorial losses, and ultimately seizing Berlin and confronting the western Allies over Germany and central and Eastern Europe. Yet those earlier historical accounts that attempted to diminish the Soviet contribution contrasted ironically with the avid attention American soldiers fighting in northwestern Europe in 1944–1945 paid to the Soviet offensives. American GIs gratefully acknowledged that every step closer the Russians drew to Berlin brought them closer to the end of their struggle in the West.

Furthermore, the end of the fighting remains a contentious issue among historians. A number of them have argued that Eisenhower erred in not attempting to beat the Russians to Berlin. Others have concluded that seizing Berlin would not have altered the essential postwar division between a Soviet buffer zone in Eastern Europe and a Western Europe dominated by the United States. Still others have acknowledged that the Soviet Union's destruction of the bulk of the German military machine spared the lives of Anglo-American soldiers. Finally, any sensible appraisal of the conclusion of the war in Europe must rest upon the realization that, perhaps with the exception of Lt. Gen. George Patton, whose bellicose assertions about "booting" the Russians out of Europe have achieved immortality through the feature film *Patton*, no one in his right mind desired to prolong the most monstrous conflict in history.

Historical interpretations of the First and Second World Wars in the last quarter century and particularly in the last decade have undergone significant changes since the original narratives were written. Recent interpretations of the most devastating and widespread wars in history, each one the most "total" war in history to that point, when placed in the broadest possible global context, necessarily revise the historian's perspective of the wars as a whole and require the constant reworking of narratives and arguments. This ongoing process constitutes the lifeblood of history, occasionally rendering studies and interpretations long canonized in the profession questionable and dated. Such challenges to what have become canonical interpretations take time to percolate through the profession and the general public, and then only to find themselves in turn revised or replaced by revisionist approaches incorporating even newer information or perspectives. In this essay, I would like to argue for a more comprehensive and interconnected approach to both World Wars that incorporates the latest research in an effort to comprehend the origins, course, and impact of the two most extensive and costly wars in human history and ultimately to suggest new ways in which historians might view these conflicts as part of larger, longer-term historical processes.

Distant Origins—The Twin Revolutions

The two world wars represent the culminating point of the twin revolutions that mark the beginning of the modern age—the French and Industrial— which propelled Europe to global domination by the beginning of the twentieth century. The French Revolution epitomized the ideas of modern nationalism and popular sovereignty, and the French Republic inaugurated national conscription in 1792, as it resorted to the *levée en masse*, first to defend against invasion by the armies of the monarchies of Europe and then to spread revolutionary ideas through conquest during the wars of the French Revolution and Napoleonic era. By the end of the nineteenth century, liberalism had fragmented, and monarchical forces had harnessed nationalism as a tool to buttress their conservative rule. National conscription consequently became the rule, but harnessed to the preservation of conservative and reactionary monarchies like Germany, Austria-Hungary, and Russia, as well as to more liberal states like France. Great Britain alone did not resort to national conscription, as fears of coups and dictatorial rule had long prompted limits on the size of its armies and the English Channel separated it from continental rivalries and its vaunted navy protected it and projected its power globally in the quest for empire.

As the masses participated increasingly in national politics, nationalism became integral, exclusionist, and racist, as popularized social Darwinism encouraged different nationalities to perceive themselves as superior to others. With national conscription, armies had the potential to grow exponentially in wartime, as the summoning of national reserves meant that men from the ages of twenty to forty-five could wage war in the name of the nation and race. Victory was seen as essential; defeat would threaten the destruction of a civilization deemed synonymous with one's own culture. Generals were committed to offensive war, because it was widely held that only an aggressive offense conducted by spirited and highly disciplined soldiers who were willing to die for their cause could win decisive victories. The cause for all the Western powers and rapidly modernizing competitors like Japan was the defense of the nation state, and of the race and empire beyond the nation state. It was imperative that soldiers would be armed with the latest and best weapons that industry could manufacture.

The industrial revolution occurred essentially in two stages, or connected revolutions: a first industrial revolution in Britain over the turn of the eighteen and nineteenth centuries; and a second phase propelled by science and improved technology initiated in the last quarter of the nineteenth century. The first revolution, which dated from ca. 1760–80 to 1830–50, was propelled by the cotton industry and then railroad construction. It also witnessed the beginning of the production of superior small arms and artillery and overlapped the wars of the French Revolution and Napoleon, which provided a military market for the products of industrialization. In the American Civil War in 1861–1865, which historians consider the first "modern" war and the progenitor of the world wars of the twentieth century, the combatant powers resorted to siege warfare, mines, barbed wire, iron ships, and even Gatling guns, the forerunners of the machine gun. The Civil War and the three German Wars of National Unification from 1864 to 1871, which witnessed rapidly improving artillery and rifles, also demonstrated the signal importance of railroads, which revolutionized logistics. Governmental priority for military considerations in German railroad development, which reflected the power of the Prussian army, resulted in the construction of twin track railway lines on major routes in order to move troops, weapons, and supplies rapidly to the German frontiers, while French railway lines leading to the eastern frontier remained single track.

The second stage, which began in the 1870s, witnessed the dramatic expansion of iron and steel production, in which Germany eclipsed British leadership in Europe, and the development of the chemical and electrical industries, in which Germany seized outright leadership. Germany's highly developed system of technical high schools and universities, and the close connections among research institutes, universities, and industry led to the formation of the first joint research teams and propelled the new military and industrial power to the forefront of technological and industrial modernization.

The years at the turn of the nineteenth and twentieth centuries witnessed the invention of dynamite, the dynamo, synthetic dyestuffs, the growing importance of petroleum, the piston engine and the automobile, the airship and the airplane, and a feasible submarine. One can scarcely imagine the great wars of the first half of the twentieth century, not to mention modern economy and society, in the absence of the above inventions. Dramatic increases in iron and steel production, and in particular the development of hardened steels, resulted in speedy improvement of both naval artillery and armor. As the year 1914 approached, European industry, drawing upon primary products from the far reaches of the global economy, became capable of mass production hitherto unimagined.

The inventions that industry could potentially manufacture on a mass scale, especially new ones like flying machines, prompted speculations of future weapons whose destructiveness would lead either to the end of war or the end of humanity. British novelist H. G. Wells captured such prospects in two novels, *The War in the Air*, published in 1907, and *The World Set Free*, which appeared just before the outbreak of war in 1914. The first novel evoked visions of global air war waged by giant German dirigibles, Japanese powered kites flown by samurai swordsmen, and American flying machines that ultimately destroy the world in a conflagration of bombs, riot, and revolution. In the second novel, Wells foresaw the world similarly ravaged by nuclear war. In both cases, small islands of humanity survived to begin anew the struggle for civilization amid the ruins of a world demolished by the products of its own technological and scientific genius. Inhabitants of Europe, of Germany and Eastern Europe in particular, and of the Asian mainland and Japan experienced just such apocalypses during World War II.

MORE IMMEDIATE ORIGINS—A NEW CONSTELLATION OF POWERS

The study of the origins of both world wars should begin at the turn of the seventh and eighth decades of the nineteenth century. By the 1860s, two western European states, Great Britain and France, had already attained the status of world powers. Great Britain, because of its financial wealth, industrialization, and ability to project imperial power abroad through its superb navy, had established a global realm with its keystone in India, the "jewel in the crown."

The French possessed major colonies in Africa and in Cochin-China, or southern Vietnam.

In Eastern Europe, the Russian empire spanned the continental heartland of Europe and Asia and expanded its frontiers to the south and east, while the Austro-Hungarian Hapsburg Empire dominated south central Eastern Europe. The Ottoman Empire reigned over Asia Minor and the Middle East, with some territories remaining in the Balkans and North Africa. Across the Atlantic Ocean, the United States was locked in a bloody Civil War from 1861 to 1865 that would determine its future: either a united, continent-spanning great land and naval power; or two antagonistic regional rivals.

Diplomacy and warfare changed the face of central Europe where in the 1860s two new states emerged—the German Empire in north central Europe in 1871 and Italy in southern Europe in 1870. In both cases, liberal and republican attempts at national unification had failed during the Revolutions of 1848, but two decades later the most powerful kingdoms in Germany and Italy—Prussia and Piedmont-Sardinia—led the drive to unify their divided peoples in nation states. Two masterful aristocratic diplomats—the Prussian Junker Otto von Bismarck and the Sardinian Camillo di Cavour—guided these creations.

On the international scene, the newly formed German Empire, whose policies Bismarck shaped during his tenure as "Iron Chancellor" from 1871 to 1890, became a force for peace and stability in Europe, as he now sought to protect and preserve the state he had brought into being. As the power of the Ottoman Empire waned in southeastern Europe, Bismarck kept Russia and Austria-Hungary from warring over Balkan territories that he deemed "not worth the bones of a single Pomeranian Grenadier." He also remained relatively disinterested in overseas possessions in the face of increasing popular pressure to join the race for empire in the 1880s. For Germany, in the eyes of its creator, continental preeminence sufficed. Italy emerged in the shadow of Germany, for it lacked the military and industrial might and resources to become truly a great power. Yet future Italian rulers, imbued with the vision of the ancient Roman Empire, would aspire to and often behave as if Italy had already become a great power.

The formation of Germany and Italy within one year dramatically changed the international configuration of power in Europe. Great Britain retreated into splendid isolation from Europe and concentrated on imperial concerns; the French also expanded their empire after their defeat at the hands of Prussia; Austria-Hungary survived as a dual monarchy reigning over southeastern Europe; and the Ottoman Empire was ejected from the Balkans by the smaller states there and fell back on its territory in Asia Minor and the Middle East.

The Russian Empire and the United States, in a sense the flanking powers of Europe, expanded toward frontiers of mythic proportions: the Russians to the east and south, the United States to the west. The North's victory in the Civil War cemented the United States' position as a power of hemispheric, potentially global reach, with great wealth of raw materials and the industrial expertise to exploit them. The North American colossus could not only continue to fulfill the destiny of the Monroe Doctrine of 1823 to "defend" the Western Hemisphere, but also to project its economic reach westward across the continent and the Pacific Ocean. Shortly after mid-century, in fact, the United States had played a singularly important role in the emergence of the first Asian power to enter international politics—Japan.

As of the mid-nineteenth century, Japan had successfully closed itself to the rest of the world for the past two hundred and fifty years. Japanese rulers were watching the European penetration of China with great concern, as Russian, British, French, and American merchants approached Japan as a potential trading partner, but Japan, wracked by social discord and economic unrest, wanted no part of any of these "barbarians." American merchants and missionaries, however, believed that God willed them to expose the "unfortunate" Japanese to the wonders of Christianity and western technology through trade. Commerce would export "superior" American institutions to the Pacific and enable the United States to "fulfill its high destiny—the universal extension of the principles of American freedom."[2] In 1852, President Millard Fillmore ordered a naval expedition to Japan, offering "friendship and commercial intercourse," or, should the Japanese decline the offer, "severe chastisement."[3] American Manifest Destiny demanded friendship or war.

The subsequent visit to Japan of Commodore Matthew C. Perry's fleet of modern warships pressured the Tokugawa Shogunate, the military leaders who ruled in the name of the Tokugawa Emperor, to sign a treaty between Japan and the United States on March 31, 1854. American hubris and avarice, backed by the threat of superior force, had forced Japan into an openness that its statesmen recognized as perilous, but to which they saw no alternative. In 1856, the barbarians descended upon Japan, as Russia, France, and Britain demanded and secured similar treaties.

The internal struggles in Japan caused by this opening to the outside world ultimately led to the aristocracy's overthrow of the Shogunate in 1868. The new young emperor, who took the name Meiji, "era of enlightened rule," proclaimed the abolition of the Shogunate and the "restoration" of power to the Heavenly Sovereign himself. The "restoration" in fact looked to Japan's future, as the "young men of 1868" aspired to create prosperity through trade and industry and to protect national sovereignty by preventing further foreign encroachment. Ultimately they desired for Japan to become a great and respected member of the international community.

Over the next two decades, Japan's constitutional government evolved into a modern cabinet system through reforms based on French and German precedents. The Meiji government formed a conscript army and rapidly bridged the gap between Japan and the West through "modernization from above," by acquiring and emulating western science, technology, and industry. The Japanese state, after establishing a national bank and currency, stimulated the development of private industry, most particularly the future *Zaibatsu*, four great conglomerates that would form a financial and industrial nucleus in the Tokugawa era that enabled Japan to compete in the international marketplace. In 1889, a new constitution of the Japanese empire, based on the Prussian model, proclaimed the emperor as divine sovereign with the power to appoint officials and a cabinet independent of the parliament. On the international scene, the new constitution was intended to demonstrate Japan's modernity to the rest of the world, and signal the emergence of a non-Western power in East Asia.

The formation of the modern German, Italian, and Japanese states in 1868–1871 should be seen as the starting point for an analysis of the origins of both the First and the Second World War, as all of the states that would play critical roles in the wars' origins were now in place. All three of the late arrivals on the international scene would seek to revise the balance of power in their favor, often even against the will of the existing powers. In a state system of incessant international rivalry and tension, fundamental disagreements ultimately led to only one means of resolution—war.

THE "NEW IMPERIALISM" AND THE ORIGINS OF GLOBAL WARS

In the 1880s, the world entered the era of the "New" or "High Imperialism," in which the European powers and the United States further expanded their dominion over the globe. A "new navalism" accompanied the era of "New Imperialism," as American Captain Alfred Thayer Mahan's classic, *The Influence of Sea Power upon History, 1660–1783* (1890), extolled, based on the British experience, the importance of capital ships—battleships and battle cruisers—to achieve global hegemony to a receptive international audience. Not only were the powers contending with one another at sea, they were also confronting one another on land as they divided the rest of the globe among themselves. The world was becoming an increasingly volatile place.

The reasons and justifications for imperial expansion varied: the pursuit of raw materials and markets, geopolitical advantage accruing from the conquest of certain strategic territories, and increased national prestige. European states, and the United States and Japan, endowed with superior technology, naval and military power, and most fundamentally "surplus" population, conquered and colonized the rest of the globe, particularly much of Asia and chunks of Africa. Europe's population had risen from 190 million inhabitants in 1815 to 400 million in 1914, increasing its share of the world's population from twenty to twenty-seven percent, and the European powers threw their demographic weight about globally.

The "New Imperialism" sprouted from, and in turn enhanced, the racist nationalism prevalent in Europe and the rest of the Western world in the last quarter of the nineteenth century. In an era of the ascendancy of doctrines purported to be "realist" or "scientific," devotion to the nation state acquired "scientific" rationalizations, exemplified by social Darwinism and "scientific" racism. Humans were pugnacious and competitive; war, an alleged response to evolutionary pressures, became a biological necessity. Metaphors of "a relentless struggle for existence," the "survival of the fittest," and the "law of the jungle" now applied to human conflict. Racist thought asserted not only the fixed characteristics and hierarchy of so-called races but also the prevention of miscegenation (the mixing of the races). Fears of inbreeding with inferior races or possible conquest by them became rampant, while determination to improve the race led to the rise of eugenics and proposals to weed out its "weaker" members. Conquered and subject peoples became evidence of the racial and moral superiority of their conquerors, whose dominance stemmed in fact from possession of superior weapons such as armored ships, steam-powered gunboats, cannon, and machine guns. But the argument was circular, as technological, industrial, and military supremacy was thought to prove racial superiority. In the third quarter of the nineteenth century, such racism rendered nationalism more exclusionist within countries and national differences more exaggerated and supremacist in international affairs.

With the advent of the "New Imperialism," Germany, Italy, and Japan found themselves at a disadvantage compared to the established powers. First, the leading imperial powers already enjoyed colonial possessions dating from earlier imperialist epochs, which provided bases for further expansion. Even the smallest of western European states, such as the Netherlands, Spain, and Portugal, possessed the remnants of earlier imperial grandeur in overseas domains in Africa and Asia. King Leopold II of tiny Belgium personally owned the gigantic realm of the African Congo, which he ruled through his private company. Leopold's rule of the Belgian Congo, immortalized in Joseph Conrad's classic novel *The Heart of Darkness*, epitomized the potentially genocidal nature of imperialism. Between 1880 and 1920, Belgian atrocities—slave labor, plunder, the murderous suppression of rebellion, attendant famine, vicious practices such as hacking off the hands of children—depopulated the Congo by half, from some twenty million to ten million people.[4]

On the Eurasian continent, imperial powers ruled racially and ethnically diverse empires. The flashpoint where the Austro-Hungarian, Russian, and Ottoman empires met lay in the Balkans. With the receding of the Ottoman tide, for example, Austria-Hungary had first assumed administrative responsibility for Bosnia in 1878 and then annexed Bosnia in 1908, angering its Slavic neighbor Serbia and Serbia's ally Russia. Germany forced Russia to accede to this fait accompli, but Russia undertook a modernization of its army and industry that would provide it with the largest army in Europe by 1917.

In comparison to extensive and far-flung empires, the German Empire in the 1870s encompassed primarily Germans within its continental boundaries, with Poles in the East and Alsatians and Lorrainers in the west. The Germans had seized these western provinces from France in 1871 and were busy "Germanizing" them. The "Polish Question" and Germany's eastern frontier posed volatile issues, as a ninety percent Protestant Prussian population had proved unable to assimilate its Catholic Polish minority.

When Wilhelm II ascended the German imperial throne in 1890, the young emperor discarded the aging, cantankerous Bismarck and embarked upon an era of personal rule. An avid disciple of Mahan, Wilhelm was determined to build a German navy to challenge Britain on the seas. German imperial dreams of a "place in the sun" that would reflect German industrial and military might propelled the nation's drive for a navy and colonies abroad. The Germans gained colonies in Southwest, West, and East Africa, among the islands of the Pacific, and a small foothold in East Asia. In Southwest Africa, between 1904 and 1907, the German army, demonstrating that it could act as brutally as any other imperial power, annihilated the Herero tribe in campaigns that historian Isabel Hull deemed a precursor of Nazi genocide during World War II.[5]

Yet the Germans invariably confronted other powers who had already plucked the sweetest fruit from the imperial tree. German acquisition of colonies consequently did not slake their imperial lust; instead, it only whetted their appetite, as became evident in German dreams of *Mitteleuropa* and *Mittelafrika*, Central Europe and a belt of German colonies across central Africa. In order to secure a larger piece of the imperial pie, the German government inserted itself bluntly into Moroccan affairs in 1905 and 1911, prompting the British and French, who were equally determined to shut Germany out of Morocco, to band together and force the Germans to back down. The mutual resentment among the powers after 1911 convinced many observers that European war was inevitable. The Germans believed that they were "encircled" and needed to break the ring around them, while the British and French became equally determined to maintain the status quo.

Italian governments coveted lands in the Balkans and in Africa, particularly Ethiopia on the Horn of Africa, and Tripoli and its territory of Libya due south of Italy across the Mediterranean. Italy's first major venture in imperial conquest, the invasion of Ethiopia, ended in catastrophe, as Ethiopian soldiers, armed and equipped by other European powers, slaughtered Italian forces at the battle of Adowa in 1896 and thereby inflicted not only bloody defeat but lasting humiliation upon the Italians. In 1911, the Italian government moved to conquer its own slice of North Africa from the Ottoman Turks in Libya. In April 1911, Italian Prime Minister Giovanni Giolitti, who understood the significance of the Ottoman Empire for the peace of Europe, presciently observed that an Italian attack against the Ottomans might lead to a clash in the Balkans that would provoke a confrontation between the two power blocs and a European war. Such thoughts did not deter Italian aggression in September, and the successful war lasted more than year.[6]

By 1912, the European great powers were busily arming themselves for the inevitable Armageddon.[7] Arms races do not necessarily lead to or cause wars, and the Anglo-German naval race ended in 1912, when the British had clearly won. The German High Seas Fleet still posed a challenge to the superior Royal Navy, but the British planned a naval blockade of Germany to counter any challenge. The German government refocused on strengthening its army, the key to survival in the accelerating land armaments race with France and Russia. The ominous portent of a powerful Russian army by 1917 propelled some German leaders toward thoughts of a pre-emptive war by 1914.

Germany and Austria-Hungary confronted France and Russia, but the alliance system was not fixed at the fringes in 1914. Italy, although allied to the Central Powers, coveted Austro-Hungarian territory in the Tyrol and on the Balkan littoral. Despite the British government's close military and naval ties to France, British Foreign Secretary Lord Grey did his very best to appear independent and unattached on the diplomatic scene. Finally, the Ottoman Empire, its navy tied to Britain and its army to Germany, had committed to neither alliance, although Germany had been pursuing it.

The arms races and alliances were significant factors in the origins of the coming war, but the crux of the matter lay in the Balkans, as Giolitti had foreseen in 1911. Two Balkan wars in 1912–13 left the Ottoman Turks with a precarious foothold in Europe and a tired but triumphant Serbia confronting Austria-Hungary over Bosnia. The assassination of Austro-Hungarian heir to the throne Archduke Franz Ferdinand on June 28, 1914, provided the occasion for the ultimate confrontation between Austria-Hungary and Russia over Serbia, and, some historians have argued, the pretext for desperate German leaders to strike while they still had a chance in August 1914.

German and Italian aspirations for imperial expansion, especially German, had direct and immediate repercussions on the balance of power because of their location in Europe. The implications of Japan's development in East Asia for a global balance of power would only gradually become manifest by the turn of the century, as a Japanese army trained by German advisors and equipped with German artillery and a Japanese navy trained and built by the British materialized. Japan projected its power onto the East Asian mainland first against China's weak vassal state Korea, which a German General Staff advisor to the army described in 1885 as "a dagger pointed at the heart of Japan."[8] Japan provoked a war with China over Korea in August 1894, quickly crushed the Chinese army and navy, and signed a treaty in April 1895 granting it the Liaodong Peninsula in Manchuria and the island of Taiwan and securing Korean independence from China. Japan, to the delight of its increasingly patriotic population, had become the first non-western imperial power of the era. Within a month of the treaty, however, Russia, supported by France and Germany, forced Japan to return Liaodong to the Chinese and a year later the Russians occupied the Liaodong Peninsula and Manchuria.

The Sino-Japanese War launched a decade of rampant imperialism in China, which, in order to pay its indemnity to Japan, borrowed heavily from European bondholders. In 1898, five states—Russia, Germany, Britain, Japan, and France—seized or claimed spheres of influence including major ports, railways, and mines. These intrusions culminated in the abortive anti-foreign Boxer Rebellion of 1900, which troops from the Western powers and Japan crushed, then looted Beijing, and forced a punitive peace in 1901.

In 1902, the British, embarrassed by their difficulty in winning the Boer War in South Africa, emerged from their "Splendid Isolation" by allying with Japan. Both states confronted Russia: British India, over a volatile Afghanistan; and Japan, over Manchuria. The Japanese navy protected Britain's naval flanks in the western Pacific and Indian Ocean so that the British could concentrate their fleet in the North Sea to meet the growing German threat. Britain was tacitly acknowledging its inability to maintain global naval supremacy in general and in East Asia in particular. The alliance reflected Japan's rising credibility as a force in East Asia, tacitly granted it a free hand in Korea and Manchuria, and positioned it to confront Russia. Japan's inclusion in what had long been solely a European alliance system also symbolized the transition from a European to a global balance of power.

In January 1904, the Japanese government went to war with Russia. It severed diplomatic relations on February 6, its fleet attacked Port Arthur on February 8, and the government officially declared war on February 10. The Russo-Japanese War, like the American Civil War, foreshadowed the First World War as a war of attrition on land costly to both sides, and of naval battle epitomizing Mahan's doctrine. On the modern battlefield of trenches, barbed wire, mines, powerful artillery, rapid-firing weapons, and increasingly accurate rifles, both the Japanese and the Russian armies suffered enormous casualties, and the conflict on land bled in favor of the much larger Russian army. At sea, however, in the battle of Tsushima Straits on May 27–28, 1905, Adm. Tōgō Heihachirō's fleet obliterated the Russian Baltic fleet, sinking thirty-four and damaging eight of forty-five Russian ships, at the cost of three torpedo boats. On board one of the Japanese cruisers, a young naval ensign, Yamamoto Isoroku, who would plan and command the attack at Pearl Harbor in 1941, lost two fingers and was wounded in the leg. The war had reached stalemate, and the Russian Revolution of 1905 prevented Russia from continuing a land war in Asia.

At the request of both sides, American President Theodore Roosevelt mediated between the two warring powers, and in the resulting Treaty of Portsmouth of September 5, 1905, the Japanese secured the Shandong (Kwantung in Japanese) Peninsula and the tsar's rail and mining rights in southern Manchuria. The Japanese people, swept away with expectations of even more gain in this, Japan's first truly national war, rioted in disappointment at the terms.[9] The rest of the world saw matters differently; for the first time, a "colored" people had won a war with a "white" or European people. Kaiser Wilhelm of Germany, rebuking his cousin Tsar Nicholas of Russia for allowing such disaster to befall him, raised fears of a "Yellow Peril" threatening the world. The Japanese, of course, had long feared the "White Peril" threatening Asia. In November 1905, the Japanese government reduced Korea to a protectorate and annexed Korea in August 1910 as a colony.

Nevertheless, as relentlessly as the Japanese strove for equality with the Western powers, they found that status elusive in an era of rampant racism because whatever their achievements, they could not become white. The British might recognize the Japanese as allies out of necessity, but Britain's offshoots and trading partners—the United States, Australia, and Canada—faced Japan in the Pacific, and all three states held rabidly racist attitudes towards Asians and sought to exclude them or at least limit their immigration.

Such racist attitudes posed an ominous portent for the future of Western relations with Japan, as the impact of American racism upon its domestic and international policy toward the Japanese demonstrated.[10] Japan's newly won pre-eminence in Asia combined with American domestic hysteria over substantial Japanese immigration to California from 1891 to 1914 to increase American racist fears and deeds. To "navalist" Alfred Thayer Mahan, the Pacific Ocean, particularly the giant China market, offered the critical future arena for American expansion of trade and colonial empire. Japan, now the dominant regional power in Asia, posed the most immediate challenge to that prospect. Japanese naval leaders, rabid disciples of Mahan and mirroring their American counterparts, concluded that the United States' imperialism would ultimately lead to a Japanese-American naval clash.

Confrontations in Hawaii over the rights of the substantial numbers of Japanese immigrants in the islands led Mahan, who feared an influx of Asians in Hawaii and the United States, to declare that the controversy was the "preliminary skirmish" in a coming "great" and "inevitable" struggle between the civilizations of East and West. A U.S. Naval War College study in 1897 raised the possibility of war with Japan, while in 1898, with the Spanish-American War, the United States annexed Hawaii, and acquired the Philippines and Guam in the western Pacific.

The California legislature passed laws discriminating against Japanese immigrants in 1906 and 1913, thereby violating an equal treatment clause in the Japanese-American Treaty of 1894 and prompting vigorous protests from Japan, which in turn triggered anti-Asian riots and war scares in the United States. While Mahan railed about the "Yellow Peril" and the threat that immigration would render the United States "west of the Rocky Mountains . . . Japanese or Asiatic," President Theodore Roosevelt requested a war plan against the Japanese. Navy planners obliged by conceiving the first War Plan Orange, which envisaged a Blue (United States)–Orange (Japan) war scenario. Edward S. Miller, author of the authoritative history of War Plan Orange, concluded, "[t]he legacy of the bigotry of 1906 was profound because it set the United States to planning war against Japan."[11] Many Japanese naval officers correctly perceived the visit of Roosevelt's "Great White Fleet" of sixteen battleships during a world cruise as thinly veiled intimidation, and Japanese imperial defense policy and fleet exercises of 1907–1908 postulated the United States as the hypothetical enemy.

American naval planners assumed that the United States would fight Japan to preserve policies of Japanese exclusion in the United States, the Monroe Doctrine, and the Open Door in China, and that the Japanese desired to dominate the Western Pacific and prevent American military intervention in China. By 1911, American planners postulated that Japan would attack America's Pacific islands and overrun the Pacific in order to further its aims in Manchuria. Accordingly, War Plan Orange provided a potential American riposte through the Central Pacific, recapturing the islands, then annihilating the Japanese fleet in a major battle, and strangling Japan through naval blockade. Mahan recognized that the balance of power in Asia rested on the balance of power in Europe, and a withdrawal of European navies from the Western Pacific in the event of a European war would leave Japan and the United States confronting one another across the Pacific.

In the grips of another war scare and during further naval planning in 1914, Mahan warned the new assistant secretary of the navy, his "apt pupil" Franklin Delano Roosevelt, of the danger of war with an expansionist Japan. President Woodrow Wilson, angered at the plotting for war that undermined his stand on neutrality, shut down the planning and muzzled naval officers, including Mahan, who died on December 1, 1914. The damage, however, had been done: the naval officers' postulation of the roots of a Pacific war in a Japanese national character, which in fact constituted a mirror image of American qualities, persisted until war in 1941 confirmed it.

Both Germany and Japan experienced a rapid modernization and rise to international power that left traditional elites in power internally and undermined the international balance of power by threatening the status quo. In both cases, the powers that benefited from the current status quo—in particular Great Britain, France, and the United States—refused to accommodate the revisionist powers. Only war could resolve such a confrontation. In 1914, when war began as Germany, hoping to pre-empt the rise of Russian power in the East, contested the balance of power against its European rivals globally, American naval officers anticipated a war with Japan. The Japanese had proved themselves prepared to risk challenging "superior" powers to war, willing to strike pre-emptively to gain an advantage, and adept at winning. By 1914, the state of Japanese-American relations clearly indicated an ominous future in the Pacific. Yet certain cultural movements in Europe and Asia also presaged an even more unstable and menacing future world beyond the origins of the war of 1914.

The race for overseas empire, the major form of imperialism at the turn of the century, co-existed with another ideology of imperialism, one more inchoate and recent, but which had the potential to disrupt further the European and Asian continents. The "Pan" movements that emerged in the late nineteenth century challenged traditional monarchist great power relationships. European "Continental" imperialisms, Pan-Germanism and Pan-Slavism, in their determination to unite all ethnic Germans in one state and all Slavs under Russian leadership respectively, would destroy the status quo in central and eastern Europe because they postulated eternal conflict between Teuton and Slav. These "Pan" movements formulated their ideals in opposition to the "West" and emphasized the mythic, the cultural, and even the philosophical dimensions of national bonds that transcended existing political boundaries in an ideological effort to create a greater union capable of competing in international politics.[12] The Pan-Germans, more ominously, adopted anti-Semitism after 1908, a step which portended the rabid movement that would emerge full-blown with defeat and revolution in Germany and Austria in 1918–19 and become one of the forerunners of the Nazi movement.

Yet a third Pan-movement appeared which historians have tended to ignore in comparison to the two European continental imperialisms. Pan-Asianism differed from the European "Pan" movements because it prominently included the island nation of Japan. Its early proponents before the turn of the twentieth century imagined an Asian civilization of the past that excelled in culture and philosophy, in contrast to a materialist, individualist, and soulless Western civilization. This initial ideology evolved in two different if related directions, and became more specific in its definition. The first emphasized Sino-Japanese cultural and racial solidarity and advocated that the two "stand together against the arch-enemy of the white race."[13] The second strand, however, was directly linked to the rise of Japan as a military and industrial power. Japan would build its military power and encourage its Asian neighbors to reform themselves in order to withstand the Western onslaught. If the Asian countries refused Japanese entreaties, Japan would use force to compel them to modernize. Japan's "civilizing mission" would thus forge "Asia for the Asians," but in the same brutal and exploitative manner as the Europeans and Americans treated peoples they deemed "lesser races." The "Pan" movements birthed cultural attitudes that looked beyond what would become the First World War to a second and greater conflict.

In conclusion, both of the coming world wars would be wars waged for empire, wars of increasingly global scope in the age of "New" or "High" imperialism, which the warring powers waged with large conscript armies armed with the latest weapons that scientific, technological, and industrial societies could manufacture en masse.

THE FIRST WORLD WAR

Understanding the First and Second World Wars requires not only a comprehensive global approach to the wars, their origins and aftermaths, but also the intertwined discussion of the fighting and home fronts; in the case of the latter, the domestic factors—political, military, social and cultural, economic—that affected the prosecution of the war in the various combatant nations. Scientific and technological developments also figured prominently in prewar expectations and wartime conduct.

In 1914, the world was truly Eurocentric, as Europe reigned as the economic and cultural center of the world and physically dominated the rest of the globe through the imperial possessions of European powers large and small. Europeans, convinced of their superiority in all realms biological, cultural, technological, industrial, and military, logically could, and did anticipate their continued global pre-eminence for the foreseeable future. Then, in a fit of hubris, they shattered their global domination in two world wars between 1914 and 1945.

Rather than the time-worn notion that European statesmen and soldiers presumed in 1914 that they were embarking on a short war of at most six months, a significant number of them understood that they might be risking a leap into a cauldron of violence that would consume them all. They took that risk almost cavalierly and unleashed a monstrous conflict that endured four and a half years, consumed inconceivable amounts of European and global blood and treasure, destroyed the fabric of Europe as it had existed for a hundred years, and precipitated revolution, collapse, and smaller conflicts in Europe and elsewhere.

The First World War began and ended as a global conflict that imperial powers waged with their armies and navies in Europe, Africa, the Middle East, and Asia, and on the oceans of the world.[14] The European powers relied on their colonial possessions for men and materials for military service and industrial labor as they mobilized their societies and imperial possessions for global war. The balance of power from the start weighed against the Central Powers and in favor of the Entente. Germany was supported by two—Austria-Hungary and the Ottoman Empire—and later three, with Bulgaria, much weaker powers. Germany's army, navy, and industry had to carry its allies, who could contribute manpower and some industry in the case of Austria-Hungary, but little else. In the crucial realm of food and raw materials, the strongest of the Central Powers, Germany and Austria-Hungary, became the most vulnerable to blockade, and thus potentially the weakest of the major powers.

The Entente comprised the strongest financial, commercial, imperial, and naval power in Great Britain, the largest and most populated in Russia, and in France the second strongest imperial power with the best airplane and aero-engine industry. The Anglo-French combination endowed the Entente with a solid nucleus that could draw on its empires as inexhaustible sources of manpower, raw materials, and agricultural products. Russia added an immense threat in the east, and Italy later contributed a diversion in the south. When Russia collapsed, the United States—the Entente's financial, commercial, industrial, and material reservoir—became its salvation, the ultimate source of manpower for victory.

The superlative German army sustained the alliance of Central Powers against a world of enemies, and German offensives in 1914 positioned it beyond German borders for the rest of the war. Certain critical factors, however, that undergirded military power began to offset these advantages as the war dragged on. Governments mobilized, haphazardly at first, the home front in order to continue the conflict. They secured supplies and raw materials, while industries refocused on the manufacture of supplies for the military, or shrank and closed. The enormous wastage of men and materiel at the front often threatened to outpace conscription and production.[15]

To replace the millions of men inducted into mass armies, government and industry drew on additional labor, from women and youth to prisoners-of-war and men from the colonies for industry and agriculture. Women not only assumed critical roles in the domestic war economy of the primary European combatants and the United States, they also fought the frontline war in Russia. Women of the working classes had always worked, either in the textile industry or domestic labor, but now they replaced men in metal working and war industries, in jobs that paid better—if less than men in comparable positions—than their previous work. Wartime work also posed severe dangers to their health from long hours of hazardous work, assembly line and factory accidents, and toxic fumes from the chemicals in explosives. Women also played important roles in labor demonstrations and revolutionary movements across Europe and in Russia and Italy in particular. Middle class women, who had not worked prior to the war as a reflection of their bourgeois status, assumed managerial positions over working class women in industry or took work in the service professions. Wartime governments showered them with accolades about winning the war with their work, but invariably assumed that at the end of the war the women should return home and relinquish their work to their men returning from the war. Most women did exactly that, but many, in France in particular remained in the industrial labor force because of the high casualties, while others assumed secretarial positions in the business sector. The British government did accord women over thirty the right to vote in return for women's wartime service, but only because the men calculated that women of that age would be married and vote as their men did. Women in Weimar Germany and Soviet Russia gained the right to vote, but France did not grant women the vote until after World War II.[16]

With women at work and men at war, male youth in particular now earned their own money and could spend it and their free time without the usual adult constraints. As a consequence, juvenile delinquency rose in all the combatant countries. Wartime conditions also led to the loosening of sexual mores, and in western countries such as Britain and France, where lower class women worked in factories with men of color from the colonies, the governments attempted in vain to keep these two groups, which were thought by arbiters of morality in Europe to be highly sexed, from interacting, in particular because such contact could undermine the racial and sexual hierarchy in the colonies. Mobilization of women and workers and soldiers drawn from the colonies thus entailed risks to the imperial social order at home and abroad. Mobilization also extended to many representatives of high and popular culture, from intellectuals and professors to cartoonists and poster artists, who were put in charge of the propaganda designed to sustain mass participation in the war effort. The capacity of the empire-nations of the great powers to mobilize at all of these levels made possible the lengthy battles of attrition that resulted in unimaginable levels of casualties on all fronts through four years of conflict.

The nature of warfare, of siege-like battles that endured for months, took its toll on the combatants. The German terms for this new warfare, "*Materialschlacht*" and "*Verwüstungsschlacht*," a battle of material and devastation, captured the horrific nature of war predicated on the massive slaughter of men and the devastation of territory. Like some metal monster, or "Great Sausage Machine," as British troops referred to the Western Front, the war seemed to develop a life of its own, feeding on the bodies of men. Such expressions or images wrongly remove responsibility from decision-makers, as if technological demands robbed them of their free will. Technology may create certain imperatives or options, but it does not possess agency. Humans do, and they developed and exploited technology in the attempt to win the war.

British and American historians still debate who won the war in 1918, whether the British led the charge to victory or American men and arms determined the outcome of the war. Certainly the British forces and the Canadian Corps performed well in the Hundred Days campaign. The inexperienced American Expeditionary Force (AEF) did obtain its objectives fighting through difficult terrain, but the American force's greatest contribution lay in its effect on the German High Command. Gen. Erich Ludendorff began his major offensives in March 1918 in a vain attempt to forestall the arrival of the American army; and then the rapidly increasing numbers of American soldiers in 1918 made it clear that Germany could not win a prolonged war. Ironically, the French army played a significant if often overlooked role from 1914 through 1918. First, it held the Germans on the Western Front nearly alone through the middle of 1916. Then, despite its near collapse into mutiny in the spring of 1917, it revived under the leadership of Gen. Philippe Pétain to hold the center of the front as the link between the British and Americans in 1918. The essence of Allied Commander-in-Chief Ferdinand Foch's plan to defeat Germany lay in the power of simultaneous or consecutive offensives by all three armies to wear down the German army and give it no respite in which to recover. The French army, with its African and elite corps as spearheads, held the longest front and suffered the most casualties of the Western allies, and not only endured, but advanced to the end of the war. Foch was right—forcing the German army on the defensive and pushing it back toward the German border required the coordinated offensives of all three powers, and no one or two could have succeeded without the others.

The naval war of 1914–1918 pales in comparison with that of the clash of armies, but the conflict on the seas was genuinely global in scope and, in the case of the German submarine campaign against Britain, it had the potential to affect the outcome of the war.[17] The naval battle of Jutland in 1916 proved to be the only major encounter between the British and German surface fleets during the entire war. The Germans' superior vessels and naval technology enabled them to take a greater toll of the British ships, but the much larger British fleet remained dominant in the North Sea for the duration of the war.

The rise of the German submarine menace and unrestricted submarine warfare against commerce, in particular the attempt to bring Britain to its knees in 1917, demonstrated the importance of the undersea weapon, which had received relatively little attention during the prewar concentration on battleships. Ultimately, the Germans could never build sufficient submarines to blockade Britain, especially once the Royal Navy, at the insistence of civilians and junior naval officers, instituted Atlantic convoys. The war against commercial shipping waged by German submarines and surface raiders ranged across the global seas and was so effective in the Mediterranean that the British navy required the significant assistance of Japanese escort vessels. The latter had already played a critical role in protecting British imperial convoys in the Pacific. A small naval air war raged over the Channel and the North Sea between British flying boats and German floatplanes, while the British were already experimenting with the concept of naval aircraft carriers that could fly planes off their decks.

The demands of war hastened the progress of military technology, particularly in the realms of aviation and armor. The wartime evolution of reliable airframes, engines, and metal aircraft construction rendered the airplane an effective weapon of war and prepared the foundation for the rise of commercial aviation after the war.[18] The tank, essentially an armored and armed tractor, even in its rudimentary state, provided much needed support for attacking infantry from its introduction in 1916 through the end of the war. The introduction of flame-throwers, light machine guns, mortars, and small caliber cannon tremendously enhanced the firepower of the infantry. German introduction of gas warfare proved deadly in 1915, although gas proved difficult to control from the outset. The rapid allied response in kind, the development of increasingly effective gas masks, and improved troop discipline in response to gas attacks gradually reduced losses to the increasingly potent chemical mixtures that the combatants propelled at one another. Hence gas became primarily a harassing weapon by 1918. In a steadily growing air war, airplanes fought for supremacy over and behind front lines, while German dirigibles and multi-engine bombers staged the first embryonic strategic bombing campaigns against British urban populations and industries in an abortive attempt to drive Britain from the war. In 1918, British government officials sorely desired to set fire to German towns to teach the "Boche" a lesson. Ultimately the tank, ground attack airplanes, and ample artillery provided the Entente infantry with the coordinated support they required to break the stalemate against a starving and exhausted Germany that could no longer continue the military conflict at the front or the war of production on the home front by 1918.

Between 1914 and 1918, military establishments and industries combined to evolve ever deadlier and more effective weapons and then to produce them in massive quantities. The development of the airplane, the tank, and the submarine prepared the way for future warfare on land, in the air, and under the sea. The First World War demonstrated unequivocally that technological progress did not necessarily equate with human progress, but could instead enable more death and destruction.

The increasingly total mobilization and brutalization of the European combatants, with attendant atrocities against soldier and civilian, began in imperial wars, accelerated in the First World War, and continued with the rise of totalitarian regimes in the interwar decades, and culminated in the Second World War. Combatants described enemies and their practices as barbaric and savage, rather ironic epithets in light of the wholesale slaughter and atrocities that European imperialists had committed against the indigenous inhabitants of Africa and Asia. The Germans committed atrocities against civilians in 1914 and then deported forced laborers, including women, from the occupied zones in Belgium and France. The British "hunger blockade" and the German submarine campaigns sought to starve civilians, while German and British aerial bombardment struck indiscriminately at the civilian population. To the east, the Ottoman Turks, beginning in 1915, massacred between a half a million and a million Armenians in a barbaric and primitive attempt at genocide. In 1939, Adolf Hitler, whose Nazi empire would modernize and industrialize mass murder, queried, "After all, who today still remembers the destruction of the Armenians?"[19]

Historian Avner Offer asserts that despite the industrial nature of the war, the Western allies' superior resources in key areas, including foodstuffs, raw materials, and population decided the outcome of the war. Food caused "the greatest discontent" among the civilian population and constituted the "weakest link" in the German war economy. In Offer's judgment, the Allied blockade and resulting food shortages played a key if indirect role in Germany's collapse.[20] Shortages of food and fuel first undermined public morale and then health in Germany and Austria-Hungary. Governmental inability to manage the shortages through rationing led to domestic unrest which disrupted production and undermined governmental authority as civilian populations demanded peace in their desperate struggle against privation. Propaganda campaigns did little good, because people could not eat or heat with propaganda. Finally, the shortages affected the armies: indirectly, as soldiers worried about their starving families at home; and directly, as they suffered from malnutrition and increased susceptibility to disease despite their priority in rations.

The Western Front in Europe remained the most significant theater of war as the major industrial powers clashed along a confined front of some five hundred miles; the war on the Eastern Front, second in importance; and the war on the Southern Front and in the Balkans, third. Yet the First World War was definitely a global war on land from the beginning. The conflict set Africa and the Middle East aflame, drew Indian soldiers into combat in the Arab heartlands and southeast Africa as well as Japan in East Asia, and the United States in the western hemisphere. Great Britain's white dominions—Australia and New Zealand, Canada, and South Africa—achieved greater autonomy as a result of their participation in the war. Their soldiers' service—the ANZAC sacrifice at the disastrous battle of Gallipoli in 1915 and the Canadian Corps' contribution to the "hundred days" offensive in 1918—had paid for their countries' greater autonomy in blood.

More than a million African soldiers fought for the colonial powers on various fronts in Europe,[21] the Middle East, and in Africa itself, and even more served as bearers or porters. The war in East Africa, in which German commander Paul von Lettow-Vorbeck's army of African *askaris* conducted a guerilla campaign against British-led Indian troops, Belgian colonial forces and white South African troops, concluded only after the armistice in Europe and led to famine, disease, destruction, and depopulation.[22] Africans' participation in the conflict also imparted a new sense of black African nationalism, but only their participation in a second world war would result in political equality and independence from their European rulers. The war had redrawn the map of Africa as it would remain in the twentieth century, and it had sown the "ideas concerning the self-determination of peoples and the accountability of colonial powers," which would influence events later in the century.[23] West Indian soldiers' wartime experience in Africa and the Middle East led to the rise of black nationalism in the West Indies, and after the war soldiers of the British West Indies Regiment "began the national liberation struggle that eventually led to the demise of colonial rule in most of the British Caribbean."[24]

Some 1.5 million Indians served the British Empire on fronts in Europe, Africa, and the Middle East. The war also brought heavy taxes, war loans, requisitions of grain and raw materials, and inflation. The British government, rather than introduce the gradual development of self-governing institutions in India as it proclaimed it would in 1917, instead resisted such change. At Amritsar, the brutal Lieut. Governor of the Punjab, Brig. Gen. Reginald Dyer, slaughtered nearly 400 and wounded some 1,200 unarmed Indians engaged in a peaceful demonstration. Unlike the white dominions, India's sacrifice would earn it not autonomy but repression. Such developments propelled the rise of Mahatma Gandhi, who called off his own early movement of non-violence and non-cooperation in the face of spreading violence.[25]

As events in Africa, India, and the West Indies demonstrated, the war, allegedly fought to make the world safe for democracy, protected and extended the global rule of whites over other races despite the resistance of many of the colonized peoples. The United States loomed as a particularly egregious example of whites' vicious repression of black aspirations for equality.[26] In the United States, the mere thought of arming African American soldiers for combat rather than assigning them to labor duties aroused the fear and ire of Southern politicians because of its threat to the racist status quo, particularly in the South. Vicious race riots and lynchings dotted the wartime and postwar American landscape, as white Americans stymied with violence any aspirations that African Americans had toward equality as a result of their participation in the "war for democracy."

In this context of the rampant racism of the imperial era, the race riots in the United States and the Amritsar massacre in India emerge as repressive measures that attempted, but failed, to drown in blood and fear any aspirations of emancipation and equality that participation in the Great War evoked. Ho Chi Minh, a waiter in Paris during the Paris Peace Conference, found his petitions for the freedom of Indo-China ignored, although the French had recruited his countrymen to fight in the Balkans and to labor in France.

The Ottoman Empire lost more than half of its territory and population during the war, most particularly in the Arab Middle East to Britain and France. The war witnessed the violent birth of the contemporary Middle East under British or French control, in particular a British mandate establishing a Jewish homeland within Palestine. The Turks, under the leadership of Gen. Mustapha Kemal or Atäturk, who had risen to prominence at Gallipoli, had to fight for the survival of their homeland against the British, French, and Greeks. Ultimately they won their struggle for an independent state, which included control of the Anatolian heartland, as Kemal became president of modern Turkey in 1922.[27]

As the continuing conflict in Asia Minor indicated, only the struggle on the Western Front in Belgium and France and the Southwestern Front in Italy concluded at the armistice of November 11, 1918—Armistice Day to western European countries and the United States. The fighting in Eastern Europe continued until the years 1921–1923. The violence of the war surpassed any in human history. Although casualty statistics vary with the source, the best estimates suggest that more than ten million men died in the war: 2.3 million Russians; 2 million Germans; 1.9 million French; 1 million Austro-Hungarians; 800,000 Britons; 770,000 Ottomans; 450,000 Italians; and 126,000 Americans.

Although the casualties in the Second World War would exceed those in the First, only in Russia/the Soviet Union did the daily losses in 1941–45 (5,635) exceed those in 1914–18 (1,459). The number of wounded totaled about forty percent of the men mobilized, and probably half the survivors suffered psychological problems which doctors, most of whom remained convinced that such problems stemmed from cowardice or character flaws instead of the stress of sustained bombardment and combat, could not treat effectively. By contrast with the Second World War, soldiers sustained the overwhelming number of casualties, although Serbia, which suffered the most proportionately of any European state, lost fifteen percent of its prewar population with the deaths of 125,000 soldiers and 650,000 civilians.

The war had traumatized entire societies, and entire societies mourned, as the war touched everyone, leaving behind millions of widows and even more orphans. The conflict set entire peoples in motion as refugees, driven from their land and homes. Yet devastation, death, and dislocation occurred not only in Europe, but globally, in Africa, Asia, and the Middle East, wherever the heavy hand of European empire had extended. The casualty statistics cited above are limited to western states; none exist for Africa, the Middle East, and Asia, where imperial bureaucracies cared only about the colonized peoples' ability to fight and labor, and not a whit about their deaths. A case in point remains the influenza pandemic of 1918–1919, which claimed 21.5 million victims globally, most of them in Asia, and particularly in India, where 12.5 million people, weakened by wartime privations and suffering, died. In the years 1914–1919, humans wreaked a catastrophe of epidemic proportions on themselves in the First World War, which concluded in the midst of an epidemic of catastrophic proportions.

The First World War was indisputably a global war. Yet broader and more encompassing interpretations of the war of 1914–1918 have just begun to penetrate the Western, particularly the American, popular imagination, which still tends to conceive not even of a European war, but more narrowly of a war fought on the Western Front in France and Belgium that started in August 1914, stopped at the armistice of November 11, 1918, and concluded with the Treaty of Versailles in June 1919.

PEACE? YES, BUT . . .

The Peace of Paris in 1919 seemed to promise the possibility of the restoration of the antebellum world, but the war had rendered a return to "normalcy," to "business as usual," impossible.[28] The German and Austro-Hungarian empires had collapsed in defeat, while the Russian empire had descended into revolution and civil war. A defeated but defiant Germany, temporarily down but not out, perceived itself as a victim of the *Diktat* of the Versailles Settlement even as it stood literally alone, untouched by the destruction that the Treaty blamed it for unleashing upon the rest of Europe. Austria-Hungary had disintegrated into its component parts, and no one missed the seemingly doomed and ramshackle multi-national and multi-ethnic anachronism of the Dual Monarchy until after it ceased to exist. Too late, many observers recognized that Austria-Hungary had provided an economic unity now absent to the fragmented tiny and largely agricultural economies—Czechoslovakia excepted—of the successor states of southeastern Europe, which left them prey to the economic manipulation of the strongest industrial power in the region—Germany.

Yet the most cataclysmic events had occurred in Russia,[29] as the tsarist autocracy collapsed under the burden of the war, its transportation system incapable of transporting food to the cities or supplies to the front. Tsar Nicholas, who had spent the war since 1915 as a useless appendage at the high command and left power in the capital to his wife, the monk Rasputin, and a series of corrupt governmental ministers, abdicated in the face of popular demonstrations in March 1917. He had lost the support of his army high command. Into the power vacuum at the top stepped first a dual regime of a provisional government, or Duma, which represented the one-eighth of the Russian population at the top of society who could vote, and a spontaneous system of Soviets which represented the other seven-eighths, the "dark masses" of workers and peasants.

Although some historians have maintained that Russia could have evolved into a constitutional monarchy—a doubtful prospect in light of the refusal of the tsar to share power—such pipe dreams became truly untenable in such a divided society in the grips of war and revolution. The Bolshevik Party seized power in October 1917 because it possessed the best leaders in Lenin and Trotsky, party organization, and connections to the workers factory committees and soldiers' Soviets in the key cities of Petrograd and Moscow. The Bolsheviks would have to fight a brutal three-year civil war to cement their rule in the new Soviet Union, and the Russian Civil War more than the revolution became the forge which tempered the party to surmount future challenges with an iron will and no quarter. Bolshevik radicals, who proclaimed their undying hostility to the capitalist, imperialist world, had seized the reins of power and fought off the uncoordinated thrusts of Russian monarchist and Allied intervention forces around the boundaries of the critical Moscow-Petrograd axis.

The Bolshevik government did not receive an invitation to the Paris Peace Conference, but the shadow of Bolshevik Russia and the fear and loathing of a radicalized "Judeo-Bolshevik" Russia, as European and American conservatives labeled Soviet Russia, loomed over and plagued the peace-makers. From the very formation of the Soviet Union, Western conservatives and liberals, Winston Churchill and Woodrow Wilson alike, not to mention rising fascists like Benito Mussolini and Adolf Hitler and Japanese militarists, sought the demise of communism and of the Soviet Union.[30] On the other hand, the Russian Revolution and its ideals of a classless society and an end to imperialism inspired Sun Yat-sen and Chiang Kai-shek, leaders of the Kuomintang (Nationalist Party) who were struggling to unify China under a fragile republic that they had founded in revolution in 1911.

The only two powers to emerge strengthened from the War of 1914–1918 were the United States and, to a lesser extent, Japan. The victorious Entente powers Britain and France owed America huge war debts; and both Japan and the United States had captured markets vacated by a Europe pre-occupied with war. The war severely undermined European global domination to an even greater extent than was evident in 1919, when the Peace of Paris and later the League of Nations granted the colonies of the defeated powers to the victors as colonial mandates, thereby propelling the British and French empires to their territorial zeniths.

In fact, Versailles established a system in the colonial realm that left the exhausted and newly debtor nations Britain and France ruling expanded empires that they were barely capable of controlling. In the 1920s, the western European imperial powers—Britain, France, Italy, and Spain most critically—fought brutal colonial wars to maintain their imperial control in the Middle East and North Africa in particular. The British and French traded threats about bombing one another and almost came to blows in 1923 over disputed territory in the Middle East. The British, in their search for cost-saving expedients to govern the empire, resorted to the Royal Air Force to subdue various "primitive" tribes in the Middle East and Central Asia and even contemplated the use of air power to subdue the Irish as well. Something had to give, and ultimately the British government substituted rhetoric for real fortifications in the Far East in the 1920s and 1930s, most particularly at the "impregnable" fortress of Singapore—a decision that would return to haunt Britain during the Second World War.

The European powers' withdrawal from East Asia in 1914 had positioned Japan, already the primary power in East Asia, to dominate a drastically weakened China by 1915. The war further enabled it to occupy some German possessions in East Asia and the Pacific Islands at the expenditure of limited military effort. All of these developments antagonized and threatened American and British interests, as did the Japanese postwar commitment of sizable forces against the Soviet Union in Siberia that lasted until 1922, some three years after all of the other powers had agreed upon to end the intervention. The Western powers' tendency to ignore the Japanese at the Paris Peace Conference, their rejection of a Japanese attempt to insert a non-discrimination clause in the League of Nations covenant, and the British abrogation of the Anglo-Japanese alliance in favor of multi-power pacts signed at the Washington Naval Conference of 1921–22 in an attempt to corral Japanese expansion in Asia all foreshadowed later tensions that would lead to conflict. On the other hand, the very outcome of the world war and Woodrow Wilson's pronouncements for democracy strengthened Japanese proponents of British-style parliamentary government in their political struggle against their authoritarian opponents and threatened Japanese militarists, who remained dissatisfied with Japanese imperial possessions and anticipated a race war against the United States.

The obvious links between the First and Second World Wars have given rise in some historical circles, particularly in France, to the concept of a thirty years' war, with a "twenty years' peace" in between. Certain core assumptions—that the first war led inexorably to the second because the German thrust for continental and global power persisted, that the slaughter and issues of the first allowed no resolution other than a second round of warfare, and consequently that Versailles and the Paris Peace Conference concluded one phase of a persisting conflict and initiated the origins of the next—prompt this interpretation. Such assumptions can easily lend themselves to a linear interpretation of the inevitability of the Second World War at the conclusion of the First.

Certainly the Great War led to the rise of fascism and communism and the weakness and disarray in the democracies in Europe, fundamental developments that enabled the outbreak of the Second World War in Europe in 1939.[31] After the First World War, a weakened Britain preoccupied with its empire and an isolationist United States intent on withdrawing all presence except financial from Europe left a gravely wounded France to confront an embittered, unrepentant, and only temporarily impaired Germany. Historian John Keegan, referring to the legacy of intense political rancor and racial hatred, upon which Adolf Hitler played in Germany, ultimately judged the Second World War "the direct outcome of the First" and "in large measure its continuation." Keegan further considered totalitarianism "the political continuation of war by other means." He concludes that the First World War initiated "the manufacture of mass death" that the Second World War "brought to a pitiless consummation."[32] Systems of forced labor, censorship, justification by an elaborate ideology, and the perversion of language had begun with colonialism in Africa and Asia and intensified during the First World War. These systems became part and parcel of militarism in Japan and totalitarianism in Nazi Germany, Soviet Russia, and Fascist Italy, where the term "totalitarianism" originated, although Mussolini's Italy paled before its two more powerful counterparts in its ability to control, mobilize, and terrorize its own population and that of other countries.[33]

Images of the Great War abounded in the Second World War, in particular that of the hardened front fighter in Germany. German soldiers marching east carried paperback copies of Ernst Jünger's epic memoir of his service on the Western Front, *The Storm of Steel* (1929), in their backpacks. Sons of soldier fathers retread the same ground as their parents, in some cases the very same battlefields where their fathers had fallen. The savage and bloody struggle in the rubble of Stalingrad in 1942–43 resurrected German historical recollections of Verdun in 1916, and a few of the same German soldiers who had fought at Verdun would fight again at Stalingrad.

In Europe and the United States, the generation of leaders—political and military—of World War II had generally been born in the last quarter of the nineteenth century and forged in the fire of the First World War and conflicts it birthed, such as the Russian Revolution and Civil War. Hitler and Mussolini had been front soldiers, the latter briefly; Roosevelt, assistant secretary of the navy; and Churchill, who had already seen action in India and the Boer War, was First Lord of the Admiralty, then a battalion commander on the Western Front, and finally Minister of Munitions in the Lloyd George government. Stalin had been a political commissar during the Russo-Polish War. Hermann Goering and Arthur "Bomber" Harris, chiefs of the Luftwaffe and Royal Air Force (RAF) Bomber Command in World War II, respectively, had been aviators, the former an ace fighter pilot. Bernard Law Montgomery had fought in the British army, while Philippe Pétain had commanded French units at Verdun and later became Commander-in-Chief of the French Army on the Western Front.

By the mid-1920s, many Frenchmen firmly believed that the Germans would come again. The small classes of French conscripts in the late 1930s, the result of absent potential fathers, soldiers killed in 1914–18, provided palpable evidence of the Pyrrhic nature of France's victory in 1918. The French collapse in 1940 and the collaborationist Vichy Regime of 1940–44 have overshadowed their valiant sacrifice in 1914–18, but both developments of the 1940s are unimaginable and incomprehensible without reference to the debacle of a victorious but prostrate France after the First World War. Marshal Philippe Pétain, the only major French figure of 1914–1918 still alive, capitulated to and collaborated with the Germans. The pessimistic old soldier believed that he had saved France from further blood-letting at the hands of an even more formidable Germany that would inevitably defeat Britain and rule Europe.[34]

Yet Colonel Charles de Gaulle, Pétain's early protégé, refused to accept defeat in 1940 and proclaimed continuing French resistance from Britain. De Gaulle, who attributed the German defeat in 1918 to moral collapse, believed in the concept of a thirty years' war. If the invasion of 1940 continued the German assault of 1914–18, de Gaulle's resistance resumed his personal unfinished war. Captured as an infantry captain after being wounded at Verdun in 1916, he had spent the rest of the war attempting to escape from German captivity. Proponent of a professional, armored elite force, de Gaulle had a score to settle with the Germans, and continued the struggle from Britain and several locations in France's colonial empire.[35]

Such continuities notwithstanding, historians should always be wary of linear interpretations, which lend a sense of inevitability to developments that only hindsight can assure. No straight line, no linear progression, directly connects the First and Second World Wars, even in Europe. The stability of the

Weimar Republic, however questionable, from 1924 to 1929, the various treaties from Locarno in 1925 that culminated in the Kellogg-Briand Pact of 1928, and the disarmament movement of the late 1920s and early 1930s offered prospects of averting another global war. Admittedly, German rearmament proceeded apace after the war in secret collaboration with the Soviet Union, as the two pariahs, united by their status as outcasts and their common hatred of and refusal to accept the existence of Poland, the "Monstrous Bastard of Versailles," pooled their resources to develop the mobile armies and weapons of the future. Nevertheless, even the typical German conservative who desired the revision of Versailles, thought in terms of restoring German power and territory in Europe and abroad, but certainly not of global war.[36]

THE GREAT DEPRESSION AND THE PATH TO WAR IN ASIA AND EUROPE

The cataclysmic impact of the Great Depression should give serious pause to those who espouse a linear interpretation of history from 1919 to 1939 postulating a direct, immediate connection between Versailles in 1919 and war in 1939. The fateful years 1929–1930 posed a distinct divide, when movement toward possible continued peace suffered irreparable blows. The crash of the American Stock Market in October 1929 signaled the onslaught of the Great Depression in the United States. Wall Street exported the disaster to central Europe by calling in American short-term loans that had initially been established in the Dawes Plan of 1924 to stabilize the German currency. Central Europeans had invested them in long-term capital intensive projects, and the German and Austrian economies consequently collapsed like a house of cards, the harshness of their depression second only to the United States. Within a decade, Germany had experienced hyperinflation culminating in 1923 and great depression beginning in 1930. The former was directly linked to the ways the Germans had financed the first war; the latter was a product of financial connections established in postwar agreements of 1924. Economic histories of the era have placed the responsibility for the Great Depression, for turning what would have been a recession into a calamity, at the feet of the United States, which instead of retracting its loans in the recession actually needed to extend more to counter the recessionary cycle. Yet the Depression antedated John Maynard Keynes' advocacy of counter-cyclical fiscal policies, which few countries rushed to adopt even after he had enunciated them in the mid-1930s.[37]

A second significant development occurred in Germany in October 1929—the death of German statesman Gustav Stresemann. Stresemann, a conservative former monarchist who had served as chancellor and then as foreign minister of the Weimar Republic from 1923 to 1929, had balanced between

Russia and the western powers to negotiate concessions to improve Germany's international position peacefully. Stresemann had placed Germany firmly within the western economic camp led by the United States and Great Britain, as he acknowledged the enormous economic strength and potential of the American colossus. The linked combination of depression, which undermined such dependence on the west, and the removal from the German political scene of Weimar's greatest statesman, who had espoused that policy, opened the door to instability and alternative solutions to Germany's difficulties.

The Weimar government floundered in the face of rampant unemployment, as a series of chancellors appointed by President Paul von Hindenburg ruled by emergency decree under Article 48 of the Weimar constitution. In the end, however, the conservative camarilla around Hindenburg chose to appoint a demagogue through whom it hoped to control the German people to surmount the crisis, very much as the Italian king Victor Emmanuel and conservatives around him had seized upon Benito Mussolini and the Fascist movement in 1922. Adolf Hitler and the Nazi party managed to gain thirty-seven percent of the popular vote in 1932, and thus a plurality. That election catapulted Hitler to the chancellorship in 1933. One year later, when Hindenburg died and the parliament building burned to the ground, Hitler seized sole power in Germany.

Any analysis of the origins of the Second World War in Europe must begin with Adolf Hitler, and the plethora of Hitler biographies reflects his importance in guiding German policy to unleash war in 1939.[38] Historians occasionally disagree about the terminology they use to describe Hitler—some refer to him as a German nationalist, others as primarily an Anti-Semite. Yet the description that fits him best—Pan-German—emphasizes his role as heir to those Pan-Germans before 1914 who combined advocacy of the unification of all Germans in Europe in one *Reich* and German imperial expansion eastward on the continent to achieve *Lebensraum*, with rabid anti-Semitism. German defeat in 1918 and the appearance of the Bolshevik regime in Russia only added fuel to the Pan-German fire. "Judeo-Bolshevism" now threatened Europe and the world with a revolutionary ideology promulgated allegedly by the hated *Untermenschen*, the Jews. In the past, German anti-Semites had condemned Jewish plutocrats and financiers and Social Democrats as internal threats to the body politic. Now they envisioned themselves surrounded by the *Erzfeind*, the arch-enemy, from outside, in Soviet Russia and Roosevelt's United States.

Hitler's ideology and aims reflected this Pan-German conception of a hostile social Darwinist world of enemies out to destroy Germany. Stresemann had thrown Germany's lot in with the West; Hitler now planned to use the Western model of imperial conquest against the West and the world. Historians now rely not only on *Mein Kampf*, Hitler's autobiographical proclamation of his intentions of 1925, and his earlier writings, but on his unpublished

Zweites Buch of 1928 to fathom his intentions.[39] He admired the British conquest of empire in India, where the British ruled millions of Hindus and Muslims, and by extension the *Herrenvolk* dominions of Australia, Canada, and South Africa, where the British had exterminated, marginalized, or enslaved the native inhabitants.

The latest works on the Nazi economy and empire emphasize Hitler's particular admiration of the United States, whose experience he planned to emulate in the twentieth century.[40] In North America, British settlers had imported a slave population from Africa, exterminated the native Americans, and expanded steadily westward to acquire tremendous living space, with farmland and natural resources that enabled the United States to become a superpower. Hitler planned to do the same through conquest of the East, exterminating "Judeo-Bolsheviks" and enslaving the "sub-human" Slavic populations to work for his superior Aryan race. From this continental heartland, Germany could contest world power against the British Empire and the United States.

Hitler could only achieve such grandiose goals through war. Consequently, once he had seized total power in Germany, in particular by gaining the abject obedience of the vaunted German army, he set out to throw off the shackles of Versailles, rearm Germany for the coming inevitable war, and launch Germany on a relentless path of conquest. In the short run, he proved himself opportunistic and flexible in his ability to create or seize upon occasions to further his aims, but those ultimate aims of global conquest with Germany as the instrument to create his Aryan super-state remained fixed. Regardless of how Hitler's opponents responded—and much has been made of British and French appeasement of Hitler at Munich in 1938, which occurred because neither power believed itself prepared for war against Germany, regardless of arguments to the contrary posed from hindsight—Hitler intended war.

The Great Depression also unhinged the constitutional government of Japan, enabled the renewed ascendancy of Japanese militarists, and led to a decade of domestic turmoil and violence, and imperial expansion on the Asian continent. The main lesson that Japanese militarists had drawn from the German defeat in 1918 was the necessity of autarchy, the ability of a state to survive economically on its own in a hostile world of enemies. Japan needed living space and raw materials for its cramped and growing island population, and by the end of the 1920s, it looked to Manchuria to provide both. The Japanese army and navy led a virtually autonomous existence in the government, because only the emperor could rein them in. Consequently, the officers of the Kwantung army on the continent provoked a war over Manchuria in 1931 and conquered the region. Japan then proceeded to colonize the territory, mine its raw materials, and industrialize its new colony of Manchukuo.

Some Japanese historians date the beginning of Japan's Second World War from 1931, because their determination to conquer, protect, and then expand their conquest of Manchuria launched enduring conflict, first with China, then the Soviet Union, and ultimately with the United States.[41] In the Russo-Japanese War of 1904–05, Japanese soldiers and the Japanese Red Cross had treated captured and wounded Russian soldiers in such exemplary fashion that the Russian tsar donated a substantial sum to the Red Cross. In the colonization of Manchuria and ensuing conflicts in East Asia and in the Pacific, the Japanese army's treatment of enemy soldiers and civilians in its brutal conventional and counter-insurgency campaigns recalled its brutality toward its recalcitrant Korean subjects. Japanese soldiers further began to exalt dying for the emperor, raising it to the level of cult status, and the murderous treatment of prisoners-of-war further reflected the brutal treatment which Japanese soldiers underwent at the hands of their superiors. Later, in the war against the colonial powers and the United States, the Japanese exacted revenge for the humiliating manner in which white people had treated them by humiliating, abusing, and killing white prisoners-of-war. The Japanese militarists had resurrected the brutal characteristics of the ancient warrior code of Bushido, to which the conduct of Japanese soldiers reverted in the quarter century after the Russo-Japanese War.

As the Japanese expanded into Chinese territory, they provoked war in 1937 with the forces of Chiang Kai-shek's Kuomintang government, whose efforts to unify China had prompted the Japanese to pre-empt such developments. Yet the Kuomintang had already confronted the Chinese Communist Party under Mao Tse-tung. Now both Chinese parties would have to fight the Japanese while preparing for the ultimate struggle for China. The so-called "China Incident" of 1937, which minimizes the fact that this launched a Sino-Japanese war, marks the beginning of the war in Asia for historians who do not accept the 1931 date.

The Japanese army discovered, however, after a series of bloody battles and conquests, punctuated by the "Rape of Nanking" in 1937,[42] that it could not swallow China. It had conquered the coastal cities and ports, but could not penetrate the Chinese hinterland, where Chiang's government had fled to Chungking, which the Japanese could bomb from the air, but not reach by land. Stalemate ensued in 1938, at which time the Japanese army turned to the northwest, toward its foremost enemy, the Soviet Union, which had become the primary source of aid to the Kuomintang and whose Outer Mongolian protectorate bordered Manchukuo. In May 1939, the Kwantung army escalated the clashes along the disputed border into a bloody four-month battle that became known in Japan as the Nomonhan Incident and in the Soviet Union as the Battle of Khalkin Gol. Gen. Georgi Zhukov's superior forces, in particular Soviet armor, crushed the Kwantung army by the end of August 1939, and the two sides signed a formal cease-fire in mid-September.[43] This encounter dissuaded the Kwantung army from testing the Russian forces in East Asia again, and the Japanese army consequently became more amenable to the navy's plans to move south to conquer the oil resources of the Dutch

East Indies and the raw materials of the British and French colonies in southeast Asia. Such conquests would ultimately bring Japan into conflict with the United States, a war that the Japanese navy and marines would have the major responsibility of waging. In the Soviet Union, Josef Stalin was now free to concentrate on Europe, and, should it become necessary, to transfer Soviet far eastern forces to his western front to help combat any invasion from that direction.

The Depression thus threw both Germany and Japan into the hands of extremists, but the Japanese launched their imperial war in East Asia in 1931 or at the latest, 1937, two years before the Germans invaded Poland. In fact, Soviet troops crushed the Japanese at Nomonhan just days before the German invasion on September 1, 1939. Western historians of both world wars deem Europe paramount in the origins and outcome of both conflicts—an understandable focus in light of the centrality of Europe in a world that it had dominated for nearly two centuries. While this may certainly be more appropriate in regard to the war of 1914–1918, such a perspective proves more problematic in attempts to comprehend the Second World War, an even more global and "total" war.

A Eurocentric approach has prompted many European historians, with some crucial exceptions such as Niall Ferguson,[44] to adhere to September 1939 as the start of the Second World War. Ferguson believes that acceptance of 1937 as the start of the war is overdue. Others point out that Hitler's Nazi Germany was not only the strongest Axis power, but the one with global pretensions to domination, while the Japanese focused on expansion in eastern Asia and the western Pacific. The difficulty with this latter assessment lies in the contemporary perspective of the Allies that while Germany was certainly the more formidable opponent, both Germany and Japan sought world power and the division of the globe.

Yet a historian might look forward through the windshield of history to the relative decline of Europe and the rise of Asia rather than through the rear view mirror at European world dominance. In that case, the opening of the second Sino-Japanese War—the first occurred in 1894–95—at the latest in July 1937, and ultimately of the war on the mainland of East and Southeast Asia, becomes far more significant. In fact, the selection of 1931—the Japanese invasion and colonization of Manchuria in 1931, eight years before the war in Europe, and ten years before Pearl Harbor—renders explicit the connection of the war in Asia and the Pacific to the struggle for empire and Japan's imperial aspirations on the Asian continent. Japanese aggression, the League's dilatory investigation of the aggression, and Japan's subsequent departure from the League of Nations in 1933, initiated the process of discrediting and undermining the League in the 1930s.

The Italian invasion of Ethiopia in 1935 continued the dismantling of the League. The Italian dictator Benito Mussolini's designs on the Mediterranean, *Mare nostrum* to Italians, and East and North Africa, prompted him to invade

Ethiopia in 1935 and intervene in the Spanish Civil War in 1936. The Italians' brutal conquest of Ethiopia, as its Emperor Haile Selassie vainly pleaded for help from the rostrum of the League, included the use of poison gas in an all-out effort to crush the Ethiopians. The war, which some might view as a colonial conflict, could also be viewed as the beginning of the Second World War in Africa, as it would lead further to Italian attacks on the British empire in east and north Africa in 1940. These moves provoked a strong British response from its own dominion and colonial troops, which in turn necessitated the intervention of German general Erwin Rommel's Afrika Corps in the ultimately vain attempt to pull Italian chestnuts out of the fire.

The case of the Spanish Civil War of 1936–1939 proves equally intriguing.[45] Many members of the International Brigades believed that the war was actually the first stage of fascist aggression in Europe when they volunteered to defend the Spanish Republic against Gen. Francisco Franco's right-wing revolt. Yet historians tend to dismiss the Spanish Civil War as at most a prelude to the Second World War. The war has thus far remained primarily a subject for historians of Modern Spain, a Spanish affair with an international overlay as Mussolini and Hitler aided Franco and Stalin assisted the Republic, while the British, French, and American democracies remained neutral.

On the other hand, Franco could not have begun his war without the indispensable aid of the Italian air force in transporting his vaunted Spanish Foreign legionnaires from Spanish Morocco to fight in Spain. The African and fascist connection thus proves significant from the start in Franco's uprising. The neutrality of the democracies certainly reinforced Hitler's and Stalin's sense of the decadence of the Western democracies in light of their refusal to defend one of their own. Finally, historians have occasionally portrayed the Second World War as a European civil war, and the brutality of the struggle between right and left in Europe from 1939 to 1945 certainly lends some credibility to such a perception. If such is the case, however, then perhaps the Spanish Civil War may be more intimately connected to the origins of the war in Europe in 1939 than historians have been willing to contemplate.

In any case, the above evidence does enable the historian to put to rest the notion of a Twenty Years' Peace. This Eurocentric perspective ignores the continuing conflicts through 1923 that the First World War ignited, and then in particular conflict in East Asia that began earlier in the 1930s. Concentration on Europe does not suffice to study the origins of the Second World War or understand a war that in the magnitude of its ferocity and sheer breadth dwarfed its predecessor. The Second World War wrought death and destruction in Asia second only to eastern and central Europe and far greater than the conflicts in western Europe and the Pacific, although histories of the war have yet to reflect this proportionality.

THE SECOND WORLD WAR AND ITS AFTERMATH

A good case exists for viewing the Second World War as two separate but indirectly connected wars—one in Europe and the other in Asia—that came together to form a global war in the second half of 1941.[46] The German invasion of Poland on September 1, 1939 stands as the accepted date for the origins of the European war. Historian John Lukacs has labeled the period September 1939 to June 1941 as the last European war, and has even portrayed the conflict as a personal struggle between Churchill and Hitler.[47] Both ideas seem rather overblown. Hitler's main war aims from the outset lay in the east, not the west. Second, while the general public tends to personalize and demonize wartime enemies, historians do not need to cater to that tendency, unless, of course, Churchill, Hitler, and Stalin were actually leading their men on the battlefield like the kings of yore.

Nazi Germany waged naval war from the start on a global scale, and the Germans faced two essential land fronts: an eastern European that included Poland, the Baltic and the Balkans, and ultimately the Soviet Union; and a western European from Scandinavia in the north through northwestern Europe, with Britain and France as its major foes. As in the First World War, the German submarines and surface raiders seriously threatened allied supply routes, only once again to meet defeat because of their inadequate numbers and the allied resort to convoys and long-range aircraft to protect merchant shipping. The Nazi war machine would fight on the vast eastern and western fronts and in North Africa as well, in its attempt to achieve Hitler's grandiose designs of world power. Hitler sent Rommel to Africa to rescue the Italians, but Rommel's attempts to conquer Egypt and cross the Suez Canal fit nicely with incredible Nazi geopolitical designs of establishing a land bridge to Asia when the forces conquering the Soviet Union met those advancing victoriously from the Middle East. The key to Hitler's success lay in the conquest of all Europe to the Ural Mountains, to create a gigantic European continental power with the living space, resources, and slave labor ultimately to contest global power with the American colossus.[48]

Historians, adhering to the chronology of the war in Western Europe and a "European war" as such, often view the invasion of Poland as the precursor to the "Phony War" in the West and then the assault on northern and then western Europe. Yet, as more recent studies of the Nazi conquest of Poland demonstrate,[49] the vicious nature of the Nazi conquest and occupation of Poland actually places it more logically as part of the Nazi-Soviet division of eastern and central Europe, but more significantly as the prelude to the later Nazi war of annihilation in the Soviet Union. The northern and western European phase of the land war, like the German invasion of Poland, was extremely short, lasting from April through June 1940. Military historians have paid some attention to the rapid German conquest of Scandinavia and the abortive

Allied operations there, but most have focused on the fall of Belgium and France. The most significant revelations these studies have yielded concern the *Blitzkrieg*, or "lightning war," that the German army and air force conducted to crush the western allies. Many previous historians had elevated the *Blitzkrieg* to Germany's guiding concept of war and mobilization from the very beginning, stressing that it allowed the Nazis to avoid total mobilization by conquering each opponent rapidly. In fact, the latest works make it abundantly clear that the Polish campaign was not conducted in lightning fashion, and that General Erich von Manstein's idea of a daring armored attack launched from the Ardennes with overwhelming air support to split the British and French forces met considerable resistance from German military planners. Even after General Heinz Guderian and Hitler supported it, and while Rommel executed it brilliantly, fears that the armored spearhead might be severed from the flanks prompted a delay to regroup that cost the Germans the capture of the British Expeditionary Force (BEF) before it escaped at Dunkirk.[50]

Once accomplished, however, German planners then arrogantly assumed that the German war machine could replicate this successful mode of warfare even in the more primitive logistical conditions of the great expanse of the Soviet Union. With continental Western European collaborators directly under the Nazi thumb, the Germans initiated plans for the invasion of the Soviet Union in July 1940 and finalized them in December. Meanwhile, with British naval supremacy an often forgotten but fundamental fact, the aerial Battle of Britain determined in only three months that Germany could not invade Britain, leaving the German air force to continue the bombing of Britain in "The Blitz" and Hitler to pursue the invasion of his ultimate enemy, the Soviet Union. On June 22, 1941, three million men, the largest force amassed to that date in history, invaded the Soviet Union to achieve Hitler's long-cherished dream.

Hitler's conquest of Western Europe in June 1940 had global implications, because western European states—Britain, France, and the Netherlands—possessed global empires, in particular in Africa, Asia, and the western Pacific. Contrary to myth and legend, the British isles did not stand alone in June 1940; they could call on the support and resources of an empire of five hundred million people.[51] The aim of striking at the global empires of the states of western Europe, particularly those of Britain and France, united Germany, Italy, and Japan and provided some unity to the war as early as 1939–1940.

The repercussions of June 1940 in Asia served to expand the Sino-Japanese War ultimately into a war for Asia and the western Pacific. The German conquest of western Europe in June 1940 precipitated Japan's penetration of Southeast Asia, which ultimately transformed the confrontation between Japan and the United States over Japanese aggression in Manchuria and China into bloody conflict. Japan's potential access to vital Southeast Asian raw materials sparked the American attempt to deter further Japanese expansion by embargoes and an attempt to bankrupt Japan internationally, actions which in turn prompted the Japanese to strike Pearl Harbor on December 7, 1941, to push the United States out of the western Pacific.[52]

The Japanese attack on Pearl Harbor might have come out of the blue for many Americans. Yet the confrontation in the 1930s between Japan and the United States over Manchuria and China, and ultimately war in 1941, were only the most recent manifestations of tensions between Japan and the United States over East Asia and the Pacific that dated back to, and had been building, since the nineteenth century. Hitler's invasion of the Soviet Union in June 1941, in combination with the Japanese attack on Pearl Harbor in December 1941 and Hitler's subsequent declaration of war on the United States on December 11, make 1941 the year in which the Second World War completely emerged as one global war to be fought to the finish by the Allies and the Axis.

The collapse of the Soviet Union and the end of the Cold War in 1990–1991 enabled fundamental changes in Western interpretations of the war in Europe, as it freed Western historians to paint a more accurate picture of the relative weight of the Russian and of the Western contributions to the war effort. Recent European historians such as Max Hastings acknowledge the very real and dominant role of the Soviet Union in the war in Europe. Other historians such as William Hitchcock and Stephen Fritz are revising and moving beyond the heroic accounts and interpretations of the Western Allies' liberation of Europe in favor of a much more nuanced and analytical appraisal of the war in northwest Europe from the D-Day invasion to the aftermath of the German surrender.

The most recent histories of the European war now readily acknowledge that the Soviet Union bore the brunt of the war against the Nazi war machine from 1941 to the very end of the conflict even after D-Day. The Nazi-Soviet war in Eastern Europe from 1941 to 1945, which was also the main front in the Nazi mass murder of the European Jews, was an atrociously brutal war of annihilation against which other conflicts paled. The Holocaust, which consumed six million European Jews and another six million Poles, gypsies, homosexuals, leftist and liberal politicians, and Russian civilians in a genocide that began with murder squads and culminated in industrial slaughter, has merited and received substantial study. Some authors, labeled "intentionalists," assert that all Germans were "eliminationist anti-Semites" from the very beginning,[53] while others, called "functionalists," conclude that the cloak of total war enabled the Nazis to pursue the "total" elimination of an entire race of people. The weight of evidence lends credence to the functionalist camp.[54] Furthermore, historians no longer view the SS and its indigenous allies as the sole executioners in the Holocaust and have explicitly demonstrated that regular German soldiers, and at times collaborators in conquered countries, were also guilty of these crimes, contrary to the claims of the German generals who helped Western historians write the early accounts of the Russo-German war.

That the Soviet Union never recognized a separate Holocaust of European Jews seems a product of the fact that the Nazi invaders slaughtered at least thirty million Soviet soldiers and civilians, including Soviet Jews. The enormity of these figures—six and thirty million, respectively—renders them difficult to grasp, but they provide fundamental insight into a truly "total" war. Historian Norman Davies correctly emphasizes that the great weight of the war and all its atrocities descended on eastern Europe and the small states there as well as the Soviet Union.[55]

In each of the great battles of Moscow in 1941 and Stalingrad in 1942–43, the Red army lost a million men repelling the Nazi invader. At Kursk in July 1943, the greatest tank battle in history put an end to the German offensives in the East and signaled the beginning of Soviet offensives that would ultimately destroy the German army. The plethora of excellent studies on Soviet operations by David Glantz and his co-authors enable recognition of Soviet achievements as well as disasters.[56] For example, Operation "Bagration" in 1944 was an impressively large and well coordinated offensive that overwhelmed the German central group armies, freeing Soviet soil and driving the Nazi conquerors back to Poland, as well as pre-occupying the Germans as D-Day in western Europe approached. The Soviet armies now excelled the Germans at the Germans' game, armored warfare, mobilizing huge armies with aerial support and skillfully disguising the main points of attack through deception. The huge tank armies of Soviet generals like Zhukov and Rokossovky, supported by mobile artillery towed by tractors and soldiers riding in American trucks, would punch deep into the German rear as Field Marshall Mikhail Tukachevsky, who had been brutally executed in Stalin's purges, had postulated, sowing confusion and panic, and then roll up the German armies. Max Hastings's masterful study of the last year and a half of the war in Europe even asserts that Zhukov was probably the most skillful commander and Josef Stalin the most adept leader of the war, notwithstanding the serious flaws of both men. They were brutal men, well suited to the brutal nature of the Second World War.[57]

The war in the West—the campaigns in North Africa, Sicily, Italy, and ultimately in northwest Europe—now becomes truly a second, and secondary front, and however important, an appendage to a much larger and more ferocious war in the East. For the sake of comparison, in the course of World War II, Britain lost 400,000 casualties, fewer than half of its First World War total, and the United States suffered the same number of combatant deaths in both Europe and the Pacific. The invasions of North Africa, Sicily, and Italy provided the necessary build-up of resources and trained men for the Western allies to confront the Germans in northwest France.[58] Had the Western allies attempted a cross-Channel invasion earlier, as American commanders desired and Churchill and British commanders feared, the Germans would likely have repelled it. The Italian campaign, contrary to Churchill's claims of Italy as a "soft underbelly," proved a hard-fought and costly slugging match often in mountainous terrain that favored the German defenders and prohibited allied tank operations. Fortunately, when Churchill attempted to turn from Italy to the Balkans, Roosevelt and the American commanders prevented what would become a disaster and insisted that only through a second front in northwest Europe, which they had been promising Stalin since 1942, could they effectively help the Soviet Union defeat the Nazis while keeping it out of western and northern Europe.

In the meantime, Royal Air Force Bomber Command, starting in 1940 and hitting its stride in 1942–43, and the U.S. Eighth Air Force, beginning in 1942 and hitting its stride early in 1944, struck the German homeland in an increasingly massive and coordinated strategic bombing campaign. RAF bomber crews, their mission assigned by Churchill and under commander Arthur "Bomber" Harris, whom they called "Butcher," sought to burn German cities to the ground in night attacks, thereby disrupting German war production and "dehousing," or killing a few hundred thousand German civilians in the process. Harris claimed that the RAF could win the war and preclude an invasion of western Europe. It could not, but the attempt to do so cost the lives of nearly fifty percent of British bomber aircrew. His counterparts in the U.S. Air Force also believed in the efficacy of bombing, but they advocated daylight "precision" bombing, which turned out to be rather imprecise given the near constant cloud cover over the continent and the consequent imprecision of the vaunted Norden bombsight. Furthermore, the American bombers required effective fighter escort to targets deep in Germany, which they only received early in 1944 with the arrival of the Merlin engined P-51 Mustang. At least the Americans suffered proportionately many fewer casualties and escaped the opprobrium that the RAF Bomber Command received for wantonly killing civilians in its night bombing to Dresden in February 1945. Historical accounts of the Eighth Air Force, such as Donald Miller's gripping narrative *Masters of the Air*,[59] invariably exhibit a triumphal tone, while accounts of Bomber Command strike a more somber note, as exemplified by Kevin Wilson's book, *Men of Air: The Doomed Youth of Bomber Command*.[60]

What the allied air forces did do most effectively, however, was to secure overwhelming aerial mastery of the skies above the beaches of the French coast and carry out the destruction of the French transportation system in the months before D-Day. Allied aerial mastery remained so absolute during the war in western Europe that the German army always functioned at a serious disadvantage compared to allied soldiers, who could summon fighter bombers staging in "cab rank" over the battlefields to dive and destroy German troop and armor concentrations. American science, technology, and industry enabled the United States to field an army of only ninety-nine divisions, far smaller than Germany or the Soviet Union, but its small size presumed huge Soviet numbers, because infantry, regardless of support from other arms, invariably took the highest total casualties and the United States had to resort to various expedients from taking men designated for service in other arms and putting them in infantry units with little training. The most experimental, and the most successful, of this example of unit mixing was Eisenhower's temporary integration of white infantry companies with the addition of a "fifth" platoon of African American volunteers for service in frontline combat in 1945.[61]

D-Day, June 6, 1944, the opening of the long desired second front in northwest Europe, remains the largest and most ambitious amphibious operation ever staged. Yet historians now depict the Normandy landings and the western Allies' prolonged and costly struggle to break out of the "bocage" country in France as flawed, if ultimately successful, operations. On D-Day, the allies benefited from aerial mastery and the support of offshore naval artillery. Omaha Beach, the costliest landing of the five beaches, in Adrian Lewis's detailed and analytical account, now becomes a "flawed victory."[62] In the overall experience of D-Day, Montgomery's failure to take Caen as rapidly as he had predicted now appears as a disaster, despite Monty's arrogant refusal to acknowledge it, or any of his other failures for that matter. The further destruction of the city through allied bombing impeded the British advance and helped the German defense, just as the bombing of Monte Cassino in Italy had provided determined German defenders with rubble and ruins in which to hide. The slow, bitter struggle through the hedgerows of the "*bocage*" country cost both sides, while devastating the French countryside and displacing the French inhabitants.[63]

German defenders in a few elite units, what remained of the once vaunted German army after three years in the Russian meat-grinder, proved worthy opponents for often raw and inexperienced allied soldiers as the struggle proceeded inland. German weaponry, from tanks to machine guns, was superior to allied equipment, an advantage that allied mass production neutralized, if at the cost, for example, of American tank units whose Shermans proved no match for German Tiger and Panther tanks.[64] The American "way of war" employed industrial superiority to out-produce the enemy, even if the weaponry delivered was not necessarily superior to that of the enemy.

While allied soldiers, particularly Americans, tended to view the Germans as being "just like us," they soon learned that fanatical SS units had no compunctions about murdering prisoners and civilians, practices they had perfected on the Eastern Front. As the fighting continued, American soldiers responded in kind, not just toward the SS, but toward regular German soldiers, and even German civilians. The closer the war drew to a victorious conclusion, the less American soldiers tolerated German resistance that could not alter the inevitable but that often proved fatal to them. In particular, the fanatical resistance of Nazi youth, either in SS reserve officer or Hitler Youth units, armed with Germany's more powerful version of the American bazooka, often cost advancing American units dearly in urban, village, or forest fighting. Under such circumstances, the Americans responded with devastating artillery barrages and fighter-bomber attacks. Once in possession of their objective, they took reprisals, and German attempts to surrender after killing American soldiers were met with a bullet to the head.

Recent scholarly accounts render American soldiers more human than heroic, capable of looting, pillage, and rape as well as brutal combat in difficult conditions. After the war, Western leaders could portray their offensives as a crusade to liberate Europe and the inmates of the concentration camps, but the American GI, fighting for the men alongside him, understood the war as a dirty job that he had to finish and survive in order to return home. This soldier in the latest scholarly works on the American soldier and the American way of war is the more nuanced and comprehensible GI of numerous memoirs.[65] For far too many Americans, Stephen Ambrose's multiple publications about American airborne and ranger units, portrayed in Steven Spielberg's classic film *Saving Private Ryan* and HBO's *Band of Brothers* series, have conflated these elite units with the entire army, thereby rendering a disservice to the average "dogface," wonderfully depicted by cartoonist Bill Mauldin's "Willy and Joe,"[66] who actually bore the brunt of the infantry war.

The latest western historical accounts now often include the experience of the liberated peoples and of German soldiers and civilians as well as the allied side from commanders to infantrymen. Frenchman Olivier Wieviorka's translated work *Normandy: The Landings to the Liberation of Paris*[67] exemplifies this approach. Perhaps the ultimate example to date of the end of the war is American William I. Hitchcock's *The Bitter Road to Freedom*,[68] which presents the European war in 1944–45 in nuanced and encompassing fashion, incorporating the military and civilian experience of all involved in the liberation of Western Europe and in the immediate aftermath of war. Hitchcock clearly demonstrates the brutality, degradation, and cost of war, even in the just cause of liberation from the Nazi yoke. The reader is left with no illusions about the nature of war, and his work provides a welcome and necessary antidote to heroic and triumphal accounts.

Historical studies now present detailed and encompassing accounts of the end of the war in the west—Stephen G. Fritz's book *Endkampf*,[69] Derek S. Zumbro's *Battle for the Ruhr*,[70] and Max Hastings' overarching study of 1944–1945[71]—present a stimulating and balanced, if revisionist interpretation, of the end of the war in Europe that encompasses the Eastern and Western European fronts. The Nazi-Soviet war, given the ideologies of the opponents, had been by definition a war of annihilation, and when the Soviet Union won, eastern and central Europe, caught between the two strongest armies in the world for six years, lay in ruins, prostrate at the feet of the Soviet conqueror, while Western Europe, not quite as prostrate, lay at the feet of the American and British liberators. And Europe nearly descended into chaos, as civil war broke out in Greece, and millions of "Displaced Persons" were swept up in the wartime and postwar dislocation, border changes, and population movements that dwarfed previous historical developments. Within three years of the German surrender, the division of Europe into a Soviet and a Western, essentially American sphere had hardened into a Cold War, which ended only with the collapse of the Soviet Union in 1991.

Now the allied powers had to turn to the Pacific and Asia, to finish the Japanese empire that had expanded into the western Pacific and Southeast Asia after Pearl Harbor. In the process, Japanese armies had seized such major British colonial cities as Singapore and Hong Kong with ridiculous ease, and their lightning conquest of Dutch Indonesia and Vichy French acquiescence to Japanese "requests" to occupy Indo-China humiliated European imperialists in front of their Asian subjects.

Historians of World War II, in accord with wartime leaders Winston Churchill and Franklin Roosevelt, relegate the Pacific Theater and Japan to secondary status, a war to be won after crushing Hitler's Germany. That basic prioritization, while it accurately reflected the relative strengths and ambitions of the Axis powers and of the allies' war effort, has relegated conflict in Asia to tertiary status and importance in the United States and Great Britain. Yet the war on the mainland of East and Southeast Asia led to the deaths of some thirteen million people, second only to the Nazi-Soviet War.

Churchill's and Roosevelt's choice incurred costly consequences for Great Britain and other European powers in their imperial realms in Asia and thus momentous change in the global balance of power. Japan's extended war in China and conquest of Southeast Asia led to the loss of British, French, and Dutch prestige and power in their colonies there and the inability of the United States to replace their domination with its own at the end of the war. The allied leaders' decision also resulted in the denigration of the China-Burma-India Theater (CBI), rendering the brutal struggle under exceedingly difficult conditions over this extensive part of the globe and its inhabitants "forgotten" to those who did not fight there and were focused on Europe and the Pacific. Histories of the Second World War have reflected these priorities, with the consequence that the CBI became "the Forgotten War." Incorporating the knowledge from recent works on the CBI not only gives a generation of aging soldiers who fought those battles their due, but also restores the nature and significance of these theaters to contemporary readers.

The naval and island campaigns that the U.S Navy, Marines, and army waged across the vast Pacific demonstrated the enormous industrial might of the United States and its ability to manufacture, man, and supply huge fleets of ships across incredible expanses of ocean and stage amphibious assaults on heavily defended islands. The struggles for the islands that the Marines and a few Army divisions waged became small battles of annihilation, as epitomized by the Japanese refusal to surrender and determination to kill as many of the American enemy opponents as possible. The closer the American forces drew to Japan, the more ferocious the clashes became.[72] When the United States confronted the likelihood of astronomical casualties on both sides in an invasion of the Japanese home island, the new U.S. President Harry Truman chose not to wait for submarines and naval tactical air forces to sever Japan from the continent by blockade and starve it to death, but to drop two atomic bombs, on Hiroshima and Nagasaki, in August 1945.[73]

Historical debates about whether the United States needed to drop one or both bombs essentially become moot when one considers the atmosphere of the time. Strategic bombers were burning Japanese cities to the ground, causing enormous casualties to no apparent political effect, and the Truman administration wanted to conclude the war in Asia as quickly as possible. No American soldier in Europe looked forward to fighting the Japanese, and the United States desired not only to avoid the casualties of an invasion but also to prevent the Soviet Union—whose entry into the war in East Asia Roosevelt had earlier negotiated to help end the Japanese threat—from conquering all of East Asia.

The Pacific Theater has greatly overshadowed the far more deadly conflict in Asia that had spawned it, perhaps because primarily British imperial forces, rather than Britain itself and the United States, actually fought the war against Japan in Asia. Mainly Indian and even African divisions fought the war in the jungles, paddies, and hill country of Southeast Asia. The war in Southeast Asia, like the war on the Eastern Front in Europe, reminds us that World War II, like its predecessor, remained very much an imperial war. Germany, Italy, and Japan, went to war to gain empire, either by conquering and subjugating regions like Russia, which previous generations had not envisaged as imperial domains but as empires themselves, or by wresting the colonies from older, decrepit empires like Britain and France. The Japanese conquest of Asia, regardless of how brutally the Japanese treated the other Asians whom they viewed as their racial inferiors in the process, humiliated and demonstrated the vulnerability of the European imperialists.[74] Independence movements across Southeast Asia gained momentum with the Japanese defeat and spilled over into the postwar era, ultimately drawing the United States into the last stage of Vietnam's thirty-year struggle for independence.

Churchill's goal, and the aim of the French, whether Vichy or Free, was the preservation of their respective empires, regardless of Roosevelt's often stated refusal to fight to preserve the British or the French empires. Colonial soldiers from Africa and Asia fought in Europe on behalf of Britain and France. Millions of Indian soldiers fought in Europe, North Africa, the Middle East, and in Asia to defend the British Empire, while wartime requisitions of materials and foodstuffs contributed to widespread wartime famine in Bengal, China, and Vietnam. Yet Winston Churchill could not tolerate the thought of Indian independence after major Indian support for the British in two world wars. The British withdrew hurriedly from India only as it fragmented into the separate and warring states of India and Pakistan in 1947, while British soldiers, often in conjunction with surrendered Japanese troops, attempted but ultimately failed to restore imperial rule across Southeast Asia after 1945.[75]

North and Sub-Saharan African soldiers composed the majority of troops in the French Expeditionary Force [FEF] that fought in Italy and southern France. British and American insistence that the French force that liberated Paris be white caused the French 2nd Armored Division to "whiten" its ranks. Charles de Gaulle's refusal to acknowledge soldiers who were not "Frenchmen" in the FEF effectively stymied recognition of African soldiers for their contribution to the liberation of France. In fact, Africa's role in the war is often reduced to the setting for the North African campaign, despite the fact that the French and British mobilized their indigenous African troops for combat in Europe and Asia and milked the indigenous economies for raw materials and foodstuffs. De Gaulle's initial base of support beyond Britain lay in French Equatorial Africa, where France's only native governor general, Félix Éboué, was the first to declare support for the Free French. Yet in the postwar era, the French refused to allow independence for their African or Asian possessions. They consequently fought, and lost, two brutal wars consecutively in Indo-China and Algeria. Ironically, the contributions of colonial soldiers in World War II gained them less recognition than similar achievements in the war of 1914–1918 because of the implications of their service in an era of increasing nationalism and demands for independence from imperial rule.

In the Second World War, gender and race played significant roles as they had in World War I. Women assumed critical roles in the domestic war economy of the primary European combatants and the United States. Even Nazi Germany, despite its slogan of "Children, Church, Kitchen" (*Kinder, Kirche, Küche*) for women, mobilized them to work in industry and agriculture. In the Soviet Union, some 800,000 women fought the war on the Eastern Front as soldiers, aviators, and support troops from nurses to NKVD (Peoples Commissariat for Internal Affairs) interrogators.[76] Women grievously suffered the war's consequences as civilian victims of strategic bombing campaigns conducted by the Germans, British, and Americans. Finally, women experienced the focused brutality toward them displayed in the Soviet occupation of Germany in 1945 and the Japanese conquest of much of Asia, most particularly in the "Rape of Nanking" and the Japanese army's use of tens of thousands of "comfort women" to serve as prostitutes for Japanese soldiers.

Racism, in the guise of the social Darwinist culture of the imperial world, figured even more prominently in World War II than it had in the Great War. Anti-Semitism was integral to Hitler's Nazism and thus the entire European war, and the unique nature of the Holocaust renders the second war qualitatively different from the first in the Nazis' concerted and industrialized campaign to exterminate the Jews of Europe as well as other social groups and "races." But examples of racism abounded beyond the Holocaust, as the refusal of European imperialists to grant independence to their peoples of color after the war indicated. Completely forgotten, in fact, was the serious divide between supporters of the British Empire and Nazi sympathizers in South Africa, one so serious that many of the racist supporters and ranks of the South African government that later imposed apartheid in 1948 had been Nazi loyalists during the war.

American conduct at home and abroad and in the war in the Pacific showed that the United States had made little or no progress in its treatment of citizens of color in the interwar years.[77] Violence erupted again in the United States during World War II as African Americans sought to enter the booming wartime labor market, and African American soldiers serving at home and abroad encountered the same demeaning treatment they had received from white Americans in World War I. American wartime internment of Japanese Americans who lived on the west coast, while the army recruited Japanese American soldiers to fight in Europe and to translate in the Pacific War, exemplified the willingness of the American government to infringe upon the constitutional rights of Japanese Americans while expecting Nisei youth to fight for a country that treated their families reprehensibly. In return, the Nisei fought superbly, and the 442nd Combat Group became the most highly decorated unit in the American army in World War II.[78]

By extension, the Pacific War became a bitter struggle with racial overtones on both sides. Some American military historians persist in contending that race played no role in the American conduct of the Pacific War, which they attribute to Japanese methods of warfare, the struggle to the death of the island war, and the brutal Japanese treatment of prisoners of war. No one contests the obvious point that Japanese attitudes of racial superiority toward other Asians and Caucasians led to their brutal conduct in Asia and the Pacific. In light of the evidence of American racism toward the Japanese that antedated the First World War, it is preposterous to assert that somehow American conduct toward the Japanese was devoid of racism and that American soldiers, products of a racist culture, suddenly discarded such attitudes when at war with the Japanese! John Dower's magisterial work presents a balanced and fair approach to the topic of race as a factor in both the Japanese and American conduct of the war.[79] Only the resistance of traditional military historians to the incorporation of the work of cultural historians can lead to such absurd denials. The United States remained a bastion of white racism that, like European imperial regimes, only began to change when forced to by the rising tide of people of color around the globe after the Second World War.

The United States itself, as its clash with Japan over China indicated, pursued its own vision and version of empire through capitalist domination of foreign markets. Roosevelt refused to defend the British or French empires, but the anger and dismay displayed in the United States during the McCarthy era over the "loss" of China when the Communists won the Civil War of 1947–49 and drove Chiang Kai-shek and his nationalist forces off the mainland to

Taiwan, or Formosa, indicates the strength of American designs on China. That rage replicated the American anger of the "Red Scare" towards the Soviet Union in the post–World War I era, and conservatives in both cases behaved as if the United States had some claim upon the future of newly independent states and consequently looked for someone to blame for the "loss" of states which were not the United States' to lose. To this day, most Americans' perspective of the war in China probably consists of awareness of the small number of American mercenary pilots who formed the "Flying Tigers" and of General Joseph Stilwell's negative attitude toward Chiang Kai-shek as described in Barbara Tuchman's book, *Stilwell and the American Experience in China, 1911–1945* (1972). Comprehension of some bitter truths about American policy toward China during and after the war demands reading studies that incorporate the Chinese perspective, such as Jay Taylor's recent work, *The Generalissimo: Chiang Kai-Shek and the Struggle for Modern China*.[80] Both the Korean and the Vietnam wars were the products of the post–World War II era, as the struggle in Korea began, and ended, at the 38th Parallel, where the Soviet invasion of East Asia had ended in 1945. The Vietnamese people regarded the United States as simply a successor to the former (and defeated) French colonizers and eventually replicated the French defeat there. If the war in Europe had evolved into the Cold War for more than four decades, the war unleashed independence movements in Asia and Africa that the European colonial powers, and later the United States, fought, in vain, for decades after 1945.

The study of the First World War draws historical observers into the apogee of the age of imperialism and imperial power, while the study of the Second World War places them in the era of its decline and decolonization. The world wars had begun in 1914 with European ascendancy and a German bid to pre-empt a rising Russia. The wars ended in 1945 with Europe in ruins, the United States and the Soviet Union astride the continent, and European global dominion irretrievably undermined in Africa, Asia, and the Middle East.

The lessons that thirty-one years of war—bounded on each end by the two costliest, deadliest, and most destructive wars ever waged—offer are many, but to date few Americans seem to have learned them. Imperialism and imperial ventures spawn war, and no war is ever a "good" war. War may be necessary or unnecessary depending on the broader historical circumstances, and it should always be undertaken only as a final, not a first, option. Finally, diplomacy should always be the preferred option, and diplomacy, which entails conciliation, can only rarely be equated with "appeasement," as some analysts obsessed with Munich in 1938 have done. Many Europeans, particularly the Germans, as well as the Japanese, appear to have learned these lessons. Of course they, having brought war upon themselves, have experienced it directly in all its horrors. Any illusions they had about the glorious and heroic nature of war, the catastrophe they experienced crushed, along with their countries, cities, and families and friends. The United States had been most fortunate to avoid their experience, but it has also failed to learn the lessons that their experience offers. The study of the history of the World Wars offers the opportunity for the intelligent student to learn such lessons without having to experience such disasters at first hand. But it also poses questions perhaps unanswerable in their very nature: how much do we learn from the experience of others, and can we even learn from our own experience?

NOTES

I would like to thank Michael Adas for his helpful comments on and careful editing of an earlier draft of this essay. The references cited in the footnotes should provide a guide to further reading on the various themes in the essay.

1. A.J.P. Taylor, *The Origins of the Second World War* (New York: Simon and Schuster, 1996 [1968]).

2. Cited in James L. McClain, *A Modern History of Japan* (New York: W. W. Norton, 2002), p. 136.

3. Cited in McClain, *Japan*, p. 137.

4. On the Belgian Congo, see Adam Hochschild, *King Leopold's Ghost: A Story of Greed, Terror, and Heroism in Colonial Africa* (Boston: Houghton Mifflin, 1999).

5. Isabel V. Hull, *Absolute Destruction: Military Culture and the Practices of War in Imperial Germany* (Ithaca, NY: Cornell University Press, 2006).

6. For a balanced interpretation of the war's origins that includes these events, see James Joll, *The Origins of the First World War* (London: Longman, 1984).

7. On the armaments race, see David G. Hermann, *The Arming of Europe and the Making of the First World War* (Princeton, NJ: Princeton University Press, 1996), and David Stevenson, *Armaments and the Coming of War: Europe 1904–1914* (Oxford: Clarendon Press, 1996).

8. McClain, *Japan*, p. 296.

9. McClain, *Japan*, p. 301.

10. The following discussion is based on two essential works: Sadao Asada, *From Mahan to Pearl Harbor: The Imperial Japanese Navy and the United States* (Annapolis, MD: Naval Institute Press, 2006), pp. 3–25, 47–51; Edward S. Miller, *War Plan Orange: The U.S. Strategy to Defeat Japan, 1897–1945* (Annapolis, MD: Naval Institute Press, 1991), pp. 19–30.

11. Miller, *Orange*, p. 22.

12. Eri Hotta, *Pan-Asianism and Japan's War 1931–1945* (New York: Palgrave Macmillan, 2007), p. 20.

13. Eri Hotta, *Pan-Asianism*, p. 39.

14. For global histories of World War I, see John H. Morrow Jr., *The Great War: An Imperial History* (London: Routledge, 2004), and Hew Strachan, *The First World War* (London: Penguin, 2005).

15. On wartime mobilization, see John Horne (ed.), *State, Society and Mobilization in Europe during the First World War* (Cambridge: Cambridge University Press, 1997), and Roger Chickering and Stig Förster, *Great War, Total War. Combat and Mobilization on the Western Front, 1914–1918* (Cambridge: Cambridge University Press, 2000).

16. On women in wartime, see Margaret H. Darrow, *French Women and the First World War: War Stories of the Home Front* (Oxford: Berg, 2000); Laura Lee Downs, *Manufacturing Inequality: Gender Division in the French and British Metalworking Industries, 1914–1939* (Ithaca, NY: Cornell University Press, 1995); Ute Daniel, *The War from Within: German*

Working-Class Women in the First World War, trans. Margaret Reis (Oxford: Berg, 1997); Claire A. Culleton, *Working Class Culture, Women, and Britain, 1914–1921* (New York: St. Martin's Press, 1999); and Nicoletta F. Gullace, *The Blood of Our Sons: Men, Women, and the Renegotiation of British Citizenship during the Great War* (New York: Palgrave Macmillan, 2004).

17. For naval histories of World War I, see Paul G. Halpern, *A Naval History of World War I* (Annapolis, MD: Naval Institute Press, 1994), and Richard Hough, *The Great War at Sea* (London: Oxford University Press, 1983). On the Battle of Jutland, see Keith Yates, *Flawed Victory: Jutland, 1916* (Annapolis, MD: Naval Institute Press, 2000).

18. On the air war, see John H. Morrow Jr., *The Great War in the Air: Military Aviation from 1909 to 1914* (Tuscaloosa: University of Alabama Press, 2008 [1993]).

19. Jean-Jacques Becker, Gerd Krumeich, Jay Winter, Annette Becker, and Stéphane Audoin-Rouzeau (eds.), *1914–1918: La trés Grande Guerre* (Paris: Le Monde Editions, 1994), p. 84.

20. Avner Offer, *The First World War: An Agrarian Interpretation* (Oxford: Clarendon Press, 1989), pp. 1, 2, 23–24, 38, 53.

21. For example, on France, see Richard S. Fogarty, *Race and War in France: Colonial Subjects in the French Army, 1914–1918* (Baltimore, MD: Johns Hopkins University Press, 2008).

22. On the war in Africa, see Edward Paice, *World War I: The African Front: An Imperial War on the Dark Continent* (London: Pegasus, 2008), and Hew Strachan, *The First World War in Africa* (New York: Oxford University Press, 2004).

23. M. Crowder, "The First World War and Its Consequences," in *General History of Africa VII. Africa under Colonial Domination*, ed. Adu Boahen (London: Heinemann, 1985), pp. 283–311.

24. W. F. Elkins, "A Source of Black Nationalism in the Caribbean: The Revolt of the British West Indies Regiment at Taranto, Italy," *Science and Society* 34 (1970): 99-103.

25. On India, see Judith M. Brown, *Modern India: The Origins of an Asian Democracy* (Oxford: Oxford University Press, 1994 [1985]).

26. On the United States in general during the war, see David M. Kennedy, *Over Here: The First World War and American Society* (New York: Oxford University Press, 1980), and Robert H. Zieger, *America's Great War: World War I and the American Experience* (New York: Rowman and Littlefield, 2000).

27. On the Ottoman Empire in the war, see David Fromkin, *A Peace to End All Peace: The Fall of the Ottoman Empire and the Creation of the Modern Middle East* (New York: Henry Holt, 1989); Justin McCarthy, *The Ottoman Peoples and the End of Empire* (London: Arnold, 2001); and Edward J. Erickson, *Ordered to Die: A History of the Ottoman Army in the First World War* (Westport, CT: Greenwood Press, 2001).

28. On Versailles, see Manfred Boemeke, Gerald D. Feldman, and Elisabeth Glaser (eds.), *The Treaty of Versailles: A Reassessment after 75 Years* (Cambridge: Cambridge University Press, 1998); Ruth Henig, *Versailles and After: 1919–1933* (London: Routledge, 1995 [1984]); and Margaret McMillan, *Paris 1919: Six Months That Changed the World* (New York: Random House, 2001).

29. On Russia in war and revolution, see Sheila Fitzpatrick, *The Russian Revolution* (Oxford: Oxford University Press, 1994 [1982]); W. Bruce Lincoln, *Passage through Armageddon: The Russians in War and Revolution, 1914–1918* (New York: Simon & Schuster, 1986); and Alexander Rabinowitch, *The Bolsheviks Come to Power: The Revolution of 1917 in Petrograd* (New York: Norton, 1978).

30. On Woodrow Wilson's reaction to the Bolshevik Revolution, see David S. Foglesong, *America's Secret War against Bolshevism: U.S. Intervention in the Russian Civil War, 1917–1920* (Chapel Hill: University of North Carolina Press, 1995).

31. On Fascism, see Stanley G. Payne, *A History of Fascism, 1914–1945* (Madison: University of Wisconsin Press, 1995), and Robert O. Paxton, *Anatomy of Fascism* (New York: Vintage, 2006).

32. John Keegan, *The First World War* (New York: A. A. Knopf, 1999), pp. 3–4, 8–9.

33. On Totalitarianism, see Bruce F. Pauley, *Hitler, Stalin, and Mussolini: Totalitarianism in the Twentieth Century*, 3rd ed. (Arlington Heights, IL: Harlan Davidson, 2009), and David Roberts, *The Totalitarian Experiment in Twentieth Century Europe: Understanding the Poverty of Great Politics* (London: Routledge, 2006).

34. On Pétain, see Charles Williams, *Pétain: How the Hero of France Became a Convicted Traitor and Changed the Course of History* (New York: Palgrave Macmillan, 2005). On Vichy France in general, see Robert Paxton, *Vichy France*, rev. ed. (New York: Columbia University Press, 2001).

35. On De Gaulle, see Jean Lacouture, *De Gaulle: The Rebel, 1890–1944*, trans. Patrick O'Brian (New York: W. W. Norton, 1993).

36. For a global study of the interwar period that does not emphasize a "Twenty Years' Peace," see Roger Chickering and Stig Förster, *The Shadows of Total War: Europe, East Asia, and the United States, 1919–1939* (Cambridge: German Historical Institute and Cambridge University Press, 2003).

37. On the Great Depression, see Charles Kindleberger, *The World in Depression, 1929–1939*, rev. enl. ed. (Berkeley: University of California Press, 1986).

38. At the present, the foremost biography of Hitler is Ian Kershaw, *Hitler: A Biography* (New York: W. W. Norton, 2008).

39. On Hitler's "Second Book" and his foreign policy, see Adolf Hitler and Gerhard Weinberg, *Hitler's Second Book: The Unpublished Sequel to Mein Kampf* (New York: Enigma Books, 2006), and Gerhard Weinberg, *Hitler's Foreign Policy 1933–1939: The Road to War* (New York: Enigma Books, 2005).

40. Adam Tooze, *The Wages of Destruction: The Making and Breaking of the Nazi Economy* (New York: Viking Penguin, 2006). Mark Mazower, *Hitler's Empire: How the Nazis Ruled Europe* (New York: Penguin Press, 2008).

41. On Japan's war, see Louise Young, *Japan's Total Empire: Manchuria and the Culture of Wartime Imperialism* (Berkeley: University of California Press, 1998); Peter Duus, Ramon H. Myers, and Mark R. Peattie (eds.), *The Japanese Wartime Empire, 1931–1945* (Princeton, NJ: Princeton University Press, 1996); Haruo Tohmatsu and H. P. Willmott, *A Gathering Darkness: The Coming of War to the Far East and the Pacific, 1921–1942* (Lanham, MD: SR Books, 2004); and Saburō Ienaga, *The Pacific War, 1931–1945: A Critical Perspective on Japan's Role in World War II* (New York: Pantheon, 1978).

42. On the "Rape of Nanking," see Iris Chang, *The Rape of Nanking: The Forgotten Holocaust of World War II* (New York: Penguin, 1998), and Takashi Yoshida, *The Making of the "Rape of Nanking": History and Memory in Japan, China, and the United States* (New York: Oxford University Press, 2009).

43. Alvin D. Coox, *Nomonhan: Japan against Russia, 1939* (Stanford: Stanford University Press, 1985).

44. Niall Ferguson, *The War of the World: Twentieth Century Conflict and the Descent of the West* (New York: Penguin, 2006).

45. On the Spanish Civil War, see Paul Preston, *The Spanish Civil War: Reaction, Revolution, and Revenge*, rev. enl. ed. (New York: W. W. Norton, 2007).

46. The essential history of World War II is Gerhard Weinberg's magisterial work, *A World at Arms: A Global History of World War II*, 2nd ed. (Cambridge: Cambridge University Press, 2005). Also see the essays in Roger Chickering, Stig Förster, and Bernd Greiner, *A World at Total War: Global Conflict and the Politics of Destruction, 1937–1945* (Cambridge: German Historical Institute and Cambridge University Press, 2005). Also see Richard Overy, *Why the Allies Won* (New York: W. W. Norton, 1995).

47. John Lukacs, *The Last European War, September 1939–December 1941* (New Haven, CT: Yale University Press, 1976). John Lukacs, *The Duel: The Eighty-Day Struggle between Churchill and Hitler* (New Haven, CT: Yale University Press, 1990).

48. On Germany at war, see Richard J. Evans, *The Third Reich at War* (New York: Penguin, 2009) and *Germany and the Second World War Vol. IX/I. German Wartime Society*

1939–1945: Politicization, Disintegration, and the Struggle for Survival, ed. Jörg Echternkamp, trans. Derry Cook-Radmore (Oxford: Clarendon Press, 2008). For a complete history of the Third Reich, see Richard J. Evans' earlier volumes, *The Coming of the Third Reich* (London: Penguin, 2003) and *The Third Reich in Power, 1933–1939* (London: Penguin, 2005).

49. Alexander B. Rossino, *Hitler Strikes Poland: Blitzkrieg, Ideology, and Atrocity* (Lawrence: University Press of Kansas, 2003).

50. Karl-Heinz Frieser with John T. Greenwood, *The Blitzkrieg Legend: The 1940 Campaign in the West* (Annapolis, MD: Naval Institute Press, 2005).

51. Ashley Jackson, *The British Empire and the Second World War* (London: Hambledon Continuum, 2006).

52. On Japan, the United States, and economic preparations for war, see Michael A. Barnhart, *Japan Prepares for Total War: The Search for Economic Stability, 1919–1941* (Ithaca, NY: Cornell University Press, 1987); Jonathan Marshall, *To Have and Have Not: Southeast Asian Raw Materials and the Origins of the Pacific War* (Berkeley: University of California Press, 1995); and Edward S. Miller, *Bankrupting the Enemy: The U.S. Financial Siege of Japan before Pearl Harbor* (Annapolis, MD: Naval Institute Press, 2007).

53. For the best example of "intentionalist" thought, see Daniel J. Goldhagen, *Hitler's Willing Executioners: Ordinary Germans and the Holocaust* (New York: Knopf, 1996).

54. See Christopher R. Browning, *The Origins of the Final Solution: The Evolution of Nazi Jewish Policy, September 1939–March 1942* (Lincoln: University of Nebraska Press, 2004). For an excellent recent study of the Holocaust, see Saul Friedländer, *The Years of Extermination: Nazi Germany and the Jews, 1939–1945* (New York: HarperCollins, 2007).

55. Norman Davies, *No Simple Victory: World War II in Europe, 1939–1945* (New York: Viking Penguin, 2007).

56. Examples of David M. Glantz's prolific works, all published by the University Press of Kansas in Lawrence, KS, are: *Stumbling Colossus: The Red Army on the Eve of World War* (1998), *Colossus Reborn: The Red Army at War, 1941–1943* (2005), *Battle For Leningrad, 1941–1944* (2005), *Zhukov's Greatest Defeat: The Red Army's Epic Disaster in Operation Mars* (2005), and *Red Storm over the Balkans: The Failed Soviet Invasion of Rumania, Spring 1944* (2006). With Jonathan M. House as co-author, Glantz has published, once again with Kansas, *To the Gates of Stalingrad: Soviet-German Combat Operations April–August 1942* (2009), *When Titans Clashed: How the Red Army Stopped Hitler* (1998), and *The Battle of Kursk* (2004).

57. Three excellent studies of the Soviet Union at war are: Richard Overy, *Russia's War: Blood upon the Snow* (New York: TV Books, 1997); Chris Bellamy, *Absolute War: Soviet Russia in the Second World War* (New York: Alfred A. Knopf, 2007); and Catherine Merridale, *Ivan's War: Life and Death in the Red Army, 1939–1945* (New York: Metropolitan Books, Henry Holt, 2006).

58. On the Mediterranean Theater, see Douglas M. Porch, *The Path to Victory: The Mediterranean Theater in World War II* (Konecky and Konecky, 2008).

59. Donald L. Miller, *Masters of the Air: America's Bomber Boys Who Fought the Air War against Nazi Germany* (New York: Simon & Schuster, 2006). On American aviators on all fronts, see John C. McManus, *Deadly Sky: The American Combat Airman in World War II* (Novato, CA: Presidio Press, 2002).

60. (London: Weidenfeld and Nicolson, 2007). See also John Terraine, *The Right of the Line* (London: Hodder and Stoughton, 1985).

61. David P. Colley, *Blood for Dignity: The Story of the First Integrated Combat Unit in the U.S. Army* (New York: St. Martin's Press, 2003).

62. Adrian Lewis, *Omaha Beach: A Flawed Victory* (Chapel Hill: University of North Carolina Press, 2007).

63. See Carlo d'Este, *Decision in Normandy: The Real Story of Montgomery and the Allied Campaign* (New York: Penguin, 2004). Also see footnote 62.

64. See Belton Y. Cooper, *Death Traps: The Survival of an American Armored Division in World War II* (New York: Ballantine Books, 1998).

65. On the GI's war in Europe, see Peter Schrijvers, *The Crash of Ruin: American Combat Soldiers in Europe during World War II* (New York: New York University Press, 1998).

66. Bill Mauldin, *Willie and Joe: The WWII Years*, ed. Todd DePastino (Seattle, WA: Fantagraphics Books, 2008).

67. Olivier Wieviorka, *Normandy: The Landings to the Liberation of Paris*, trans. M. B. DeBevoise (Cambridge, MA: Belknap Press of Harvard University Press, 2008).

68. *The Bitter Road to Freedom: A New History of the Liberation of Europe* (New York: Free Press, 2008).

69. Stephen G. Fritz, *Endkampf: Soldiers, Civilians, and the Death of the Third Reich* (Lexington: University Press of Kentucky, 2004).

70. Derek S. Zumbro, *Battle for the Ruhr: The German Army's Final Defeat in the West* (Lawrence: University Press of Kansas, 2006). Also see David Stafford, *Endgame, 1945: The Missing Final Chapter of World War II* (New York: Little, Brown, 2007).

71. Max Hastings, *Armageddon: The Battle for Germany, 1944–45* (London: Macmillan, 2004).

72. On the war for the Pacific islands, see Donald L. Miller, *D-Days in the Pacific: Guadalcanal, Tarawa, Saipan, Iwo Jima, Okinawa* (New York: Simon & Schuster, 2005), and Thomas W. Zeiler, *Unconditional Defeat: Japan, America, and the End of World War II* (Wilmington, DE: Scholarly Resources, 2004). For the American soldier at war in Asia and the Pacific, see Peter Schrijvers, *The GI War against Japan: American Soldiers in Asia and the Pacific during World War II* (New York: New York University Press, 2005).

73. For the latest work on the dropping of the atomic bomb, see Andrew J. Rotter, *Hiroshima: The World's Bomb* (Oxford: Oxford University Press, 2008). Also see Ronald Takaki, *Hiroshima: Why America Dropped the Atomic Bomb* (New York: Back Bay Books, 1996).

74. On the war in Asia and its effect on the British Empire, see Christopher Bayly and Tim Harper, *Forgotten Armies: The Fall of British Asia, 1941–1945* (Cambridge, MA: Belknap Press of Harvard University Press, 2005); Philip Snow, *The Fall of Hong Kong: Britain, China and the Japanese Occupation* (New Haven, CT: Yale University Press, 2003); Alan Warren, *Singapore 1942: Britain's Greatest Defeat* (London: Hambledon & London, 2002); and Louis Allen, *Burma: The Longest War 1941–45* (London: J. M. Dent, 1984). For a superb overview of the end of the war in Asia and the Pacific, see Max Hastings, *Retribution: The Battle for Japan, 1944–45* (New York: Alfred A. Knopf, 2008). Also see H. P. Willmott, *The Second World War in the Far East* (London: Cassell, 1999).

75. Two fine studies of the war's end and immediate postwar era in Asia are Christopher Bayly and Tim Harper, *Forgotten Wars: Freedom and Revolution in Southeast Asia* (Cambridge, MA: Belknap Press of Harvard University Press, 2007), and Ronald H. Spector, *In the Ruins of Empire: The Japanese Surrender and the Battle for Postwar Asia* (New York: Random House, 2007). For the specific case of Korea, see Allan R. Millett, *The War for Korea, 1945–1950: A House Burning* (Lawrence: University Press of Kansas, 2005).

76. For example, see Reina Pennington, *Wings, Women, and War: Soviet Airwomen in World War II Combat* (Lawrence: University Press of Kansas, 2007).

77. A fine general study of America's war that challenges common assumptions about it is Michael C.C. Adams, *The Best War Ever: America and World War II* (Baltimore, MD: Johns Hopkins University Press, 1994). Also see Ronald Takaki, *Double Victory: A Multicultural History of America in World War II* (New York: Little, Brown, 2000).

78. Among the most recent books on the wartime internment of the Japanese Americans, see John Howard, *Concentration Camps on the Home Front: Japanese Americans in the House of Jim Crow* (Chicago: University of Chicago Press, 2008), and Greg Robinson, *A Tragedy of Democracy: Japanese Confinement in North America* (New York: Columbia University Press, 2009). On Japanese American soldiers, see Bill Yenne, *Rising Sons: The Japanese*

American GIs Who Fought for the United States in World War II (New York: Thomas Dunne Books, St. Martin's Press, 2007).

79. John W. Dower, *War without Mercy: Race and Power in the Pacific War* (New York: Pantheon, 1986).

80. Jay Taylor, *The Generalissimo: Chiang Kai-Shek and the Struggle for Modern China* (Cambridge, MA: Belknap Press of Harvard University Press, 2009). See also Jonathon Fenby, *Chiang Kai-Shek: China's Generalissimo and the Nation He Lost* (New York: Carroll and Graf, 2004).

CHAPTER 6

Locating the United States in
Twentieth-Century World History

CARL J. GUARNERI

This chapter describes, and hopes to further, a budding relationship between American and world history. Since the 1940s, most conventional U.S. histories have begun with the idea that the nation has developed fundamentally apart from the rest of the world, outside the norms or constraints of global history. Challenging this exceptionalist premise, a movement to internationalize the study of American history has gained ground among scholars and teachers since the 1990s. It has been stimulated by public debates over American multiculturalism and globalization, growing American involvement in transnational movements, and concerns about the impact of American policies abroad—an issue that predated the events of 9/11 but was dramatized by them. Inside academia, the globalizing impetus has arisen from the vogue of Atlantic history among scholars of colonialism and slavery and, most powerfully, from the growth of world history in the core curriculum. Crystallizing these trends, the *La Pietra Report* of the Organization of American Historians in 2000 called for historians to rethink the traditional boundedness of American history and connect it to the world beyond.[1] Increasingly, historians have responded by tying American events to global trends, pursuing American movements across national borders, and analyzing U.S. history comparatively.

A corresponding move is taking place from the world history side, although its momentum is not as strong. The much-debated *National Standards for History* (1996) declared that world history should include American history as an integral part and reminded teachers that "the history of the United States was not self-contained but fully embedded in the context of global change."[2] Despite this, many world history teachers continue to subordinate the United States, citing the need to cover a large number of societies and the assumption that students "get" the U.S. story in American history classes. This neglect, along with world history textbooks with a regional or civilizational approach that compartmentalizes the United States in its own chapters, only reinforces the divide between U.S. and world history. Recent world history textbooks move toward bridging that gap by offering truly global narratives that improve the integration of American history into world history's interpretive schemas.[3] Meanwhile, after more than a decade of influential scholarship on empires and trade in the early modern period, world history scholars have begun to shift their sights to the nineteenth and twentieth centuries. Their broadly framed studies of native peoples' dispossession, industrialization, imperialism, migration and diasporas, and environmental change include the United States as an important site.[4]

To be sure, by the twentieth century, the United States could not be ignored as a factor in world history. In 1900, it was the world's largest industrial producer, and over the next hundred years it developed into a superpower that owned colonies, operated overseas military bases, intervened in two world wars, and through its policies and exports affected the lives of people around the globe. U.S. economic power helped to shape the century's technological and consumer revolutions and the globalized capitalism ascendant at its end. Meanwhile, decades of overseas wars, immigration, and trade made foreign events, products, and cultures an important presence in American life. Twentieth-century world history cannot be written without the United States, nor can American history leave out the world. Narratives from either perspective should tell a story that is intertwined, although not identical. The idea is not to absorb national history into world history, but to sustain a fruitful dialogue between the two. From the American history side, this means producing globally embedded analyses of the nation as the site of historical change, as a developing subject in its own right, and as an agent in the wider world.

This globalizing project does not exclude the study of foreign relations, the most traditional form of international history. It adds to it, however, histories of transnational exchanges of goods, people, and ideas; processes that the United States had in common with the rest of the world; effects of the exercise of American power abroad; and reciprocal impacts between the United States and other societies. While rejecting the exceptionalist idea that the United States stands outside of history, it does not discard the notion of national uniqueness—for the United States or for other nations. Instead, it proposes a more nuanced and globally contextual view than exceptionalism's preordained polarity between "us" and "them." A more cosmopolitan American history helps us see the United States amid larger patterns and to discover the weave of similarities and differences that have created its national fabric.

One caution seems in order. In rejecting exceptionalist claims that the United States developed outside the path of world history, historians must avoid swinging to the opposite—but related—myth that world history is "a mere extension of the triumphalist narrative of the American experience."[5] Triumphalism, which overestimates America's success and assumes that the world's peoples want to, should, or will become "just like us," has the potential to redirect world history into an apology for U.S. global hegemony, much as exceptionalism turns national history into nationalist celebration. Ultimately, the aim of bringing U.S. history and world history together is not to explode national myths like exceptionalism or triumphalism. The point is to understand the relation of Americans to other peoples—including connections and similarities as well as differences—and to trace their nation's changing position on a globe dotted with other nations, a world that was shrunk considerably by twentieth-century wars, revolutions, and technological innovations. An accurate, globally informed U.S. history should be framed not as America *versus* the world or America *as* the world, but as America *in* the world.

THREE PERSPECTIVES: COMPARATIVE, TRANSNATIONAL, GLOBAL

Historians who attempt to situate the United States in the wider world enter a conversation about world history that has been going on for decades. It is not surprising, then, that they have generally followed methodological routes that were first marked out by world historians. World history overviews tend to divide into two camps: those that examine comparative regions or "civilizations" and those that stress transregional contacts as motors of global change. Meanwhile, as world historians have expanded regional stories toward the global, they have debated what large narratives can encompass the whole. These three emphases—which we can loosely label comparative, transnational, and global—undergird the growing monographic literature on an enlarged U.S. history and are embodied in the first overviews of a more globalized American narrative.[6]

Each approach is, at least in part, a product of specific historical forces and ideas. Comparative history, the oldest, gained momentum from the vogue of social science methods and comparative sociology in the 1950s and 1960s and the ascendance of social history, with its cross-cultural categories of race, class, family, and gender. Transnational history has taken its impetus from the challenges of post-1960s globalization and the many impacts, experiential and intellectual, that denser exchanges have brought to Americans and the world. Finally, although some global narratives predate the 1970s, the emergence of world history as a curricular requirement gave global history scholarship a forceful *raison d'etre*. None of these approaches would have endured if scholars had not found national and culture-bound categories a hindrance; or to put it positively, had they not found it fruitful to pursue historical subjects across national boundaries.

Comparative History

Each approach has its own concerns and problems, with somewhat different implications for a globalized history of the U.S. twentieth century. Simplifying drastically, we can describe comparative history as an attempt to discern similarities and differences between two or more historical contexts or developments, and perhaps to find a larger meaning that applies to all. By now, comparative history of the United States has added to its early preoccupation with frontiers and slavery the study of nation building, emancipations, and—moving into the twentieth century—feminist movements, immigration patterns and policies, labor and protest movements, and welfare states. Like global and transnational historians, comparativists aim to expand history's explanatory lexicon by looking beyond the nation. Implicitly or explicitly they attack the premise of an exceptionalism that locates the United States as fundamentally outside global trends or norms.

Still, comparative history faces criticism from scholars who advocate a "transnational turn." As a general method, it is charged with producing static analysis that accepts history's outcome instead of presenting the alternatives available to people in real-time narratives. Critics also point out that the units of analysis comparativists select determine the questions they ask and the conclusions they reach. Both criticisms zero in on the nation as the prime culprit, suggesting that comparative history, wittingly or not, helps to construct national identity, affirms an essentialist national "character" or "creed," and assumes the centrality of the nation to history. Critics complain that comparative history, applied specifically to U.S. topics, reinforces exceptionalist premises. Tendencies evident in some comparative histories—such as privileging the nation as the unit of analysis, homogenizing its internal differences, taking it as the norm against which others are measured, emphasizing the national distinctiveness over shared global experiences, and ignoring reciprocal influences with other societies—have produced skepticism about the value of undertaking comparative work as U.S. history "goes global."[7]

Does comparative history necessarily make its Americanist practitioners complicit with exceptionalism? It is not hard to find recent comparative works where American differences are predetermined, exaggerated, or even essentialized. Seymour Martin Lipset's overdrawn contrast between U.S. and Canadian value systems is a case in point. Even Eric Rauchway's generally nuanced analysis of American trade and immigration betrays the exceptionalist bias announced in the book's title: *Blessed among Nations*.[8] Yet historians should be careful not to throw out the nation with the nationalist bathwater. Nations, not least the United States, create institutions and identities that structure their residents' lives and choices. National differences can matter a great deal, and they sometimes point to unique features. The long-running debate over "why there is no socialism in the United States" is marred by its all-or-nothing formulation—socialist organizations, in fact, gained ground in the era of World War I. Yet the scholarly controversy has brought to light distinctive features of American class relations, culture, and polity in operation from the 1880s to the 1930s. The racial and ethnic diversity of American workers, the separation of American unions from political parties, the pull of individualist ideologies, peculiarities of the American electoral system, and—not least—successful repression of socialism as "un-American" combined to limit socialism's appeal when compared to Western Europe.[9] The question of why the United States alone among industrialized nations has no national health care system may spur a similarly productive debate about the second half of the twentieth century.[10]

Comparative works can affirm important national differences without placing the United States outside the family of nations. Donald Meyer argued that "the history of modern women is best told as parts of the histories of separate nations," since capitalism, patriarchy, and socialism were decisively shaped by national cultures and governments.[11] The history of immigration and citizenship from the 1880s onward highlights crucial American variations, such as the guarantee of citizenship for all children born in the United States, within a spectrum of policies set by immigrant-receiving nations that otherwise evinced a broad consensus.[12] Comparative studies that include the United States among Western nations that industrialized, accepted immigrants, expanded the national government, and adopted welfare state measures emphasize common trends across national boundaries. Their comparisons produce a spectrum of contexts, outcomes, and explanatory features instead of a bimodal schema in which all others cluster together and the United States is a radical outlier.[13]

Nor does factoring in the nation-state commit historians to finding it the key variable. Relatively weak government powers in the United States and Latin America compared to Europe help to explain their high rates of violence, but the "weak state" theory has trouble accommodating the fact that the United States has the world's highest rates of criminal prosecution and incarceration.[14] Similarly, it may seem plausible to explain Americans' greater religiosity compared to Europeans by pointing to effects of the constitutional separation of church and state, but the gap became evident only in the late nineteenth century and widened dramatically after World War II. By the 1990s, Americans were about five times more likely than Europeans to be active members of a religious group.[15] This trend suggests that social and cultural changes on both sides of the Atlantic loom larger than national political frameworks in explaining religious adherence. Even in nation-based comparative studies, demographic factors, ethnic origins, economic activities, and geographic differences—all related only indirectly to national governments or policies—often emerge as key explanatory variables.

George Fredrickson's studies of the United States and South Africa remain the gold standard for comparative work, in part because they demonstrate that binational comparisons can illuminate both cases and avoid the pitfalls of exceptionalism.[16] In general, however, multinational comparisons move outward more easily to global themes and lend themselves less readily to exceptionalist dichotomies between "us" and "them." Examining several similar cases can move scholars toward discovering commonalities and variations along a continuum. In fact, comparative work opens possibilities for relativizing exceptionalism itself by comparing the American sense of "chosenness" with other ideologies of national specialness and superiority, such as republican France, South Africa under Boer control, or modern Israel. In such instances, as Glenda Sluga has written, "comparative histories of nations and of national identities also invite reassessments of the units out of which they are constituted—that is, the nations/states that are the subjects of comparison."[17]

Transnational History

A more explicit reassessment is proposed by transnational history, a term that has recently come into vogue in the United States. Because "transnational" describes an impulse more than a method, its definition is fluid and covers a variety of examples. Transnational history is set off from others by the motion and scale of its subjects. Generally, it explores the movements of people, goods, processes, and institutions that cross oceans and borders. Prominent twentieth-century subjects in the emerging transnational literature include commodity trade and technology transfer, travel, diasporas and migration systems, imperial relations, the impact of global mass culture, international social movements such as feminism or religious fundamentalism, and global nongovernmental organizations (NGOs).

Variants of transnational history have arisen simultaneously in different national and historiographic contexts, and there is confusion over labels. Some scholars stake out separate realms for "international history," which studies formal interstate relations; "entangled history," which analyzes mutually constitutive national or imperial trajectories; "cross-national" history (a variant of the French "histoire croisée" or German "transfer history"), which analyzes reciprocal political, social, and cultural impacts; and transnational history, which concentrates on the objects and dynamics of circulation rather than national origins and impacts. Other scholars use "transnational" as an umbrella term for all of these.[18]

Perhaps most important, the relation between transnational and national history varies according to different studies and models. In some versions, it enlarges the space of national history by stressing how the nation is affected by events abroad and exerts influence elsewhere. To take one example, the strong American nation-state of the twentieth century was made transnationally as immigration, security concerns, and global economic competition led the United States and other nations to take firm control of their borders.[19] "Entangled history," as currently proposed for empires and nations, fits within this formulation of transnational history, which keeps the nation as a focal point but includes external contexts and reciprocal influences. So, too, does the move to describe the mutual effects of imperial and national history—the impact of involvements abroad upon metropolitan society and culture, and vice versa—that has reinvigorated British studies and is now energizing a body of work that explores connections between the domestic and international workings of American empire.[20]

Among the most valuable contributions of U.S.-oriented transnational history are works that examine the global impact of American consumerism and mass culture in the twentieth century. Originating in the 1970s from a blanket indictment of American cultural exports as a form of "cultural imperialism," studies of the historical transmission of American fast food, music, movies, and television programs evolved into more nuanced explorations of their multiple meanings, resonances, and uses abroad. Scholarship on cultural reception suggests that American mass culture means different things in different national, ethnic, class, gender, and generational contexts. Popular culture's audiences select or reinterpret its messages to fit their own social, political, or personal circumstances. U.S. television programs can reinforce anti-Americanism or stimulate consumer fantasies, and American jazz, rock and roll, and rap music have taken complex journeys from their homeland to far-flung destinations. Moreover, so-called "Americanization" has traveled on a two-way street, as rock and roll refashioned and reexported by The Beatles and the Rolling Stones, pop music from Brazil and Jamaica, Japanese animation, and Spanish-language television made huge inroads in the American market. Transnational cultural studies have charted this two-way traffic, documented its mutual influences, and examined its hybrid forms as symbols of the interplay of the global and national in a hyperconnected world.[21] Such studies provide material for enriching national and global history simultaneously.

Transnational history can also imply the desire to transcend the nation, not simply to situate it among vectors of reciprocal impact. Flows of people or goods, multinational institutions, and global "imagined communities" can be seen to raise particular spheres of life out of local or regional contexts into a transnational realm. When this network becomes the historian's main subject, the nation is reduced to one among many relevant sites. Circuits of migration and exchange, for example, have their own chronology and logic in which national interventions are only partly formative. The growing literature on ethnic diasporas, which began with studies of African migration and has spread to Chinese, Italian, Indian, and Irish studies, suggests the contrasting directions that transnational history is pursuing. Some diaspora studies integrate migrants' strong ties to their homelands or their allegiance to panracial/ethnic identities into national narratives, showing how they challenge theories of assimilation, suggest new concepts of multiculturalism, and at times spark nativist opposition. The varied outcomes that the same ethnic diaspora produces in different national settings can suggest fruitful comparisons. These approaches to diasporas—even ones that link diasporas to "deterritorialized nation-states"— nod toward traditional comparative studies and imply substantial compatibility with nation-based history.[22]

Other studies envision ethnic diasporas as challenges to the nation-state and harbingers of "transnational citizenship," although there is much debate over what this concept entails.[23] Whether taken literally as dual or multiple citizenship or figuratively as a deterritorialized social identity based on ethnicity or something else, this version of transnationalism subordinates national frames of analysis. At every landing, formerly neatly national attributions are replaced by multiple affiliations or by participation in international networks of migrants who share regional origins or occupational and religious characteristics. These identities, sustained by rapid communication and frequent mobility, can supersede national allegiances or render them irrelevant. The nation, some argue, is being "unmade" as well as made transnationally. Diasporas, along with other transnational phenomena such as criminal networks, religious movements, and multinational corporations, regularly cross national boundaries, use global networks of communication and transportation, and are only partially subject to national laws. According to some theorists, they point the way toward a "postnational" era that will require a correspondingly nonnational, even global, form of narrative.[24]

In a similar vein, scholars have increasingly examined borderlands as sites of cross-national flows, hybrid identities, and regional commonalities, qualities that call into question the boundedness of nation-centered history and symbolize, some say, the decreasing efficacy of nation-states in a globalized world.[25] The American Southwest, which has long been a region of contested boundaries and overlapping peoples, provides a favorite example. In one sense, the U.S.-Mexican borderland epitomizes a transnational liminal zone where immigration, trade, and popular culture blur boundaries and create arenas of interpenetration and interdependence. Taco Bell restaurants in Mexico, Mexican soap operas in the United States, ethnic intermarriages, and new transnational identities such as "Chicano" or "Latino" complicate unitary national narratives on both sides of the border. Yet borders are also where dominant national groups "draw the line" by enforcing national security and mainstream definitions of culture and identity. On the U.S. side, intensified exchanges have triggered defensive responses such as tightened border control, English-only laws, and refusal of public aid to "undocumented" residents. Like globalization writ small, stepped-up flows across the U.S.-Mexican border have produced multiple effects: the growth of a multinational capitalism whose managers move enterprises to the cheapest labor market or entice desperate workers across national borders, the creation of a transnational space with its own hybrid commonalities, and the emergence of heightened nationalist anxieties as a result of such interpenetrations.

National institutions and nationalist sentiments remain very much in this mix. Critics point out that the new transnational history may overestimate the importance of supranational institutions in an age when nation-states remain powerful. Some warn against hitching the wagon of transnational history to the simplified teleology of globalization, which is often unidirectional and homogenizing. Transnational studies have expanded the repertoire of American history, covering topics that range from diasporas, borderlands, and global pop culture to tourism, missionaries, and the Rotary. They have also enlarged the explanatory frame for narratives of reform and public policy that have customarily been told in insular national terms.[26] Although these are exciting moves, it is too soon to know whether transnational studies may compel a more fundamental rethinking of American history or produce major overarching descriptive frameworks or explanatory interpretations in which the United States can be located afresh.

Global History

In the meantime, global "grand narratives" already in circulation provide a third methodological reference point for an enlarged U.S. history. These ask us to locate the nation inside frameworks that world historians invoke to describe processes that have tied regions and continents together in the modern era. Among them are the "dual revolution" of political and industrial transformation that began around 1750; modernization theory and other schemas of political or economic development; geopolitical histories of competing nation-states and empires; world systems analysis and other narratives of domination, dependency, and resistance; and the history of globalization itself.

Some of these have special salience for twentieth-century U.S. history. Achieving prominence in the 1950s and 1960s, modernization theory reflected the industrialized West's confidence that its road to wealth and democracy offered a multistage model that other societies could follow. Rigid and ahistorical, modernization theory is mainly of interest today as an ideology whose influence can be traced in U.S. policies toward colonial subjects and developing nations. It legitimized the widespread belief among twentieth-century Americans that the world's peoples envied the American standard of living and longed to imitate American life.[27] Still, in the loose form of a transition from "traditional" to "modern" societies, a process that began in Western societies and spread by force or emulation to the rest of the world, with the concomitant task of explaining rapid versus "lagging" development, the general notion of modernization (and its cousin, "Westernization") remains embedded as a deep structure in some narratives of twentieth-century world history. It is still visible in works that celebrate America's rise and project it as a model for the rest of the world.[28]

World systems theory challenged modernization by turning attention to unequal economic relationships. According to this schema, an integrated world capitalist economy coalesced after the fifteenth century, dominated by the rich and powerful "core" nations of Western Europe, which gradually brought distant regions on their "periphery" into dependence upon its financial and commodities market.[29] Like modernization theory, the specifics of the world systems approach have been heavily criticized, but its broad outlines remain influential. Loosely applied to the United States, a world systems perspective starts with North America as an outpost on the global periphery that slowly but surely became enmeshed in the web of colonization, mercantilism, and the slave trade. After independence, the United States embarked upon a course followed by other "semiperipheral" states: consolidating the nation-state, developing export production, industrializing, and asserting control over its regional hinterland. By World War I, the United States emerged as an important member of the European core group and a global power in its own right. Carried forward, world systems analysis interprets the global economic and political crises of the 1970s as the decline of U.S.-Western European hegemony and the beginning of a multipolar world order. A grand narrative based on world systems scaffolding would thus trace the U.S. path from the periphery to the core of the world economy ("from settler colony to global hegemon") and then confront it with a chaotic era of emerging powers (China, India, Brazil), financial crises, and competing regional blocs.[30]

The developing phases of the world economy were paralleled by and embodied within shifting interstate systems. At first by necessity and increasingly by choice, Americans sought to define their place in existing frameworks of alliance and competition among states and empires. Geopolitically, placing the United States in world history involves examining its role in nineteenth-century Europe's "balance of power" between competing nations, the "new" imperialism of the late 1800s targeted largely at Africa and East Asia, the alliances that led to World Wars I and II, the global cold war between communism and capitalism, and the unstable post-1970s world order that featured the United States as the lone superpower but not the sole determinant force in world politics.

In both arenas—the world economy and the international state system— the United States began its national career at the margins of power and emerged early in the twentieth century to join other great powers at the center. This rise to global power links U.S. history to two other world historical trajectories, those of empire and globalization.

Empire is a thread in world history that extends from ancient to modern eras. Elastic in definition as well, it describes relations that range from territorial conquest and overseas rule to more subtle and consensual ways of controlling other peoples by means of international alliances, economic domination, or "cultural imperialism." As the United States grew in power, it practiced all these forms of control, despite Americans' general reluctance to use the "e" word. In the nineteenth century, the nation expanded westward to the edge of the continent, then graduated in the 1890s to formal overseas colonization. In the twentieth century, frequent U.S. intervention abroad, leadership of the cold war alliance, and attempts to export American institutions and culture world- wide all have elicited intense public debate over the existence, nature, scale, and workings of an American empire. It is not surprising that world history teleology figures prominently in this controversy. An American empire has been said to culminate the westward course of imperial power since Rome; it has been cast as a successor to Britain's global regime or positioned as one pole of an East-West or North-South rivalry that will dominate the global future. Meanwhile, calibrating America's position at any given moment on a recurrent imperial/great power cycle from "rise" to "fall" has become a mini-industry among scholars and pundits.[31]

Today's globalized economy, which some see as a manifestation of Ameri- can empire, introduces another shared history in which to locate the United States. Historians have pointed out that "globalization," a coinage that emerged in the 1980s to describe the rapid linkage of the world's peoples and econo- mies, has a long past. Some contend that the interlinked global economy de- scends from the interoceanic contacts of the "first globalization," the Euro- pean overseas expansion after 1500 that mingled distant populations and ecosystems. There is greater agreement that another era of globalization spanned the period of the new imperialism, roughly from the 1870s to World War I, and that its recent resurgence began, after the contractions of depression and the disruptions of world wars, sometime after 1945.[32]

In contrast to many popular formulations, this reading of globalization is discontinuous and nonlinear. It also intersects with major junctures in Ameri- can history, suggesting that the United States can be used as a prism for under- standing globalization. Thomas Bender has noted that the first globalization tied the New World colonies to world history from their founding. More im- portant for our purposes, Michael Geyer and Charles Bright have made the case in an influential essay that genuine global integration emerged for the first time during the "second globalization," from the new technologies, ideas, and institutions that North Atlantic societies (Western Europe and the United States) projected outward in their formal and informal empires of the mid- to late nineteenth century, and in the competitive responses they generated around the world. Ever since, the interplay between nationalism as a means of mobili- zation, identity, and resistance, and larger global forces has been a defining tension of the modern era.[33]

This chronology highlights the period since the mid-nineteenth century as the first truly global epoch, in which virtually all the world's peoples were ma- terially and consciously connected. It suggests the possibility of replacing the periodization centered on a "long nineteenth century" (1750–1914) that dom- inates current world history textbooks—and a "short twentieth century" based on geopolitics (1914–1991)—with a "long twentieth century" narrative (circa 1850–present) that concentrates on the new global interconnectedness and its ramifications. This schema better accommodates the pre-1914 origins of enduring worldwide social trends and economic structures. It also highlights developments that survived the oscillations of the world wars and cold war, whose events chop up textbooks into short-term units that often lose sight of long-term trends.[34]

This chronology also frames the challenge of describing the relationship between modern U.S. and world history. What Geyer and Bright call "the condition of globality" congealed at the very time the United States joined the great power scramble for markets and colonies. To be sure, Western European nations, especially Great Britain, were the strongest promoters of late nineteenth-century globalization. The British Empire, steamships, the Suez Canal, the gold standard, and other forces and conventions joined the world on European terms. Yet, "Anglobalization" paved the way for eventual U.S. hegemony.[35] After the economic deglobalization of depression and world war, the United States began to call the most important shots that integrated the world—or at least the noncommunist world, since the cold war attempted to reshape globalization in bimodal fashion. U.S. hegemony in the post–World War II world was short-lived, however. It was damaged by defeat in Vietnam and the monetary and energy crises of the 1970s. Many scholars argue that the United States lost dominant control over the globalizing process at the very time its corporations, culture, and currency were going "transnational."

It is revealing that both the world systems and globalization theories fix upon the 1970s as a dividing line between eras of Western/U.S. hegemonic and multifocal globalization. For advocates of the so-called "new global history," the 1970s are critical for a different reason. Using satellite communications and supranational institutions as critical measuring rods, they argue that genuine globalization dates only from that period. Some interpret the entire span from the 1500s to the 1970s as a "pre- or proto-global" era.[36] It is far too soon to tell whether this theory will hold. Right now, there is more evidence—and greater utility for historians—for initiating discussion about globalized changes in the second half of the nineteenth century, keeping its end point open. Clearly, the definition, dynamics, and periods of globalization will continue to be debated, and each formulation will have implications for placing the United States in world history.

Global grand narratives offer the most encompassing and systematic way to embed national histories within world history. Yet historians do not have to agree that world history moves in unison through stages of development to nudge modern American history toward global contexts. Along with most nations, the United States has participated in what Charles Tilly has called the "large processes" of modern history.[37] Such developments as industrialization, urbanization, state building, the demographic transition, militarization, imperialism, and the changing status of women are the staples of world history textbooks. The United States is too infrequently and too cursorily incorporated into these chapters, which have the potential to identify crucial interactions, chart national variations, and suggest the wider context of national issues and debates. American history textbooks, for their part, relegate global parallels to sidebars and boxed features.

Thomas Bender and John Gillis, among others, have urged American historians to keep transnational trends and processes consistently in view as frameworks for assessing U.S. developments.[38] Scholars exploring the growth of the American state, migration flows, the rise of consumerism and big business, the spread of mass schooling, the workings of American imperialism, and other large twentieth-century themes have demonstrated the value of framing these subjects globally.[39] This approach can be practiced "inside/out" or "outside/in"; that is, by enlarging local or regional histories toward international contexts or by announcing global themes whose ramifications can be traced in local arenas. Either way, relating national history to global processes does not dissolve the nation but fosters a globally informed national history, one that does not arbitrarily stop at the nation's edge to search for causes, effects, and significance.

A Convergence of Perspectives?

The three models discussed here are not mutually exclusive. Searching for wider comparisons, connections, and contexts are different ways of moving U.S. history toward the global, each with its distinctive set of questions and perhaps its own bias on the continuum from national distinctiveness to shared global trends. But there is ample common ground among them and opportunity for complementary work. All three approaches tend to denaturalize or denormalize the nation; all work within contexts that expand beyond it; and all chip away at the myth of an America isolated from the forces affecting other lands. Practitioners of each approach often incorporate others as a minor thread, and increasingly all three perspectives are joined in single narratives. Globally informed studies of the Great Depression, for example, describe it as a national and global economic crisis, compare governments' responses, and trace mutual policy influences—sometimes on the same page. And the burgeoning literature documenting the transnational youth movement and the "Revolutions of 1968" offers globalized explanatory frameworks as well as national comparisons along the way.[40]

Rather than engaging in special pleading for one of these approaches, historians should think of them as working on different levels but having the potential to join a mutually beneficial conversation. Global history proposes grand narratives and describes large processes that offer opportunities for national variations, regional comparisons, and transnational studies. Comparative history qualifies sweeping claims about globalized uniformity and uses nations or regions to particularize generalizations about historical processes and movements. Transnational histories look both ways; they mine new transborder subjects for global narratives while suggesting national comparisons along the way and adding the crucial topic of reciprocal impacts. Scholars and teachers enlarging the range of twentieth-century U.S. history can take advantage of all three.

THE UNITED STATES AS A WORLD POWER: PATTERNS OF ENGAGEMENT AND INFLUENCE

Historian Geoffrey Perret has written that "America's wars have been like rungs on a ladder by which it rose to greatness."[41] If "greatness" means global power and influence, the Spanish-American War of 1898 and World Wars I and II indeed represented momentous steps. In 1898, the United States officially graduated from continental expansion to overseas empire; in 1917, the nation first entered a war on the European continent; and in 1941, it joined a global military alliance aimed at defeating a coalition of authoritarian regimes in Europe and Asia.

True enough in its broad outlines, Perret's statement requires additions to correspond with the realities of twentieth-century America. For one thing, it needs a backstory: America's military victories were built upon a deeper history of pursuing trade and other national interests overseas as well as its expanding industrial capacity. For another, it must discuss the ideological impulse that spurred the U.S. quest for influence. America's wars, like its foreign relations generally, were energized by pride in the nation's cultural and political institutions and the desire to spread them worldwide. Yet the drive for global hegemony was only one side of the story. Despite their nation's growing international involvement, many Americans remained proudly parochial. War was a route to global power, but it was also the way Americans learned geography, according to a popular jest. Each step toward global engagement was accompanied by political debates over whether the negative effects of colonies, alliances, wars, or membership in international organizations outweighed their benefits. Once undertaken, these outward ventures tested the American public's limited patience for wars "over there," long-term international commitments, and even global interdependence.

The Rise of the United States to Power

What factors and forces lay behind the rise of the United States to global power by the early twentieth century? American history textbooks often treat industrialization as a domestic process and imply an abrupt switch from overland expansion to overseas empire. Both approaches mislead students by focusing internally and by beginning the story too late. Addressing the question should send scholars back in time to sketch the foundations of America's growing prowess during the "long twentieth century." The question is also impossible to answer from a purely domestic perspective, requiring consideration of processes outside the nation and its interactions with the rest of the world.[42]

Like that of all European great powers that emerged between the seventeenth and nineteenth centuries, the story of America's emergence was internationally entangled. U.S. leaders also generally followed European precedents. Compared to Western European powers, American ascendancy was unexceptional in its reliance upon seizure of lands from indigenous peoples, economic growth, military might, overseas colonization, and other forceful projections into the global arena of capitalism and competitive nation-states. It culminated in entry into European wars, a move that earlier Americans had repudiated but one where—as Perret noted—military victory confirmed global status. Despite these broad similarities, America's rise was relatively rapid, comparable to Japan's half-century trip from the sidelines to the center of global politics. And America's location opened opportunities for influence on two oceans as well as in its own hemisphere.

The young nation's location on the North Atlantic littoral placed it in a world of great power models and positioned it to receive Europe's excess capital, advanced technology, and labor-seeking migrants. On the Caribbean and Pacific shores, as recent histories emphasize, overseas expansion was a direct result of the nation's westward push. Proslavery "filibusters" made the first American attempts to acquire Caribbean lands, the California gold rush encouraged Americans to build a Panama railroad, and the West Coast became a staging ground for American missionaries, whalers, merchants, and business owners in the Pacific. To support U.S. trade with Asia, the government imposed commercial treaties upon China, Japan, and Hawaii and purchased Alaska from Russia. Competition loomed large in expanding the U.S. global role. In calling for an "Open Door" policy of equal Western trade privileges in China in 1899, the United States was looking to compensate for its recently closed continental frontier. It was also playing catch-up with European imperialists, just as the scramble to annex the Philippines was meant to cut off threatened Japanese and British moves.[43]

In actuality, America's ascendancy was aided by its second-stage timing. With the exception of Hawaii, nearly all U.S. overseas lands were acquired from a prior colonial power. More broadly, the United States benefited from following in Britain's footsteps. Britain's supremacy in naval power provided relative peace and "free security" for the young nation. American businesses overseas profited from the spread of the English language as well as British-led conventions in banking, transport, and currency conversion. U.S. leaders followed Britain in demanding open markets and extraterritoriality, and England provided the model for building up U.S. naval power to protect national interests overseas. From the forced opening of Japan in the 1850s to gunboat diplomacy in the Caribbean in the 1910s to the "invasion" of Europe by American music and movies in the 1920s, the U.S. government's aggressive trade policies—also drawing on British precedent—paved the way for global economic clout.

America's industrial might was another foundation of its global power. By 1900, the United States became the world's largest industrial producer. American farm exports receded to about half of the U.S. total, replaced increasingly by manufactured goods. Abundant natural resources, inexpensive immigrant labor, European investment, technological borrowing and innovation, and a corporation-friendly government fueled American industrial growth. By diversifying into manufacturing (with the help of high tariffs) and retaining ownership of its businesses, the United States avoided the dependence upon European (especially British) control that plagued farm and mine export industries in many Latin American nations. The sheer size of the U.S. domestic market encouraged the rise of giant businesses whose consumer-friendly appeals and mass production techniques enabled them to penetrate the world market.[44]

American overseas investments soon followed, and by 1914, they began to exceed incoming foreign monies. Canada, Mexico, and Central America became the first places where American holdings eclipsed Britain's, supporting the thesis that U.S. influence in the hemisphere was not simply an extension of the Monroe Doctrine but a training ground for global power.[45] Finally, loans to America's allies during World War I transformed the nation from a debtor to the world's largest creditor, giving Americans substantial indirect power over borrowing nations and intensifying U.S. involvement in their domestic affairs. Those loans combined with other factors to push the nation into the European war—an unprecedented escalation of U.S. overseas commitments. After the war, American companies rushed in to fill the vacuum in Europe and to compete in Europe's former colonies.

It is worth noting that the culminating boost to U.S. global power came through events initiated elsewhere, primarily through Europe's catastrophic self-destruction in the course of two world wars. Both wars spurred decolonization movements by dismembering the losers' empires and bankrupting the victors. In both cases, Americans emerged from war comparatively unscathed and economically paramount, primed to take advantage of trade opportunities and confident in the superiority of their institutions.

Still, only after World War II did American leaders unhesitatingly assume the role of global political leader that the nation's ideological, military, and economic resources seemed to justify. Because the United States commanded such a powerful economic and technological base by the early 1900s, the question has arisen why it took the nation decades to assume international hegemony. Offered as reasons why the United States did not, and perhaps politically could not, take on the position of global hegemon between the wars were: the failure of Woodrow Wilson's campaign to join the League of Nations, America's relative lack of dependence upon foreign trade, the reluctance of U.S. bankers to stabilize the interwar global economy, the nation's inward turn toward protectionism during the Depression decade, and the continuing cultural and political hold of isolationism in the face of gathering war clouds in Europe and Asia.[46] It may also be true that the question itself exaggerates the extent of Britain's control over the pre-1914 global economy and the degree to which the United States could dictate terms for the interwar world. In any case, the issue merits further study, not least because it has implications for the nature of U.S. global power, including the theory that the United States was a reluctant world leader.[47] The idea that American presidents had the means of global hegemony at their disposal but lacked a domestic mandate, though certainly debatable, points to a persisting pattern of ambivalence among Americans about their nation's place in the world.

Global Engagement and National Insularity

Traditional narratives of American foreign affairs in the first half of the twentieth century portray the nation oscillating from involvement in World War I to isolationism in the 1920s and early 1930s and then again, more seriously and permanently, to global engagement after World War II. Historians have qualified the isolationist tag given to the interwar years in many ways, from detailing U.S. trade policies to chronicling U.S. interventions in Latin America. Nevertheless, ongoing tensions between global integration and national insularity have been a prominent motif of American attitudes and policies throughout the long twentieth century. Nation building, and even empire building, in a global era involved a shifting mix of openness and closedness. In the late nineteenth century, the United States was a prime beneficiary of globalization, but at the same time, its high tariffs protected domestic industries. American imperialist takeovers or military interventions brought out significant opposition at home. In many cases, formal U.S. engagement with the wider world ebbed and flowed as American policy makers perceived foreign developments as threats or opportunities and as different domestic groups' agendas toward the world won out in electoral contests.

The struggle between inclusive and exclusionary immigration policies provides one of the richest examples. Moved by domestic debates as well as economic and geopolitical considerations, the nation's door to newcomers swung on its hinge through the long twentieth century: first toward closure from

Chinese exclusion in the 1880s to the sweeping restrictive laws of the 1920s, which were tightened in the 1950s by cold war concerns; then toward openness in 1965 when the quota system was jettisoned and a surge of Latino and Asian migrants occurred; then (potentially) toward closure again when economic fears and waning Anglo ethnic dominance converged with obsession with national security following 9/11 to reignite a nativist movement. Despite widespread celebration of immigration as a national trademark and the open door as the American ideal, the history of immigration policy showed a continuous struggle between competing visions that was resolved only tentatively and temporarily.[48]

One way to reconcile policy oscillations and contradictory impulses has been proposed by Ian Tyrrell, who suggests that the American state and society reversed their orientations toward the outside world after World War I.[49] Before that watershed, transnational social and economic people-to-people contacts were legion even as the nation-state asserted its traditional detachment from the international community. Beginning in 1917, the U.S. government joined international agreements and formed alliances, but the American people turned aggressively inward to cultural exceptionalism. According to Tyrrell, contradictory impulses were visible in the years between 1925 and 1970. On the one hand, World War II and the cold war hugely extended America's global outreach. America's economic prowess spread technological changes and consumer capitalism to Europe and Japan, and American leaders endorsed multilateralism through membership in the United Nations (UN). On the other hand, midcentury Americans celebrated their uniqueness and zealously guarded their culture from foreign contamination and "un-American" ways. The study of geography and foreign languages—never an American strength—declined despite the growing presence of U.S. soldiers, diplomats, and business leaders abroad. Strongly exceptionalist versions of national history prevailed. A narrowed patriotism limited Americans' global cultural integration.

According to this interpretation, only with renewed globalization and heightened global competition in the late twentieth century did both the American state and society look outward. Even then, Americans brought to their global encounters new versions of the old tension between their pride in national distinctiveness and their resentment of global interdependence. In a resolutely global era, the American public's long-standing habits of selective attention to world affairs, simplistic categories for analyzing them, and self-righteousness endured, producing what one historian calls "an odd combination of parochialism and arrogance."[50] Whether or not Tyrrell's periodization holds, he and other scholars have alerted us to Americans' deep-seated ambivalence about the global world they inhabit and that their policies helped to create.

Ideology, Culture, and U.S. Foreign Relations

U.S. policy makers have been more consistently attentive to foreign developments than most Americans, but they, too, have confidently proclaimed America's superiority. Henry Luce's famous 1941 essay, "The American Century," which called for the United States to use its preeminent power and prestige to spread its ideas through the postwar world, was hardly original.[51] Luce, the child of American missionaries in China, gave voice to crusading impulses and missionary ideals that had infused American imperialism in the 1890s and justified America's entry into World War I. Whether U.S. policy makers preferred influence by example, unilateral action, or international cooperation, they consistently blended concern for U.S. national interests with a strong dose of faith in the nation's principles and practices and the desirability of disseminating them.

Since 1990 historians of American foreign relations have loosened the grip of cold war "realists" on their field by reengaging it with ideologies and *mentalités*. Impressed by cultural continuities, they have found a core of common principles and ideas that endure beneath the twists and turns of American twentieth-century foreign policy. According to Michael Hunt, three basic components of this shared ideology are: (1) Americans' vision of national greatness, (2) their propensity to view the world's population through a hierarchy of race, and (3) their growing distrust of foreign revolutions.[52]

Since the early nineteenth century, American nationalism revolved around twin ideas—an exceptionalist assertion of national uniqueness and an expansionist sense of mission—that at first appear contradictory, but turn out to be opposite sides of the same coin.[53] American institutions were the result of unique social conditions and a peculiar national "genius," but once articulated they could be adopted anywhere as catalysts of progress. New nations have often infused their emergence with a sense of destiny, but Americans developed an especially passionate conviction of their world historical importance as a model for others. Confidence in liberal democratic government, capitalist enterprise, and technological progress underwrote a century-long parade of policies designed to spread America's example, from U.S. imperial rule in the Philippines at the beginning to nation building in Iraq at the end. Woodrow Wilson remains the most compelling presidential spokesman for this strain of thinking, but his principles, if not his methods, have been widely shared.[54]

Racial hierarchies, like exceptionalism, migrated from domestic conversations to overseas enactments. Claims of white racial superiority, honed against African Americans and nonwhite native peoples at home, were also shaped in reaction to European and Asian immigration that threatened Anglo-American hegemony.[55] These prejudices were transferred overseas to stigmatize the peoples of Latin America, Asia, and Africa and to legitimize U.S. initiatives of conquest, colonization, or Westernization.

Recent histories of American thinking about foreign peoples have added hierarchies of culture to Hunt's category of race. In varied ways, U.S. historians have adopted Edward Said's concept of "Orientalism" to explore cultural bias in American policy making. Studies of American images of the Middle East or Asian peoples, for example, suggest how an imperialist mentality has projected Western fears, needs, and preconceptions onto foreign peoples, then used this imaginary construct to form or to justify patronizing or oppressive policies.[56] Tropes of gender have also woven their way into policy makers' discussions, demonstrating the "dynamic interrelationship between the creation of foreign policy and the construction of gender."[57] Gendered images have been used both to degrade the other and to elevate the self: to imbue nonwhite peoples with stereotypes of female inferiority or to celebrate civilized "manliness" and fortify it through conquest.[58] Conceived in broad terms that encompass race, gender, and religion—and moving into cutting-edge areas such as sensory perceptions—the study of cultural formations that influenced Americans' behavior toward other peoples is among the most promising directions of current foreign relations scholarship.

Like their views of national outsiders, Americans' readings of foreign revolutions have filtered distant events through domestic traditions.[59] Although their nationhood was won in a pioneering anticolonial revolution, many Americans chose to hold it up as a "moderate" model against which all others were found lacking. Especially after Russia's Bolshevik Revolution, American leaders feared the "menace" of communism, which they identified with socialism, dictatorship, and atheism—all "un-American" practices. Once the United States asserted itself as the enforcer of global order after World War II, revolutions abroad threatened regional stability and global trade, both essential to hegemonic powers. By the mid-twentieth century, the nation born in revolution became a powerful opponent of third world uprisings. U.S. leaders continued to promote republican institutions worldwide, but they had to look like theirs and be adopted peacefully.

Scholars who emphasize political economy would amend this triad of core beliefs to include a stronger economic component. In William Appleman Williams's "open-door" interpretation, which remains influential, U.S. policy makers consistently sought access to foreign markets to secure domestic prosperity and business support.[60] Walter LaFeber, Emily Rosenberg, and others have broadened the open-door idea into a loose creed that advocated government promotion of free enterprise at home and abroad, incorporating technology, investment, and access to markets. Whether called "liberal developmentalism" (Rosenberg) or something else, this creed complements Hunt's triad when it is unhitched from Marxist determinism and not offered as a single-factor explanation.[61]

Emphasis on core beliefs that underpinned U.S. policies does not dismiss foreign policy controversies but helps to frame them. Americans on both sides of such debates often shared basic values but differed over their specific application. American exceptionalism cut both ways in 1898, fueling arguments for the nation's imperial mission as well as objections over its "descent" into empire. So did racism, which could rationalize either the Anglo-Saxon "white man's burden" or the dread of colonial racial intermixture. To a considerable extent, policy differences were about means rather than ends. Should U.S. republican institutions be spread by example or force? "Exemplarists" insisted on the former, along with John Quincy Adams and most nineteenth-century statesmen; "vindicators" followed Woodrow Wilson in arguing that foreigners needed to be taught through intervention to elect good rulers.[62] Should the United States become involved in European rivalries and wars? Those called "isolationists" in the twentieth century believed that foreign commitments would place the American model in danger by risking centralization at home or empire and exhaustion abroad. Their opponents saw the defeat of foreign dictators as an essential prelude to preserving American democracy and spreading its influence. Finally, are U.S. interests in foreign relations best pursued by unilateral actions or by international negotiations and compacts? Unilateralists feared ceding American national initiatives, sovereignty, and values to international organizations; multilateralists (often called "Wilsonians" or internationalists) responded that such institutions quicken international exchange and spread democratic habits of cooperation and compromise.

Nor does consideration of ideology dismiss the "realist" influence in U.S. thinking, by which policy makers downplayed idealism in favor of hard-nosed considerations of geopolitics, such as great power competition for territory and resources, the balance of power, or spheres of influence. "Realist" strategizing was especially prominent during cold war jockeying against the Soviets. It could be used to justify such disparate policies as alliances with anticommunist dictators or nonintervention in Eastern European revolts against Soviet control. Despite these shifting maneuvers, the bedrock rationale remained ideological: the idea that a fundamental global contest was under way between diametrically opposed systems, with the American capitalist, democratic model superior to communism. Perhaps the most glaring example of privileging this ideological conflict was the U.S. war in Vietnam, where a doctrinaire disposition to see communism as ubiquitous and monolithic mired the nation in its longest and least successful war. Every nation's foreign policies emerge from the intersection of national aims and ideals with situational constraints and opportunities. Scholars impressed by the so-called "cold war consensus" argue that U.S. leaders were especially adept at fusing—and sometimes masking—national self-interest with idealistic principles.[63] Both admirers and critics of U.S. hegemony agree that the habit endured beyond the cold war.

The moralistic tinge of U.S. foreign policy discourse has had double-edged effects. On the one hand, it motivated critics at home and abroad to pressure U.S. leaders to live up to their professed ideals. Advocates of racial desegregation, human rights, religious pluralism, open-door immigration, and other causes have turned to American foundational documents or presidential speeches for textual support. The "Wilsonian moment" is one such transnational episode, when in the wake of World War I, anticolonial leaders in Egypt, India, China, and Korea seized upon the Fourteen Points' principle of "self-determination of peoples" to press for national autonomy.[64] On the other hand, moralism has often deluded the American public into thinking that since their nation's policies are well meaning, resistance stems from unabashed self-interest or an irrational anti-Americanism. Moralistic rhetoric obscures the actual record, leading Americans to grossly overestimate their nation's foreign aid budget, for example, or its record in promoting global human rights and environmental improvement.

Reciprocal Impacts: America in the World/ The World in America

The projection of U.S. power and values abroad was not the sole trajectory of America's global engagement. Among the most promising subjects of transnational history are circuits of mutual influence—the ways in which "outside" influences affected the domestic United States at the same time that American actions shaped developments elsewhere. Economic historians remind us that the United States has always been part of the global economy, subject to its cycles of expansion and recession, currency crises, and ebbs and flows of capital. Foreign inroads into the American market are as ubiquitous as Japanese autos or clothes made in China.[65] The global entanglement of social and political changes has been less obvious but equally significant. As the United States exerted power overseas, "America in the world" had its counterpart in "the world in America."

Literary scholars have pioneered explorations of the domestic impact of U.S. imperialism, but social and cultural historians are catching up. Kristen Hoganson describes how well-to-do American women of the late nineteenth and early twentieth centuries, like their counterparts in Britain, showed their sophistication by displaying household objects imported from "exotic" overseas locales, including U.S. imperial lands. Paul Kramer's study of the U.S. regime in the Philippines suggests how racial policies forged in the island encounter came to the mainland through cultural exhibits at world's fairs, which then helped to spur anti-Asian immigration policies. And Gary Okihiro traces Hawaii's lingering echoes in twentieth-century American culture—from surfing, hula, and sports to racial thinking—at the same time the islands themselves became Americanized.[66]

These examples, like the flow of American pop culture and music outward and then, in transformed ways, back again (discussed above under the heading

"Three Perspectives: Comparative, Transnational, Global"), demonstrate that "cultural imperialism" is a two-way street. The export of American religion, especially evangelical Protestantism and Mormonism, to the third world at the same time that Americans imported Buddhism and Asian religious traditions provides a slightly different model of mutual influence, more parallel than entangled. Immigration is another case of reciprocal social impact. Migration to the United States has been "pushed," at least in part, by the impact of U.S. moves abroad, such as cheap exports of grain that forced peasants in Europe and Mexico off their land, or U.S. military actions in Europe, Asia, and Central America that created refugees who seek safety in the United States. At the same time, twentieth-century migrants—especially the postwar influx from Latin America and Asia—have made the United States a more diverse nation in appearance, languages, and customs. "Whenever I hear about North American penetration in Latin America," the writer Gabriel García Márquez quipped, "I laugh into my coat lapels because the real cultural penetration is that of Latin America into the United States."[67] By widening the spectrum of who Americans could be, postwar global immigrants changed the United States as much as it changed them.

The cold war caused a huge leap in U.S. commitments abroad, so it is not surprising that it had sweeping domestic effects. "Containment culture" did its work not just through the postwar Red Scare but also in popular movies, television shows, and military toys.[68] The "imperial presidency" took shape at the height of the cold war, when Congress ceded war-making powers to the White House, the national security and defense establishment consumed much of the federal budget, and executive foreign policy put the nation in a seemingly permanent state of war.[69] More positively, historians have documented the effects of cold war propagandizing in aligning federal officials behind the civil rights movement's desegregationist agenda. Stung by charges from third world critics and Soviet propaganda that the leader of the so-called "Free World" tolerated racist practices at home, the U.S. State and Justice Departments filed supporting briefs in most of the major civil rights cases, including *Brown v. Board of Education of Topeka*.[70]

Overall, the dominant flow of influence shifted from the nineteenth century, when the United States was primarily an importer of money, goods, and ideas, to the late twentieth century, when it was a major exporter, able to project its economic and cultural power worldwide. This did not prevent reciprocal effects, but it changed their character to include opposition as well as acceptance. In the second half of the twentieth century, resentment of U.S. cultural exports (to France, for example) or U.S. policies of warfare and regional development (in the Middle East) returned as resistance to U.S. trade and foreign policy initiatives.[71] In a roughly similar way, transnational NGOs, whose numbers increased rapidly after 1960, launched criticisms of many U.S. policies concerning nuclear arms, human rights, humanitarian aid, and the environment. Some of these NGOs, such as Friends of the Earth and the Committee for a Sane Nuclear Policy, were formed in the United States, while others, such as Greenpeace (Canada), *Médecins sans Frontières* (France), and Amnesty International (Great Britain), were founded elsewhere; most established affiliates in other countries. The rise of such organizations was a marked feature of globalization, serving notice that historians should examine their effects on American and global politics.[72]

Paradoxes of a Global America

Coexistence of a strong drive to global power and American resistance to global constraints has been especially evident during post-1970 globalization. The former energized U.S. promotion of free-market capitalism through the International Monetary Fund (IMF) and other means, continuing U.S. interventions in Latin America and new ones elsewhere, and a "war of choice" and nation-building mission in Iraq. The latter justified ignoring European allies on Middle East policies, refusing to join international agreements on criminality and the environment, and disparaging the United Nations, which the United States helped to found in 1945, but which it can no longer dominate.

Several scholars have resorted to the language of paradox to encapsulate this mixed record. Commenting on "the Paradox of a Global USA," Bruce Mazlish remarks that "the most powerful actor on the global stage seems resolutely determined not to live in the world it is helping to create through globalization." Akire Iriye writes that the internationalization of goods and ideas "was more synonymous with Americanization before the 1950s, but became less so after that" because it came to involve "many features that were not generated, or welcomed, by Americans." Both complain that when U.S. policy makers could not control the terms of globalization, they turned against it.[73]

Two related paradoxes underscore the limits of American power under globalization. One based on economics recounts how U.S. promotion of new technology and free-market capitalism sowed the seeds of competition in other lands. As American entrepreneurs had imitated and outcompeted the British in the second half of the nineteenth century, so did Japanese and others to the United States in the second half of the twentieth. Thanks to globalization, the United States is in danger of becoming the victim of its own success. Another paradox points out the inability of the United States, despite its hegemonic aims and military prowess, to control a globalized world. After scanning the diffusion of political clout to regional powerhouses like China and Japan or continental blocs such as the European Union, Joseph Nye lists a series of threatening international political and environmental trends. He concludes that America's might is "too great to be challenged by any other state, yet not great enough to solve problems such as global terrorism and nuclear proliferation" without "the help and respect of other nations."[74]

These paradoxes point to the need for Americans to rethink the notion that the global ought to be their national story writ large. In a broad sense, the conflicted U.S. relationship with globalization is not unique, but one that is faced by all nations. How do nation-states groomed to promote national ideals and interests confront questions of sovereignty, security, and mutual dependence that are raised by today's hyperconnected world? Three factors make the American case different and especially important. First, the United States is not an ordinary nation, but the most powerful presence in today's global arena. How its leaders address its relationship to globalization will have enormous consequences, constituting a potent force that may contribute to common solutions for global peace, equality, and sustenance or work against them. Second, since the United States took the lead in postwar globalization through its promotion of free trade, consumer capitalism, the "information revolution," and even—at first—the UN, its rejection of multilateralism strikes many foreign observers as inconsistent and self-serving, adding fuel to global anti-Americanism. Finally, the basic concepts of American identity that have undergirded its foreign policies, which are rooted in exceptionalism and missionary nationalism, seem to conflict with the current trend toward a global interdependence that does not depend upon U.S. leadership or conform to American views. Because the American public and their policy makers of the twentieth century, as in the nineteenth, saw their nation as unique and exemplary rather than simply one nation among many, forging a new relationship with the rest of the world for the twenty-first century will be not be an easy task.

A Nation among Others: Cohorts and Competitors

"Where in the world is America?" ask two prominent scholars probing the nature of today's global connections.[75] "Everywhere" may seem to be the proper response, given the global reach of U.S. military and political power and the spread of American pop and consumer culture by the end of the twentieth century. One productive way to address the question historically would be to depict the expanding radius of U.S. foreign policies over the course of the century. Especially after World War II, U.S. power extended into areas previously deemed marginal to national concerns, such as the Middle East and Africa. Meanwhile, the U.S. orientation toward East Asia underwent dramatic reversals, reflecting the decline of Europe and resurgence of Asia as a center of economic power. Another, quite different tack might be to examine the influence of mythic images of America around the world—a sort of reverse "Orientalism."

This section offers instead a comparative approach to locating the United States globally, one that examines resemblances and common histories between societies that shared key features with the United States and have been similarly situated toward global developments. The medieval historian Marc Bloch once noted that the most illuminating comparisons are those between societies with common influences and substantial basic similarities. Four such reference groups seem most appropriate for comparing to the path of modern American history: (1) other British New World "white settler societies"; (2) postemancipation societies in the New World black diaspora; (3) Western European nations that forged transatlantic connections with the United States and underwent similar political, social, and industrial trends; and (4) the new political and industrial world powers of the twentieth century, Japan and Russia. (Japan is discussed here, but Russia is covered below in "Five Topics for an Integrated U.S. and Global History.")

Cohorts and Competitors

Canada, Australia, and New Zealand share important features with the United States. All four so-called "settler societies" originated as temperate-zone colonies established under frontier conditions primarily on British foundations and were populated mainly by Europeans, who outnumbered and dispossessed native peoples. Each combined, albeit uneasily, British inheritances with those of later immigrants from Europe and Asia. All eventually separated from the British Empire but remained dependent upon Europe for investment capital, foreign trade, and cultural styles.[76] In the late nineteenth and early twentieth centuries, ties among the group became particularly strong, evidenced by mutually influenced policies toward indigenous peoples, simultaneous early women's suffrage campaigns, similar experiences of labor unions and land reform, active transnational networks of social reformers, and common adoption of restrictive immigration laws, particularly against Asians.[77]

After World War I, however, divergence became a major trend of the settler-society cohort. The United States emerged as the only one to become a mature industrialized economy and world power. America took on a role closer to imperial Britain's, gradually replacing it as Canada's dominant trading partner and source of direct investment in its staple, mineral, and manufacturing sectors. In other ways, however, the settler-society cluster remained a distinctive unit, a dual history as colonists and colonizers positioned their white majorities uniquely in the global decolonization story. In the twentieth century, all four nations faced the challenge of developing "post-settler" cultural attitudes and policies. All sought to include Asian and other immigrants of color in a society committed to "multiculturalism"—a Canadian coinage of the 1980s. All struggled to rectify past actions toward indigenous peoples by according them land and legal rights, including self-government.[78] Comparative and connective histories of these projects could be mutually enriching and also widen the context of recent U.S. history.

In one crucial respect, the United States differed from Britain's "white dominions" and resembled more closely its colony in South Africa: both were lands divided racially between white settlers and the descendants of African peoples, many of them slaves. The African American intellectual W.E.B. Dubois recognized that American racism was "but a local phase of a world problem" that surfaced in South Africa's settler colonies and throughout the black Atlantic.[79] Within this group, there exist revealing comparative studies of the immediate postemancipation years.[80] Moving into the twentieth century, a trove of comparative work has analyzed the dynamics of white supremacy during America's Jim Crow years (1880s–1960s) and the South African apartheid regime that took shape in the early twentieth century and became formalized by the 1950s.[81]

Such comparisons, and others still to be undertaken, have many topics to cover: the complex legacy of slavery, the evolving history of racial categories, the dynamics of regimes of segregation and racial stratification, the problematics of constructing national identities among African-descended peoples (DuBois' famous "double-consciousness"), and the making and remaking of hybrid Afro-mestizo-European cultures. Transnational history adds the crucial insight that people and ideas are constantly in motion. Racial concepts and practices developed at home figured prominently in U.S. imperial ventures in the Philippines and Cuba. Meanwhile, twentieth-century circuits of migration provide the context for understanding international movements such as Garveyism, which had enormous appeal in the Caribbean as well as the United States, and which shaped the outlook of Ghana's first prime minister, Kwame Nkruma, during his American residency. Pan-Africanism in the first half of the century and the influence of Gandhi among South African, Indian, and U.S. people of color at midcentury demonstrate the interconnectedness of racial and anti-imperial struggles.

Historians have recently demonstrated how important midcentury anticolonial movements were in shaping the U.S. civil rights movement and spurring African American protests against U.S. policies in Africa. In the other direction, leaders of independence movements in Africa and Asia cited the American civil rights protests as inspirations or models.[82] Awaiting study in comparable detail is the "international turn" of the late 1960s and 1970s, whereby the neo-Marxist theories of Franz Fanon and others influenced liberation leaders in the black diaspora, including Steve Biko in South Africa and Malcolm X and Eldridge Cleaver in the United States. Such topics not only suggest fruitful synergies between transnational and comparative history but also reaffirm that diaspora studies open up new spaces for a global U.S. history.

In the twentieth century, Western Europe remained a crucial reference point for American history and identity. Although the framework of Atlantic history ends by current convention with the abolition of slavery in Brazil in 1888, transatlantic connections hardly disappeared. Mass overseas migration from Europe continued, peaking in the 1910s. European art, literature, philosophy, and architecture, along with social welfare policies, made influential "Atlantic crossings" in the first half of the century, pulled by American wealth and provincial hunger and often pushed by the ravages of war and fascist regimes.[83] Politically and economically, however, the prevailing winds of influence in the North Atlantic shifted eastward. After World War II, the United States became the indisputably dominant economic power and diplomatic partner of Western Europe. From the Marshall Plan and the North Atlantic Treaty Organization (NATO) to the "invasion" of Europe by American consumerism and mass culture, the "irresistible empire" of American hegemony shaped Western European culture and politics in crucial ways.[84] For at least a few midcentury decades, it seems possible for historians to speak of an "American Atlantic."

Despite these transatlantic ties, Americans continued to hinge their national identity on polarities between the Old and New Worlds. When urbanization, industrial capitalism, and political centralization coursed through the Atlantic world in the early twentieth century, they were framed by exceptionalist discourse. Many Americans feared that factories, class divisions, and big government were "Europeanizing" their society, while Europeans, watching the invasion of American consumer goods and democratic culture, sounded alarms against "Americanization."[85] These paired warnings were actually indications of convergence, not difference. They disguised broadly similar—and often mutually influencing—responses on both sides of the North Atlantic, including the rise of big business and consumer capitalism, changes in women's roles, the growth of labor unions, and the development of stronger states. Differences of timing or degrees of change only reinforced overarching similarities.[86]

This underlying pattern of convergence persisted into the post–World War II years, expanding to include the entry of married women into the paid labor force, a common sexual revolution and youth revolt in the 1960s, and even similar concerns over immigration and multiculturalism. Yet, during these years, three key transatlantic differences emerged, and they became more pronounced as the cold war wound down. First, continental Europeans' commitment to the welfare state intensified in the face of the neoliberal Reagan-Thatcher "revolution" of the 1980s, leading to trade policy disputes with the United States and stronger affirmations of a cultural gap based upon divergent "social models." Second, the collapse of the Soviet Union, together with memories of the world wars' destruction, eroded Europeans' support for military spending, while the United States continued its pattern of military interventions worldwide. European leaders increasingly preferred diplomacy and negotiation to force in international disputes, and most differed with U.S.

presidents on Middle East policy, including the Iraq War of 2003. Finally, the expansion of the European Union (EU) beyond shared passports and currency toward an integrated federation portended a resurgent, unified, and more independent Europe. How would the EU exercise global power? Would it endanger the long-standing North Atlantic alliance between the United States and Western Europe? Would its example of continental integration spread to South America or elsewhere and become a building block of a new global order in the twenty-first century? At the end of the century, some U.S. foreign policy analysts predicted that the EU would increasingly come into conflict with the United States and resist its economic and geopolitical objectives.[87] Skeptics labeled this portrait overdrawn, but the trend it embodied paralleled the perception that a multipolar world was crystallizing in the post–cold war decades.

Another of the century's emergent great powers, Japan, invites comparison with the United States, which entered the global arena in the same late nineteenth-century era.[88] Both nations attained great power status rapidly and in broadly similar ways: via industrialization, military victories over neighbors, and imperial takeovers facilitated by naval might—although Japan faced greater resistance from existing Western powers. As second-stage industrializers responding to British domination, U.S. and Japanese businesses mixed openness to foreign capital and technology with reliance upon government protectionism and subsidies. Both nations were also secondary players in the Western imperialist scramble who made their greatest inroads in nearby islands and shores (Japan in Korea and the Pacific, the United States in Central America and the Caribbean). Like the other imperialist powers, Japan and the United States developed ideologies of racial superiority that justified ruling subordinate peoples while their technological advances allowed them to pose as modernizers of "backward" peoples. Given their work ethic, economic success, and expansionist tendencies, it becomes understandable that the two nations became antagonists and (eventually) intense but peaceful rivals in global trade.

Nevertheless, key geographic, historical, and cultural differences set the two nations apart. A huge nation straddling two oceans, the United States possessed far more agricultural and mineral resources and a larger domestic market than Japan, and thus was less dependent upon empire or trade. The American population was augmented by millions of job-seeking immigrants, whereas Japan, growing explosively on a small cluster of islands, sought outlets for emigration overseas. Japan's bid to become "the England of the Pacific" was cut short by World War II. Stripped of empire and military might, it became reliant upon U.S. protection against China or other potentially hostile powers, a dependent position that nevertheless freed investment funds for economic development. Japan's spectacular postwar growth, from one-third of Britain's output in 1950 to three times the British gross domestic product (GDP) in the 1980s, was built upon political stability, educational successes, and technological innovation. Lastly, while the Japanese proved remarkably successful at combining industrial growth with indigenous cultural traditions—perhaps *because* they did so—their way of life became an alternative to Western modernization that influenced other Asian peoples but had limited appeal elsewhere. Americans, in contrast, developed a modernized Western cultural style that sought, and often achieved, enormous global influence.

For these reasons as well as the anticipated rise of China, some Western observers have predicted long-term "middle power" status for Japan and continued global preeminence for the United States. Perhaps, but such one-on-one comparisons may obscure the new terms of globalized competition, which reward economic growth more than military success, the multifocal nature of economic globalization, and the rapid rise of East Asia more generally, which may challenge the long period of Western global dominance.

Comparisons between the global United States of the mid-twentieth century and the prior century's British Empire may be more appropriate. Allusions to the British Empire popped up as soon as Americans opted for colonialism in 1898, and they became commonplace when the United States became the dominant global force following World War II. They gained special salience when, in response to attacks of 9/11, President George W. Bush pursued an aggressive military and geopolitical strategy. This unilateral turn opened public debate over the existence and desirability of an "American empire," a regime based on enforcing global order on U.S. terms. At the century's end, the policy dispute between anti-imperialists and "neoimperialists" echoed the controversies of its opening years, when Americans had argued over annexing the Philippines.[89]

In its half century of rising global engagement, did the United States follow the imperial model of Great Britain, whose economic and naval power controlled half the globe by the time of World War I? Neoimperialist historians stressed the successes of the British Empire and urged American leaders to follow its lead. Concentrating upon the "liberal" regime that Britain promoted after the Irish famine (1845–1849) and the Indian Rebellion (1857), they described how Britain's planting of parliamentary institutions and a free press in its colonies prepared them for self-rule, while British power spread free markets and the rule of law around the globe. This "liberal imperialism" allegedly dovetailed with the idealism of Woodrow Wilson as well as later U.S. presidents' various interventions to support representative government and the capitalist market.[90]

Even after setting aside this overly rosy view of British imperial rule and U.S. interventions, there are important differences between the two cases. Most obvious is the weakness of U.S. formal imperialism. At the end of the twentieth century, the United States controlled far less territory than Britain did at the height of its empire—less than 7 percent of the world's land (including the mainland United States), compared to 23 percent ruled by tiny Britain in 1913. Americans have been more reluctant than the British to invest in the nation's overseas territories or to relocate there. Unlike Victorian imperialists, American leaders have been under constant pressure to extricate themselves as quickly as possible from episodes of intervention that threatened to develop into long-term rule. "Empire," however, fails to capture the unprecedented global dominance of the United States since 1945. U.S. military power today is more dominant than Britain's ever was, operating from an unequaled string of bases around the world and wielding far more firepower than its rivals. Economically, too, the United States outpaced its competitors by a bigger margin: its share of total world output was more than 22 percent in 2000, compared with 8 percent for Britain in 1913.[91]

America's control over other lands has been exerted mainly through military, economic, and cultural pressure, not direct colonial rule. Britain's "empire project" also included a web of investment, trade, and financial dependence in addition to formal colonialism.[92] Since each power enjoyed a turn at setting the terms of global exchange, a more appropriate strategy than comparing empires may be to compare their two "hegemonies." Many scholars argue that this term, originally used to describe Athenian leadership of ancient Greece, conveys better than empire the influence that great powers exert beyond force and territorial conquest. World systems theorists prefer it because it emphasizes the constantly evolving competition for control over the interstate system and the world economy in the absence of a true world empire (such as the Romans or Hitler aspired to). Other prominent scholars also believe that hegemony best captures the ability of a military and economic giant like the post-1945 United States to impose an international order that benefits itself, provides "public goods" such as growth and stability, and elicits cooperation or at least acquiescence from other nations.

How, then, do British and U.S. hegemonies compare? Are there persuasive analogies between the so-called "Pax Americana" (1945–present) and the "Pax Britannica" (1815–1914), Britain's employment of its naval might, the balance-of-power system, and global trade to keep European rivals from waging all-out war for a century?[93] In the "Pax Americana" era, the United States has used cold war alliances, military interventions, economic pressures, and international organizations such as the IMF to contain rivals and to shape the global order to its liking. Among Britain's practices that corresponded to later U.S. actions was its deal making with local elites worldwide to secure their cooperation, its aggressive promotion of free trade, its leadership in making the gold standard the basis of international exchange (later extended by the United States in the Bretton Woods system), and the "selling" of its advanced technology and liberal system of government. To most observers, however, the scope and exercise of U.S. power in the second half of the twentieth century far eclipsed Britain's at its apex, highlighting a unique global situation. Nineteenth-century England was by no means militarily dominant in Europe. With the brief exception of the Crimean War (1853–1856), Britain avoided great power wars—until it was drawn into World War I, which proved fatal to its economy and empire. While the United States did not *seek* great power wars, America's productive might and military prowess allowed it to crush its rivals Germany and Japan in World War II and outlast the USSR in the cold war. At the same time, the benefits of its trade and technology lured potential rivals such as China into peaceful relationships. The collapse of European powers and their empires permitted the United States to occupy a unique position as a global "superpower" that was not possible before 1945. America's "hard power" combined with its distinctive "soft power"—the appeal of its model of capitalist culture and modernity—to fill the kind of geopolitical vacuum that nineteenth-century Britain never faced.

Of course, the jury is still out on the ultimate fate of American hegemony. The British example in the nineteenth century sparked a great power scramble that led directly to World War I. Since the end of the cold war, the United States has cultivated peaceful relations with emerging powers such as China and India. There remain, however, serious problems of "blowback" (resistance to American interventions), global problems beyond the hegemon's ability to solve unilaterally, and the prospect of a global order without a hegemonic center. Some scholars believe that a "post-American world" emerged in the 1970s, others that American dominance will persist into the foreseeable future.

In the last quarter of the twentieth century, questions about superpower "decline" and what nation might succeed the United States as global leader spawned enough books and theories to constitute a veritable industry. Paul Kennedy's *Rise and Fall of the Great Powers* (1987) stirred controversy by suggesting that the United States was following Hapsburg Spain, Napoleonic France, and the British Empire into history's dustbin.[94] The unsuccessful U.S. war in Vietnam signaled "imperial overstretch," the situation where a great power's military commitments outran its economic resources, and the resurgence of Germany and Japan showed how new technologies could be better exploited by nations unburdened by militarism. Yet, no sooner did Kennedy's dismal prognosis appear than the U.S. economy surged from booms in banking and computers, Japan and Germany stagnated, and America's free-market capitalism regained prestige. Most dramatically, the collapse of the Soviet Union in 1991 left the United States victorious as the sole global superpower. Then, as if to mock long-term prognosticators, at the century's end, the terrorist attacks of September 11, 2001, triggered a domestic recession and led U.S. policy makers into long and costly wars in Iraq and Afghanistan, raising the specter of overreach once more. Amid commentators' warnings about imperial decay—and sometimes in the same books—there appeared rays of hope for the United States as a continuing great power, from confidence in its technological innovation and "soft power" to arguments that potential rivals such as China, the EU, or India were fatally flawed and destined to remain second-tier.[95]

At the century's end, grand theories of imperial overstretch, sea powers versus land powers, and hard versus soft power linked U.S. and global history in provocative ways. Yet despite their self-proclaimed realism, political commentators seemed unable to keep up with events, locked into a great power scheme of analysis that the new global connectivity and the emergence of regional nodes of power may have rendered obsolete. In a globalized world and in a multipolar international system, the overriding question may not be "who is the next global leader?" but "how can nations and peoples live together equitably and peacefully?" Whether U.S. and world historians can discern routes from the past to such a future remains to be seen.

FIVE TOPICS FOR AN INTEGRATED U.S. AND GLOBAL HISTORY

After exploring "inside-out" strategies that enlarge U.S. history toward global comparisons and connections in the previous two sections, this discussion now turns to an "outside-in" approach that begins with some major world history topics and situates the United States within them. Unlike the preceding sections, this one adopts a narrative style in order to suggest alternatives to conventional textbook accounts. How might new narratives look that better incorporate global contexts in twentieth-century U.S. history and ask simultaneously what impact the United States had on world history? The five mini-essays that follow reach in a modest and necessarily abbreviated way toward a response. By discussing capitalism, technology, war, feminism, and the environment, they attempt to incorporate insights from recent scholarship as they sketch a blended U.S./global story. These short narratives are intended as examples of the kind of history I am advocating. They should be read as invitations to scholars and teachers to bring U.S. history into a richer dialogue with world history, to explore other twentieth-century topics, and to construct their own globalized narratives.

Transformations of Capitalism in the American Century

To track the vicissitudes of American capitalism and its entanglement with the global economy and politics in the twentieth century is an enterprise far beyond the scale of this chapter. Yet three themes can be sketched as essential pieces of that larger undertaking: the role of Americans in promoting mass consumer capitalism; the midcentury contest among capitalism, fascism, and communism; and the U.S. place in postwar economic globalization.

As industrialism spread through the Western world in the late nineteenth century, Americans took the lead in three areas. First, while Britain, Germany, and Japan also built industries using the new technologies of electricity, steel, and chemicals, American businessmen, more than the others, formed giant corporations that dominated major industries. Second, the United States became the first nation to evolve a large sector of its economy devoted to white-collar work. By 1900, more Americans were employed in clerical work, sales, and service than in manufacturing, a position England did not reach until the 1930s and Germany until the 1960s. This development blurred class antagonisms and expanded the pool of consumers. Finally, Americans pioneered mass production techniques that manufactured cheap and convenient consumer goods.[96]

The preeminent example of the last was the automobile, developed largely by French and German engineers but embraced by Henry Ford, whose Model T (1908) made cars affordable to the masses and whose continuous assembly line produced one every ten seconds. European leaders admired this scheme of mechanized production and labeled it "Fordism." Supplemented by Frederick W. Taylor's theory of "scientific management," which reduced physical work to small steps that could be optimized for efficiency, Ford's methods became influential in Canada, Europe, Japan, the Soviet Union, and various outposts of the developing world.[97] Ford also played a crucial role in joining mass consumption to mass production by pioneering the five-day workweek. A half day of work on Saturday was allotted to British industrial workers by law in 1874. Its American counterpart did not arrive until the 1910s, but during the next decade, a full two-day weekend became standard in heavily unionized industries and in Ford's automobile factories. Ford foresaw that good pay would appease bored or overworked employees, while long weekends encouraged their spending on items like automobiles. The weekend narrowed the gap between mass production and consumption by viewing workers also as consumers. To close it entirely, advertising, catalogs, and chain stores stimulated consumer desires and distributed goods through an efficient retail network.[98]

Like the weekend or Ford's automobiles, many emblems of the new consumer capitalism—from advertising to movies and department stores—were pieced together by innovators on both sides of the North Atlantic. Americans were the pioneers of some but not all, but since they were often most successful at producing and marketing them, America became a trope for the modern capitalist culture of mass consumption and a forecast of the effects of economic competition in the industrialized world.[99]

Quite abruptly, the Depression of the 1930s and the world war that followed it presented this capitalist order with its severest challenge. The Depression caused a crisis of confidence from within, while the war defined an external struggle between liberal capitalism and two competing programs of political and economic modernity—fascism and communism—which had emerged from the ruins of World War I.[100] Despite their differences, all three ideologies promised prosperity, modernity, and national unity. Profoundly authoritarian in practice, Soviet communism and fascism were antithetical to liberal values, but in the 1930s, they appeared to harness state power to produce employment more effectively than the capitalist democracies. The global economic crisis seemed to confirm communist theories that the capitalist cycle of boom and bust would eventually collapse in a heap. The Depression also discredited the old economic liberalism of free trade and laissez-faire, since the economy did not right itself automatically and governments that waited for it to do so were overturned. The economic crash hit the United States especially hard because the nation had built a very limited social safety net and because it called into question the self-reliant "American Dream."

It has often been pointed out that Franklin Roosevelt's New Deal, which created an array of job and social welfare programs, set out to reform capitalism (which FDR called "the profit system") in order to save it. In the long run, it succeeded: the New Deal did not end the Great Depression—only mobilization for World War II brought full employment—but it enabled Americans to survive the decade-long economic crisis without fundamentally altering their economic or political systems. In practice, the Depression wrought broadly similar effects on most Western governments—centralized control, public works programs, pension plans—but the key issue was whether authoritarian leaders would employ them to destroy unions, collectivize the economy, and bolster undemocratic rule. The U.S. and British Commonwealth states survived without turning to authoritarianism and lived on to defeat fascism on the battlefield—ironically, with a decisive assist from their communist rival, the Soviet Union.[101]

The communist challenge remained, and for decades after World War II, democratic capitalism evolved during a less-violent but equally important battle against communist "command economies." The general strategy adopted in Western Europe and the United States was to combine welfare state protections for workers with the managed capitalism of John Maynard Keynes, the British economist who advocated that governments increase spending and adjust tax policies to stabilize the business cycle. Long after the crisis of the 1930s, the combination of economic management and social protection proved to be social liberalism's most enduring legacy. "We are all Keynesians now," President Richard Nixon reportedly proclaimed in 1971. The effectiveness and staying power of the Keynesian consensus may well have helped

Western capitalist economies outlast the Soviets in the cold war. In any case, when the policy pendulum swung back toward free-market liberalism as the cold war wound down, a speculative frenzy ensued that ended with a U.S. banking and real estate bust in 2008 and the onset of the worst global economic crisis since the 1930s.

During the post–World War II boom, dramatic developments were at work to reignite economic globalization and multiply its effects. Television advertised consumer goods and broadcast entertainment almost everywhere. Jet travel sped up migration and allowed multinational corporations to move manufacturing to low-wage nations. Computers permitted instant transfers of capital and gave formerly isolated places access to global information.[102] The United States took the lead in the postwar expansion of globalized capitalism. Eager to dominate new markets, Americans oversaw the spread of free trade and the flow of raw materials through financial institutions like the World Bank and the General Agreement on Tariffs and Trade (1947), which was replaced by the World Trade Organization (WTO) in 1995. The United States pioneered advances in computer and satellite technology that replaced industrial manufacturing as the driver of economic growth. American fast food became so popular abroad that McDonald's operated in 103 nations and fed 1 percent of the world's people each day. The worldwide appeal of basketball player Michael Jordan illustrated the interlaced globalization of sports, manufacturing, and marketing by U.S.-based corporations such as Nike.[103] Even more than during the 1920s, America's freewheeling consumer society, broadcast by movies and television, projected a model for many of the world's people. Of course, there were important exceptions. For cultural conservatives and nationalist leaders in other Western nations, and in non-Western regions where Islamic fundamentalism was strong, resentment of globalized consumer capitalism became a staple of anti-American protests.

By the 1970s, however, it was already apparent that U.S. domination of economic globalization was diminishing. The Organization of Petroleum Exporting Countries (OPEC) embargo exposed America's dependence on imported oil. Free trade spread technological capabilities to rising economies in Japan, Korea, and India. In the ensuing decades, foreign cars, electronics, textiles, and other manufactures made huge inroads into the U.S. market. U.S.-based multinational corporations moved facilities to third world nations where wages were low and taxes and regulations minimal. The largest of these companies took in more money than the output of many nations and grew beyond the control of governments. Due to the globalized market for labor and goods, the United States became more dependent upon the world economy than at any time in the twentieth century: foreign trade rose from 11 percent of GDP in 1970 to 20.5 percent in 1980 and 26 percent by 2000.[104] For first time since World War I, the United States became a debtor nation in 1985, importing goods and using foreign (especially Chinese) investment to sustain Americans' high standard of living—a precarious arrangement that nearly collapsed when the credit bubble burst in 2008.

Instead of an American regime, the new globalized economy emerged as a complex and decentralized web of relationships beyond one nation's control. Its effects have been hotly debated by scholars, political leaders, and ordinary people for two decades. Champions of globalization point to raised standards of living in many nations, the diffusion of new technologies and information, the creative energies of global entrepreneurs, and the formation of new hybrid transnational cultures. Critics respond with evidence of worsening inequality between and within nations, globalization's damage to local economies and cultures, its domination by powerful international corporations, its jeopardizing of food safety, and its diffusion of criminal networks.[105] These debates make clear that the new global interdependence has severe costs as well as benefits. Public protests against the costs took a quantum leap with huge demonstrations by labor and environmental organizations at the WTO meeting in Seattle in 1999.

Combating the ill effects of globalization and steering the global economy toward social justice will require more inclusive and transparent forms of international cooperation than WTO meetings and G-8 summits. The United States, along with other Western powers, has consistently backed away from proposals to construct a new global order that accommodates the needs of developing nations. Demands to radically increase nonmilitary aid, end subsidies for American farmers that flood foreign markets with cheap grain, control U.S.-based multinationals, or support global agencies that regulate working conditions have been seen as jeopardizing America's position in the world economy, redistributing legitimate profits, or giving advantages to emerging rivals of the United States. An encouraging exception was the United States' agreement in 2005 to cancel the entire $40 billion debt owed by eighteen poor nations to the World Bank, the IMF, and the African Development Fund. Only time will tell if this move presaged a shift by U.S. policy makers away from the unilateralist and free-market doctrines of recent decades.

American Technology in a Century of War and Destruction

The twentieth century has been labeled an "age of extremes" in which improvements in technology, living standards, and the status of women were countered by ideological disillusionment, genocide, and total war. Americans were fortunate to enjoy much of the former and largely escape the latter. Few Americans would agree that the twentieth century was "the most terrible century in Western history," and many would be surprised to hear the period from 1914 to 1945 called "the age of catastrophe."[106] The world wars that bracket this era took an appalling global toll. As many as 9 million people died in World War I and more than 60 million in World War II; more than half in the latter conflict were civilians. Yet the continental United States, secure behind its ocean borders, was spared the horrors that plagued Eurasian peoples: invasion by marauding armies and airplanes with bombs, mass destruction of cities and farms, genocide, famine, and brutal occupations and dictatorships. The United States not only suffered fewer military casualties than any major belligerent but it was also the only nation that emerged richer and stronger from these decades of global conflict.

Despite this fortunate exemption, the United States was a major contributor to each stage of the twentieth century's escalation of the deadly techniques of warfare. America's entry into World War I showed the possibilities of mobilizing the home front through new mass media (radio and movies) and the use of government powers to assure war production. In World War II, America's role as the "arsenal of democracy" and its innovations in naval and air warfare added to the appalling destruction. In the century's second half, the U.S. bid for global hegemony played a pivotal role in militarizing the planet. The invention of nuclear weapons sparked an arms race that spread to the Soviet Union and other major powers and came perilously close to triggering a planetary catastrophe. Spurred by the globalizing momentum of the cold war and the "military-industrial complex," American engineers developed sophisticated high-tech weapons that raised the twentieth century's mechanized, impersonal form of warfare—and its toll of civilian casualties—to a new level. Preeminent military power had double-edged effects, deterring potential enemies, but also tempting American leaders to take on commitments where military measures could not resolve political struggles and where air power and advanced weapons did more harm than good. Ironically, and often tragically, Americans helped to make the world—and their nation—a more dangerous place, even as they set out to police it.

The twentieth-century version of total war, which mobilized whole societies and employed destructive new weapons, had devastating implications. Among them was the idea that the home front's involvement in war production justified bombing enemy factories and cities, a rationale that evolved inexorably toward simply terrorizing civilians. Aerial bombing against cities, used previously in Japan's invasion of China and the Spanish Civil War, took on enormous dimensions in World War II. Long-range bombers like the B-24 and B-29 were among the Americans' most destructive technological innovations. American and British raids on Cologne, Hamburg, Dresden, and Berlin, which mixed firebombs with explosives, killed 600,000 persons, mostly civilians, and U.S. incendiary raids on Tokyo killed 80,000 in one day. Such carnage paved the way for U.S. President Harry Truman to view the atomic bomb as just another wartime weapon when he readily approved the attacks on Hiroshima and Nagasaki that helped to force Japan's surrender in August 1945.[107]

After the war, the nation's sole possession of nuclear weapons emboldened U.S. leaders to pledge to contain communism globally and to threaten to use nuclear weapons during proxy conflicts in Korea, the Taiwan Strait, and elsewhere. "Brinksmanship," the Eisenhower administration's strategy of brandishing nuclear threats, tamed the Defense Department budget and sent no U.S. troops into a ground war—both desirable goals after the costly Korean War—but as Eisenhower acknowledged, American leaders would have to use nuclear bombs should their bluff be called. After the Soviets matched the United States with their own bomb in 1949, a long and costly arms race proceeded. Bigger bombs as well as better delivery systems were the goal as each side competed to produce hydrogen bombs, intercontinental bombers, submarine-launched missiles, intercontinental ballistic missiles, antisatellite weapons, and multiple warhead systems. The United States kept ahead in almost every category, but never enough for its leaders to remain at ease. Nevertheless, in the aftermath of the frightening Cuban Missile Crisis of 1962, it became clear that the possession of atomic weapons was useful mainly as a deterrent to prevent the other side from risking a first strike. This doctrine of "Mutually Assured Destruction" eased the path to the détente years of the late 1960s and early 1970s, when the United States and the USSR began negotiating test bans and limits on nuclear deployment. Even then, the race continued with the development of new satellite technology and missile defense shields, raising the risk of renewing tension and overturning existing bilateral agreements.

As for the "secret" of the bomb itself, because scientists around the world pursued it and nations sought to control their own security, the genie quickly escaped from the bottle.[108] Britain, France, China, Israel, and India joined the club of nuclear nations between 1953 and 1974. Pakistan became a nuclear power in 1998, heightening fears that tensions with India could provoke a catastrophic exchange. In recent years, North Korea has tested atomic weapons and Iran has moved toward building them. The Nuclear Non-Proliferation Treaty, forged in 1968 and later renewed, is signed by five nuclear powers including the United States, but not by four others (India, Pakistan, Israel, and North Korea). Faced with proliferation, American leaders adopted the strategy of building international coalitions to approve sanctions to deter so-called "rogue states" from developing nuclear weapons. Apart from the rogue state scenario or an accidental detonation, there also lurked the frightening possibility that a nonstate terrorist group might acquire a nuclear bomb and ignite it in a suicide attack. Long after the cold war, the world remained in danger of nuclear destruction, but in ways no one had foreseen in 1945.

Although U.S. armed forces shrank in the aftermath of World War II, military spending remained high. Escalating cold war tensions justified manning hundreds of military and naval bases abroad and enlarging the private sector devoted to military research and development. When Eisenhower warned in

1960 that a "military-industrial complex" was eroding American democracy, the process was already well under way. The Defense Department, government research agencies, air and arms industries, pork-minded congressmen, and university laboratories all collaborated to ensure a steady stream of funds that kept the U.S. military formidable and technologically advanced.[109] Rising arms sales abroad also sustained the industry: by the early twenty-first century, U.S. sales reached more than $30 billion annually, more than twice as much as Russia, the next leading global supplier. During the cold war, America's economy was put on a seemingly permanent wartime footing that, it was argued, was good for domestic prosperity and necessary for national security. The end of the cold war did surprisingly little to change this as the lone remaining superpower undertook a new series of military interventions (and some humanitarian ones) and girded itself and its allies against terrorist threats.

During this never-ending military buildup, the United States excelled at developing advanced, mechanized forms of warfare that minimized American casualties and maximized others. The B-52 strategic bomber (introduced in 1955), designed for high-altitude, long-distance missions, led the way. Later, saturation bombings were replaced by "smart" technology such as precision laser-guided bombs, cruise missiles, and unmanned aircraft. On the ground, armored vehicles and satellite-guided mobile artillery aided American troops. Critics claim that such weapons made war impersonal, dealing death by remote control and substituting the excitement of video games for the horror of up close combat. Push-button warfare limited U.S. military casualties, a feature that appealed to the American public and politicians. Supporters also cited the ability of the new weapons to hit targets precisely and limit "collateral damage," but in practice, faulty mechanics, unreliable intelligence, and overuse led to many civilian deaths.[110]

In retrospect, the U.S. military's growing reliance upon air strikes stands out as a dominant trend. During the Vietnam War, U.S. planes dropped more than twice as many tons of bombs as the Allies during World War II. One result was lopsided "kill ratios," since thirty or forty Vietnamese people died for every U.S. soldier. Another was the increased ratio of civilian deaths, which accounted for more than 80 percent of the war's casualties. Yet despite this carnage, such bombing did not cripple the enemy's ability to fight.

The fact is that air strikes and massive firepower from advanced military weapons have rarely proved effective against guerrilla tactics, where enemy combatants operate in dispersed units, melt into the civilian population, and take refuge in protected bunkers or friendly villages. Such warfare, along with its nearly invisible partner, guerrilla terrorism, has become the tactic of resort for local insurgent groups and international terrorist cells arrayed in "asymmetric" combat against powerful nations. Success in the conventional Persian

Gulf War of 1991 lulled U.S. military analysts into thinking that the Iraq War of 2003 would be similarly brief. Yet for years after U.S. forces easily overran Baghdad, they struggled to control an insurgency against the U.S. occupation in which far more Americans and Iraqis lost their lives. The Taliban's insurgency and al Qaeda's hideouts in Afghanistan appear equally resistant to U.S. air raids.

Meanwhile, the shocking terrorist attacks on New York and Washington on September 11, 2001, demonstrated that the United States was not exempt from the killing of civilians that had been a prominent feature of the twentieth-century world. As disbelief and anger gave way to reflection, Americans began to realize that the technology of air travel and cell phones, exploited by non-state enemies, obliterated the security formerly provided by oceans and missiles. Taking on the role of global hegemon, their nation had become more, not less, vulnerable to attack. The "paradox between the unprecedented power of the United States and the fact that the civilian population [is] . . . at unprecedented risk of assault by foreign adversaries" will certainly shape, and perhaps temper, U.S. foreign policy decisions for decades to come.[111]

The United States and the Global Cold War

The end of the cold war has made possible fresh interpretations of the fierce rivalry between the United States and the Soviet Union that forged a fifty-year bipolar geopolitical system. Recent scholarship is less intent on assigning blame or taking sides in the superpower rivalry. And world history offers perspectives that broaden the cold war's temporal and spatial contexts beyond conventional U.S.-based narratives. Standing back from the positions of its main protagonists, it becomes apparent that the cold war was a mix of new and familiar features that together raised the stakes for all involved.[112] First, there was the traditional great power competition that stemmed from the Americans' and Soviets' geopolitical situation. Both nations sought to fill the power vacuum left by the war's course of destruction through Europe and Asia. As the only great power left in Eurasia, Russia seized the opportunity to extend its dominance at its western and eastern borders, while the United States, the world's premier economic and military force, aspired to construct a global order that would assure its continued prosperity and security. This included checking Soviet power in Europe and Asia by adopting traditional balance-of-power tactics. Second, the cold war was an ideological struggle between the two survivors of the decades-long contest among capitalism, communism, and fascism. Great power hostility was intensified because both sides defined the clash as a climactic struggle between competing systems and both declared that the forces of history and righteousness were on their side. Third, because of nuclear technology, the cold war went far beyond previous great power standoffs by endangering human existence itself. A precarious "balance of terror" replaced the balance of power that traditionally held empires in check, and nuclear weapons threatened to escalate each superpower confrontation into a global catastrophe.

Finally, as the superpower rivalry expanded outward to absorb other nations and regions, it began to resemble earlier imperial struggles. The Americans and Soviets accused one another of being imperialists, and both had a point. Each sought to control its regional "front yard" as a sphere of influence—the Americans in the Caribbean and the Soviets in Eastern Europe. Both used pressure to extend their way of life to peoples in Latin America, Asia, and Africa and to enlist them as trade partners and political allies. Like prior European imperial powers, they built overseas bases that stationed troops and ships in distant corners of the world, giving the cold war a global reach.

This imperial dimension has attracted historians writing in the cold war's wake who seek larger contexts for understanding it. Geir Lundestad labels U.S. involvement in Western Europe an "empire by invitation" since Western Europeans wanted the United States to provide a postwar economic boost and a military shield against the Soviets. Building on this argument, John Lewis Gaddis contrasts the U.S. and Soviet blocs in Europe as empires by "invitation" and "imposition," respectively, noting that in Eastern Europe Stalin and his successors set up satellite states that abolished representative government, disregarded human rights, and enforced Soviet dictates.[113] Although it is plausible for Europe, the contrast between benign and coercive empires is questionable in Latin America, Africa, and the Asian periphery. In those regions, the cold war rivalry became entwined with the simultaneous breakup of Europe's colonial empires, and the Americans and Soviets intruded, often uninvited, into local economies and politics. Odd Arne Westad has shown how the cold war moved new third world nations from the margins to the center of the superpowers' attention as each intervened to validate its ideologies and gain military bases, resources, or votes in the UN.[114]

In principle, both superpowers were dedicated to overthrowing empires, the United States through its ideal of national self-determination and the USSR through Marxist-Leninist anti-imperialism. In actuality, both nations viewed nationalist movements as pawns in their geopolitical chess match. Marxist-Leninist ideology encouraged third world peoples to blame their economic woes on capitalist exploitation, and the Soviets' command economy offered a way to control rapid modernization. But cold war competition encouraged the Soviets to intervene where Soviet-style communism was bound to fail and, in the case of Afghanistan, to try to suppress a nationalist revolt against their puppet regime. Meanwhile, Americans channeled government propaganda, foreign aid, and modernizing projects toward emergent nations, but the hostility of U.S.

leaders toward national liberation movements, which were feared as procommunist, and their support for racist or despotic anticommunist regimes in developing nations from Iran, the Congo, and South Africa to Nicaragua and Cuba, crippled the quest for influence. More than any other event, the U.S. war in Vietnam demonstrated its leaders' willingness to subordinate their traditional anticolonial stance to the cold war's polarized geopolitics.

Because both the Americans and Soviets intervened in local struggles and sought to dictate terms for aid, their policies struck many third world peoples as "a continuation of colonialism through slightly different means."[115] Confronted with demands that they choose sides, some emerging nations did, while others remained nonaligned or played the Americans and Soviets off against one another. Still others became hot spots where local guerrilla movements armed and financed by the superpowers contended for control, which escalated the violence and in many cases brought no improvement to ordinary peoples' lives, no matter which side won.

As the cold war dragged on, its superpower protagonists confronted imperial "overstretch." In Vietnam and Afghanistan, the United States and the USSR proved unable to win protracted, unconventional wars against third world nationalist movements. Meanwhile, the arms race drained funds from their domestic economies. This double burden took its most obvious toll in the Soviet Union, which abruptly imploded in the late 1980s, withdrawing from Afghanistan, unable to suppress nonviolent uprisings in Eastern Europe, and struggling with rising domestic discontents. The question of American responsibility for the Soviet collapse remains controversial. Some U.S. scholars believe that President Reagan's resumption of the arms race and rivalry for the third world exhausted Soviets' resources. Most historians focus on the USSR instead; they see the failing Soviet economy at the root of its collapse, give the arms race a supporting role, and point to the reforms of Soviet leader Mikhail Gorbachev as the trigger.[116] Despite both sides' foreign clashes and commitments, the cold war boiled down to the issue of how well capitalist and communist systems performed *inside* the superpower nations and their allies. In the end, the Soviet system could not keep up with the capitalist West under the new globalized market economy and could not contain demands from its own and dependent peoples for greater autonomy and a better life.

The cold war ended without destroying the world, but in the face of American triumphalism, it is important to note the heavy price it exacted in resources and lives. The Red Scare, the "military-industrial complex," and the "imperial presidency" left permanent scars in American life. Beyond U.S. borders, the cold war damaged American relations with several Latin American countries, India, and much of Africa and the Middle East. Misguided alliances with anticommunist dictators blocked needed economic and political reforms in the developing world. Millions of third world people, mostly peasants, died in civil wars that were escalated with superpower weapons and aid. The collapse of communism did not mean that history had "ended" with the triumph of democratic and capitalist values, as some pundits declared.[117] Authoritarian governments, rising anti-Western sentiments, resurgent ethnic and religious tensions, and increasing economic inequality between rich and poor nations— each in part a legacy of the cold war—loomed as potential challenges to those values. Meanwhile, the cold war habit of demonizing nations and militarizing international disputes persisted into a post–cold war world where the United States remained the lone superpower.

American Feminism and the Transnational Women's Movement

In the post–World War II world, new transnational social movements such as the youth counterculture, black nationalism, environmentalism, and global feminism were mobilized by increased global trade and communication. The new transnationalism followed an earlier wave of international organizing by Pan-Africanist, socialist, and women's organizations of the early twentieth century that stalled in the Depression and war years. The international women's movement, in which Americans played a leading role and that scholars have begun to document, provides a good example of the resurgence of international organizing as well as the strategic issues that American activists faced as they attempted to bridge divisions between "the West and the rest."

Nineteenth-century feminists in the Anglo-American world divided their emphasis between the moral improvement of society and achieving woman suffrage. In the 1880s, American activists moved to the international stage by inspiring chapters of the Women's Christian Temperance Union (WCTU) in Canada, Australia, and New Zealand and establishing the International Council of Women, which spawned the International Woman's Suffrage Association (1902). Less formally, radical feminists agitated for suffrage and against militarism in the socialist Second International (1889–1916) and the Woman's International League for Peace and Freedom (1915).[118] All these groups were dominated by elite Protestant women from the United States, Britain, and northern and Western Europe (with a small contingent from Australasia), and their congresses were held in Europe and North America. Members conducted the long campaign for suffrage in their respective nations, but they adopted ideas and tactics from each other, including the militant protests of British suffragettes. The linked trajectories of European and American feminists became clear when both groups used women's participation in World War I to goad their governments into granting women the right to vote.[119]

Organized feminism in the United States and the West generally lost momentum by the end of the 1920s. At that point, most North Atlantic nations had achieved universal suffrage and their women's movements experienced a letdown when no major social transformation resulted. World War I stimulated international organizing for banning war and advocating woman suffrage in newly created nations, but the crisis of depression and World War II put women's rights agitation on hold, with the notable exception of suffrage victories in South America.

When the transatlantic women's movement revived in the 1960s, it had deeper social support and a wider-ranging agenda than its predecessors. Rising economic expectations led American and European families to have fewer children, and more married women entered the paid workforce. Women's educational gains also underlaid the feminist surge. Meanwhile, the invention of oral contraceptives in the 1960s—a development traceable back to the American Margaret Sanger's work of the 1910s—promised dramatic change. Middle-class women had been limiting family size in various ways for decades, but with "the pill," sexual intercourse was decisively separated from reproduction. Reliable birth control made women's careers more feasible and encouraged freer attitudes toward sexual expression.

As the new American and European movements developed in tandem, they branched into factions that championed either reformist feminism in the equalitarian mode or a new radical feminism (sometimes called "women's liberation") that preached revolution and critiqued conventional notions of womanhood, sexuality, and family life. Transatlantic parallels were striking, despite differences in national contexts. British, French, and Italian feminists had stronger ties to socialists and labor unions, while American feminists were more apt to indict patriarchy rather than capitalism. Most of these feminist movements ended up concentrating on legal battles over discrimination and abortion rights. Meanwhile, radical feminists' emphasis on autonomy and their frank acceptance of lesbianism challenged basic cultural and political conventions—a stance that popularized concepts like "sexism" and validated the trend toward looser sexual norms, but also aroused mainstream opposition.[120]

American and European feminists also encountered criticism when they brought their agendas to the global stage. At a series of International Women's Conferences sponsored by the UN beginning in 1975, Western feminists negotiated with a far more diverse group of delegates than at the early twentieth-century congresses. Women from developing countries in Asia, Africa, and Latin America concentrated their struggles on combating hunger and disease, gaining access to education, and winning fundamental legal rights rather than achieving the second-stage political and social advances promoted by Western feminists. Together with African-descent women in the United States and Britain, problems of poverty, racism, and motherhood concerned them more than sexual liberation or professional advancement. In addition, some third world representatives resented Western feminists' campaigns against polygamy, unequal inheritance, or female circumcision, which appeared as yet another form of Western cultural imperialism. Feminists gathered at international conferences also experienced splits between reformism and radicalism analogous to those that weakened national movements: should they take aim at local discriminatory laws and customs or attack the injustice of the global economic system?[121]

Despite these divisions, Western and non-Western feminists found common ground when they linked women's progress to international agreements on human rights that took shape in reaction to the horrors of world war and genocide. The Universal Declaration of Human Rights, drafted by an international committee chaired by Eleanor Roosevelt and adopted by the UN in 1948, condemned discrimination by sex and applied civil and political rights to all.[122] The UN-sponsored conferences that began in Mexico City in 1975 and ended in Beijing in 1995 developed an ambitious consensus platform that included peace and international social justice as well as economic opportunities and basic rights for women. In 1993, the UN Declaration on the Elimination of Violence against Women condemned rape, battery, and forced prostitution. By 2006, 183 nations had signed a UN Convention to Eliminate Discrimination against Women. These agreements, along with monitoring mechanisms, validated global feminism and gave NGOs and local feminists the ammunition to pressure governments. But many were hedged with reservations and most were not enforced despite their status as international law.[123]

Feminists' obstacles mounted when a global backlash erupted in the 1970s led by defenders of traditional family and sex roles. As the world economy slid into recession, the Anglo-American public retreated to conservative views, asserting that the liberal social changes of the 1960s had gone too far. The pope, conservative leaders in Catholic nations, and Protestant evangelical sects in the United States opposed Western feminists' emphasis on reproductive rights, especially birth control and abortion. In Islamic countries, fundamentalist imams condemned Westerners' practice of gender equality and loose sexual mores and defended the seclusion or restriction of women. As Western feminism went global, it caused wider ripples of opposition as well as genuine changes.

In many ways, global feminism can be taken as emblematic of late twentieth-century transnational social movements. Organizations based on transnational solidarities of gender, like those of race or religion, addressed local conditions and problems at the same time their members sought wider allegiances and influence. Many Americans developed dual identities that blended their membership in transnational groups, including global feminist organizations, with citizenship in the United States. As globalization proceeded, more and more people around the world negotiated the enlarged scale of their existence by adopting a similar "cosmopolitan" strategy. Twentieth-century transnational feminism achieved notable successes by linking local agendas with global ones, but they also demonstrated the problem of enforcing international agreements and the difficulty of building transnational coalitions across global divides of culture and wealth.

Global Environmental Crisis and the National Response

The second half of the twentieth century was marked by accelerated environmental deterioration and growing recognition of its human causes. For more than a century, industrialized nations, including the United States, promoted economic growth and exploited land, water, mineral, and energy resources with few restraints. By the late twentieth century, the environmental costs of this headlong rush were becoming apparent and their global effects obvious.[124]

One aspect of the problem was the depletion of the planet's biological and mineral resources. In the twentieth century, global energy use grew by a factor of fourteen. Dependence upon fossil fuels climbed with coal-fired electrical power and gasoline-powered vehicles. The world was quickly running out of oil: experts expected production to peak around 2020 and decline irrevocably after that. Coal supplies were more plentiful, but their use contributed heavily to air pollution. The strain on the world's oceans became evident when unregulated overfishing of the Grand Banks off the North American coast destroyed habitats and virtually closed down the international codfish industry, creating a chain reaction that led to overfishing of other species in the world's oceans. The parallel destruction of tropical rain forests and grassy plains threatened animals and plants with massive extinction, reducing the biodiversity that preserves the earth's ecosystems and fosters human health. Studying the depletion of oceans, forests, and minerals, some scientists warned that an environmental collapse was under way that paralleled those that overtook earlier civilizations such as the Romans and Mayans.[125]

A second, related feature of the crisis was the environmental damage that human activity exacted. Oil spills from giant tankers killed millions of fish, while gas leaks at Bhopal, India (1984) and a nuclear explosion at Chernobyl, Ukraine (1986) made regions toxic to plants and humans. Pollution that rose into the atmosphere turned local hazards into transregional and even global ones. Acid rain, caused by sulfur dioxide from burning coal, ruined water and killed wildlife hundreds of miles downwind from power plants. Industrial and consumer use of chlorine and bromide opened an "ozone hole" over the North and South Poles that permitted increased levels of dangerous ultraviolet light to enter the earth's atmosphere. Most alarming, scientists warned that greenhouse gas emissions from cars, farms, and factories were causing an increase in the earth's atmospheric temperature that is melting glaciers and raising sea levels to the point where they may inundate many of the earth's coastal regions and cities. Global warming also threatens long-term climate changes that will turn lakes and farmlands arid.[126]

As the leading industrial and consumer economy at the end of the twentieth century, the United States used a disproportionate amount of the world's resources. With less than 5 percent of the global population, the United States accounted for 30 percent of the world's energy use and produced 20 percent of its greenhouse gases and perhaps half of the other polluting chemicals. (By 2005, China passed the United States in total, but not per capita, carbon emissions.) Americans' consumption habits wreaked ecological damage in developing nations, whether directly through U.S. oil, rubber, and banana companies or indirectly through purchases of minerals, foods, and tropical hardwoods.[127] It is clear, moreover, that the planet's resources will give out if American habits spread globally. China alone would use up the present world production of oil if its people consumed at the same rate as Americans. Yet leaders of developing nations argue that rich industrial powers like the United States should lead the way toward environmental change, and some declare that moderating pollution is a lower priority than catching up to the West's living standards.

Disproportionate responsibility and long-term national interest suggest that the United States should take aggressive measures to reduce its dependence upon oil and to lighten its environmental footprint more generally. In many cases, however, the U.S. government has lagged behind other nations in joining international commitments to mitigate environmental damage. An early success was American leaders' agreement to the Montreal Protocol (1987), which phased out the production of ozone-depleting chlorofluorocarbons (CFCs) within a decade. More recently, the Bush administration, committed to deregulation at home and fearing reduced corporate profits, refused to accept the Rio de Janeiro Convention of 1992 that protected the biodiversity of plants and animals, disputed the existence of global warming, and withdrew from the Kyoto Protocol of 1997, by which the United States had pledged to reduce its release of carbon-based gases by 7 percent. There are signs that the Democratic administration elected in 2008 may redirect U.S. policy on energy and the environment toward domestic sustainability and international agreements. Meanwhile, reacting to protests and publicity by the growing number of environmental groups, the American public appears more committed to conservation and the development of renewable energy than the federal government. California legislators passed a law in 2006 that aligned its energy production goals with the Kyoto accords, and across the nation individuals and communities began to turn to waste recycling, hybrid cars, and solar power.

The environmental crisis calls out for national leadership and international cooperation, but the commitment to growth, which drove the U.S. economy to global preeminence and that is now shared by most of the world's people, poses the dilemma of reconciling ever-increasing human wants with protection of the environment. This dilemma, along with national rivalries and stepped-up economic competition under globalization, has hindered the drafting of binding international agreements to date as well as official U.S. support for them. Yet American and other nations' leaders who seek international cooperation on trade, development, or law enforcement may well be pressured to engage in international negotiation and compromise on environmental issues in return. As globalization proceeds, its damaging effects may provide incentives for all nations to exchange some of their freedom of action for assurances of others' goodwill and the ultimate goal of collective survival.

CONCLUSION

A decade before the twentieth century opened, U.S historian Frederick Jackson Turner, surveying the era's increased global contacts, declared that local and national histories "can only be understood in the light of the history of the world." "All [nations] are inextricably connected, so that each is needed to explain the others."[128] Turner's views were shared by other historians of the period 1880–1917 who interpreted American development as an instance of global social and political evolution. After World War I, this worldly impulse began to wane. Instead of Turner's cosmopolitan reflections, the exceptionalist views of his "frontier thesis" carried the day. The idea that history should discover unique national paths rather than common global patterns dominated American historiography from the 1940s to the 1980s. Ironically, but not surprisingly, at the same time that the United States was assuming global economic and political leadership, historians asserted its superior development outside the norms of history and chose to focus upon what made the American nation unique.[129] Only toward the end of the twentieth century did a more cosmopolitan perspective begin to revive, as historians responded to the prospect of a multipolar political order in the wake of the cold war, witnessed the impact of events abroad on American life, and experienced a new and accelerated round of globalization.

An enlarged U.S. history has emerged from this conjuncture to describe more accurately how American history has embodied the fact of human connectedness. It presents the opportunity to rethink American history for a global age. As this survey of recent scholarship has indicated, no single method, theory, or master narrative prevails among its practitioners. They seek instead new ways of historical inquiring that challenge American exceptionalism by asking how U.S. history relates to what happened elsewhere in order to reveal its distinctive features and to understand the full range of its causes and effects. A welcome corollary of this historiographic project is a renewed conversation between U.S. and world history that has produced new methods, theories, and subjects for a globally embedded national history. For some of its practitioners, an internationalized U.S. history promises a civic benefit, too.[130] Is it possible to recover the cosmopolitan impulse that Turner expressed in the 1890s and redirect it to important historical issues of our own day? Purged of the ethnocentric and evolutionist premises that tainted American historiography in Turner's era, the new national history might also be chastened by the century of extremes that ensued—especially its negative effects, which included wars, genocides, economic oppression, and environmental degradation. Many—but not all—of these were spurred by overheated national rivalries and ambitions. In the twenty-first century, as a globalized U.S. history documents how the fate of Americans has been entwined with others, it may encourage Americans to blend their national allegiance with commitment to the global commons.

NOTES

1. Organization of American Historians and New York University, *La Pietra Report: Project on Internationalizing the Study of American History* (New York: n.p., 2000), 7–8. For essays from the La Pietra conferences, see Thomas Bender, ed., *Rethinking American History in a Global Age* (Berkeley: University of California Press, 2002).

2. National Center for History in the Schools, *National Standards for History, Basic Edition* (Los Angeles: NCHS, 1996), 44, 175.

3. Jerry H. Bentley and Herbert F. Ziegler, *Traditions and Encounters: A Global Perspective on the Past*, vol. II, 4th ed. (Boston: McGraw-Hill, 2008); Robert Tignor et al., *Worlds Together, Worlds Apart: A History of the World*, vol. II, 2nd ed. (New York: W. W. Norton, 2008).

4. See, for example, John C. Weaver, *The Great Land Rush and the Making of the Modern World, 1650–1900* (Montreal: McGill-Queen's University Press, 2003); Peter Stearns, *The Industrial Revolution in World History*, 3rd ed. (Boulder, CO: Westview Press, 2007); Dirk Hoerder, *Cultures in Contact: World Migrations in the Second Millennium* (Durham, NC: Duke University Press, 2002); Patrick Manning, *The African Diaspora: A History through Culture* (New York: Columbia University Press, 2009); J. R. McNeill, *Something New under the Sun: An Environmental History of the Twentieth-Century World* (New York: W. W. Norton, 2001).

5. Organization of American Historians and New York University, *La Pietra Report*, 7.

6. For contrasting emphases on comparative, transnational, and global approaches, respectively, see Carl Guarneri, *America in the World: United States History in Global Context* (New York: McGraw-Hill, 2007); Ian Tyrrell, *Transnational Nation: United States History in Global Perspective since 1789* (Basingstoke, UK: Palgrave Macmillan, 2007); and Thomas Bender, *A Nation among Nations: America's Place in World History* (New York: Hill and Wang, 2006).

7. For definitions, criticisms, and defenses of comparative history, see Theda Skocpol and Margaret Somers, "The Uses of Comparative History," *Comparative Studies in Society and History* 22 (1978): 174–197; George Fredrickson, *The Comparative Imagination* (Berkeley: University of California Press, 1997); Deborah Cohen and Maura O'Connor, eds., *Comparison and History: Europe in Cross-National Perspective* (New York: Routledge, 2004); and Micol Siegel, "Beyond Compare: Comparative Method after the Transnational Turn," *Radical History Review* 91 (Winter 2005): 62–90.

8. Seymour Martin Lipset, *Continental Divide: The Values and Institutions of the United States and Canada* (New York: Routledge, 1990); Eric Rauchway, *Blessed among Nations: How the World Made America* (New York: Hill and Wang, 2006).

9. John H.M. Laslett and Seymour Martin Lipset, eds., *Failure of a Dream? Essays in the History of American Socialism* (Garden City, NY: Doubleday, 1974); Jean Heffer and Jeanine Rovet, eds., *Pourquoi n'y a-t-il pas de socialisme aux Etats-Unis/Why Is There No Socialism in the United States?* (Paris: Editions EHESS, 1987); Seymour Martin Lipset and Gary Marks, *It Didn't Happen Here: Why Socialism Failed in the United States* (New York: W. W. Norton, 2000); and Robin Archer, *Why Is There No Labor Party in the United States?* (Princeton, NJ: Princeton University Press, 2008).

10. See Paul Starr, *The Social Transformation of American Medicine* (New York: Basic Books, 1982); Jill Quadagno, *One Nation, Uninsured: Why the U.S. Has No National Health Insurance* (New York: Oxford University Press, 2006).

11. Donald Meyer, *Sex and Power: The Rise of Women in America, Russia, Sweden, and Italy* (Middletown, CT: Wesleyan University Press, 1987), 629.

12. Aristide R. Zolberg, *A Nation by Design: Immigration Policy in the Fashioning of America* (Cambridge, MA: Harvard University Press, 2006); Marilyn Lake and Henry Reynolds, *Drawing the Global Colour Line: White Men's Countries and the International Challenge of Racial Equality* (Cambridge: Cambridge University Press, 2008); Adam M. McKeown, *Melancholy Order: Asian Migration and the Globalization of Borders* (New York: Columbia University Press, 2008).

13. See, among many titles, Mansel G. Blackford, *The Rise of Modern Business in Great Britain, the United States, and Japan* (Chapel Hill: University of North Carolina Press, 1988); Walter Nugent, *Crossings: The Great Transatlantic Migrations, 1870–1914* (Bloomington: Indiana University Press, 1992); and Wolfgang Schivelbusch, *Three New Deals: Reflections on Roosevelt's America, Mussolini's Italy, and Hitler's Germany, 1933–1939* (New York: Picador, 2006).

14. Available from Ranking America Web site, http://rankingamerica.wordpress.com/category/law-and-justice/. See also William J. Novak, "The Myth of the 'Weak' American State," *American Historical Review* 113 (June 2008): 752–772.

15. Peter N. Stearns, *Western Civilization in World History* (New York: Routledge, 2003), 93.

16. George M. Fredrickson, *White Supremacy: A Comparative Study in American and South African History* (New York: Oxford University Press, 1981); and *Black Liberation: A Comparative History of Black Ideologies in the United States and South Africa* (New York: Oxford University Press, 1995).

17. Glenda Sluga, "The Nation and the Comparative Imagination," in *Comparison and History*, ed. Cohen and O'Connor, 108.

18. For a discussion of some of these terms but no consensus, see "*AHR* Conversation: On Transnational History," *American Historical Review* 111 (December 2006): 1441–1464.

19. Tyrrell, *Transnational Nation*, 118–133. See also McKeown, *Melancholy Order*.

20. See, as representative titles, Amy Kaplan and Donald E. Pease, eds., *Cultures of United States Imperialism* (Durham, NC: Duke University Press, 1993); and Kristen Hoganson, *Consumers' Imperium: The Global Production of American Domesticity, 1865–1920* (Chapel Hill: University of North Carolina Press, 2007).

21. See Rob Kroes, R. W. Rydell, and D.F.J. Bosscher, eds., *Cultural Transmissions and Receptions: American Mass Culture in Europe* (Amsterdam: VU University Press, 1993); and Richard Pells, *Not Like Us: How Europeans Have Loved, Hated, and Transformed American Culture since World War II* (New York: Basic Books, 1997). For the theoretical underpinnings of this work, see John Tomlinson, *Cultural Imperialism: A Critical Introduction* (Baltimore, MD: Johns Hopkins University Press, 1991).

22. Linda Basch, Nina Glick Schiller, and Cristina Szanton Blanc, *Nations Unbound: Transnational Projects, Postcolonial Predicaments, and Deterritorialized Nation-States* (New York: Routledge, 1993); Robin D.G. Kelley, "How the West Was One; The African Diaspora and the Re-Mapping of U.S. History," in *Rethinking American History*, ed. Bender, 123–147.

23. Robin Cohen, *Global Diasporas: An Introduction* (Seattle: University of Washington Press, 1997), proposes a comparative typology and discusses recent "deterritorialized social identities." On transnational citizenship, see Etienne Balibar, *We the People of Europe? Reflections on Transnational Citizenship* (Princeton, NJ: Princeton University Press, 2004), and Wayne Hudson and Stephen Slaughter, eds., *Globalization and Citizenship: The Transnational Challenge* (New York: Routledge, 2007).

24. Arjun Appadurai, *Modernity at Large: Cultural Dimensions of Globalization* (Minneapolis: University of Minnesota Press, 1996); Ulf Hedetoft and Mette Hjort, eds., *The*

Postnational Self: Belonging and Identity (Minneapolis: University of Minnesota Press, 2002); Adam M. McKeown, *Chinese Migrant Networks and Cultural Change: Peru, Chicago, Hawaii, 1900–1936* (Chicago: University of Chicago Press, 2001).

25. See, for example, the special issue on "Rethinking History and the Nation-State: Mexico and the United States as a Case Study," *Journal of American History* 86 (September 1999).

26. See, for example, Daniel T. Rodgers, *Atlantic Crossings: Social Politics in a Progressive Age* (Cambridge, MA: Harvard University Press, 1998).

27. For overviews, see P. W. Preston, *Development Theory: An Introduction* (Cambridge, UK: Blackwell, 1996); and Colin Leys, *The Rise and Fall of Development Theory* (Bloomington: Indiana University Press, 1996). For cold war applications, see David C. Engerman, ed., *Staging Growth: Modernization, Development, and the Global Cold War* (Amherst: University of Massachusetts Press, 2003); and Nils Gilman, *Mandarins of the Future: Modernization Theory in Cold War America* (Baltimore, MD: Johns Hopkins University Press, 2003).

28. J. M. Roberts, *The Triumph of the West* (Boston: Little, Brown, 1986); David Fromkin, *The Way of the World: From the Dawn of Civilizations to the Eve of the Twenty-First Century* (New York: Knopf, 1998). In dissent, see Theodore H. Von Laue, *The World Revolution of Westernization* (New York: Oxford University Press, 1987).

29. Immanuel M. Wallerstein, *The Modern World System*, 3 vols. (New York: Academic Press, 1974–1989); and, more succinctly, *World-Systems Analysis: An Introduction* (Durham, NC: Duke University Press, 2004).

30. Michael Adas, "From Settler Colony to Global Hegemon: Integrating the Exceptionalist Narrative of the American Experience into World History," *American Historical Review* 106 (December 2001): 1692–1720. Giovanni Arrighi, *The Long Twentieth Century: Money, Power, and the Origins of Our Times* (London: Verso, 1994), sees the United States as the latest in a line of capitalist world system hegemons.

31. For debate over the current "American empire," see notes 89 and 91 below.

32. For brief introductions to globalization, see Jürgen Osterhammel and Niels P. Petersson, *Globalization: A Short History* (Princeton, NJ: Princeton University Press, 2005); and A. G. Hopkins, ed., *Globalization in World History* (London: Pimlico, 2002).

33. Bender, *Nation among Nations*, 15–60; Michael Geyer and Charles Bright, "World History in a Global Age," *American Historical Review* 100 (October 1995): 1034–1060.

34. For supporting arguments, see Arrighi, *The Long Twentieth Century*; Charles S. Maier, "Consigning the Twentieth Century to History: Alternative Narratives for the Modern Era," *American Historical Review* 105 (June 2000): 807–831; and Peter N. Stearns, "Long 19th Century? Long 20th? Retooling That Last Chunk of World History Periodization," *History Teacher* 42 (February 2009): 223–228.

35. Niall Ferguson, *Empire: The Rise and Demise of the British World Order and the Lessons for Global Power* (New York: Basic Books, 2003), xxiii.

36. See Bruce Mazlish, *The New Global History* (New York; Routledge, 2006).

37. Charles Tilly, *Big Structures, Large Processes, Huge Comparisons* (New York: Russell Sage Foundation, 1984).

38. Bender, *Nation among Nations*; John R. Gillis, "What Will It Take to Globalize American History?" in *Globalizing American History: The AHA Guide to Re-Imagining the U.S. Survey Course*, ed. Peter N. Stearns and Noralee Frankel (Washington, DC: American Historical Association, 2008), 93–116; Carl J. Guarneri, "Internationalizing the United States Survey Course: American History for a Global Age," *History Teacher* 36 (November 2002): 37–64.

39. Don H. Doyle and Marco Antonio Pamplona, eds., *Nationalism in the New World* (Athens: University of Georgia Press, 2006); Hoerder, *Cultures in Contact*; Peter N. Stearns, *Consumerism in World History: The Global Transformation of Desire* (London: Routledge, 2001); Stearns, *Schools and Students in Industrial Society: Japan and the West, 1870–1940* (Boston: Bedford Books, 1998); Julian Go and Anne Foster, eds., *The American*

Colonial State in the Philippines: Global Perspectives (Durham, NC: Duke University Press, 2003).

40. John A. Garraty, *The Great Depression* (Garden City, NY: Anchor Books, 1987); Eric Hobsbawm, *The Age of Extremes: A History of the World, 1914–1991* (New York: Vintage Books, 1994), 85–108; Jeremi Suri, *The Global Revolutions of 1968* (New York: W. W. Norton, 2007), and "The Rise and Fall of an International Counterculture, 1960–1975," *American Historical Review* 114 (February 2009): 45–68.

41. Geoffrey Perret, *A Country Made by War: From the Revolution to Vietnam—the Story of America's Rise to Power* (New York: Random House, 1989), 558.

42. Despite a vast literature on America's rise to world power, few scholars have placed it in global context. For a good beginning, see Michael Hunt, *The American Ascendancy: How the United States Gained and Wielded Global Dominance* (Chapel Hill: University of North Carolina Press, 2007).

43. Bender, *Nation among Nations*, 214–223; Robert E. May, *Manifest Destiny's Underworld: Filibustering in Antebellum America* (Chapel Hill: University of North Carolina Press, 2002); Aims McGuinness, *Path of Empire: Panama and the California Gold Rush* (Ithaca, NY: Cornell University Press, 2007).

44. Edward J. Davies, *The United States in World History* (New York: Routledge, 2006), 41–76, offers comparative insights on American industrialization.

45. Compare Gaddis Smith, *The Last Years of the Monroe Doctrine, 1945–1993* (New York: Hill and Wang, 1994), with Greg Grandin, *Empire's Workshop: Latin America, the United States, and the Rise of the New Imperialism* (New York: Henry Holt, 2006).

46. Charles P. Kindelberger, *The World in Depression, 1929–1939* (Berkeley: University of California Press, 1973), 297; D. C. Watt, *Succeeding John Bull: America in Britain's Place, 1900–1975* (Cambridge: Cambridge University Press, 1984).

47. For a forceful rebuttal, see Andrew J. Bacevich, *American Empire: The Realities and Consequences of U.S. Diplomacy* (Cambridge, MA: Harvard University Press, 2004).

48. John Higham, *Strangers in the Land: Patterns of American Nativism, 1860–1925* (New York: Atheneum, 1973); Reed Ueda, *Postwar Immigrant America* (Boston: Bedford/St. Martin's, 1994), 18–57; Zolberg, *A Nation by Design*, 166–431.

49. Tyrrell, *Transnational Nation*, 185–186.

50. Bender, *Nation among Nations*, 300.

51. Henry R. Luce, "The American Century," *Life* 10 (February 17, 1941): 61–65.

52. Michael H. Hunt, *Ideology and U.S. Foreign Policy* (New Haven, CT: Yale University Press, 1987).

53. See Adas, "Settler Colony to Global Hegemon," 1692–1697.

54. Tony Smith, *America's Mission: The United States and the Worldwide Struggle for Democracy in the Twentieth Century* (Princeton, NJ: Princeton University Press, 1994); Frank Ninkovich, *The Wilsonian Century: U.S. Foreign Policy since 1900* (Chicago: University of Chicago Press, 2001). On the technological component, see Michael Adas, *Dominance by Design: Technological Imperatives and America's Civilizing Mission* (Cambridge, MA: Harvard University Press, 2006).

55. Matthew Frye Jacobson, *Barbarian Virtues: The United States Encounters Foreign Peoples at Home and Abroad, 1876–1917* (New York: Hill and Wang, 2000).

56. Melani McAlister, *Epic Encounters: Culture, Media, and U.S. Interests in the Middle East since 1945* (Berkeley: University of California Press, 1995); Christina Klein, *Cold War Orientalism: Asia in the Middlebrow Imagination, 1945–1961* (Berkeley: University of California Press, 2003). See Andrew J. Rotter, "Saidism without Said: Orientalism and U.S. Diplomatic History," *American Historical Review* 105 (October 2000): 1205–1218.

57. Laura McEnaney, "Gender," in *Encyclopedia of American Foreign Policy*, ed. Alexander DeConde et al. (New York: Scribner's, 2002), 124.

58. John W. Dower, *War without Mercy: Race and Power in the Pacific War* (New York: Pantheon, 1986); Andrew J. Rotter, "Gender Relations, Foreign Relations: The United States

and South Asia, 1947–1964," *Journal of American History* 81 (September 1994): 518–542; Kristin L. Hoganson, *Fighting for American Manhood: How Gender Politics Provoked the Spanish-American and Philippine-American Wars* (New Haven, CT: Yale University Press, 1998).

59. David Brion Davis, *Revolutions: Reflections on American Equality and Foreign Liberations* (Cambridge, MA: Harvard University Press, 1990). For a revealing case study, see Timothy Mason Roberts, *Distant Revolutions: 1848 and the Challenge to American Exceptionalism* (Charlottesville: University of Virginia Press, 2009).

60. William Appleman Williams, *The Tragedy of American Diplomacy* (New York: Dell Publishers, 1962).

61. Walter LaFeber, *The American Search for Opportunity, 1865–1913*, vol. II of *The Cambridge History of American Foreign Relations* (Cambridge: Cambridge University Press, 1993); Emily S. Rosenberg, *Spreading the American Dream: American Economic and Cultural Expansion, 1890–1945* (New York: Hill and Wang, 1982).

62. H. W. Brands, *What America Owes the World: The Struggle for the Soul of Foreign Policy* (Cambridge: Cambridge University Press, 1998).

63. N. Gordon Levin Jr., *Woodrow Wilson and World Politics: America's Response to War and Revolution* (New York: Oxford University Press, 1968), 237; Ninkovitch, *The Wilsonian Century*.

64. Erez Manela, *The Wilsonian Moment: Self-Determination and the International Origins of Anticolonial Nationalism* (New York: Oxford University Press, 2007). See also Alan Dawley, *Changing the World: American Progressives in War and Revolution* (Princeton, NJ: Princeton University Press, 2003).

65. Lance E. Davis and Robert Gallman, *Evolving Financial Markets and International Capital Flows: Britain, the Americas, and Australia, 1865–1914* (Cambridge: Cambridge University Press, 2001). On Japanese cars, see Wanda James, *Driving from Japan: Japanese Cars in America* (Jefferson, NC: McFarland, 2005).

66. Hoganson, *Consumers' Imperium*; Paul A. Kramer, *The Blood of Government: Race, Empire, the U.S. and the Philippines* (Chapel Hill: University of North Carolina Press, 2006); Gary Y. Okihiro, *Island World: A History of Hawai'i and the United States* (Berkeley: University of California Press, 2008).

67. Interview with García Márquez by Enrique Fernandez, *Village Voice*, July 3, 1984.

68. Alan Nadel, *Containment Culture: American Narrative, Postmodernism, and the Atomic Age* (Durham, NC: Duke University Press, 1995); Tom Engelhardt, *The End of Victory Culture: Cold War America and the Disillusioning of a Generation* (New York: Basic Books, 1995).

69. On the imperial presidency, see Hunt, *American Ascendancy*, 140–150. The phrase is from Arthur Schlesinger Jr., *The Imperial Presidency* (Boston: Houghton Mifflin, 1973).

70. Mary L. Dudziak, *Cold War Civil Rights: Race and the Image of American Democracy* (Princeton, NJ: Princeton University Press, 2000); Azza Salama Layton, *International Politics and Civil Rights Policies in the United States, 1941–1960* (Cambridge: Cambridge University Press, 2000).

71. Philippe Roger, *The American Enemy: A Story of French Anti-Americanism*, trans. Sharon Bowman (Chicago: University of Chicago Press, 2005); Chalmers A. Johnson, *Blowback: The Costs and Consequences of American Empire* (New York: Metropolitan Books, 2000). See also, "*AHR* Forum: Historical Perspectives on Anti-Americanism," *American Historical Review* 111 (October 2006): 1041–1129.

72. On the rise and impact of NGOs, see Akira Iriye, *Global Community: The Role of International Organizations in the Making of the Contemporary World* (Berkeley: University of California Press, 2002).

73. Bruce Mazlish, Nayan Chanda, and Kenneth Weisbrode, eds., *The Paradox of a Global USA* (Stanford: Stanford University Press, 2007), 1, 47.

74. Joseph S. Nye, *The Paradox of American Power: Why the World's Only Superpower Can't Go It Alone* (New York: Oxford University Press, 2002), 40.

75. Charles Bright and Michael Geyer, "Where in the World Is America? The History of the U.S. in the Global Age," in *Rethinking American History*, ed. Bender, 63–99.

76. Peter N. Stearns, "The Settler Societies: The West on Frontiers," in *World History in Brief: Major Patterns of Change and Continuity*, 6th ed. (New York: Pearson Longman, 2007), 429–436; Carl J. Guarneri, "The United States among New World Settler Societies, 1783–1914," unpublished paper, 2007.

77. Lake and Reynolds, *Drawing the International Colour Line*; Ian Tyrrell, *Woman's World, Woman's Empire: The Woman's Christian Temperance Union in International Perspective, 1880–1930* (Chapel Hill: University of North Carolina Press, 1991); Peter J. Coleman, *Progressivism and the World of Reform: New Zealand and the Origins of the American Welfare State* (Lawrence: University Press of Kansas, 1987).

78. Augie Fleras and Jean Leonard Elliot, *The Nations Within: Aboriginal-State Relations in Canada, the United States, and New Zealand* (Toronto: Oxford University Press, 1992); Janice Stein et al., *Uneasy Partners: Multiculturalism and Rights in Canada* (Waterloo, CA: Wilfrid Laurier University Press, 2007).

79. Robin D.G. Kelley, "But a Local Phase of a World Problem: Black History's Global Vision, 1883–1950," *Journal of American History* 86 (December 1999): 1045–1077.

80. Carl N. Degler, *Neither Black nor White: Slavery and Race Relations in Brazil and the United States* (New York: Macmillan, 1971); Rebecca J. Scott, *Degrees of Freedom: Louisiana and Cuba after Slavery* (Cambridge, MA: Harvard University Press, 2008).

81. Fredrickson, *White Supremacy*; John W. Cell, *The Highest Stage of White Supremacy: The Origins of Segregation in South Africa and the American South* (Cambridge: Cambridge University Press, 1982); Anthony W. Marx, *Making Race and Nation: A Comparison of South Africa, the United States, and Brazil* (Cambridge: Cambridge University Press, 1998).

82. Brenda Gayle Plummer, *Rising Wind: Black Americans and U.S. Foreign Affairs, 1935–1960* (Chapel Hill: University of North Carolina Press, 1996); Penny von Eschen, *Race against Empire: Black Americans and Anticolonialism, 1937–1957* (Ithaca, NY: Cornell University Press, 1997); Kelley, "How the West Was One," 136–139.

83. Nugent, *Crossings*; Annie Cohen-Solal, *Painting American: The Rise of American Artists, Paris 1867–New York 1948* (New York: Alfred A. Knopf, 2001); Bernard Bailyn and Donald Fleming, *The Intellectual Migration: Europe and America 1930–1960* (Cambridge, MA: Harvard University Press, 1969); Rodgers, *Atlantic Crossings*.

84. Victoria de Grazia, *Irresistible Empire: America's Advance through 20th–Century Europe* (Cambridge, MA: Harvard University Press, 2005); R. Laurence Moore and Maurizio Vaudagna, eds., *The American Century in Europe* (Ithaca, NY: Cornell University Press, 2003).

85. Europeanization was the background to Frederick Jackson Turner's "frontier thesis" and other essays. See *Frontier and Section: Selected Essays of Frederick Jackson Turner* (Englewood Cliffs, NJ: Prentice-Hall, 1961). On "Americanization," see Roger, *The American Enemy*.

86. Laurence Veysey, "The Autonomy of American History Reconsidered," *American Quarterly* 31 (Fall 1979): 459–477; Stearns, *Western Civilization*, 93–95, 117–118.

87. Charles A. Kupchan, *The End of the American Era: U.S. Foreign Policy and the Geopolitics of the Twenty-First Century* (New York: Alfred A. Knopf, 2003).

88. Good starting points for this comparison are Akira Iriye, *Pacific Estrangement: Japanese and American Expansionism, 1897–1911* (Cambridge, MA: Harvard University Press, 1972); and Walter LaFeber, *The Clash: A History of U.S.-Japan Relations* (New York: W. W. Norton, 1997).

89. For a historical analysis in favor of empire, see Niall Ferguson, *Colossus: The Price of America's Empire* (New York: Penguin Press, 2004). For opposition, see Chalmers A. Johnson, *The Sorrows of Empire* (New York: Metropolitan Books, 2004).

90. Ferguson, *Colossus*, 24–26, 169–199.

91. Comparisons with Britain and other imperial powers are elaborated in Johnson, *Sorrows of Empire*, 15–37; Ferguson, *Colossus*, 1–29; Bernard Porter, *Empire and Superempire: Britain, America and the World* (New Haven, CT: Yale University Press, 2006); and Charles S. Maier, *Among Empires: American Ascendancy and Its Predecessors* (Cambridge, MA: Harvard University Press, 2006).

92. John Darwin, *The Empire Project: The Rise and Fall of the British World-System, 1830–1970* (Cambridge: Cambridge University Press, 2009).

93. For a range of responses, see the essays in Patrick Karl O'Brien and Armand Clesse, eds., *Two Hegemonies: Britain 1846–1914 and the United States 1941–2001* (Aldershot, UK: Ashgate, 2002).

94. Paul Kennedy, *The Rise and Fall of the Great Powers: Economic Change and Military Conflict, 1500 to 2000* (New York: Random House, 1987).

95. Joseph S. Nye, *Bound to Lead: The Changing Nature of American Power* (New York: Basic Books, 1990); Amy Chua, *Day of Empire: How Hyperpowers Rise to Global Dominance—and Why They Fall* (New York: Doubleday, 2007); Fareed Zakaria, *The Post-American World* (New York: W. W. Norton, 2008).

96. Blackford, *Rise of Modern Business*; Aristide A. Zolberg, "The Roots of American Exceptionalism," in *Pourqoi n'y a-t-il pas de socialisme aux Etats-Unis?* ed. Heffer and Rovet, 106–114; David A. Hounshell, *From the American System to Mass Production, 1800–1932: The Development of Manufacturing Technology in the United States* (Baltimore, MD: Johns Hopkins University Press, 1984).

97. Steven Watts, *The People's Tycoon: Henry Ford and the American Century* (New York: Knopf, 2005); Robert Kanigel, *The One Best Way: Frederick Winslow Taylor and the Enigma of Efficiency* (New York: Viking, 1997). For Ford's impact abroad, see McNeill, *Something New under the Sun*, 316–319; Greg Grandin, *Fordlandia: The Rise and Fall of Henry Ford's Forgotten Jungle City* (New York: Metropolitan Books, 2009).

98. Witold Rybczynski, *Waiting for the Weekend* (New York: Viking, 1991), 109–161; Roland Marchand, *Advertising the American Dream: Making Way for Modernity, 1920–1940* (Berkeley: University of California Press, 1986); De Grazia, *Irresistible Empire*, 130–183, 226–283.

99. Stearns, *Consumerism in World History*, 44–59, 66; Rob Kroes, *Them and Us: Questions of Citizenship in a Globalizing World* (Urbana: University of Illinois Press, 2000), 154.

100. This two-pronged struggle is best framed in Hobsbawm, *The Age of Extremes*, 54–177, 225–256.

101. Schivelbusch, *Three New Deals*; Garraty, *The Great Depression*; Bender, *Nation among Nations*, 293–294.

102. For vivid descriptions of postwar globalization and its effects, see Benjamin R. Barber, *Jihad vs. McWorld: How Globalism and Tribalism are Reshaping the World* (New York: Ballantine Books, 1996); and Walter Truett Anderson, *All Connected Now: Life in the First Global Civilization* (Boulder, CO: Westview Press, 2003).

103. Walter LaFeber, *Michael Jordan and the New Global Capitalism*, rev. ed. (New York: W. W. Norton, 2002).

104. Alfred E. Eckes Jr. and Thomas W. Zeiler, *Globalization and the American Century* (Cambridge: Cambridge University Press, 2003), 209.

105. For essays offering contrasting views on key issues, see David Held and Anthony McGrew, eds., *The Global Transformations Reader: An Introduction to the Globalization Debate*, 2nd ed. (Cambridge, UK: Polity Press, 2003).

106. Hobsbawm, *Age of Extremes*, 1, 6.

107. Michael S. Sherry, *The Rise of American Air Power: The Creation of Armageddon* (New Haven, CT: Yale University Press, 1987); Conrad C. Crane, *Bombs, Cities, and Civilians: American Airpower Strategy in World War II* (Lawrence: University Press of Kansas, 1993), 120–142, 161–162.

108. See Andrew J. Rotter, *Hiroshima: The World's Bomb* (New York: Oxford University Press, 2008), 270–303.

109. Hunt, *American Ascendancy*, 129–133.

110. Michael S. Neiberg, *Warfare in World History* (London: Routledge, 2001), 90–93.

111. Adas, *Dominance by Design*, 339–415 (quotation, 387).

112. The following section is a revised and condensed version of my treatment of "The Cold War as Imperial Rivalry" in *America in the World*, 247–262.

113. Geir Lundestad, "Empire by Invitation? The United States and Western Europe, 1945–1952," *Journal of Peace Research* 23 (September 1986): 263–277; John Lewis Gaddis, *We Now Know: Rethinking Cold War History* (New York: Oxford University Press, 1997), 52.

114. Odd Arne Westad, *The Global Cold War: Third World Interventions and the Making of Our Times* (Cambridge: Cambridge University Press, 2005).

115. Westad, *Global Cold War*, 396.

116. Michael J. Hogan, ed., *The End of the Cold War: Its Meanings and Implications* (Cambridge: Cambridge University Press, 1992), gathers a range of historians' reflections.

117. Francis Fukuyama, "The End of History?" *National Interest*, 16 (Summer 1989): 3–18.

118. Tyrrell, *Woman's World, Woman's Empire*; Leila J. Rupp, *Worlds of Women: The Making of an International Women's Movement* (Princeton, NJ: Princeton University Press, 1997); Ellen Carol DuBois, "Woman Suffrage around the World: Three Phases of Suffragist Internationalism," in *Suffrage and Beyond: International Feminist Perspectives*, ed. Caroline Daley and Melanie Nolan (New York: New York University Press, 1994), 252–274.

119. Richard J. Evans, *The Feminists: Women's Emancipation Movements in Europe, America and Australasia* (London: Croom Helm, 1979), 211–228; Bonnie G. Smith, *Changing Lives: Women in European History Since 1700* (Lexington, MA: D.C. Heath, 1989), 396–397; Christine Bolt, *The Women's Movements in the United States and Britain from the 1790s to the 1920s* (Amherst: University of Massachusetts Press, 1993).

120. Olive Banks, *Faces of Feminism: A Study of Feminism as a Social Movement* (Oxford: Blackwell, 1986); Susan Kent, "Worlds of Feminism," in *Women's History in Global Perspective*, ed. Bonnie G. Smith, vol. I (Urbana: University of Illinois Press, 2004), 302–306.

121. See, for example, Mallika Dutt, "Some Reflections on United States Women of Color and the United Nations Fourth World Conference on Women and NGO Forum in Beijing, China," in *Global Feminisms Since 1945*, ed. Bonnie G. Smith (London: Routledge, 2000), 305–313.

122. Mary Ann Glendon, *A World Made New: Eleanor Roosevelt and the Universal Declaration of Human Rights* (New York: Random House, 2001).

123. Elisabeth Friedman, "Woman's Human Rights: The Emergence of a Movement," in *Women's Rights, Human Rights: International Feminist Perspectives*, ed. Julie Peters and Andrea Wolper (New York: Routledge, 1995), 18–35; Jean H. Quataert, *The Gendering of Human Rights in the International Systems of Law in the Twentieth Century* (Washington, DC: American Historical Association, 2006), 17–33.

124. McNeill, *Something New under the Sun*, is an excellent overview. For the United States, see also Philip Shabecoff, *A Fierce Green Fire: The American Environmental Movement*, rev. ed. (Washington, DC: Island Press, 2003).

125. Clive Ponting, *A New Green History of the World: The Environment and the Collapse of Great Civilizations*, rev. ed. (New York: Penguin, 2007); Jared Diamond, *Collapse: How Societies Choose to Fail or Succeed* (New York: Penguin, 2005).

126. Elizabeth Kolbert, *Field Notes from a Catastrophe: Man, Nature, and Climate Change* (New York: Bloomsbury, 2006); Andrew E. Dessler and Edward A. Parson, *The Science and Politics of Global Climate Change: A Guide to the Debate* (Cambridge: Cambridge University Press, 2006).

127. Richard P. Tucker, *Insatiable Appetite: The United States and the Ecological Degradation of the Tropical World* (Berkeley: University of California Press, 2000); Myrna I. Santiago, *The Ecology of Oil: Environment, Labor, and the Mexican Revolution, 1900–1938* (Cambridge: Cambridge University Press, 2006).

128. Turner, "The Significance of History," in *Frontier and Section*, 21.

129. See Ian Tyrrell, "Making Nations/Making States: American Historians in the Context of Empire," *Journal of American History* 86 (December 1999): 1015–1044.

130. Bender, *Nation among Nations*, 300–301.

CHAPTER 7

The Technopolitics of Cold War

Toward a Transregional Perspective

GABRIELLE HECHT AND PAUL N. EDWARDS

Technological change played a major role in the defining events of the twentieth century, especially in war. Two world wars, the cold war, and colonial and postcolonial conflicts around the globe were all characterized by innovation in the technologies of destruction, from tanks and ballistic missiles to mass-produced automatic rifles and portable antiaircraft rockets. As the century wore on, conflicts spread well beyond the battlefield. Weapons of mass destruction rendered specious most distinctions between military fronts and protected rear areas. Mass production dropped the price of small arms into the bargain basement, while free markets made them readily available.

Across nearly four decades of cold war, military hardware became an economic sector unto itself. By the mid-1980s, global annual military budgets reached nearly $1 trillion. This figure included almost $350 billion in global annual expenditure on weapons and military hardware, but ignored untold billions in arms trade on a global black market.[1] Notions of a "military-industrial complex"—already a commonplace in the early 1960s—only hinted at the depth of the entanglements between technology, military power, political authority, and civil society that had developed by the cold war's end.

Perhaps precisely because these entanglements are so salient, historians rarely try to explain the course of technological change itself. Recent scholarship on globalization, for example, makes much of the idea that evolving transport and communication infrastructures promoted globalization processes.[2] But like most historiography, this scholarship usually treats technology as a hermetic "black box." Technology appears as an explanatory factor, yet rarely are the inner workings of technological innovation and diffusion tied directly to what is being explained. Narratives and tropes of progress, widely discredited in political and social history, still find broad and unexamined acceptance with respect to technological change.

Nowhere has this been more striking than in studies of the cold war. Historians regard the superpower arms race as one of the cold war's central features. Yet outside the subspecialty of the history of technology, most have treated its military technology as an exogenous force. In such accounts, nuclear weapons appear as ready-made tools for politicians, end products of the byzantine military-industrial complex, or awe-inspiring sources of iconography. Politicians and diplomats figure as the most significant actors, and popular images of things nuclear constitute cold war culture. Until recently, this approach produced studies of the cold war focused primarily on so-called nuclear states (those possessing atomic weapons)—especially, of course, the United States and Soviet superpowers. Other parts of the world made an appearance primarily as proxy sites for superpower struggles, or thorns in the sides of the two titans.

Revisiting the Cold War: Technology and Transregional Perspectives

The traditional account of the cold war begins with the partition of Europe after World War II. Initially intended as a temporary custodial arrangement, the partition became quasi-permanent by 1947–1948, as the Soviet Union installed communist governments throughout Eastern Europe and the U.S.-backed Marshall Plan brought Western Europe under American influence. The U.S. policy of "containment" committed the United States to limiting the spread of communism by all possible means, anywhere in the world. The cold war became in rhetoric, and often in practice as well, a global, total contest between competing ideologies, economies, and cultures. With the first successful Soviet nuclear test and the Chinese communist revolution in 1949, closely followed by the outbreak of war on the Korean peninsula, tensions between the emerging superpowers escalated dramatically. An unprecedented arms race began in both conventional and new, high-tech weapons that included not only nuclear explosives but also jet aircraft, ballistic missiles, and nuclear-powered submarines.

The cold war continued with the Cuban Missile Crisis of 1962 and U.S. entry into the Vietnam conflict in 1965. In the 1970s, a period of détente ensued, but the nuclear arms race continued without a break. The Soviet invasion of Afghanistan in 1978 renewed tensions, initiating a period sometimes known as "Cold War II" or the "Carter-Reagan Cold War."[3] During this period, U.S. military budgets soared to dramatic heights, even as popular protests against nuclear weapons intensified. In 1985, Mikhail Gorbachev came to power, restructuring the Soviet economy and relaxing restrictions on political speech. By some accounts, this ultimately led to the collapse of the Soviet

Union in 1991. Many historians date the cold war's end to the dismantling of the Berlin Wall in 1989, following the collapse of the East German communist regime, part of a wave of democratic quasi-revolutions in Eastern Europe during that year.

Recently, historians have called for reexamining the cold war from perspectives that reduce the centrality of the superpower struggle. The dominance of cold war politics probably led contemporaries to focus too closely on its largest military actors, namely the United States, Europe, and the Soviet Union. From other points of view—especially that of the global South—processes such as decolonization and development were more salient. Historians have begun to move beyond treating the South merely as proxy sites for cold war conflicts, instead exploring how national politics and culture in places like Vietnam and Algeria shaped cold war practices "from below." This approach is becoming known as the "new international history."[4] It provides important new perspectives, but still does not examine the role of technology in global conflict.

One area of social science scholarship *has* endeavored to include technological change as an object of analysis: "science and technology studies," or STS. This field includes historians, sociologists, anthropologists, and others interested in understanding technological systems and their relationship to social, political, and cultural dynamics. STS has devoted considerable attention to cold war science and technology, but this too has generally centered on the United States, Europe, or the Soviet Union. Because they seek to unpack the inner political and social workings of technology, these scholars tend to focus on case studies and microprocesses. The macroview offered by global and transregional history is nearly nonexistent in this literature.

This chapter, then, aims to put two scholarly fields in dialogue in order to explore cold war technopolitics in a transregional perspective. We hope thereby to stimulate new ways of teaching about and conducting research on the cold war. First, we survey the political and social history of cold war technology. Second, and simultaneously, we seek to improve our understanding of cold war technopolitics by approaching them from a transregional point of view. Due to space constraints, we focus here on just two technical systems: nuclear technologies and computers. These comprise our areas of expertise, but they also represent two of the cold war's most significant technological systems (the third being space and missile technologies, which we can only treat in passing).

ANALYZING TECHNOLOGICAL CHANGE

For our purposes, foremost among the tools of STS is the *sociotechnical systems approach* developed by Thomas Parke Hughes and his colleagues.[5] This perspective directs us to view technologies not as individual devices, but as vast, interdependent networks of artifacts, institutions, people, and social systems. The nuclear system thus includes not only warheads and reactors but also uranium mines, missiles, electric power grids, weapons testing sites, and waste disposal facilities. It also includes regulatory agencies, national laboratories, corporations, military commanders, scientists, technicians, and miners, as well as communities located near mines, reactors, waste dumps, and nuclear missile silos. Similarly, as sociotechnical systems computers include not only central processors but also peripheral devices (printers, disk drives, and so forth), software corporations, manufacturing facilities, maintenance technicians, geographical clusters and cultures such as Silicon Valley, the all-important system operators who manage networks, data-entry workers, chip manufacturers, and software developers are located all over the world. Indeed, computers and computerized networks—not only the Internet, but others such as those of the major credit card systems, banks, and financial markets—have become fundamental infrastructures in the developed world, with tendrils reaching around the globe. From this perspective, devices, institutions, and altered social relations form a complex sociotechnical system, where causal relationships look more like mutual construction than like technological determinism.

Properly deployed, the sociotechnical systems approach can help trace links between apparently unconnected historical actors, such as American nuclear weapons designers and the Congolese hard-rock uranium miners who supplied their raw materials. Where the former derived enormous power from their technical knowledge and technological resources, the latter suffered from their lack. How do actors derive power from technical knowledge? In what does their power consist? Familiar historical categories such as race, class, institutions, and culture can help explain these relations. But they are not enough. In sociotechnical systems, power derives from the control of knowledge, artifacts, and practices. This hybrid form of power has cultural, institutional, and technological dimensions. We call it *"technopolitics."*[6]

Technopolitics is the strategic practice of designing or using technology to enact political goals. Such practices are not simply politics by another name. They produce artifacts whose design features matter fundamentally to their success, and to the ways in which they act upon the world.

When political actors work with engineers to solve problems, such as how to manage the command and control of nuclear-armed military forces on a global scale, they orient each other to particular solutions. As politicians and designers work together—very often indirectly, mediated through institutions—emerging technical capabilities both create and constrain political possibilities. At the same time, technical capabilities expand and take on directionality to the extent that they acquire political support and effectiveness; unsupported designs come to seem impractical (even if they are not) once large resources have been committed to another alternative.

Very often, if not always, neither politicians nor engineers foresee the full implications of this process, which we call *"mutual orientation."*[7] For example, during the cold war, both the United States and the Soviet Union constructed global systems to provide early warning of nuclear attack. As warning time windows shrank to mere minutes, both sides automated these systems and preprogrammed their military responses. A major technopolitical implication foreseen by neither side was that these highly automatic warning systems effectively became tightly coupled to each other. Military activity by one side provoked an immediate response from the other; this could produce a rapid series of upward-ratcheting movements that very nearly led to accidental nuclear war on a number of occasions.[8]

This chapter deploys these ideas in its survey of scholarship on the nuclear age and the computer age. World War II military projects boosted nuclear technologies and digital computers from prototype to operational systems. In the immediate postwar period, military development continued to dominate both systems. They soon grew closely connected, as computerized control made possible global nuclear command and unintentionally integrated the superpowers into a single, tightly coupled cybernetic unit: apocalypse on a hair trigger. Starting in the 1950s, national governments began to invest heavily to advance their civilian applications.

At that point, the histories of nuclear systems and computers began to diverge. After enjoying a "bandwagon market" in the 1960s, orders for nuclear power reactors began to drop off. Until very recently, only a few nations envisaged building new ones. Nuclear power has remained a system that can operate only on a very large scale, with massive state involvement. Despite the best efforts of civilian manufacturers, nuclear power could not seem to shed its symbolic ties to nuclear weapons. In contrast, computers rapidly managed to cast off the symbolic baggage of military association. They enjoyed spectacular commercial success in the 1960s, when they too were an expensive "big technology," attractive mainly to large corporations and governments. Several commercial booms ensued and in the 1980s, desktop "personal" computers became consumer products and corporate computer networks laid the groundwork for the modern Internet. So despite the continuing significance of military computing, the profound success of computers as commodities ultimately brought them out from under the shadow of their original military sponsors.

Five decades ago, both nuclear power and computers were the subjects of utopian visions. Power would be "too cheap to meter." Robots would run our factories and artificial minds would solve our problems. By the 1970s, economic and technical problems, environmental hazards, and major social movements had shattered nuclear utopianism. But cyber-utopianism shook off every fear, gathering strength even into the present. Whereas nuclear technologies proved mainly divisive, computer technologies emerged—at least in the popular imagination—as a global unifying force and a symbol of libertarian freedom.

We divide our discussion of these developments into three thematic sections. First, we examine the arms race, a central technopolitical dynamic of the cold war in which nuclear and computer systems were closely intertwined.

Second, we explore the complex relationships among expertise, power, and democracy that characterized nuclear and computer technopolitics in the cold war. Third, we address the ways these technopolitics were involved in the reshaping of nationalisms, colonialisms, and international relationships.

Our survey is by no means exhaustive. Instead, we have chosen works that, when grouped together, can help scholars and teachers develop fresh perspectives on the role of technology in the cold war. We have taken an interdisciplinary approach, including not only history but also sociology, anthropology, and political science as appropriate. We have endeavored when possible to offer comparative perspectives on nuclear and computer history, but the current state of historiography severely limits our efforts: computer history in particular is dominated by U.S. material. We can only hope that the holes in our survey will inspire future studies of technopolitical systems in transregional perspective.

TECHNOPOLITICS AND THE ARMS RACE

The U.S.-Soviet arms race constituted the central technological and military dynamic of the cold war. Not only among historians but also among the lay public, considerable controversy still rages around its origins. One passionate debate concerns the U.S. decision to drop atomic bombs on Hiroshima and Nagasaki. Were these bombs necessary to end the war? Did the U.S. nuclear attack initiate the cold war, or did the Soviet Union start it during the Allied occupation of Europe? This well-trodden historical terrain underlies many investigations of cold war technology, often driven by the all-important question: was the arms buildup necessary to prevent a World War III?[9]

Though ultimately unanswerable, this counterfactual question nonetheless provides a key entry point into any analysis of arms-race technopolitics. The United States alone spent $5.8 trillion developing the complex technological systems—from missiles and submarines to computers and communications satellites—required to support its nuclear arsenal.[10] The public rationale for most of these expenditures was that this arsenal guaranteed the security not only of the United States but also of Europe and even the entire globe, by "deterring" the USSR from using its own arsenal to achieve its expansionist aims.

In fact, national security was only one among many factors driving weapons development and deployment. Others included interservice rivalry, "technological enthusiasm," national prestige, and the entrenched interests and routines of the military-academic-industrial "Iron Triangle."[11] These forces not only guided decisions about how many and what kind of weapons to build but also shaped the design of weapons and delivery systems, sometimes in unexpected ways.

Consider the following example. In the 1950s, the United States constructed the world's first computerized continental air defense system, to track and shoot down nuclear-armed Soviet bombers. At the time, most engineers believed that computers were far too slow and too unreliable to do the job. Why, then, deploy them for this difficult and ultraimportant task?

The answer reveals a complex technopolitical choice. Charged with finding technological solutions to the defense of an entire continent, rival groups of civilian engineers advocated different solutions. One involved new, high-risk digital computer technology, while the other promised to automate and improve the existing slow but reliable analog systems. Frightening intelligence estimates of Soviet technological capabilities created a powerful sense of urgency. Although these estimates turned out to be overblown, they generated pressure for radical change and helped promote massive investment in new technology. Public anxiety about a possible Soviet surprise attack led politicians to promise active air defense. Behind the scenes, though, no knowledgeable officer expected any air defense to shoot down more than 20 percent of enemy bombers. Meanwhile, air force "prompt use" strategy—known only to commanders at the highest levels—assumed that the United States would strike first, destroying Soviet bombers before they left the ground and rendering air defense unnecessary.[12]

The initial proposal for a computerized warning system came not from the military, but from civilian engineers at the Massachusetts Institute of Technology (MIT), whose existing computer project was threatened by a funding crisis. Seeking a new sponsor, these engineers generated a blue-sky proposal for a centralized, computerized system for early warning, tracking, and interceptor control.[13] Within the air force, debates raged over the new idea, which would consolidate command of aircraft in control centers on the ground. Many officers resisted removing air defense from the hands of pilots. They also distrusted then new and untested computer technology. Far from being a foregone conclusion, the eventual decision to proceed with the computerized SAGE (Semi-Automatic Ground Environment) system represented a simultaneously technological, political, and ideological choice.[14] Among its immense ramifications was the award of a contract for the forty-six enormous SAGE computers to IBM. This contract played a decisive role in IBM's ascent to dominance of the world computer market in the 1960s.[15]

Or take a second example, from the second decade of the arms race: the U.S. development of missile guidance technologies in the 1960s. One might assume that perfecting nuclear weapons inevitably required increasing the accuracy of missiles. In fact, however, more accurate missiles were by no means an obviously desirable goal; increased accuracy had major strategic and economic implications. Early nuclear strategy derived from World War II carpet bombing of cities, designed not only to destroy weapons factories but also to kill and terrorize civilian populations. Yet highly accurate missiles could potentially destroy the opponent's missiles, even in hardened silos before they could be launched. Targeting missile silos rather than cities allowed strategists to make the politically useful claim that theirs was a genuine military strategy, rather than simple terrorism. At the same time, it meant that one side's surprise attack could, in principle, eliminate the other's retaliatory capability and "win" a nuclear war. This encouraged the hair-trigger "use 'em or lose 'em" policy of "launch on warning." Thus, political factors largely unrelated to U.S.-Soviet relations shaped missile guidance technology. In turn, engineers and military leaders used this politically shaped technology to redesign nuclear strategy and lay claim to the expertise required to defend the Western world. In this manner, guidance systems were technopolitical: technologies designed to fulfill particular political purposes. Their politics, however, were often unremarked, even obscured: experts framed their designs as technological imperatives, the result of the inevitable path of technological progress.[16]

Obscuring the political dimensions of such technological changes, long-standing beliefs about industrial capitalism merged seamlessly with the liberal democratic ideologies driving the cold war in the West. Since at least the nineteenth century, U.S. discourse on technological development had emphasized ingenuity, entrepreneurship, and the free market: superior technology equated directly with marketplace success, and vice versa. American scientists and engineers, generally held in enormous esteem after their decisive roles in World War II, garnered further legitimacy and authority by distancing themselves from "politics." They pictured science as a disinterested search for truth, and technology as its practical application. Technology itself was "value-neutral"; only its users could determine its application for good or for ill. (Nonetheless, technology's association with science almost always gave it a positive valence by default.) On this distinctively American view, technological change involved politics only when its designers *explicitly stated* political or ideological goals. Notions of efficiency and progress, frequently invoked to justify technological change, were naturalized along with the liberal market capitalism that provided their motive force. This was the ideological backdrop that made it possible for air defense or missile guidance to appear apolitical in the United States.[17]

NUCLEAR WEAPONS AND COMPUTING IN THE SOVIET BLOC

American nuclear technopolitics may therefore surprise some readers, but findings that Soviet nuclear technology was politically shaped will shock no one. Cold war discourse framed the United States as apolitical, and the Soviet Union as profoundly ideological; it therefore followed that its technologies would have deeply political dimensions and be fundamentally "flawed" as a result. Recent scholarship makes clear that this opposition—political versus apolitical—is not a useful one in distinguishing between American and Soviet technological developments. Both were the result of technopolitical processes, albeit in different ways.

As soon as Stalin had grasped the military implications of the Hiroshima and Nagasaki bombs, he gave the Soviet atomic weapons project top priority. Obsessed with the conflict between socialism and capitalism, Stalin isolated Soviet scientists from their Western colleagues. Thus, Soviet scientists and engineers designed nuclear weapons largely on their own (although spies like Klaus Fuchs sometimes provided useful technical knowledge). Under Stalin, a "command-administrative" structure guided development strategies. With his approval, the administrator in charge of this structure directed scientists and engineers to pursue numerous design alternatives simultaneously—against their better judgment—in order to build weapons as quickly as possible. The Stalinist regime's political practices reverberated throughout the Soviet nuclear system, most notoriously in the use of prison labor at uranium mines and construction projects.[18]

After Stalin's death, Khrushchev's administration sought a more open approach to scientific and technical development. This approach not only encouraged increased international contact but also enabled scientists and engineers to be more active in setting policy agendas for nuclear development. Specific information on weapons systems remains scarce, but a recent study of Russian nuclear power suggests ways that the Soviet system gave nuclear development a distinctive technopolitical profile. Party officials regarded nuclear power as the means to build a fully communist society: nuclear technology could revive "poorly performing" industries, for example, and irradiating foods could compensate for inefficiencies in agriculture. Soviet visions of nuclear panaceas thus resulted in what one author has labeled "atomic-powered communism."[19]

Cold war technopolitics was equally evident in the Soviet bloc's approach to computerization. By the late 1940s, Soviet engineers (here, too, isolated from their Western counterparts) had developed their own, largely independent line of computer research.[20] A small indigenous computer industry developed, but by the late 1960s, the prevalent approach involved functional copying and/or direct acquisition of Western technology, especially IBM machines. Ultimately, Soviet production and use of computers always lagged well behind the United States, Europe, and Japan. While much remains to be learned about the reasons for this major difference in technological orientation, informed speculation in recent scholarship suggests that technopolitics played a decisive role.

Even today, computerization is never a simple choice about machinery. Instead, it always represents a complex repositioning of the division of labor between human beings and machines. This can affect how work tasks are understood, organized, and executed at every level, from individuals to large institutions.[21] This was especially true in the 1950s, when the full capabilities of digital computers remained unexplored and their limitations were unknown.[22] During that period, the Soviet military apparently made a deliberate decision not to pursue the rapid and far-reaching computerization of command and control systems characteristic of its U.S. counterpart.[23] Only when Khrushchev ordered substantial cuts in military personnel and conventional weapons in the early 1960s did military commanders begin to integrate computers into guidance systems. Even then, "computers were used largely to control weapons, not in command-and-control systems. In the latter field, introduction of computers would have upset existing information circulation patterns and threatened existing power structures," according to Slava Gerovitch.[24]

Another factor was the slow realization that the truly difficult problems of computing did not regard hardware, but problem definition and software coding and debugging. As one Russian military expert has written, in the 1950s, "heads of military system projects generally focused their attention on hardware development. . . . They took software development too lightly, did not allot necessary specialists and time, were not eager to estimate the necessary investments and resources. Programmers' labour was deemed to be very simple and cheap." Yet, ultimately, the cost of programming complex military systems far exceeded that of the computers themselves.[25] By the 1970s, about 100,000 programmers worked for the Soviet military forces. Thus—as was also the case with nuclear technologies—the full costs and implications of the entire sociotechnical system of computing became clear only slowly. Although Soviet military forces took full advantage of computers by the 1970s, economic constraints, limits on available expertise, poorly organized computer manufacturing infrastructure, and the politics of existing command-control structures interacted to restrict the role of computing in Soviet command-control systems.

One result of this technopolitical construction of computing was that until the late 1960s, the Soviets produced relatively small numbers of computers for civilian use. Experience with the machines was therefore acquired more slowly. Only in the late 1960s and early 1970s, with the Ryad series of mainframes, did the Soviets (together with their satellites) begin a serious attempt at widespread computerization.[26] This, too, was tied directly to ideology via the notion of "scientific-technological revolution," which Goodman has characterized as "perhaps the most important ideological extension of Marxism-Leninism since the early days of the USSR."[27]

In a wider global context, it is the ceaseless American efforts to dissociate technology from politics that appear anomalous—not the Soviet acknowledgment of their interplay. This is especially clear in nuclear weapons development: the engineers, scientists, administrators, and politicians who shaped the military atom outside the superpowers appeared fully aware of the technopolitical dimensions of this process.

BEYOND THE SUPERPOWERS: NUCLEAR POLITICS IN FRANCE, ISRAEL, AND INDIA

Arguing that U.S. nuclear capability would suffice to defend the Western world, American policy makers discouraged even their closest foreign allies from developing atomic bombs. But for Britain and France, more was at stake than simple security: a need for independence, anxieties about global status and decolonization, the prestige of nuclear scientists and engineers, and strong desires to develop modern scientific and technological infrastructures played important roles in their decisions to develop atomic weaponry. Britain exploded its first bomb in 1952; France in 1960. Other nations followed suit: China, Israel, South Africa, India, and Pakistan—to name only those with confirmed weapons programs. In all of these instances, the actual development and deployment of nuclear weapons came about through the sophisticated, self-conscious prosecution of complex technopolitics. In particular, a widespread tactic for pushing weapons programs through involved using ambiguities in engineering design to camouflage or shape political goals. We illustrate this point by considering weapons development in France, Israel, and India.[28]

France officially became the world's fourth military nuclear power in 1960, when it tested its first atomic bomb in the Algerian desert. The French appeared to have developed their bomb in record time, having announced their intention to do so a scant two years earlier. But examining French nuclear technopolitics reveals a longer history. At least as early as 1951, high-level engineer-administrators in the French Commissariat à l'Energie Atomique (CEA) expressed serious interest in developing atomic weaponry, partly to re-create a distinctive national identity after the traumas of World War II, partly to counter the transformation (and later, loss) of France's empire, and partly to secure independence from superpower wrangling. But the various prime ministers who led the country in the 1950s were unwilling to commit publicly to a military program. Rather than force the issue, CEA leaders adopted a versatile approach to civilian nuclear development by choosing a reactor design that could—at least in principle—produce both electricity and weapons-grade plutonium. Depending on the audience and the political climate, these reactors could be presented as purely civilian, purely military, or somewhere in between. CEA leaders skillfully deployed this flexibility to ensure continuity in the reactor program, as well as the *de facto* pursuit of a nationalist military nuclear policy well before the government was willing to commit to any such thing. The reactors thereby enacted policy in a way that classic political processes could not. When France officially announced its intention to build a bomb in 1958, CEA engineers were already well along the road. Thus, no single moment marked the political decision to acquire a bomb—but nor did the French bomb grow inevitably out of an existing technological infrastructure.[29]

Similarly, Israeli nuclear weapons did not result from careful strategic planning, but rather from a sediment of small decisions responding to immediate political and technological circumstances. Indeed, similarities between Israeli and French nuclear development were not coincidental: in the 1950s, France shared not only reactor technology but also nuclear expertise with Israel. At the same time, Israeli nuclear leaders also learned the technopolitics of ambiguity, just as in 1950s France, Israeli nuclear decisions were made by the expert elites, not by politicians. But while French nuclear decision making shifted to include more classically political input in the 1960s, no such shift occurred in Israel. By 1970, "a tradition had been established which held that the political arena was not the appropriate forum in which to decide [Israel's] nuclear policy." Like the French, Israeli nuclear leaders claimed that their reactors—in reality, optimized for producing bomb-grade fuel—were prototypes for electrical generation. But Israel went much further, refining technopolitical ambiguity to a high art. For example, Israeli engineers did not test their atomic bombs, because the act of testing would have been tantamount to an official declaration that Israel "had the bomb." Such a declaration might only spur Arab neighbors to begin military nuclear development. Unlike France, Britain, and China (which all tested their bombs to establish great power status), Israel's particular circumstances suggested that a state of permanent technopolitical ambiguity would bring greater geopolitical benefit.[30]

For France and Israel, military nuclear capability was only partly motivated by national security. Similarly, two recent studies of India's nuclear program argue that national security provided only a thin justification for developing an atomic bomb. There, even more than in France and Israel, policy making remained in the hands of a small "strategic enclave" of scientists and engineers. In the 1950s and 1960s, the primary goal of these men was to put India on the international scientific and technological map. Like their counterparts elsewhere, they saw an independent nuclear program as a means of defining national identity.

Of course, newly independent India was in a radically different geopolitical position from other nuclear powers. Indian scientists and technologists believed that their nuclear work would shape their nation's postcolonial emergence through a distinctive hybrid of "science, modernity, and indigeneity."[31] The precise nature of that hybridity, however, remained open to debate. Some elites thought that India should distinguish itself from the West by taking the moral high ground, renouncing military nuclear capability. Others thought that India required the military atom to attain prestige commensurate with its size. Tensions and power struggles between these two camps meant that the Indian bomb project proceeded in fits and starts. Thus, Indian leaders claimed that the 1974 test was a "peaceful nuclear explosion." Not until 1998 did the nation officially acknowledge—and test—its military nuclear capability. Throughout these decades, however, the symbolic utility of a nuclear bomb greatly outweighed any military value, since its most likely targets were Pakistan or China—making it impossible for India to use the bomb without risking severe damage on its own soil. Domestic factors outweighed national security needs, and indeed the nuclear elite kept the military removed from its development efforts. In the end, domestic rivalries, based partly in competition over who could count as an expert authority, shaped India's nuclear capability and the cultural meanings that surrounded it.[32]

Comparing these various programs highlights the close association between nuclear technology and national identity. At first glance, this may seem paradoxical. How could the same technology provide a distinctive emblem for several different nations? The answer lies in the hybrid, technopolitical nature of nuclear development. *How* technological choices were made matters as much as *which* choices were made. Responding to a variety of domestic problems, such as loss of prestige, wartime devastation, decolonization, or the need to establish a new state, technical and political elites sought to create distinctive national nuclear programs. This certainly did not mean that elites agreed on the character of national identity. Nuclear choices were often entangled with debates over how best to shape the nation, and over which institutions or social groups were best equipped to do the shaping. Nuclear debates regularly invoked symbols of nationalism, both old and new. The French compared reactors to the Arc de Triomphe; the Russians likened them to samovars; in China, leaders spoke of "the people's bomb."[33] In each of these cases, elites used the symbolic and material apparatuses of nuclear systems to perform new conceptions of national identity. Such nationalist discourse played an important role in marshaling domestic enthusiasm for costly nuclear projects in both the military and civilian spheres.

A Sociotechnical Systems Perspective
on Nuclear "Security"

Rhetoric notwithstanding, then, nuclear weapons have typically served purposes well beyond national security. As George Perkovich argues, this point is crucial in the context of nuclear proliferation. Analysts who view states' interests in nuclear weapons solely in terms of national security miss crucial dimensions of their development—and thus are unable to even propose workable nonproliferation plans. Similarly, policy makers who fail to take seriously the technopolitical and cultural dimensions of nuclear development will never produce anything more than fantasies about global disarmament (though these fantasies seem to have considerable popular appeal).

Have nuclear weapons made the world safer? Cogent arguments can be made that the fear of nuclear apocalypse, burgeoning along with the swollen superpower arsenals, deterred both sides from launching an intentional war. But the sociotechnical systems approach suggests that it is too simplistic to view nuclear weapons use as the product of clear decision-making processes by rational actors weighing purely political factors.

Consider the ghoulish combination of military and technopolitical logic that prevailed in the design of nuclear forces. In both the United States and the Soviet Union, political choices and absolutist ideologies dictated a global reach for national military power. Each side publicly portrayed its motives as purely self-protective. But military strategy had to take into account technological factors that gave an overwhelming advantage to a first-strike strategy. No effective defense against nuclear weapons was ever developed. Therefore, only an attack on delivery vehicles (first bombers, later missiles) *before they left the ground* could hope to prevent a catastrophic retaliatory strike. In the 1950s, General Curtis LeMay told a gathering of Strategic Air Command pilots that he "could not imagine a circumstance under which the United States would go second" in a nuclear war.[34] Nevertheless, official U.S. policy always proclaimed that the United States would never launch first.

By the early 1960s, three trends had emerged. Each side possessed thousands of thermonuclear warheads, making real the threat of near annihilation for the victims of an attack. Both superpowers could deliver those warheads using intercontinental ballistic missiles, capable of spanning the distance between them in half an hour; submarine-launched missiles could reach their targets in just ten minutes. Finally, computerized early warning and control systems placed the whole system on a hair trigger. The technopolitical logic of this situation made a first-strike strategy seem even more imperative. Paul Bracken has argued that during the cold war, "the likelihood of nuclear Munichs [was] exaggerated, but the possibility of nuclear Sarajevos [was] understated."[35] Other analysts concur that nuclear weapons arsenals actually "increased the likelihood of accidental war."[36]

Thus, the sociotechnical systems perspective provides deeper insight than a narrower view. Nuclear weapons alone do not make war more likely. But the nuclear weapons *system* does: hair-trigger, automatic warning and control systems; nonrecallable, ultrarapid delivery vehicles; and the social organization of command decisions. The operation of complex technopolitical systems is highly unpredictable, not because the technology has a life of its own, but because the systems are so deeply embedded in social, political, and cultural forms.[37] In the aftermath of the cold war, insufficient attention to nuclear technopolitics and their attendant unpredictability has taken on deadly dimensions. The dismantling of the Soviet Union has resulted in dubious security structures for its nuclear weapons and materials; conflicts between India and Pakistan regularly raise the specter of nuclear war; and fears about nuclear "rogue states" provide a central theme for U.S. policy makers.

If American policy makers can successfully cast nuclear proliferation issues in narrow technical and security terms, it may well be because (as discussed earlier) the dominant discourse and practice surrounding technological development in the United States continually and actively divorces technology and politics. In order to understand this dynamic better, we turn to an analysis of the changing role of technical experts in modern states.

EXPERTISE, POWER, AND DEMOCRACY

Modern states accorded key roles to technical experts long before the cold war.[38] Indeed, modernist forms of governmentality relied heavily on the creation of new state knowledge about citizens, from health and wealth to demography and geography; hence the birth of statistics.[39] Further links between technical expertise and state power developed when notions of "technocracy," or rule by technical experts, emerged in the late 1920s during the heyday of Fordism/Taylorism.[40] Although it rapidly acquired the antidemocratic connotations associated with oligarchy, technocracy originated in Progressive politics. It was seen as a way for states to guide social and technological change toward promoting the general welfare, *in opposition* to the privatized expertise represented by industry and benefiting only the industrial elite. Only state experts, asserted technocracy's proponents, could counter the increasing power of their industrial counterparts.

The power of technical experts in the modern state reached its zenith during the first decades of the cold war. In the United States and Soviet Union, wartime emergency arrangements rapidly became quasi-permanent peacetime collaborations between technology-based military forces, state-supported science research universities, and industrial laboratories.[41] From roughly 1945 to 1970, science enjoyed an aura of cognitive authority and infallibility, combined with a presumption of political and ethical neutrality. Attracted by the possibility of a privileged arbiter of truth, public officials and institutions including courts, regulatory bodies, and presidential advisors systematically and increasingly appealed to scientific expertise. This symbiotic relationship of scientific and political authority made expert advisors a veritable "fifth branch" of government.[42]

In what ways did technological development shape this "fifth branch"? First, it supported the growth of scientific knowledge, as the sciences required ever more complex, precise, and capable instruments and other tools. By automating scientific calculations, computers rapidly became a crucial tool in the growing infrastructure of "big science." In making possible the routine use of numerical simulations, they opened complex, nonlinear physical systems to detailed investigation.[43] As the productive power of science grew, so too did its political prestige. Clearly, scientists controlled a new, ever more important means of (knowledge) production. Second, technology's own growth fed from this new knowledge, as both state and private laboratories increasingly systematized the use of science to create new products. By 1959, IBM began to reinvest more than half of its profits in research and development, a then unheard-of percentage that soon came to define the modern "high-technology" firm.

Third, technological development rapidly became the means and measure of cold war geopolitical power. The superpowers competed not only in the arms race but also in everything from the space race to the quality of home appliances, and other nations followed suit. This competition helped to entrench and increase the participation of experts in governance. Exports of technical expertise to the developing world, either directly or through training programs for foreign nationals, became a major means of establishing dependencies and alliances both for the superpowers, as part of this cold war competition, and for the former colonial powers, as a means of maintaining dominance in the postcolonial era. At the same time, scientific internationalism—the view of science as a single, unified international community "beyond" partisan politics—played an important role in damping cold war tensions.

The mounting reach and importance of new, complex, and sometimes dangerous technologies during the cold war sharpened debates about relations between technology and democracy. Conflicting attitudes about this relationship had long marked Western political traditions. Utopian political discourses often interpreted new technologies as a means to increase the rationality, transparency, and efficiency of democratic government. At the same time, dystopian discourses frequently viewed these same technologies as threats to democracy, seeing them as tools for surveillance, systems subordinating human needs to their cold logic, and vehicles for social domination by technocratic elites. Early cold war ideology relied on the temporary victory of the utopian view that successful technological development depended upon, produced, and guaranteed democracy. And democracy's greatest guarantor was a nuclear deterrent.

This perceived connection between technology and democracy helped to spur and to justify the proliferation of experts within the state, in the United States and elsewhere. Yet this very proliferation eventually served to heighten anxieties about the oligarchic possibilities inherent in technocracy. The pendulum began to swing toward dystopian discourses about technology and science. By the late 1960s, important new social movements criticized overreliance on technical experts and sought to reverse or reshape the direction of technological change. Most salient among these were environmentalism and the antiwar and antinuclear movements. Perhaps ironically, these movements soon claimed their "own" technical experts.

The cold war hence witnessed three overlapping and cumulative trends. First, between 1945 and 1970, technical experts' political purview within the state expanded dramatically. Second, from the late 1960s into the 1980s, broad-based social movements effectively criticized expert power. Finally, from the 1970s into the present, credible expertise spread widely outside the state, opening technical decisions to adversarial politics.

COMPUTERS AND EXPERT POWER

In the post–World War II era, computer technology played a major role in strengthening the social power of scientific experts. This occurred throughout the developed world, and occasionally elsewhere as well, albeit differently in different places. To date, most of the historiography dealing with this phenomenon has focused on the United States, where it developed to perhaps its greatest extreme, for at least two main reasons. First, computers made mathematical analysis of scientific data far more efficient and far more powerful. They allowed scientists to apply numerical methods to a huge range of previously inaccessible domains. This process continues today, as computer modeling techniques spread into sciences such as ecology, genetics, and others that once relied chiefly on qualitative forms of analysis. Second, computers rapidly acquired a reputation for infallibility; they "could not make a mistake." By the late 1940s, popularizers and press accounts frequently termed the machines "giant brains."[44] The neurological imagery of cybernetics enhanced this association.[45] The machines thus developed an intimate symbolic connection with science, intelligence, and perfect rationality. The image of white-coated scientists standing before huge computers, waiting for answers as if worshipping at an altar, became a generally recognized trope. The sociotechnical characteristics of digital computing contributed to this effect, since until the mid-1960s, virtually all computers were large, expensive mainframes, accessible only through what some have called a "priesthood" of operators and programmers.[46]

This self-reinforcing conjunction of two forms of power—analytical and symbolic—conferred potency on computer-assisted forms of knowledge production and helped to legitimate scientific expertise in the United States. A particularly macabre example of this phenomenon was the cold-blooded production of nuclear war-fighting strategy by the RAND Corporation, a think tank founded by the U.S. Air Force in 1946. Though it quickly became clear that many millions of people would die in almost any imaginable nuclear exchange between the superpowers, RAND analysts cheerfully produced reams of computer-modeled strategic scenarios that defined "victory" as a greater percentage of survivors. Herman Kahn's books *On Thermonuclear War* (1960) and *Thinking about the Unthinkable* (1962) are perhaps the best examples of this twisted, computer-supported rationality.[47] Kahn inspired Stanley Kubrick's famous caricature, Dr. Strangelove, in his 1964 film.

RAND employed a motley collection of mathematicians, sociologists, economists, computer experts, physicists, and others, paying some of the highest salaries then available for scientists and offering intellectual freedom and outstanding resources. RAND programmers developed the software for the SAGE air defense system, eventually spinning off a separate entity, the System Development Corporation (SDC), for that purpose. At the time, the SDC constituted the largest collection of computer programmers anywhere in the world; it was the first organization to gain expertise in programming large, highly reliable computer systems.[48] By the time of the Kennedy administration, RAND's expertise was frequently imported wholesale into policy planning.[49]

Computers played key roles in the design and production of American nuclear weapons. They supported scientific work, leading to powerful new weapons technologies. John von Neumann, the Hungarian émigré mathematician, first linked electronic digital computers with nuclear weapons design when he learned, in 1944, about the secret Electronic Numerical Integrator Analyzer and Computer (ENIAC) project. Von Neumann, affiliated with the Manhattan Project, knew that computation for the first fission bombs (the "atomic" bombs used at Hiroshima and Nagasaki) was being done with hand calculators and slow electromechanical punch card apparatus. He realized that the ENIAC would provide a much faster, more flexible way to carry out this work. Although the ENIAC was not completed until after the war had ended, by then von Neumann had become deeply involved in the project. He assisted in designing its successor, the Electronic Discrete Variable Automatic Computer (EDVAC), whose architecture became the basis of most computer designs from the mid-1940s until the early 1980s. At von Neumann's urging, the ENIAC's first use (in late 1945) was a mathematical simulation of a thermonuclear ("hydrogen") bomb explosion. By the mid-1950s, Los Alamos and other weapons laboratories had built copies of his pioneering Institute for Advanced Study computer. These machines and their successors became fundamental tools of nuclear weapons designers.

At the same time, computers helped to legitimate scientists as opinion leaders in political discourse. Von Neumann himself—an outspoken anticommunist and a military hawk—became an extremely important figure in post–World War II science and technology policy. Von Neumann also maintained key connections with RAND, where game theory famously became the basis for simulations of nuclear strategy. Thus, von Neumann personified the strong connection between computers, nuclear weapons, and scientific expertise in the early cold war. His personal fame and political influence contributed directly to public perception of this relationship.[50]

During the period of American combat involvement in the Vietnam War (1965–1974), computers helped to redefine "expertise" in the U.S. armed forces. Traditional armed forces defined expertise in relation to battlefield experience. But during the Kennedy and Johnson administrations, under the leadership of Secretary of Defense Robert McNamara, they came to seek quantitative understandings instead. McNamara's Defense Department placed a high priority on collection of "data" on battlefield activity—such as the infamous body counts, maps of troop movements, and counts of vehicles destroyed—which it processed (with computers) into statistics that usually appeared to show progress toward winning the war, despite conflicts between these statistics and the frequently pessimistic reports of observers on the ground. Under McNamara, the Pentagon adopted RAND strategic concepts developed for nuclear confrontations in Europe; these turned out to be disastrously inappropriate for conflict with a highly motivated peasant guerilla army. In conjunction with new communications technologies, which permitted the White House to direct the bombing campaigns *in detail* from the other side of the planet, computers thus contributed significantly to the unrealistic strategy and performance evaluations that kept the United States mired in the war for so long.[51] As the antiwar movement peaked in the late 1960s, computer installations—by now firmly associated with military research and "establishment" power in the public consciousness—became frequent targets of sometimes violent protests. Protesters clearly registered both symbolic and real connections between nuclear weapons, computing, and the Vietnam War. In 1969, antiwar saboteurs destroyed computer equipment for nuclear missile guidance systems at a Sperry Corporation plant in Michigan. The following year, protesters firebombed a million-dollar computer center at Fresno State College.

The disastrous trajectory of the Vietnam War became one basis for changes in American public attitudes toward technological and scientific expertise that began to develop in the latter half of the 1960s. Associated as well with the youth counterculture and the environmental movement, this distrust reflected a sense of betrayal, as the dangerous downside of scientific/technological "advances" of the 1940s and 1950s became increasingly apparent. As the Vietnam War dragged on and its geopolitical counterpart, the cold war, entered its third decade with no end in sight, the equally endless quest for ever more powerful military technology came to seem more a problem than a solution for democracy and freedom. The terror associated with nuclear weapons, napalm, and other high-tech weaponry—together with fears about the environmental dangers of nuclear reactors, nuclear waste, long-lived pesticides, and the proposed supersonic transport, among others—began to override the confident sense of progress of the cold war's first two decades. In the United States, this growing challenge to the technological paths laid out by the cold war reached a first crescendo with the first celebration of Earth Day in April 1970.

Yet, as we noted above, these grassroots social movements soon understood that inchoate protest alone would rarely succeed politically against the voice of reason wielded by technical experts of the military, government, and industry. As they became more sophisticated, they began to claim their "own" expertise. Like the technocracy movement of the 1930s before them, they came to see expert knowledge as a powerful resource that they, too, could wield.

The antiwar and environmental movements also developed from within American scientific/technological elites. In 1968, a group of MIT faculty called on scientists to help "devise means for turning research applications away from the present emphasis on military technology toward the solution of pressing environmental and social problems," leading to the founding of the Union of Concerned Scientists the following year.[52] Other nongovernmental organizations such as the Club of Rome, an elite group of politically concerned industrialists and political leaders, helped to place environmental concerns on the agenda of national governments, particularly in the developed world. Based on computer models, the international best seller *The Limits to Growth* offered environmentalists an important rhetorical tool with its extremely pessimistic assessment of future dynamics in world resources, population, agriculture, and pollution.[53] Around the same time, climate scientists—basing their projections on computer simulations—began to warn of possibly catastrophic human-induced climate change within the foreseeable future.[54] Computer modeling has since become a fundamental tool for environmental scientists of all stripes.

Lay movements to debate technical issues on technical grounds marked the beginning of a new era in American politics. Expert knowledge—once seen as above the fray—now rejoined adversarial politics. Political actors engaged in contests of power and values would henceforth seek alignments and alliances with expert actors involved in contests over truth. Access not only to scientists but to their tools as well, became a key to technopolitical power.

Nuclear Expertise and Democracy

The history of opposition to nuclear technology illustrates the shift in how social movements conceptualized and used expertise over the course of the cold war. In the early years of the cold war, antinuclear opposition focused on weapons. The U.S. bombing of Hiroshima and Nagasaki triggered an initial wave of horror-induced protest against atomic bombs in the 1940s. But it was not until the mid- to late 1950s—with the development of the hydrogen bomb and the acceleration of nuclear weapons testing—that the disarmament movement gained momentum. Led by segments of the international scientific community and pacifist organizations, nuclear disarmament groups formed around the world. The earliest among these included Gensuikyo (Japan), Pugwash (a broadly international coalition that included Soviet scientists), SANE (United States), and the Campaign for Nuclear Disarmament (Britain). These groups were joined by others throughout Europe, Australia, and New Zealand.[55] Meanwhile, nonaligned nations in Asia and Africa opposed nuclear testing as a basic tenet of foreign policy, a theme of their unity, and a possible means to calm cold war tensions. At the 1955 Bandung conference of nonaligned nations, the Ceylonese representative suggested that nonaligned nations could become "mediators in the dispute between the giants of communism and anticommunism which, if fought out to an end, will deluge the world in blood and leave the earth infected with atomic radiation."[56]

Particularly in the United States, the challenges posed by disarmament groups raised anticommunist hackles. Activist groups there were subject to FBI surveillance, and some of their leaders were hauled in for questioning by the House Un-American Activities Committee. Nevertheless, by the 1960s, the nuclear disarmament movement had acquired a discernible influence on world politics. It did not achieve its ultimate goal of abolishing nuclear weapons. But scholars Lawrence Wittner and Matthew Evangelista argue that it did play significant roles in shaping international treaties and government policies on both sides of the Iron Curtain.[57]

Early disarmament campaigns were more intent on critiquing government policy than on challenging the nature and function of expertise itself, perhaps because their leadership included internationally prominent scientists who tended to focus debates on the uses of knowledge rather than on the conditions of its production. As the movement's momentum began to wane in the late 1960s after the partial victory of the Nuclear Non-Proliferation Treaty, a new style of antinuclear activism took its place. This one targeted reactors rather than bombs, and challenged the nature and operation of expert power within the state.[58]

As the military atom became increasingly entrenched in the U.S., nuclear experts in the Atomic Energy Commission (AEC) turned their attention to civilian applications of nuclear technology. Pervasive, upbeat imagery promoted the infinite benefits of "our friend the atom," as did Eisenhower's enthusiastic "Atoms for Peace" initiative. Yet the successful development of commercial nuclear power was by no means foreordained. For one thing, utilities and manufacturers were reluctant to sink huge development costs into an unproven and uncertain technology with obvious risks. AEC experts had to create a demand for nuclear power, not only by investing in research but also by active lobbying among the public, Congress, and the utility industry.[59]

The special issues involved in reactor operation (the extremely long lifetime of radioactive materials, the potential risk of plant meltdown, plant decommissioning, and long-term waste storage, among others) required new kinds of expertise. The emergence of experts in areas such as reactor safety and utility economics led to a proliferation of experts outside the AEC. Scattered across a variety of agencies and research centers, these experts might proffer conflicting opinions. Techniques such as probabilistic risk analysis could not resolve these conflicts, and it became increasingly clear that expert assessments by themselves could not produce clear choices about reactor safety. In the United States at least, the legitimacy of expert power had been based on the assertion that expertise stood above—and apart from—politics. But the attempt to define reactor safety problems along narrowly technical and economic lines rapidly collapsed, as the social dimensions of issues such as waste sites rose to the surface. Once politics stood revealed as integral to nuclear development, faith in experts as final, impartial arbiters was destroyed.[60] After the near catastrophe at Three Mile Island in 1979, the U.S. antinuclear movement saw major success. Purchasers have canceled all new reactor orders placed since 1979, although the United States has continued to derive 20 percent of its electricity from nuclear power plants constructed before that date.

Analysts explain the halt of nuclear development in the United States by a wide variety of factors. In part, increasingly visible disagreements among U.S. experts eroded public confidence. In response, the U.S. regulatory process became increasingly stringent, which in turn made licensing nuclear plants prohibitively expensive. The 1973 oil crisis together with the simultaneous rise of the environmental and antinuclear movements made nuclear power the center of partisan disputes over energy policy. And antinuclear activists knew how to build effective political coalitions at the local level, which enabled them to defeat nuclear power on a reactor-by-reactor basis.[61]

ANTINUCLEAR POLITICS IN GERMANY AND FRANCE: A STUDY IN CONTRAST

The American antinuclear movement relied heavily on countering government claims with its "own" experts, who testified in local courts. By contrast, the even more successful antinuclear movement in Germany was profoundly antitechnocratic. In 1975, activists occupied a nuclear power plant construction site at Wyhl, Germany, for over a year, successfully preventing further work. This action was followed by mass protests at the Grohnde and Brokdorf sites in 1976–1977. These early successes helped galvanize a loose-knit coalition of environmentalists, feminists, antinuclear activists, and antitechnocrats, which entered 1980 election campaigns as the first Green Party. The Greens believed strongly in local knowledge and collective decision making (*Basisdemokratie*), rejecting any special role for technical expertise. Within a few years, the Greens gained a substantial minority presence in the West German parliament, sparking similar political movements across Europe. By 1989, the twilight of the cold war, Greens held about seven thousand elected local positions in West Germany.[62]

Nuclear power failed in Germany because the Green movement successfully focused the energies of environmentalists and antinuclear weapons protesters on this circumscribed, prominent target. This strategy gained important momentum from factors such as West Germany's position on the most likely front line of nuclear war in Europe and the highly unpopular U.S. move to introduce cruise and Pershing "theater" nuclear missiles there in 1981. At the same time, German regulatory traditions involved greater cooperation between expert analysts and interested parties than in the United States. By the

1970s, two emerging politico-legal principles marked a specifically German approach to questions of expertise. The cooperation principle held that decisions should be based "on all actors being informed to the same high degree," while creating environmental measures accepted by "all those involved or affected." The precautionary principle stated that "environmental risks and damage shall be avoided as far as possible from the very outset."[63] These principles were codified in German law in 1990. Many analysts have noted that the precautionary principle, in particular, shifts the burden of expert analysis from those who oppose to those who promote the introduction of new technology.[64]

In contrast to the United States and Germany, nuclear power in France enjoyed spectacular success. In 1971, after a protracted battle among engineers and managers within the nuclear industry, Electricité de France (EDF, the state-owned electric utility) decided to abandon the gas-graphite design developed by French engineers. France purchased a license to build light water reactors from Westinghouse, and utility engineers proceeded to alter and "Frenchify" this design. In 1974, responding to the oil crisis, the government proposed the Messmer plan, which called for the immediate construction of thirteen new nuclear reactors. These led to more, and by the late 1980s, France had fifty-four reactors producing up to 80 percent of its electricity needs—a higher percentage than any other nation in the world.[65]

Antinuclear protests in the 1970s were at least as vigorous in France as elsewhere. The protest movement started early there—by 1971, local groups had begun to oppose the construction of new sites. These groups joined up with the emerging Parisian ecology movement, and by late 1974, a loose coalition of antinuclear activists had begun to oppose the Messmer plan. This coalition was soon joined by the Confédération Française Démocratique du Travail (CFDT), a national labor union with a particularly strong presence among nuclear employees. The CFDT had strongly opposed the abandonment of gas-graphite reactors; its experts included nuclear engineers and scientists who produced massive reports to show why that design was technologically and economically more efficient. Defeated in that battle, they proceeded to develop extensive critiques of radiation protection and waste disposal practices. For the CFDT, the Messmer plan would only exacerbate the health and safety problems arising from weaknesses in these practices. By 1975, the CFDT had joined forces with antinuclear activists in order to call for a moratorium on nuclear development. As the movement gained momentum, critiques broadened to include the nature of decision making in the French state, which left no entry for outside experts or activists to participate in technology policy making. This critique helped turn the tide of popular opinion, which was becoming increasingly disgruntled with other aspects of French government policy, and by 1977, opinion polls showed that most French citizens opposed nuclear power.[66]

How can we explain the success of French nuclear power in light of such opposition? Ultimately, we must look to the ways in which technology and politics were related in France. Within the state and its agencies, plenty of room existed for expert disagreement. Technology and politics were intertwined, as long as the politics in question operated within the state. Outside voices, however, had no place in state decision making; indeed, most technology policy decisions were made not by politicians but by the experts themselves. While regulatory processes might lead to alterations in reactor design or practice, they left no room to contest reactor development decisions themselves. EDF wooed public opinion back to nuclear energy site by site, with the promise of economic payoffs. Ironically, the utility was helped by developments within the antinuclear movement itself, which was hijacked by a small, extremist minority that espoused (and practiced) sabotage and increasingly violent demonstrations. Such techniques alienated public opinion. The erosion of popular support for the antinuclear movement left no more channels through which to oppose massive reactor development. CFDT experts and others had to content themselves with working within this system.[67]

EXPERTISE IN THE COLD WAR

The two generations of activists and scholars who have investigated the hidden science and technology of weapons development and testing have produced the most recent legacy of nuclear protest movements. Their investigations have revealed countless abuses of expert power during the cold war. Western cold war ideology suggested that it was only in the Soviet Union and other Eastern Bloc nations that science and technology could be "distorted" through human experimentation, environmental devastation, and insufficient attention to the safety of technological installations. Certainly, recent evidence about nuclear development in the former Soviet Union suggests that the authoritarian regime and its lack of political accountability produced poorly functioning systems that devastated workers, residents, and the environment.[68] But studies show that the United States did not have an ideal track record either. Nuclear weapons manufacturing had serious consequences for both nuclear workers and the environment in the United States.[69] Experiments carried out by the AEC included releases of radioactive iodine into the atmosphere and injections of tracer doses of plutonium into medical patients, all conducted without the knowledge of the human subjects in question.[70] Such developments are only partly attributable to inadequate research protocols and innocent mistakes. The prevailing sense that any and all nuclear research was justifiable in the context of the cold war, together with the culture of secrecy that pervaded nuclear activities, helped make such abuses possible.

The reach of expert power during the cold war thus had multiple, often contradictory dimensions. The cold war often provided a mantle of secrecy under which to engage in otherwise socially unacceptable uses of technology. But public disappointment with the technological promises of the cold war and disillusionment with the possibilities of expert power produced protest movements with international dimensions. These protests ultimately both reinforced and challenged the power of experts within the state. They reinforced it through their implicit agreement that political debates had to take place on technical grounds. At the same time, they undermined the authority of experts by pitting them against each other in public, political arenas. Against the backdrop of particular historical traditions and politico-legal infrastructures, these trends played out in different ways around the globe.

NATIONALISM, COLONIALISM, AND THE RESHAPING OF INTERNATIONAL RELATIONSHIPS

One of the major social and political dynamics of the cold war involved the reshaping of international relationships against the backdrop of changing nationalisms and decolonialization. This reshaping had important technopolitical dimensions. "Development" was the new order of the day. As expressed by Western political leaders and modernization theorists, development ideology linked scientific and technological progress with peace, democracy, and economic growth.[71] Meanwhile, the Soviet heavy-industrial model of progress differed little from that of the West on this account—except of course in its rejection of the free market. Henceforth, for poor and rich alike, technological achievement would appear to replace empire as an indicator of geopolitical power.

As a new symbol of nationalism, nuclear systems were among the quintessential enactments of this shift. With an ambivalent eye on the United States and increasing concerns about decolonization, British and French leaders in particular began to argue that the basis of international power was no longer empire, but nuclear bombs—and their nations had better make the switch before it was too late. Atom bombs would even prevent imperial states from themselves becoming reduced to colonized subjects. Witness Churchill's chief scientific advisor in 1951: "If we have to rely entirely on the United States army for this vital weapon, we shall sink to the rank of a second-class nation, only permitted to supply auxiliary troops, like the native levies who were allowed small arms but no artillery."[72] Or French parliamentary deputy Félix Gaillard, the same year: "those nations which [do] not follow a clear path of atomic development [will] be, 25 years hence, as backward relative to the nuclear nations of that time as the primitive peoples of Africa [are] to the industrialized nations of today."[73] Even as it fueled the world's most modern industry, Africa remained the eternal metonym for backwardness. Such discourse functioned by mapping two proclamations of geopolitical rupture onto each other: nuclear equals (former) colonizer; non-nuclear equals colonized (or formerly so). In practice, however, nuclear sociotechnical systems depended upon, reinforced, and reformulated colonial relationships, particularly in the domains of uranium mining and weapons testing.

If colonialism was deeply implicated in the development of nuclear systems, the same was not true for computers. Throughout most of the cold war, colonial and postcolonial relationships were notable primarily by their absence in computer technopolitics. Instead, nationalism provided the dominant theme. In the first two decades of the cold war, computer nationalism was partly fostered by military security concerns, as early advanced computers served primarily for code breaking and nuclear weapons design. U.S. export restrictions on advanced computers led to national sponsorship of computer industry development in Great Britain and France, linked directly to the independent nuclear capabilities of those nations. In the early 1960s, the association of computers with cold war military power began to sink beneath the level of public awareness, as the civilian computer industry boomed. By the early 1980s, computer manufacture had become transregionally networked, with Japanese computer manufacturers and "Asian Tiger" component suppliers and assembly plants playing central roles. These developments spurred new forms of computer nationalism, particularly as U.S. manufacturers began to feel threatened by Japanese industrial strength.

In the first three decades of the cold war, both the relative absence of colonial and postcolonial dynamics from computer development and the particular form they took in nuclear development were a complex product of technopolitics and geopolitics. Like many military technologies of the era, both systems depended upon many kinds of highly specialized expertise. Their production also required advanced manufacturing systems. By the mid-1970s, integrated circuits had to be produced in special "clean rooms" by scrubbed-down technicians wearing bodysuits; even microscopic dust particles could ruin silicon wafers. Similarly, nuclear weapons depended on the ability to machine and handle extremely dangerous materials, including conventional explosives as well as uranium and plutonium. Nuclear power demanded complex, redundant safety systems as well. Such requirements marked the generalized concentration of technical expertise and infrastructure in the developed world.

These conditions rarely existed in either colonial territories or postcolonial nations. For most of the latter, the manufacture of goods and the extraction of raw materials remained the major "development" path. In the case of nuclear systems, this meant that mineral extraction and the provision of "wastelands" for weapons testing dominated the relationships between nuclear powers and colonial or postcolonial territories. In the case of computer systems, it meant that colonial and postcolonial territories—particularly in Africa—were by and large excluded from the first few decades of technological development.

Nevertheless, both nuclear and computer systems were central to the ideologies and practices of scientific and corporate international relations. In practice, weapons and reactors were ultimately the products of internationally produced knowledge. No nation actually built nuclear technologies based solely on knowledge produced by its own experts. The key issue, therefore, concerned which nations could legitimately have access to what kinds of knowledge. Meanwhile, computers played a major, but largely behind-the-scenes, role in creating the globally networked multinational industries that emerged in the 1970s—although the "global" nature of the network was partial at best, excluding much of Africa. Operating any organization on a transregional scale requires a highly organized information system; combined with global telecommunications systems and key organizational innovations, computers offered the possibility of real-time control of multinational, networked organizations. By the mid-1970s, the latter represented an indirect but powerful challenge to the superpower governments. By parsing their manufacturing and management operations among many national locations, multinational corporations could not only reduce labor costs but also engage in what analysts call "regulatory arbitrage," choosing the most advantageous regulatory regime. As Manuel Castells and others have shown, the "informational economy" that emerged in the 1970s vastly amplified its power and reach by means of new, computer-based information technology. Not coincidentally, this technology was mainly available to the former colonial powers, the United States, and (later) to the Soviet Union. The different ways in which nationalism, colonialism, and international relations interacted within nuclear systems and computer systems represent important, parallel (if connected) trends in the role of technology during the cold war.

NUCLEAR DEVELOPMENT IN COLONIAL AND POSTCOLONIAL CONTEXT

Nuclear technologies embodied national identities by signifying progress, modernity, independence, or renewal. Nuclear nationalisms typically emphasized how scientists and engineers had worked in isolation to produce their nations' nuclear capabilities and stressed that national technological systems formed the basis for political and economic strength. The heroes of these stories— often the only visible actors—were bombs, reactors, scientists, and engineers. Nuclear nationalisms, in other words, obscured the colonial relationships necessary to their existence.

Colonial territories had been sources of radioactive materials even before World War II. Most of the world's radium had come from a single mine in the Belgian Congo. This mine also supplied most of the uranium for the Manhattan Project, and continued to produce uranium for the United States and Britain after the war. Other nations also needed colonial territories for their own nuclear development. France could pursue an independent nuclear program because it had access to uranium not just on metropolitan soil but also in its

African colonies. Britain's colonial ties to uranium-supplying regions in Africa and Australia helped maintain nuclear relations with the United States after the war. European use of African uranium continued well after decolonization. The French program, for example, used uranium from Madagascar in the 1950s and 1960s, from Gabon starting in the 1960s, and from Niger starting in the 1970s. Throughout the cold war, South Africa derived uranium from the tailings of gold mines exploited under apartheid, and sold it to the United States and Britain. Beginning in the late 1960s, the Rössing uranium mine was one of the centerpieces in South Africa's colonial occupation of Namibia. But colonial conditions existed outside of Africa too—particularly in East German mines, where the Soviet nuclear program used prison labor to extract and refine uranium ore. Finally, internal colonial dynamics also played an important role in the acquisition of uranium. Rich deposits occurred on Native American lands in the United States, aboriginal lands in Australia, and tribal lands in India.[74]

Uranium mines were among the least visible elements of the nuclear system. This invisibility had several causes: the need to keep ore reserves secret, particularly in the early cold war; the remote locations of mines; and the fact that mining uranium used many of the same technologies as other mining industries. At the other end of the fuel cycle, the opposite was true. Weapons testing was the most visible element of the nuclear system. Only a successful test could officially bring a nation into the nuclear weapons "club." Testing was thus both a rite of passage and a strong political statement. Yet testing shared one important feature with mining: it was conducted primarily in colonized, recently decolonized, or tribal spaces. The United States conducted its earliest tests in the Marshall Islands, infamously displacing Marshallese from their homelands. In the early 1950s, the testing program moved to the Nevada desert, in territories used by Indians for hunting and grazing. France exploded its first bomb in Algeria, and conducted subsequent tests in the Moruroa atoll in French Polynesia. Great Britain tested bombs in Australian Aboriginal territories. The Soviet Union tested on tribal lands in the Arctic, and China on nomadic lands near the Soviet border.[75]

Colonized, recently decolonized, and tribal lands were not the only ones subject to nuclear testing, nor were they the only sources of uranium. Yet such spaces were, without question, disproportionately represented at these two extremes of the nuclear fuel cycle. What explains their predominance? More than bad geological or geographical luck was at play. Prospectors favored land they perceived as empty, uninhabited, or underutilized; so did officials searching for propitious nuclear test sites. Places like the Nevada desert or the Arctic tundra seemed like wastelands, their inhabitants invisible. As Valerie Kuletz argues, "environmental science discourse often supports . . . discourse about desert lands as barren wastelands by organizing bioregions within hierarchies of value according to production capacity." Similar hierarchies place indigenous people and nomads "at the bottom of the ladder of economic productivity."[76]

Colonial and postcolonial territories were thus more susceptible to being seen either as barren, or natural resources ripe for exploitation—a perspective that in fact had provided much of the original rationale for European imperialism and American expansionism. In cold war developmentalist discourse, using such places for nuclear purposes would valorize them by giving them a place in the grand march of progress led by nuclear technology. Valorization could go hand in hand with nationalism. This pairing was especially striking in the hands of the French. President Charles de Gaulle prefaced his announcement of the Moruroa test site by thanking the Polynesians for having rallied to the cause of the Free French in World War II: "I have not forgotten this, and it is one of the reasons why I chose Polynesia for the installation of this site."[77] The test site was described as a gift of gratitude, one that would bring ample economic fallout, help Polynesia modernize, and give it an important role in upholding the grandeur of France.

The world's largest nuclear powers thus *needed* colonial resources and spaces. But framing this relationship in terms of dependence would have undermined the symbolic value of nuclear achievement; hence the language and practice of "development." Mines of all kinds were supposedly conducive to development by encouraging local economic activity, imparting industrial skills and work habits, and producing exportable commodities. Mining was said to be especially important for newly independent nations by giving them a base upon which to build their economies. National nuclear programs drew on this international developmentalist rhetoric, particularly when they set up uranium mines in Africa. By the 1980s, when economic indicators began to show that near-exclusive reliance on mining only exacerbated poverty by making southern economies too vulnerable to the vagaries of markets over which they had no control, nuclear programs had by and large dropped out of the uranium mining business. In their place came multinational corporations.

CORPORATE ACTORS AND GOVERNMENT SECRETS

Until the 1960s, government-driven programs had dominated uranium mining, which was directed primarily at supplying nuclear weapons. The 1960s witnessed a glut in uranium supplies. Fuel needs for the U.S. arsenal (by far the largest) were met, but reactors had not yet attained commercial viability. In the mid-1970s, as nuclear power commercialized and spread, the demand for uranium increased again. This time, multinational corporations (often in partnership with oil companies) led mining efforts. The rhetoric of development served corporations well: they styled their mines as endeavors to encourage economic and technical progress in the third world.

One set of forces that defined the international shape of the nuclear industry thus involved colonial relationships and their transformations under the new rubric of developmentalism. Another, intersecting set of forces involved the reworking of scientific internationalism under cold war conditions. Before World War II, nuclear physicists and chemists had been prominent practitioners of scientific internationalism, and many chafed at the secrecy that pervaded nuclear programs after the war. Secrecy meant isolation: at least in principle, any country wishing to develop an atomic bomb had to do so on its own, using indigenous knowledge. France, China, and later India elevated this alleged isolation to a matter of prestige, proudly proclaiming the indigeneity of their bombs and reactors. But no nation, not even the United States, developed either military or civilian nuclear systems completely on its own. Nations did not just rely on colonial holdings for raw materials—they also relied on each other for knowledge. The Manhattan Project drew heavily on the work of émigré scientists and had branches in Canada and Britain. Britain, in turn, drew on the experience provided by this wartime collaboration to develop its bombs—as did French scientists, who also benefited from later, veiled discussions with British colleagues. Israel learned from France; China, from the Soviet Union; and so on. Claiming that bombs were indigenous, therefore, usually involved obscuring the international exchanges—colonial or otherwise—needed to produce them.

These exchanges also complicated the determination of what constituted a "nuclear secret." Basic scientific knowledge concerning fission and fusion was widely available. Bomb design fell more clearly into the domain of privileged information, though as the cold war progressed it too became less of a mystery. The same applied to the techniques required to produce various bomb components (such as isotope separation to make weapons-grade fuel). By the 1960s, the most technologically difficult aspects of weapons production lay not in the basic knowledge necessary to make bombs, but in engineering and managing the gigantic systems required to build them. The most politically difficult aspects involved controlling the flow of information, materials, and expertise—not just through international arms control treaties but also through sanctions and export controls. Countries such as India, whose weapons development was condemned by the "international community" (in this context, a phrase that signified the members of the United Nations Security Council) in turn decried this condemnation as neocolonial.

While military nuclear knowledge retained an aura of secrecy throughout the cold war (and beyond), access to civilian nuclear knowledge opened up beginning with the 1955 Geneva Conference for the peaceful applications of atomic energy. This event was meant to revive internationalism in the nuclear arena. In fact, the conference involved a curious blend of nationalism and internationalism. Each country mounted its own booth, displaying scale models of its nuclear achievements to date. Papers imparted serious scientific and engineering knowledge framed in terms of national achievements. At the same time, the conference generated tremendous nuclear utopianism: thanks to unprecedented international cooperation, nuclear technology would soon solve the planet's energy problems and lead to world peace. Electricity would be "too cheap to meter." Rich nations would help poor ones develop nuclear power plants, and everyone would be better-off in the process.

Created in 1957, the International Atomic Energy Agency (IAEA) was an outgrowth of the first Geneva Conference and Eisenhower's "Atoms for Peace" program. The agency had two aims: safeguarding the world from the military atom, all the while fostering the spread of "peaceful" nuclear technology. The first aim was to act as a counterbalance to the insanity of the superpower arms race. When viewed from nations that would become nuclear pariahs—in particular, South Africa, Iran, and Iraq—this aim appeared to perpetuate global inequalities by attempting to ensure that only a few very powerful nations would have access to the most modern military hardware and the techniques of apocalypse. The second aim was considerably less contested. It combined development ideologies instantiated in institutions like the World Bank, the belief that nuclear power held the key to all progress, and long traditions of scientific internationalism in nuclear research. The IAEA appeared to hold that there was no nation, however poor, that could not benefit from at least some nuclear technology or science. In this realm, the agency acted as the main structure within which international nuclear exchange might occur. This exchange could be "purely" scientific. It could also serve as a precursor to commercial relations. And there were more and more of these as time went on: the United States, Canada, and France were particularly eager to export their reactor technologies.[78]

Nuclear technopolitics thus perpetuated and transformed the global relations of dominance inherited from colonialism, both through its material (mining and testing) and political (international organizations and treaties) practices. At the same time, the rationale for these relations changed in important ways. The colonial "civilizing mission" had been transmuted into the competing development ideologies of the cold war superpowers, including the People's Republic of China. Together with "global security" (to prevent nuclear apocalypse), it now provided the order of the day. Imbricated with nuclear systems (among others), these priorities provided one of the technopolitical infrastructures for the redistribution of global alliances of the cold war (East, West, and nonaligned).

COMPUTERS AND TECHNOLOGICAL NATIONALISM

Computers became the core of another transregional—some would say global—technopolitical infrastructure. Since the early 1990s, this infrastructure has become visible as the global Internet and World Wide Web. But the groundwork for the Internet was laid during the cold war, as the spread of electronic computers created a new standard: digital formats for data, information, and communication. These could be copied and transmitted far more easily and less expensively than under previous technological regimes, but they required vast investments in equipment, training, and conversion from older analog formats. The possibility of linking computers through networks emerged in the 1970s. Computers, networks, and other techniques for digital data processing played a major role in the rise of multinational corporations during the 1970s, helping to create what Manuel Castells has called a global economy capable of operating in real time on a planetary scale.[79]

Dimly aware of the digital juggernaut gathering momentum in America, national governments throughout the world responded in many ways. Here we focus primarily on developments outside the United States. For those who view the current internationalization of the computer industry as inevitable, what may prove most striking in these histories is how many nations developed their own indigenous computer industries. These national drives were often connected to the early military significance of computers, as well as to impulses of technological nationalism similar to the ones driving nuclear development. Technological nationalism generally failed in the computer field, largely because a single company (IBM) came to dominate the world market in the mid-1960s, introducing a powerful strategy of standardization and component compatibility in which most other companies were forced to participate in order to survive. Yet in the 1950s, before IBM had consolidated its grip and while computers were still a new, unformed technology, many nations explored their own paths into digital information technology. Even after IBM systems became the world standard, national governments sometimes sought to resist its technological regime through projects to build indigenous computer production. The following brief discussions illustrate how some of these efforts were shaped by their particular technopolitical contexts.

In the 1950s, Great Britain had a vigorous indigenous computer industry, responsible for virtually every computer installation in England until 1960. In 1945, Great Britain possessed the world's most advanced computers, built in secret for its World War II code-breaking operations. That these machines surpassed their American equivalents was first confirmed in the 1970s, when the British military declassified its documents on the Colossus I computer.[80] After World War II, the Ferranti Corporation became the first to market programmable digital computers, primarily to the British nuclear weapons program.

These and other military-sponsored projects accounted for the bulk of British computer sales. In the United States in 1956, IBM and Sperry Rand contracted to build supercomputers for atomic weapons research and code breaking. Seeking to compete, the British government funded the Muse/Atlas supercomputer at Manchester University. According to Kenneth Flamm, "when completed in 1962, Atlas was among the most powerful scientific computers in the world."[81] In the mid-1960s, Britain's National Physical Laboratory developed one of the world's first computer networks, a direct ancestor of the Internet. Yet around the same time, the fragmented British computer industry was collapsing, overwhelmed by the U.S.-based IBM. Flamm traces this decline to lower levels of integration between military research and commercial application.

A somewhat similar pattern developed in France. Despite a late entry into the new field, the French-owned Machines Bull developed commercially successful computers in the early 1960s. Apparently without government prodding or support, the company decided independently to compete with the U.S. and British military supercomputer projects. Lacking the military subsidies of these counterparts, the Bull project failed, and the French CEA (atomic energy commission) purchased its supercomputer from IBM. Disastrous financial consequences for Bull ensued, and the firm was purchased by General Electric—leaving France with no major indigenous computer producer.

In 1966, the CEA again sought to purchase an American supercomputer for its nuclear weapons program. This time the U.S. government—which opposed an independent French nuclear arsenal—refused to license the export. Although the CEA nonetheless completed its weapons calculations, secretly using an identical supercomputer already installed at a civilian firm, the incident caused a public scandal. French independence, self-determination, and national identity, already linked to nuclear weapons and nuclear power, were again at stake. In part as a result of this crisis, the government initiated a series of programs known as the "Plan Calcul" (1967–1980). The plan sponsored a new "national champion" firm, the Compagnie Internationale pour l'Informatique (CII). Despite the CII's mediocre technological and market performance, guaranteed government procurement programs kept the firm alive through the 1970s. Clearly, successive French governments found an indigenous computer industry vital to French national interests. In 1978, President Valéry Giscard-d'Estaing commissioned an influential report on the "informatization of society."[82] Characterizing "telematics"—the combination of telecommunications and information technology—as the wave of the future, the report argued that France had to seize the initiative or fall by the wayside in the coming era of computing for the masses.

In response, France launched a major, prescient technological initiative, a videotex system known as Télétel. Using the newly modernized national telephone network, Télétel offered two-way text transmission using small terminals known as "Minitels." The French Postes, télégraphes et téléphones (PTT) gave away more than six million Minitel terminals between 1980 and 1992, supplying free access to a national telephone directory and other databases. With for-pay chat services and online pornography, the system saw a tremendous boom in popularity during the 1980s. The system ultimately foundered in the mid-1990s with the advent of the more flexible Internet. But Télétel remains the first example of a computer network as a mass communication service—and a potent symbol of French technological prowess.[83]

More than any other nation, Japan explicitly connected computers with national identity. U.S. cold war policy promoted a strong Japan as an Asian buffer against Soviet expansionism and Chinese communism. The postwar Japanese constitution radically limited defense spending, while U.S. forces provided protection in exchange for military bases in the region. Japanese industry concentrated on high-technology manufacturing in areas such as automobiles and electronics. By 1966, the Japanese Ministry of International Trade and Industry (MITI) "identified the computer industry . . . as the single most important element in the future economic growth of Japan."[84] Stringent import controls and a strategy focused on component manufacture produced, by the late 1970s, a Japanese computer industry capable of going head-to-head with IBM—albeit sometimes through devious or even patently illegal means.[85]

Thus, the 1960s "economic miracle" of "Japan, Inc." began as a deliberate U.S. geopolitical goal. But as tensions mounted during the Carter-Reagan cold war, U.S. policy makers began to see Japanese technological prowess as a national security threat. Computerization lay at the heart of American military strategy. In 1981, MITI announced the Fifth Generation Computer Initiative. Budgeted at $855 million over ten years, the plan sought to leapfrog U.S. technology. The possibility that another nation might control supplies of vital components, or even come to dominate computer manufacture, was intolerable to the Reagan administration. It responded in 1983 with a $600 million Strategic Computing Initiative (SCI), organized by the Defense Advanced Research Projects Agency (DARPA). Tellingly, where the announced goals of the MITI program focused on peaceful uses, Strategic Computing planned military applications for the electronic battlefield of the future. The renewed military investment in computer research aroused widespread controversy in the United States. Though both the MITI and the DARPA plans ultimately faltered, each succeeded in linking computers to the very different national identities of their respective sponsors.

Perhaps the most vigorous independent effort to deploy computers as technopolitics—and the most dramatic failures—occurred in the Soviet Union and its satellites. Centrally planned economies seemed to cry out for computer-powered information management. Potentially, computers could open a data window through which planning bodies could view production, distribution, and consumption figures at all levels, from whole nations to factories and local distributors. Indeed, by the late 1960s, Soviet central planning bodies sought to introduce computer-based management and control systems into heavy industry almost by force. Interestingly, these attempts foundered in the 1970s for social reasons—especially massive built-in disincentives for managers on the ground. Factory directors realized that while the new systems might improve efficiency in the long run, during a long, complex introduction and adjustment period they would actually reduce productivity. In addition, these managers saw that computerization would render factory operations more transparent and accountable to central planning agencies. Local managers rightly feared that such transparency might strip them of the power to hoard scarce supplies and labor—a power critical to their success in the Soviet system. Thus, the overall sociotechnical system's contradictory goals effectively prevented adoption of an ostensibly more efficient information technology.[86]

Brazil, unlike most Latin American countries, consistently invested relatively large sums in science, and particularly in physics, during the cold war. With the advent of transistors and other computer-related solid-state technologies in the 1950s, a few Brazilian physicists decided to concentrate on solid-state physics, expressly for the purpose of developing scientific computers of their own. A late 1950s collaboration with Israeli scientists led to a joint project to build a mainframe computer in the 1960s. By then the Brazilian Navy had begun an initiative to develop indigenous computer-building capacity for national economic development. Major domestic political changes during the 1960s (most notably the military coup of 1964) shattered near-term hopes for an independent indigenous computer industry, but this project had by then become important to a substantial group of "pragmatic antidependency guerrillas" who continued to push it forward.

In 1978, the military government adopted a "market reservation" policy stringently restricting imports of minicomputers and microcomputers. (Mainframe computers were recognized as beyond the capability of indigenous manufacturers.) The military viewed an independent information technology industry as critical to both Brazilian and Latin American security. By limiting foreign competition, the market reserve approach had worked in other sectors to create indigenous industries. Brazilian nationalism made these policies widely popular; they were seen as counterhegemonic struggles against the cultural and economic dominance of the United States, and the democratic governments elected after 1984 therefore continued the policies.[87]

Market reservation also, however, produced high costs for users and created a black market in smuggled computers and computer parts. Perhaps most significant, these policies provoked a major confrontation with the United States in 1986–1987, at the behest first of IBM and later of Microsoft. After President Reagan threatened $100 million in trade sanctions, Brazilian president Sarney softened the market reserve policy substantially. Overall, the policy led to mixed success, bolstering an indigenous industry, but also generating high prices and a black market in smuggled IBM machines. In the end, Brazil's explicitly technopolitical strategy failed to overcome the dominance of the global, United States-led marketplace.[88]

In the case of South Africa, nuclear ambitions connected closely with the fate of the indigenous computer industry. Isolated by the international community due to its racist system of apartheid, South Africa adopted policies intended to preserve its regime at all costs—"total war and total strategy."[89] The government launched nuclear weapons research and production around 1974. International sanctions intended to thwart these policies included export restrictions not only on military matériel, but also on "dual-use" technologies. "Dual-use" restrictions embargoed the sale of computers, computer components, and some software (such as encryption systems) to South African police and military forces.

Using front organizations, third-party transfers, and other techniques, the government evaded most embargoes. Government users pirated key software; in the early 1990s, the Atomic Energy Corporation spent more than $1 million to buy licenses for software it was already using.[90] Military users sought supercomputers for such purposes as nuclear weapons design and battle simulation. But smaller mainframes, minicomputers, and even the desktop computers just reaching the market in the early 1980s also played significant roles in the apartheid state, a dark form of technopolitics indeed. Apartheid relied on a complex, internally contradictory classification system determining every individual's legal status as white, colored, black, and so forth. Passbooks up to ninety-five pages long recorded every legal aspect of nonwhite citizens' lives, and could be demanded by police or other officials at any time. Computer systems helped Pretoria's Department of Plural Relations and its regional Bantu Administration Boards centralize this information.[91] During the 1980s, activists in the United States and the Netherlands documented numerous ways that South African police deployed computers, from tracking individuals to tactical police communications.[92] However, mid-1980s plans for comprehensive computerization were only partially fulfilled.

Ironically, computer embargoes forced South Africa to build strong, independent capability in hardware manufacture and software design.[93] For example, the South African information technology company Dimension Data traces its success to this situation. Founded in 1983, not long after the embargoes began to take effect, DiData went on to become an $11 billion company, dominating the networking industry in South Africa while building operations in more than thirty-five countries on five continents.[94] Infoplan, a quasigovernmental corporation tightly linked to the South African military, helped to manage the regime's computer stockpile.[95] Today it remains the information technology facility of the defense forces.

In the twilight of the cold war, computers played a part in apartheid's demise. During the mid-1980s, with the help of Dutch and British activists, the African National Congress (ANC) developed an encrypted communications network, known as "Vula," employing personal computers, modems, tape recorders, and pagers (before the Internet era). By 1989, Nelson Mandela himself used Vula (through intermediaries) to communicate with other ANC leaders from his prison cell. A Vula founder notes that until 1985, a poor communication system severely hampered the ANC's effectiveness both as an army and as a political organization; Vula dramatically improved communications.[96] A few years later, apartheid was in its death throes.

South Africa, a white-dominated nation tightly integrated into the world economy through U.S. and European multinationals, was the exception rather than the rule in Africa. Very few former African colonies have significant computer capacity even today. In the technopolitics of information systems, the legacy of colonialism for Africa was not *obscured inclusion* in global systems (as in the case of nuclear development) but rather *counterintegration*. Until the 1980s, when personal computers became a commodity product that could be exported with relative ease, most computer technology relied on other infrastructure not readily available outside the developed world. This infrastructure included not only complex, advanced hardware but more important the social infrastructure of trained programmers and computer engineers. The developed world's extractive relationship with Africa created only the bare skeleton of a modern communication and information system, a bitter inheritance with which the continent now struggles.

As the foregoing examples demonstrate, throughout the cold war, technological nationalism motivated numerous attempts around the world to build indigenous computer industries. Though most ultimately collapsed in the face of the American juggernaut, some—such as the French Minitel—succeeded at least briefly. Even when they failed, however, they laid groundwork for the burgeoning infrastructure of globalization, creating digital information environments and new expectations. The fragmented, uneven distribution of today's global computer-based information infrastructure thus reflects, darkly, the history of colonialism and cold war technopolitics.

CONCLUSION

The end of the cold war has led political leaders and the mass media to talk about "new world orders," sometimes signifying the decline of superpower tensions, other times that murky process reified as "globalization." Assumptions that technological progress is unilinear and exogenous undergird this rhetoric, shaping claims that range from the necessity of antiballistic missile defense to the benefits of global connectivity. New times, we are told, call for new technologies.

Bringing the themes and scholarship we have discussed here into the classroom can help teach our students that neither the times nor the technologies are as new as they might think. Today's technopolitical order has direct roots in the cold war. Neither the proliferation of weapons of mass destruction, nor the varied international responses to this proliferation can be understood separately from this history. Weapons are not merely the tools of political leaders, and technological systems more generally have far-flung political and cultural dimensions. "Globalization" is not a single, uniform, technology-driven process;

it means different things everywhere, its technologies have long histories, and their development has social, political, and cultural dimensions and consequences. Exposing students to the relationships between technological and political change and their complex cold war history can teach them to unpack public rhetoric and ask important questions about the social processes that shape their lives.

At the same time, post–cold war developments have made it increasingly urgent for scholars to examine technopolitics in transregional perspective. As our survey makes clear, huge geographical gaps remain in our understanding of these phenomena. The analytic gaps are also large. How can we move beyond comparative analysis to understand how technopolitics connected or disconnected different regions of the globe? How can we place explorations of the microprocesses of technological change in a transregional framework? Many of these issues are too large for scholars working independently; tackling them may require not just new conceptual structures but also new, collaborative methods of research. We hope this chapter will help stimulate such endeavors.

NOTES

1. David Held, Anthony McGrew, David Goldblatt, and Jonathan Perraton, *Global Transformations: Politics, Economics and Culture* (Stanford, CA: Stanford University Press, 1999).

2. See Stanley D. Brunn and Martin Dodge, "Mapping the 'Worlds' of the World Wide Web: (Re)Structuring Global Commerce through Hyperlinks," *American Behavioral Scientist* 44, no. 10 (2001): 1717–1739; Manuel Castells, *The Rise of the Network Society*, vol. 1, *The Information Age: Economy, Society and Culture* (Cambridge, MA: Blackwell Publishers, 1996); Eszter Hargittai and Miguel Angel Centeno, "Introduction: Defining a Global Geography," *American Behavioral Scientist* 44, no. 10 (2001): 1545–1560; Held et al., *Global Transformations*; and Matthew A. Zook, "Old Hierarchies or New Networks of Centrality? The Global Geography of the Internet Content Market," *American Behavioral Scientist* 44, no. 10 (2001): 1679–1696.

3. Fred Halliday, *The Making of the Second Cold War* (London: Verso, 1986).

4. See Scott L. Bills, *Empire and Cold War: The Roots of U.S.-Third World Antagonism, 1945–47* (New York: St. Martin's Press, 1990); Mark Bradley, *Imagining Vietnam and America: The Making of Postcolonial Vietnam, 1919–1950, The New Cold War History* (Chapel Hill: University of North Carolina Press, 2000); Matthew James Connelly, *A Diplomatic Revolution: Algeria's Fight for Independence and the Origins of the Post–Cold War Era* (New York: Oxford University Press, 2002); Fred Halliday, *Cold War, Third World: An Essay on Soviet-U.S. Relations* (London: Hutchinson Radius, 1989); and Melvyn P. Leffler and David S. Painter, *Origins of the Cold War: An International History* (New York: Routledge, 1994); Michael Adas, *Dominance by Design* (Cambridge, MA: Harvard University Press, 2006); Mahmood Mamdani, *Good Muslim, Bad Muslim* (Johannesburg: Jacana Media, 2005); Odd Arne Westad, *The Global Cold War: Third World Interventions and the Making of Our Times* (Cambridge: Cambridge University Press, 2005).

5. Wiebe Bijker, Thomas P. Hughes, and Trevor Pinch, eds., *The Social Construction of Technological Systems* (Cambridge, MA: MIT Press, 1987) and Thomas P. Hughes, *Networks of Power: Electrification in Western Society, 1880–1930* (Baltimore, MD: Johns Hopkins University Press, 1983).

6. Gabrielle Hecht, *The Radiance of France: Nuclear Power and National Identity after World War II* (Cambridge, MA: MIT Press, 1998).

7. Paul N. Edwards, *The Closed World: Computers and the Politics of Discourse in Cold War America* (Cambridge, MA: MIT Press, 1996).

8. Alan Borning, "Computer System Reliability and Nuclear War," *Communications of the ACM* 30, no. 2 (1987): 112–131 and Paul Bracken, *The Command and Control of Nuclear Forces* (New Haven, CT: Yale University Press, 1983).

9. See Gar Alperovitz, *Atomic Diplomacy: Hiroshima and Potsdam: The Use of the Atomic Bomb and the American Confrontation with Soviet Power*, expanded and updated ed. (New York: Penguin, 1985); Gar Alperovitz and Sanho Tree, *The Decision to Use the Atomic Bomb and the Architecture of an American Myth*, 1st ed. (New York: Knopf, 1995); Barton Bernstein, "Seizing the Contested Terrain of Nuclear History," *Diplomatic History* 17, no. 1 (1993): 35–72; John Lewis Gaddis, *Cold War Statesmen Confront the Bomb: Nuclear Diplomacy since 1945* (New York: Oxford University Press, 1999); Gaddis, *We Now Know: Rethinking Cold War History* (New York: Oxford University Press, 1997); Stephen M. Meyer, *The Dynamics of Nuclear Proliferation* (Chicago: Chicago University Press, 1984); Richard Rhodes, *The Making of the Atomic Bomb* (New York: Simon & Schuster, 1986); and J. Samuel Walker, *Prompt and Utter Destruction: Truman and the Use of Atomic Bombs against Japan* (Chapel Hill: University of North Carolina Press, 1997).

10. Stephen I. Schwartz, ed., *Atomic Audit: The Costs and Consequences of U.S. Nuclear Weapons since 1940* (Washington, DC: Brookings Institution Press, 1998).

11. Gordon Adams, *The Politics of Defense Contracting: The Iron Triangle* (New Brunswick, NJ: Transaction Books, 1982).

12. Gregg Herken, *Counsels of War* (New York: Knopf, 1983).

13. Kent C. Redmond and Thomas M. Smith, *From Whirlwind to Mitre: The R&D Story of the SAGE Air Defense Computer* (Cambridge, MA: MIT Press, 2000) and Redmond and Smith, *Project Whirlwind: The History of a Pioneer Computer* (Boston: Digital Press, 1980).

14. Edwards, *The Closed World* and Paul N. Edwards, "From 'Impact' to Social Process: Computers in Society and Culture," in *Handbook of Science and Technology Studies*, ed. Sheila Jasanoff, Trevor Pinch, Gerald Markle, and James Petersen (Beverly Hills, CA: Sage Publications, 1995), 257–285.

15. Kenneth Flamm, *Creating the Computer: Government, Industry, and High Technology* (Washington, DC: Brookings Institution, 1988).

16. Donald A. MacKenzie, *Inventing Accuracy: A Historical Sociology of Nuclear Missile Guidance* (Cambridge, MA: MIT Press, 1990).

17. Gabrielle Hecht and Michael Thad Allen, "Authority, Political Machines, and Technology's History," in *Technologies of Power: Essays in Honor of Thomas Parke Hughes and Agatha Chipley Hughes*, ed. Allen and Hecht (Cambridge, MA: MIT Press, 2001), 1–24.

18. David Holloway, *Stalin and the Bomb: The Soviet Union and Atomic Energy, 1939–1956* (New Haven, CT: Yale University Press, 1994).

19. Paul R. Josephson, *Red Atom: Russia's Nuclear Power Program from Stalin to Today* (New York: W. H. Freeman, 2000), 43.

20. Gregory D. Crowe and Seymour E. Goodman, "S. A. Lebedev and the Birth of Soviet Computing," *IEEE Annals of the History of Computing* 16, no. 1 (1994): 4–24.

21. See Jonathan Grudin, "Why Groupware Applications Fail: Problems in Design and Evaluation," *Office: Technology and People* 4, no. 3 (1989): 245–264; Edwin Hutchins, "How a Cockpit Remembers Its Speeds," *Cognitive Science* 19 (1995): 265–288; Rob Kling, "Computerization and Social Transformations," *Science, Technology, & Human Values* 16, no. 3 (1991): 342–367; Rob Kling and Walt Scacchi, "The Web of Computing: Computing Technology as Social Organization," *Advances in Computers* 21 (1982): 3–85; and Lee Sproull and Sara B. Kiesler, *Connections: New Ways of Working in the Networked Organization* (Cambridge, MA: MIT Press, 1991).

22. Edwards, *The Closed World*.

23. Seymour E. Goodman, "Soviet Computing and Technology Transfer: An Overview," *World Politics* 31, no. 4 (1979): 539–570.

24. Slava Gerovitch, *From Newspeak to Cyberspeak: A History of Soviet Cybernetics* (Cambridge, MA: MIT Press, 2002).

25. Vladimir Lipayev, "History of Computer Engineering for Military Real-Time Control Systems in the USSR," Russian Virtual Computer Museum, available from www.computer -museum.ru/english/milhist.htm.

26. See N. C. Davis and Seymour E. Goodman, "The Soviet Bloc's Unified System of Computers," *ACM Computing Surveys* 10, no. 2 (1978): 93–122; Gary L. Geipel, A. Tomasz Jarmoszko, and Seymour E. Goodman, "The Information Technologies and East European Societies," *East European Politics and Societies* 5, no. 3 (1991): 394–438; Goodman, "Socialist Technological Integration: The Case of the East European Computer Industries," *The Information Society* 3, no. 1 (1984): 39–90; Goodman, "Soviet Computing and Technology Transfer"; and W. K. McHenry and Seymour E. Goodman, "MIS in Soviet Industrial Enterprises: The Limits of Reform from Above," *Communications of the ACM* 29, no. 11 (1986): 1034–1043.

27. Goodman, "Soviet Computing and Technology Transfer."

28. Space considerations prevent us from discussing all nations equally. For nuclear development elsewhere, see Brian Cathcart, *Test of Greatness: Britain's Struggle for the Atom Bomb* (London: Murray, 1994); Margaret Gowing, *Independence and Deterrence: Britain and Atomic Energy, 1945–1952* (London: Macmillan Press, 1974); John Wilson Lewis and Xue Litai, *China Builds the Bomb* (Stanford, CA: Stanford University Press, 1988); J.D.L. Moore, *South Africa and Nuclear Proliferation: South Africa's Nuclear Capabilities and Intentions in the Context of International Non-Proliferation Policies* (New York: St. Martin's Press, 1987); Paul Lawrence Rose, *Heisenberg and the Nazi Atomic Bomb Project: A Study in German Culture* (Berkeley: University of California Press, 1998); and Mark Walker, *German National Socialism and the Quest for Nuclear Power, 1939–1949* (Cambridge: Cambridge University Press, 1989).

29. Hecht, *The Radiance of France*.

30. Avner Cohen, *Israel and the Bomb* (New York: Columbia University Press, 1998).

31. Itty Abraham, *The Making of the Indian Atomic Bomb: Science, Secrecy and the Postcolonial State, Postcolonial Encounters* (New York: Zed Books, 1998), 156.

32. George Perkovich, *India's Nuclear Bomb: The Impact on Global Proliferation* (Berkeley: University of California Press, 1999).

33. Hecht, *The Radiance of France*; Josephson, *Red Atom*; and Lewis and Litai, *China Builds the Bomb*.

34. Herken, *Counsels of War*.

35. Bracken, *The Command and Control of Nuclear Forces*.

36. Scott D. Sagan, *The Limits of Safety: Organizations, Accidents, and Nuclear Weapons* (Princeton, NJ: Princeton University Press, 1993).

37. Charles Perrow, *Normal Accidents: Living with High-Risk Technologies* (New York: Basic Books, 1984); Gene I. Rochlin, *Trapped in the Net: The Unanticipated Consequences of Computerization* (Princeton, NJ: Princeton University Press, 1997); and Edward Tenner, *Why Things Bite Back: Technology and the Revenge of Unintended Consequences* (New York: Vintage Books, 1997).

38. The relationship between technology and political power is an old and important theme in historical and social analysis, dating at least to Karl Marx's discussions of means of production as a controlling factor in political economy. Modern discussions of this issue begin with Thomas P. Hughes and Agatha C. Hughes, *Lewis Mumford: Public Intellectual* (New York: Oxford University Press, 1990) and Lewis Mumford, *Technics and Civilization* (New York: Harcourt Brace, 1934). Like Marx, Mumford and his modern inheritors, such as Jacques Ellul, Langdon Winner, and Neil Postman, argued that some technologies carry or perpetuate an inherent political structure. See Jacques Ellul, *The Technological Society*, 1st American ed. (New York: Knopf, 1964); Ellul, *The Technological System* (New York: Continuum, 1980); Neil Postman, *Technopoly: The Surrender of Culture to Technology*, 1st ed. (New York: Knopf, 1992); Langdon Winner, *Autonomous Technology: Technics Out of Control* (Cambridge, MA: MIT Press, 1977); and Winner, *The Whale and the Reactor* (Chicago: University of Chicago Press, 1986).

39. Donald MacKenzie, *Statistics in Britain, 1865–1930: The Social Construction of Scientific Knowledge* (Edinburgh: Edinburgh University Press, 1981); Theodore M. Porter,

The Rise of Statistical Thinking, 1820–1900 (Princeton, NJ: Princeton University Press, 1986); and Porter, *Trust in Numbers: The Pursuit of Objectivity in Science and Public Life* (Princeton, NJ: Princeton University Press, 1995).

40. *Technocracy: What, Why, Who, When and How—A Brief, Illustrated Outline of the Amazing Revelations of Foremost Engineers and Economists concerning America's Past Prosperity, Present Depression, and Future Freedom* (Los Angeles: Angelus Press, 1933); Graham Allan Laing, *Towards Technocracy* (Los Angeles: Angelus Press, 1933); Allen Raymond, *What Is Technocracy?* (New York: Whittlesey House, 1933); and Howard Scott and Continental Committee on Technocracy *Introduction to Technocracy* (New York: J. Day, 1933).

41. Loren R. Graham, *The Ghost of the Executed Engineer: Technology and the Fall of the Soviet Union* (Cambridge, MA: Harvard University Press, 1993); Paul R. Josephson, *Totalitarian Science and Technology* (Amherst, NY: Humanity Books, 1998); and Stuart W. Leslie, *The Cold War and American Science: The Military-Industrial-Academic Complex at MIT and Stanford* (New York: Columbia University Press, 1993).

42. Sheila Jasanoff, *The Fifth Branch: Science Advisers as Policymakers* (Cambridge, MA: Harvard University Press, 1990). The executive, legislative, and judicial elements are the first three branches. The "fourth branch" refers to the media, especially the press, and was so named by Douglass Cater in *The Fourth Branch of Government* (Boston: Houghton Mifflin, 1959).

43. Paul N. Edwards, "Making History: New Directions in Computer Historiography," *IEEE Annals of the History of Computing* 23, no. 1 (2001): 86–88 and Peter Louis Galison, "Computer Simulations and the Trading Zone," in *The Disunity of Science: Boundaries, Contexts, and Power,* ed. Galison and David J. Stump (Stanford, CA: Stanford University Press, 1996), 118–157.

44. Edmund Callis Berkeley, *Giant Brains; or, Machines That Think* (New York: Wiley, 1949).

45. Steve Heims, *John Von Neumann and Norbert Wiener: From Mathematics to the Technologies of Life and Death* (Cambridge, MA: MIT Press, 1980) and Norbert Wiener, *Cybernetics: Control and Communication in the Animal and the Machine* (New York: Wiley, 1948).

46. Steven Levy, *Hackers* (New York: Anchor Press, 1984).

47. Herman Kahn, *On Thermonuclear War* (Princeton, NJ: Princeton University Press, 1960) and *Thinking about the Unthinkable* (New York: Horizon Press, 1962).

48. Claude Baum, *The System Builders: The Story of SDC* (Santa Monica, CA: System Development Corporation, 1981).

49. Herken, *Counsels of War.*

50. William Aspray, *John Von Neumann and the Origins of Modern Computing* (Cambridge, MA: MIT Press, 1990); Heims, *John Von Neumann and Norbert Wiener*; and John von Neumann, "Can We Survive Technology?" *Fortune* (June 1955): 106–108, 151–152.

51. James Gibson, *The Perfect War: The War We Couldn't Lose and How We Did* (New York: Vintage Books, 1986) and Martin Van Creveld, *Command in War* (Cambridge, MA: Harvard University Press, 1985).

52. MIT Faculty, "Founding Document: 1968 MIT Faculty Statement," Union of Concerned Scientists, 1968, available from www.ucsusa.org/ucs/about/founding-document-1968-MIT-faculty-statement.html.

53. Donella H. Meadows et al., *The Limits to Growth: A Report for the Club of Rome's Project on the Predicament of Mankind* (New York: Universe Books, 1972).

54. Study of Man's Impact on Climate, *Inadvertent Climate Modification* (Cambridge, MA: MIT Press, 1971).

55. Michael Bess, *Realism, Utopia, and the Mushroom Cloud: Four Activist Intellectuals and Their Strategies for Peace, 1945–1989: Louise Weiss (France), Leo Szilard (USA), E.P. Thompson (England), Danilo Dolci (Italy)* (Chicago: University of Chicago Press, 1993); Robert A. Divine, *Blowing on the Wind: The Nuclear Test Ban Debate, 1954–1960* (New York: Oxford University Press, 1978); Matthew Evangelista, *Unarmed Forces: The Transna-*

tional Movement to End the Cold War (Ithaca, NY: Cornell University Press, 1999); Andrew Rojecki, *Silencing the Opposition: Antinuclear Movements and the Media in the Cold War* (Urbana: University of Illinois Press, 1999); Meredith Veldman, *Fantasy, the Bomb, and the Greening of Britain: Romantic Protest, 1945–1980* (New York: Cambridge University Press, 1994); Lawrence S. Wittner, *One World or None: A History of the World Nuclear Disarmament Movement*, Stanford Nuclear Age Series (Stanford, CA: Stanford University Press, 1993).

56. Quoted in Wittner, *One World or None*.

57. Evangelista, *Unarmed Forces*, and Wittner, *One World or None*.

58. For an analysis of the relationship between disarmament activism, critiques of expert power and nuclear weapons development at the end of the Cold War, see Hugh Gusterson, *Nuclear Rites: A Weapons Laboratory at the End of the Cold War* (Berkeley: University of California Press, 1996).

59. Brian Balogh, *Chain Reaction: Expert Debate and Public Participation in American Commercial Nuclear Power, 1945–1975* (New York: Cambridge University Press, 1991); and Irvin C. Bupp and Jean-Claude Derian, *The Failed Promise of Nuclear Power: The Story of Light Water* (New York: Basic Books, 1978).

60. Balogh, *Chain Reaction*, 216.

61. Gary Downey, "Risk in Culture: The American Conflict over Nuclear Power," *Cultural Anthropology* 1 (1986): 388–412; Rick Eckstein, *Nuclear Power and Social Power* (Philadelphia: Temple University Press, 1997); James Jasper, *Nuclear Politics: Energy and the State in the United States, Sweden, and France* (Princeton, NJ: Princeton University Press, 1990); George T. Mazuzan and J. Samuel Walker, *Controlling the Atom: The Beginnings of Nuclear Regulation, 1946–1962* (Berkeley: University of California Press, 1984); Richard L. Meehan, *The Atom and the Fault: Experts, Earthquakes, and Nuclear Power* (Cambridge, MA: MIT Press, 1984); Terence Price, *Political Electricity: What Future for Nuclear Energy?* (Oxford: Oxford University Press, 1990); J. Samuel Walker, *Containing the Atom: Nuclear Regulation in a Changing Environment, 1963–1971* (Berkeley: University of California Press, 1992); and Spencer Weart, *Nuclear Fear: A History of Images* (Cambridge, MA: Harvard University Press, 1988).

62. Margit Mayer and John Ely, *The German Greens: Paradox between Movement and Party* (Philadelphia: Temple University Press, 1998).

63. Claudia Keil, "Environmental Policy in Germany," Resource Renewal Institute, 1999, http://www.rri.org/envatlas/europe/germany/de-index.html#_Toc474807384 (accessed May 27, 2002).

64. Wybe Th. Douma, "The Precautionary Principle," European Environmental Law Homepage, ed. Douma and Jürgen G.J. Lefevere, http://www.eel.nl/documents/cms_eel_id147_1_The%20Precautionary%20Principle.pdf (accessed May 27, 2002).

65. Hecht, *The Radiance of France*; and Jasper, *Nuclear Politics*.

66. Michael Bess, *The Light-Green Society: Ecology and Technological Modernity in France, 1960–2000* (Chicago: University of Chicago Press, 2003); Jasper, *Nuclear Politics*; Dorothy Nelkin and Michael Pollak, *The Atom Besieged: Antinuclear Movements in France and Germany* (Cambridge, MA: MIT Press, 1981).

67. Bess, *The Light-Green Society*.

68. Josephson, *Red Atom*.

69. Arjun Makhijani, Howard Hu, and Katherine Yih, *Nuclear Wastelands: A Global Guide to Nuclear Weapons Production and Its Health and Environmental Effects* (Cambridge, MA: MIT Press, 1995); and M. Joshua Silverman, "No Immediate Risk: Environmental Safety in Nuclear Weapons Production, 1942–1985," PhD diss., Carnegie Mellon University, 2000.

70. Eileen Welsome, *The Plutonium Files: America's Secret Medical Experiments in the Cold War* (New York: Dial Press, 1999).

71. Arturo Escobar, *Encountering Development: The Making and Unmaking of the Third World*, Princeton Studies in Culture/Power/History (Princeton, NJ: Princeton University Press, 1995).

72. Cited in Alice Cawte, *Atomic Australia, 1944–1990* (Kensington, Australia: New South Wales University Press, 1992), 41.

73. Cited in Hecht, *The Radiance of France*, 62.

74. Thomas Borstelmann, *Apartheid's Reluctant Uncle: The United States and Southern Africa in the Early Cold War* (New York: Oxford University Press, 1993); Cawte, *Atomic Australia*; Hecht, "Rupture-Talk in the Nuclear Age: Conjugating Colonial Power in Africa," in "Postcolonial Technoscience," ed. Warwick Anderson and Gabrielle Hecht, special issue of *Social Studies of Science* 32, no. 5–6 (October–December 2002): 691–728; Jonathan E. Helmreich, *Gathering Rare Ores: The Diplomacy of Uranium Acquisition, 1943–1954* (Princeton, NJ: Princeton University Press, 1986); and Valerie Kuletz, *The Tainted Desert: Environmental Ruin in the American West* (New York: Routledge, 1998).

75. Cathcart, *Test of Greatness*; Bengt Danielsson and Marie-Thérèse Danielsson, *Poisoned Reign: French Nuclear Colonialism in the Pacific* (Camberwell, Australia: Penguin Books, 1986); Kuletz, *The Tainted Desert*; Lewis and Litai, *China Builds the Bomb*; Makhijani et al., *Nuclear Wastelands*.

76. Kuletz, *The Tainted Desert*, 13.

77. Danielsson and Danielsson, *Poisoned Reign*, 67.

78. Lawrence Scheinman, *The International Atomic Energy Agency and World Nuclear Order* (Washington, DC: Resources for the Future, 1987).

79. Castells, *The Rise of the Network Society*.

80. Tony Sale, "Lorenz Ciphers and the Colossus," in *Codes and Ciphers in the Second World War: The History, Science and Engineering of Cryptanalysis in World War II*, available from www.codesandciphers.org.uk/lorenz/index.htm.

81. Kenneth Flamm, *Targeting the Computer: Government Support and International Competition* (Washington, DC: Brookings Institution, 1987).

82. Simon Nora and Alain Minc, *L' Informatisation De La Société: Rapport à M. Le Président De La République* (Paris: La documentation française, 1978).

83. William Cats-Baril and Tawfik Jelassi, "The French Videotex System Minitel: A Successful Implementation of a National Information Technology Infrastructure," *MIS Quarterly* 18, no. 1 (1994): 1–20.

84. Flamm, *Creating the Computer*.

85. Fujitsu, Hitachi, and Mitsubishi were all involved in theft of IBM software and computer designs, for which Fujitsu and Hitachi eventually paid more than $1 billion in damages. Charles W. Ferguson and Charles R. Morris, *Computer Wars: The Fall of IBM and the Future of Global Technology* (New York: Times Books, 1993).

86. Geipel et al., "The Information Technologies"; Goodman, "Socialist Technological Integration"; and McHenry and Goodman, "MIS in Soviet Industrial Enterprises."

87. Erick D. Langer, "Generations of Scientists and Engineers: Origins of the Computer Industry in Brazil," *Latin American Research Review* 24, no. 2 (1989): 97–111; and Edward M. Roche, "Brazilian Informatics Policy: The High Costs of Building a National Industry," *Information Society* 7 (1990): 1–32.

88. R. L. La Rovere and S. E. Goodman, "Computing in the Brazilian Amazon," *Communications of the ACM* 35, no. 4 (1992): 21–24.

89. South African National Defence Force and Maj. Gen. B. Mortimer, "South African Defence Force Involvement in the Internal Security Situation in the Republic of South Africa," South African Truth and Reconciliation Commission (1997), available from www.doj.gov.za/trc/submit/sadf.htm.

90. Seymour E. Goodman, "Computing in South Africa: An End to 'Apartness'?" *Communications of the ACM* 37, no. 2 (1994): 21–25.

91. Philip Frankel, "The Politics of Passes: Control and Change in South Africa," *Journal of Modern African Studies* 17 (1979): 199–217.

92. American Friends Service Committee, *Automating Apartheid: U.S. Computer Exports to South Africa and the Arms Embargo* (Philadelphia: NARMIC/America Friends Service Committee, 1982); and Gert Slob, *Computerizing Apartheid: Export of Computer Hardware to South Africa* (Amsterdam: Komitee Zuidelijk Afrika, 1990).

93. AlterNet Better World Communications, *South Africa: Infotech Lives after Disinvestment*, Usenet newsgroup posting on soc.culture.african, UNITEX mailing list, June 21, 1989, http://groups.google.com/groups?q=infotech+lives+after&hl=en&lr=&ie=UTF-8& selm=2357%40ccnysci.UUCP&rnum=1.

94. Beverly Goodman, "Dimension Data: Networking beyond South Africa," *Red Herring* (November 2000).

95. American Friends Service Committee, *Automating Apartheid*.

96. Tim Jenkin, "Talking to Vula: The Story of the Secret Underground Communications Network of Operation Vula" (published in 6 parts), *Mayibuye: Journal of the African National Congress* 6, nos. 1–6 (1995). Also see R. Kelly Garrett and Paul N. Edwards, "Revolutionary Secrets: Technology's Role in the South African Anti-Apartheid Movement," *Social Science Computer Review* 25, no. 1 (2007): 13–26.

CHAPTER 8

A Century of Environmental Transitions

RICHARD P. TUCKER

INDUSTRIALIZATION, CONSUMPTION AND THE NATURAL WORLD, TO 1914

Throughout history, Homo sapiens [sapiens] has adapted to natural systems and used them for human purposes. But the rise of industrialization and large-scale economic organization has given human societies steadily accelerating power over the natural world. This has meant an increasingly ominous loss of the biosphere's capacity to sustain resources for use by humans as well as other species. Global environmental change in the twentieth century accelerated some trends from the earlier industrial era, diversified others, and saw the rise of environmental management as a response to shrinking frontiers of natural resources and rising levels of pollution.

By the early nineteenth century, Western Europe could boast solid beginnings in industrialization and capital formation, rapid population growth, and urban markets. Europe's population in 1500 had been an estimated 67 million; by 1800 it reached 146 million; and by 1900 it reached 295 million. It was marked by the rise of industrial cities, led by London. Previously great cities worldwide were centers of trade and administration, but industrial technology made possible urban concentrations on a previously unknown scale. Peasants removed from the land, in England more than anywhere else, were forced either into cities to provide an expanding urban labor force or to migrate to new lands on other continents.

In anticipation of the twentieth century's explosive worldwide urban growth, urban pollution accelerated steadily, dumping massive amounts of effluent in

Europe's great rivers, the Thames, the Seine, the Rhine and others. In the nineteenth century, fossil fuels, especially coal, emerged as the supporting energy sources for the industrial regimes. Factories and railways were powered primarily by coal, which created a blanket of soot over urban regions, and produced a vast increase of respiratory illnesses, one of the most widespread of industrial epidemics.

As a result of the wide range of new industrial technologies, Western Europe was able to extend its dominion across the world's oceans and far inland on previously forbidding continental land masses. Long-distance overland and transoceanic trade of bulk products was revolutionized by the transport revolution brought on by railways and steamships, which exponentially sped shipping and reduced transport costs. The global railway system penetrated far into the Americas, Africa, and southern Asia. After the American Civil War in the 1860s (which the North won in large part on the back of its new industries and railroads), Yankee entrepreneurs followed the British into tropical lands.

The process of globalization, or the gradual unification of the world beyond Eurasia and the Middle East, toward a single integrated system of resource use, can be traced to the 1490s, when Columbus crossed the Atlantic and Vasco da Gama sailed around Africa to India. Europe's rise to global dominance is the key to the environmental history of the modern world. The rising urban populations required an expansion of food production in the countryside, increasingly from distant lands. Britain imported an increasing portion of its wheat, first from the Baltic region of Poland and western Russia, then in the nineteenth century from the United States, Canada, and Argentina.

Europe's urbanizing drift was paralleled by a population exodus to other temperate regions of the world; over thirty million Europeans migrated by the late nineteenth century. These migrants transformed North America, the southern cone of South America, southern Africa, and Australia into white-dominated settler societies. Their ideas of private property and drive to produce marketable commodities were fundamental to capitalist agriculture, grazing, and forestry. Arguing that these pursuits were markers of civilization, the settlers dispossessed indigenous peoples with more collective and subsistence-oriented approaches to land and the natural world. In terms of the environmental destiny of the lands occupied by the white settlers, European humans were only the most prominent of many invasive species, for they took with them many of their cultures' associated species of plants and animals. And, largely unconsciously, they also transported Eurasian micro-organisms, the human, plant and animal diseases that had co-evolved with them. The Americas and Oceania would be transformed, often in devastating ways, by this army of invasive species.

Frontier farmers grew food and wool for clothing for their own use, clearing forests as they moved onward onto fertile new soils. But they also produced marketable products for towns and cities, and ultimately for trans-

Atlantic export as well. Western Europe's colonies supplied more and more primary (unprocessed) products that Europe's climates and soils alone could not provide in sufficient quantities or at all, including food grains, especially wheat, coffee, and sugar. In tropical and subtropical regions, European immigrants were less accustomed to climate, soils, and diseases, so they were less likely to settle in large numbers. From the sixteenth century onward, they emphasized far more the products of tropical monocrop plantations producing market crops for European consumers. For labor they relied on enslaved Africans to clear fertile forest lands for agriculture. From the cotton belt of the southern United States across the Caribbean and Mesoamerica, as far as the sugar plantations of coastal Bahia in Brazil, the environmental history of these lands was shaped as much by involuntary African in-migration as by European settlers.

Two examples of trans-Atlantic trade illustrate the ecologically transformative power of the European exodus. Each is a prime example of the transoceanic commodity chains that integrated the world economy. The first is cane sugar, which was not produced in temperate Europe until sugar beets became common after 1800. From the 1500s onward, Western Europe's insatiable market for sugar transformed the fertile lowlands of the Caribbean and northern South America into vast plantations worked by African slaves. As the slaves cleared biologically diverse forests to plant and harvest a single species, sugar cane, they provided British and other European planters and merchants with the profits that provided significant amounts of the capital that financed the industrial revolution.

The second example is cotton. The industrial era began in earnest in the Midlands of England around 1800 with the first industrialized production of cotton clothing for consumers throughout Europe, southern Asia and the Americas. Since (like cane sugar) cotton cannot grow in the British climate; drier subtropical climates and soils were commandeered for cotton: the slave states of the southern United States, the Nile valley, and the Indus region in northwest India. In the twentieth century, production areas shifted from worn-out soils in the southeastern United States to more fertile soils in Mexico and Central America, displacing both natural forests and the small-scale, subsistence plots of local peasants.

Tropical plantation economies generally produced single products and added little nutrition to the global diet. The most dramatic and widespread example of this was the rapid spread of coffee and tea production and consumption worldwide after the Napoleonic Wars. Coffee and tea both grow best in well-drained soils and moderate temperatures, in tropical and subtropical lands—and in ecological zones above the lowlands that were being transformed by sugar, cotton, and other export crops. In some areas, such as the hills of Kerala in southwestern India, tea plantations prosper just uphill from coffee groves. Tea and coffee are tree crops, not row crops. Thus, they are not planted annually or biennially, exposing soils to annual erosion. But the initial clearing of woodlands to plant the tea bushes and coffee trees was an extremely sensitive time. Until the new roots and crowns were well established, the heavy rains of the tropics could produce devastating erosion on the sloping land and destruction of riverine systems downhill. Consumers in Europe and North America, both middle class and factory laborers, became mildly but compulsively addicted to their caffeine of choice. In that way they fueled their energies for the working day, but by nightfall had no nutritional benefit to show for it.

In contrast, there was nutritional benefit from the newly global livestock economy, which railways and steamships made possible. But the spread of cattle and sheep throughout the world's global grasslands transformed yet another major type of ecosystem from species-varied native grasslands into biologically narrower pastures, often on severely degraded soils. The explosive spread of the livestock economy reflected both internationally rising populations and rising consumption levels in Europe and urban centers of the Americas. This expansion had been a gradual process in Eurasia, where livestock had co-evolved over millennia with their fodder flora and the diseases they carried. But in the Americas, Australia, and New Zealand, there were few controls over the European ungulates and their associated species. Cattle and sheep ran wild and reproduced exponentially. Natural grasslands and woodlands were quickly overgrazed and degraded throughout the Americas, except in wet tropical forests and cold northern boreal regions. It was only in the late nineteenth century that degraded rangelands began to be restored by large-scale ranchers who created new breeds of cattle and seeded pastures with Old World grasses. The results were a great economic success, providing animal products for urban residents, or at least those who could afford to buy them in both the Americas and Western Europe. But the biotic cost was the homogenization of millions of acres of New World and Australasian grasslands.

By the late nineteenth century, both France and a newly unified Germany aggressively entered the race for European control of Africa, Asia, and the Pacific. The two decades before 1914 saw intensified European imperial rivalries for strategic control of the world's waterways and access to distant lands and natural resources. As Europe marched toward the cataclysmic end of a relatively peaceful century, the rising American economic and ecological empire watched alertly from the sidelines.

WORLD WAR I: A TURNING POINT

Throughout the history of organized societies, armies and navies have destroyed each other and each other's cities, farms, and forests as systematically as their weapons allowed. Even civilian populations had been battered, sometimes deliberately, by military forces. But "Total War," the modern industrial state's mobilization of all its human, economic, and natural resources, was displayed for the first time in 1914, when the European powers unleashed against each other the military machines that their industries had been preparing for decades and to that point they had deployed mainly against outgunned, pre-industrial societies.

The "Great War," the war that consumed European civilization starting in the summer of 1914, brought unprecedented destruction of cities and industries, farmlands and forests, as well as human lives. The destructive power that both sides brought to the trenches of northern France and beyond could hardly have been imagined half a century before. Dynamite, airplanes, machine guns, motor vehicles, chemical weapons—the list of industrial inventions brought into play in the four-year nightmare is long. High explosives shattered military equipment and industrial centers. The world's first warplane pilots learned to deliver those explosives with some efficiency. But most fundamentally this was the first war powered by petroleum, and fought with unprecedented mobility by motor cars, trucks, and tanks. Another ominous technological innovation came from the flourishing young chemical industry. The paralytic stalemate that developed in the trenches after the stop of the first German invasion of northern France was intensified by mustard gas attacks, which marked the first use of the century's most notorious weapons of environmental warfare.

In all these areas of struggle, the war brought unprecedented administrative cooperation between government agencies and private entrepreneurs, for emergency exploitation of natural resources. Governments provided priority and tax funds for military uses of industries and transport networks, and industrial innovations left a legacy of far wider uses of natural resources for the postwar world. Like previous wars, for example, but on a far greater scale, the conduct of the First World War necessitated the harvesting of massive amounts of wood. A wide variety of timber products was employed, including millions of pit props for the trenches. Foresters and logging crews felled timber far beyond peacetime norms throughout Europe, and as the war dragged on from overseas as well.

The intercontinental networks of industry, transport, and finance that had been built during the previous century enabled the warring powers to draw resources from far greater distances than in any previous war. This was even more dramatically evident after the United States entered the war in early 1917. Softwood lumber was shipped not only from forested areas of northern and eastern Europe but also from the yellow pine belt of [the] southeastern United States, where frenzied logging at rates far beyond previous rates of logging left slash piles that burst repeatedly into wildfires and subsequently caused severe erosion of the sandy soils. Collateral damage was less severe in the timber harvests in coniferous forests of [the] northeastern United States and Canada. But British Columbia's great forests were harvested intensively for the final stages of the war, and their timber was shipped to Europe by the new transcontinental railroad network and even through the newly opened Panama Canal.

Hardwoods, especially the Himalayan cedar, were made available to the British armed forces by Britain's colonial forest service in India. After cutting they were shipped from the mountain slopes of the western Himalayas down to the Indus river basin on railways that had been constructed a half century earlier to ship wheat from Punjab to Western destinations. Even the embryonic timber industry of Britain's African colonies managed, despite severe labor shortages, to provide timber supplies for the war. The emergency justified building forest roads and rail lines that otherwise would have taken far longer to finance. In this way Europe's war made possible Europe's penetration of colonial resource zones far more rapidly than otherwise would have been possible.

When the war ended with the Armistice of November 1918, much of Europe's urban and industrial infrastructure lay in ruins, requiring massive postwar reconstruction. Well into the 1920s, despite the immediate postwar depression, transoceanic timber supplies continued to flow into Europe at high levels, thus undermining American and colonial foresters' efforts to manage tree harvests through systematic rotation. But where trees are cut without severe damage to soil and water regimes, forests can recover and environmental damage can be short-term. In Alsace, for example, where military columns had sliced through tree-covered hills during the conflict, solid stands of timber grew a half century later. And in Les Landes in southwestern France, where American and French loggers had worked feverishly together in 1918, Europe's largest tree farms flourished. Yet these timber producing areas were not forests in a biological sense, but intensive stands of one to three species of fast-growing industrial inputs. The war had not only devoured forests, it had contributed to the world's accelerating biotic impoverishment.

In the war's aftermath it became clear that the world center of finance capital, the industrial world's vital basis for exploiting global resources, had shifted from London and other European cities to New York. The American economy had been far more stimulated than damaged by the war, and as a consequence the American empire was eclipsing its European rivals to become the twentieth century's predominant driver of resource extraction. Like its European counterparts in the 1920s, the American government, in tandem with leading industrialists, surveyed its military need to guarantee future supplies of strategic resources: minerals, petroleum, and natural rubber. In the extraction of these resources, and the environmental costs associated with these processes, the distinction between military and civilian uses of resources was becoming increasingly blurred.

THE INTERWAR YEARS: NORTH AMERICAN AFFLUENCE AND GLOBAL COMPETITION FOR RESOURCES

After a severe but brief depression in 1919–20, the United States emerged as the world's leading consumer economy. From Maine and Florida to California, rising affluence provided a model of mass consumption for urban-industrial societies. The lynchpin of American industry and consumer satisfaction, then as now, was automobiles. The American automotive industry, which had been given major impetus by wartime capital infusions and design innovations, emerged in 1920 with its facilities intact and enlarged, not badly damaged like its European competitors. Henry Ford's innovative, assembly-line system of mass production of inexpensive automobiles guaranteed that the auto industry would become the centerpiece of American industry and consumer culture.

The auto industry's boom was predicated on rapid expansion of petroleum supplies. Gasoline, motor oils, and industrial lubricants of many sorts could be refined from petroleum, but in most cases not from coal. So the basis of the world's transport economy shifted from nineteenth century coal to petroleum in the new automotive era (and the air transport industry that was emerging to complement it). This shift had already taken place in the military with petrol-driven warships the norm in up-to-date navies and tanks and airplanes introduced into trench warfare. Hence the story of environmental costs of coal extraction and use was joined by the story of petroleum.

Standard Oil, Gulf Oil in Texas, and their other American competitors moved first into Mexico, but when political conditions there became unstable for Yankee investors, they turned to Venezuela. After years of largely fruitless exploration supported by the current dictator and his cronies, large reserves were found around and under Lake Maracaibo. Hell-bent on maximizing drilling around and under the great but shallow lake, the oil firms and local overlords created one of the world's most notorious poisoned ecosystems, destroying virtually all other uses of the lake. Hundreds of other oil production areas and refineries around the world also resulted in high environmental costs, but the environmental history of the industry remains largely to be written.

Another major industry that necessarily complemented the boom in the auto industry was rubber. Production of tires, as well as many other uses of rubber, boomed in the 1920s. The only viable source of rubber was natural latex tapped from trees of Brazilian stock that had been planted in several Southeast Asian colonies. Since 1905 American rubber firms had invested in Sumatran plantations with the support of the Dutch colonial regime. Many thousands of acres of rain forest were cleared by indentured Javanese and Chinese workers, who labored under brutal conditions. Their work was vital to Allied success on the ground in World War I. By the 1920s, Goodyear's Wingfoot plantation in Sumatra became the world's largest.

But Americans resented the virtually complete control the Dutch and British enjoyed in international marketing and pricing of raw rubber. To break the European monopoly, Harvey Firestone, in close coordination with officials in Washington, prospected for alternative sites from the southern Philippines to equatorial West Africa. In 1926, with support from the U.S. State and Commerce Departments, he signed an agreement with the government of Liberia allowing him to develop an 87,000 acre plantation. This vast estate would remain the largest American rubber operation in the tropical world until it was crippled by the Liberian civil war in the 1990s. Vast plantations of rubber trees in industrially ordered rows displaced both native forests and the food plots of local villagers.

The rising middle class and its aspirations to affluence, mobility, and comfort created a boom in consumer demand. This expansion was largely shaped by the advertising industry, working through the steadily expanding print media, both newspapers and magazines and later radio as well. Between them they created consumer appetites seemingly without limits, for a steadily widening range of goods, which in turn were marketed increasingly by supermarket chains and department stores.

In the years after 1945, the United States would become globally recognized for having by far the highest rates of energy and resource consumption of any society in the world, thus making its relatively small population (5 to 7 percent of the world total) the largest threat to the world's environment. America's global ecological empire drew on resources from many parts of the world, which in turn attracted corporate investment and managerial experts from around the country into the high-risk, high-profit game of foreign investment. American corporations invested in urban utilities, farm machinery, shipping and banking, railroads, meat packing, mining, and numerous other extractive and manufacturing industries at home and overseas. The range of operations that the American industrial economy pursued abroad by the 1920s was so extensive that it surpassed even that of the British, the world's leading bankers and investors over the previous century.

The geographical scope and ecological consequences of the American empire were regionally concentrated. Victorian Britain had controlled a vast empire in Africa and Asia, and had largely constructed the export economies of Latin America. American interests focused largely on Latin America and the Caribbean, the Pacific, and parts of Southeast Asia. Aside from the Firestone plantation in Liberia, Americans largely ignored Africa and the Indian subcontinent. And like all Western operations in China, which comprised one of the world's other great potential markets, American enterprises were confined largely to its maritime provinces. Thus, environmental change in Chinese history was largely a self-contained history until the last years of the twentieth century.

The most widely publicized case of American use of tropical ecosystems to produce food for its domestic consumption was bananas, grown and marketed by the giant corporate duopoly of United Fruit and Standard Fruit. These two agro-corporations operated from 1900 onward throughout Central America and the Caribbean coastal lowlands of South America. Beginning in the 1950s, they additionally exploited the Pacific coastal lowlands of Ecuador, to keep up with the demands of the booming markets in the western United States. By contrast, bananas remained a far less important part of European diets, though British operations in Jamaica and elsewhere, French plantations in the Ivory Coast, and north European importers played roles in the global geography of commercial bananas. Moreover, many of the European investors were buyers, not plantation operators like the Americans, so they had less direct impact on soil, water, and vegetation changes in their source areas.

Far more bananas, of far more varieties, were grown in India and Africa. But these were almost entirely for local consumption, grown by small farmers on their multi-crop plots of row and tree crops. They had little to do with the large-scale capitalist plantations that were restricted to a single crop, demanding heavy water inputs, grown for distant markets and the nutrition of distant urban consumers, susceptible to epidemic diseases, and at the mercy of economic cycles. Ecological transformations resulting from agricultural expansion were mostly the consequence of corporate agro-business over much of the world.

The interwar years also saw the rise of natural resources management science, including major programs introduced into the colonial and tropical world. Forestry led the way. Systematic timber cropping had been practiced in Germany for at least three centuries, and spread to France and other European countries after the Napoleonic upheavals ended in 1815. The Dutch rulers of Java soon began to manage the teak forests of the island. And when the British conquerors of India faced alarming timber shortages in the 1850s, they hired leading German foresters to organize timber production in the monsoon forests of teak, Himalayan cedar, and other hardwoods. By the 1880s, American foresters were being trained by German mentors. And both moved into Cuba and the Philippines in the immediate wake of American military victories there in 1898.

During World War I, British foresters moved from India into the biologically more complex tropical rain forests of Malaya. But their silvicultural experience in India was not adequate for the great Southeast Asian rain forests. The Americans in the Philippines were ahead of them in understanding and harvesting several hardwood species that they called Philippine mahogany for marketing purposes. So Americans helped organize the British tropical forest research and management center outside Kuala Lumpur. In British, Dutch, and American centers, foresters worked closely with private sector timber traders, both Western and more often overseas Chinese. This led to rapidly accelerating production of timber products from rain forests for booming urban markets around the Pacific Basin and Southeast Asia—including Japan, the future giant in Pacific timber trade after the 1950s. This production was overwhelmingly concentrated on the few species of construction and specialty timbers that had markets. Maintaining the species diversity of natural forests was peripheral to their work for another half century, when international criticism finally emerged in response to the threat to the world's tropical forests.

Tropical agronomy developed in similar fashion in the interwar years. British agronomists and plant ecologists associated with Kew Gardens in London, working with colonial agricultural services, experimented with a wide range of crops for their viability around the tropics. Their most prominent previous success had been the transfer of rubber trees from their evolutionary home in the Brazilian Amazonia to Ceylon, Malaya, and the Dutch Indies. In the latter colony, Dutch botanists had been experimenting with introduced crop varieties since the 1840s at their botanical garden in Buitenzorg (today's Bogor) in the hills above Jakarta. A global network of economic botanic research had emerged during Victorian times. Many failures to sustain the production of varieties introduced from one continent to another gave them accumulated experience in growing commercially viable commodities. British and American agronomists pursued similar agendas around the Caribbean Basin. The British were mostly in colonial administrative posts; the Americans more often worked for private agro-corporate firms led by United Fruit's banana operations in Central America. Tropical soil science developed very slowly until the 1950s. But plant disease research was emphasized because monocrop plantations, such as bananas, in tropical climates were almost inevitably susceptible to diseases that destroyed entire plantations in short order.

The rapid expansion of consumer economies in the industrial world of the 1920s was followed by the deep collapse of capital investment and consumer demand for over a decade after the onset of the great world depression in October 1929. European colonial regimes and their extractive operations in Africa and Asia slowed severely, and imports of tropical products into the United States decreased significantly. However, this was only a temporary decline in the North's demand for tropical resources and its consequent pressure on tropical ecosystems. It would be reversed decisively by World War II.

Elsewhere in arid regions of the planet, drought cycles produced deadly environmental damage when they hit. Multi-year droughts had been a perennial feature of climate cycles in the Sahel grasslands of sub-Saharan Africa, where the cropping and grazing practices of farmers had been adjusted to the stress of lean years. But the new British and French colonial overlords knew little of those cycles and were determined to extract maximum annual production of market crops, especially groundnuts (called peanuts in North American dialects), which provided the basis for a major portion of Europe's cooking oils.

Similarly, farmers in the monsoon-fed regions of the Indian subcontinent had perennially experienced occasional multi-year rain failures. Hence, the fear of famine was deeply imbedded in India's rural culture. In response to that challenge, British engineers from the 1830s onward built the world's most elaborate system of irrigation canals in the Ganges and Indus basins, for both local food security and the export of wheat to Europe. In contrast to areas of dry farming, where the threat of drought was not alleviated, irrigated areas became largely free of naturally caused crop failures. But this progress, and the massive expansion of arable land that accompanied it, came with a price. In many locations where drainage was inadequate to cope with the intensified application of water, soils became waterlogged or salts percolated upward to the surface, poisoning the soil. Where there was stagnant water, mosquitoes bred, spreading malaria far more widely than in the pre-irrigation era. This was an unfortunate way of slowing population growth in the densely populated Gangetic region until the advent of new public health measures led by DDT [insecticide] after 1950.

In the American Midwest, vast, deep-rooted prairies of perennial grasses had been transformed into a vast grain belt to supply the eastern seaboard and European markets since the railroads were extended across the region in the late 1800s. The annual sowing of wheat, alternating with winter fallows, exposed soils to wind erosion. Then came disaster. A multi-year drought culminating in the early Depression years crippled wheat production and forced farmers off the land into a long migration to California. Unprotected soils dried out completely, and were turned into unprecedented dust storms that darkened skies as far as the east coast.

Starting in early 1933, Franklin Roosevelt, the new President, involved the government far more actively than ever before in managing both the American economy and natural resources. The Department of Agriculture, in conjunction with a network of state-level agencies and agricultural universities, created the Soil Conservation Service, with Hugh Bennett as its founding director. Bennett brought many years of experience in fighting soil erosion in the devastated pine lands of his southern homeland, and then in many locations in the Caribbean, Mexico, and Australia.

British Empire agronomists also brought extensive experience in drought-prone South Africa and India to the new challenges of the 1930s. Bennett's colleagues introduced Great Plains farmers to better soil management practices, including contour plowing and shelterbelt tree planting in a newly organized system of Soil Conservation Districts. His British colleagues, institutionally well placed to introduce new soil practices across the Empire, produced similar innovations for their widespread colonies. These efforts were derailed by the demands of World War II, but in its aftermath they became an important example of the twentieth-century trend toward innovation in response to disasters in land management practices.

WORLD WAR II

From a global perspective, the Second World War was an even more widespread ecological holocaust than the first. Theaters of war were far more widespread than before, this time spreading throughout the Pacific and Southeast Asia, as well as desert regions in North Africa. Greatly accelerated firepower made war's destructive power far more devastating than before. The air war over Europe and the Pacific was a source of destruction beyond the battlefield in comparison with the more limited use of air power between 1914 and 1918. English cities were crippled by German bombers in the Blitz of 1941–42, and in response, the British and American air forces used "conventional" firebombing to burn over one hundred German cities into ashes by 1945. On the other side of the world, as the war turned to the western Allies' favor, American planes bombed Japanese cities (built far more with wood than the stone and steel cities of Europe). By the summer of 1945, with Nazi Germany destroyed, the Allies moved to complete the submission of the Japanese. In perhaps the most momentous and controversial military action in human history, two planes ordered by President Truman dropped the first nuclear bombs, obliterating the cities of Hiroshima and Nagasaki. Stalin and his military planners were acutely aware of the explosive power unleashed by the bombings—they were Washington's other audience—and the Japanese emperor ended the struggle almost immediately on August 15.

By that time, the war had killed at least 60 million people throughout Europe, Asia, and the Pacific, some 25 million in Russia and China alone. Many additional millions were refugees, homeless and in flight. Refugee movements have always been a consequence of wars, but in the total wars of the twentieth century, refugee masses were far greater than ever before. Their impact on land and natural resources is just beginning to be studied by environmental historians. One of the largest refugee movements was in China, which suffered the war for nine years, starting with the Japanese invasion in 1937—the largest chapter in an era of turmoil and chaos that engulfed China from the collapse of the Confucian imperial dynasty in 1911 until Mao Tse-tung consolidated national control in 1949. In 1939, as the Japanese army advanced into the Yellow River basin, the Nationalist army retreated westward. Its command decided to slow the Japanese advance by destroying the ancient and intricate system of dikes that left the silt-laden river confined at a level high above the surrounding countryside. As a result, vast regions of farmland lay under water for many months, in some cases, years. Some twenty million Chinese peasants—at least those who survived drowning, raced many miles to higher ground, and spent the rest of the war in a desperate effort to avoid starvation. Their struggles for survival accelerated a centuries-long process of denuding hills and watching thin hill soils wash away.

Less tragically dramatic, World War II also saw massive worldwide mobilization of resources to meet military needs. The wide range of interwar advances in mining and harvesting, transport and marketing made possible a more nearly worldwide extraction of war materials than in the 1914–18 war. Three examples suffice to suggest the scale of operations. One of them involved forest products. German foresters were ready to harvest timber in Czechoslovakia and elsewhere in newly conquered Eastern Europe, knowing that German supplies of timber had been severely depleted in the previous war. In turn, the Soviet regime was more prepared to exploit its vast forest belt than before, since new interwar railways had made distant eastern forests more accessible. After the war, the Soviets were in a position to extend industrialization into the Eurasian boreal zone for the first time, an important shift in the overall pattern of global ecological change.

The petrochemical industries of the combatant powers developed substitutes for scarce materials. Most dramatically, the U.S. outpaced its German rival in creating high-quality synthetic rubber from crude oil. At the start of the war in the Pacific, Japan had cut off the vital supply of natural rubber from the Western Allies; without synthetic rubber the Western coalition's war machine would have been crippled. The new product filled the gap, and its success meant that in the postwar era, roughly half of the world's steadily growing demand for rubber products would be met from petroleum, and that the acreage of tropical soils devoted to rubber trees would stabilize rather than inexorably expanding.

Industrial energy supplies were also severely stressed by war's demands. But the United States in particular was able to utilize hydropower for concentrated wartime production. The pioneering regional hydropower system created by the TVA, or the Tennessee Valley Authority, had been a centerpiece of the New Deal responses to the Great Depression. Its power plants were essential for meeting the war's emergency production quotas. And in the northwest on the Columbia River, the new Grand Coulee hydro-complex assured adequate power for processing aluminum for the airplane industry.

In the aftermath of the war, just as after 1918, the world faced a Herculean task of reconstructing the cities, industries, and transport systems that had been destroyed—this time in Asia as well as Europe. Thus, there was no immediate postwar depression after 1945, for, particularly in the United States, mines and factories continued to run, and forests of all continents were logged for reconstruction timber. Finally, the great backlog of consumer demand for peacetime products assured that the factories that remained would be retrofitted from military production to civilian products or new ones built to meet the growing demand. Postwar baby booms, or upward spikes in fertility rates, have been commonplace in history. But in the late 1940s, international birth rates accelerated at the fastest pace ever, and stimulated a revival of the old Malthusian debate over rising population and the limits of resources.

THE POST-WAR BOOM

In the postwar years, the United States—its industry and population for the second time far less damaged than its European and Japanese competitors—led the world into high per capita resource consumption. This was the era of full mass consumerism. Millions of new homes were built with lumber harvested from both American and Canadian forests. New suburbs sprawled around cities, created at the expense of farm and woodland. The automotive industry boomed, providing family cars for a far wider portion of the society than in the 1920s. Supermarkets and shopping malls grew up on the periphery of older cities, providing standardized, energy-intensive fast food, wrapped in paper and plastic for the throwaway generation. Agribusiness prospered, as corporate farms swallowed up local small-scale farms to provide fruit and vegetables to consumers throughout the year. Transport costs were heavily subsidized by government-funded highway building, culminating in the Interstate Highway system of the 1950s and 1960s. The trucking industry, supplemented by commercial jet planes in the 1960s, supplied fruit and vegetables from California's central valley or subtropical Florida to consumers around the country every month of the year. National boundaries were minor hindrances to the spread of this economy. By the 1960s, the agribusiness economy spread into northern Mexico and the Caribbean, then Chile and elsewhere in the southern hemisphere, where toxic strawberries could be grown for American markets in January.

For supermarket customers, time and space were effectively abolished. But independent farmers, with their tradition of multi-cropping, were marginalized. Agribusiness giants (heavily subsidized by government crop support payments) specialized in large-scale production of single crops, defended against pests by heavy applications of chemical fertilizers and pesticides. This new lifestyle, with its multi-faceted stresses on the environment, required ever-increasing stocks of petroleum. The United States continued to tap reserves in Mexico and Venezuela. But now American firms moved into the Middle East, where giant American oil companies accelerated their competition for economic and political leverage against their competitors in western Europe.

Two other energy sources also assumed far greater importance in the postwar world. One was hydropower. Around the world in the decades after 1945, hundreds of rivers were tamed by high dams, many of them built on the high-prestige models of Hoover Dam on the Colorado River and the regional power grid of [the] TVA. American engineers and construction firms worked with the governments of dozens of countries to build showpiece projects. The newly established United Nations funneled both Americans and their European counterparts into these resource-intensive projects through the U.N. Development Program. In a parallel development, Soviet engineers planned hydroprojects for virtually every river in Eastern Europe and Siberia, building many of them for military needs as much as for consumer products.

Nuclear power also came into its own after 1945, as several designs for nuclear plants were devised. The environmental stakes in this industry were high, not only because fission technology could produce plutonium for bombs as well as power for industry, but also because the spent fuel has a half life of 10,000 years or more. No other example of industrial pollution can begin to match this challenge, which remains totally unresolved. Moreover, opponents of nuclear power questioned the safety of the plants, and were validated when the American plant at Three Mile Island released dangerous amounts of radio-activity. Then in 1984 came the meltdown of the Soviet reactors at Chernobyl, poisoning entire regions downwind.

Less apocalyptic elements of the world's accelerating consumer economy bound the temperate and tropical zones together, as technical advances made possible the extraction of a steadily increasing range of natural resources. One, with fateful consequences for the world's forests, was paper products. Rough brown kraft paper and cardboard production had expanded rapidly in the 1920s for the growing consumer economy, but until the 1960s most of the wood pulp for paper mills had been extracted from northern conifer forests. Thereafter, new techniques brought new tree species into play, beginning one of the most fateful aspects of global resource extraction since 1945. Eucalyptus and tropical pines came into widespread use. Both could be grown in large single-species plantations, and heavy construction equipment assisted in clearing multi-species forest ecosystems, to be replaced by single-species tree plantations.

The rebirth of Japan's industrial economy after the 1950s marked the entrance of a major player into the game of tropical deforestation, as its booming prosperity demanded constantly more raw material from beyond its borders. Carefully replanting its own extensive forest resources, which had been badly damaged in the war, Japan reached across the Pacific to Southeast Asia and then Latin America, as well as the conifer forests of northwestern North America for timber and wood pulp. A timber products subsidiary of the Mitsubishi industrial empire led the way into Southeast Asia. Western Europe's economic revival, strengthened by increasing regional integration under the Common Market, played a somewhat similar role in developing export production in source areas of the old colonial empires. Rising consumer demand for tropical products in Europe led to expanding imports from Africa and Latin America. In sum, for forest and agricultural products, industrial minerals and petroleum, the race to exploit resources in formerly colonized areas steadily intensified, as Japan and finally in the 1990s China joined the competition to establish neo-colonies.

A major side effect of the accelerating contrast between Northern industrial economies and Southern dependent economies was that the North became increasingly adept at exporting industrial pollutants to Third World countries, often with the consent of local governments. Industrial wastes were shipped to West African countries for dumping, with payments to local elites and often without public disclosure of their toxic contents. And heavily polluting, processing industries, such as new plants for manufacturing tropical paper pulp, were no longer located in industrialized societies but in Indonesia, Brazil, and other rain forest locations. Heavy downriver toxicity was effectively exported to local communities in tropical countries.

TROPICAL AND SUB-TROPICAL REGIONS OF THE POST-COLONIAL WORLD

The politics of environment were transformed in most of Asia, Africa, and Latin America in the era after 1945. Throughout the tropical and subtropical world, most countries' new political leaders and their economic advisors were committed to rapid economic growth, usually emphasizing industrialization. Accelerating problems of environmental damage were hardly on the horizon of public discussion in most societies worldwide until the late 1960s. Under authoritarian regimes, including those that dominated many post-colonial countries, these issues were suppressed and public protest about environmental damage was rarely tolerated.

Underlying all other trends in the post-colonial world after 1945 were rates of population growth which were far higher in Asia, Africa, and Latin America than in the long-industrialized countries (though wide regional differences among these countries were emerging). The population of Asia, which had been 903 million in 1900, rose to 1.376 billion by 1950 and 3.611 billion in 2000. The population of Africa, which had stood at only138 million in 1900, rose to 224 million by 1950, and by 2000 accelerated almost exponentially to 784 million, with the highest sustained fertility rates of any continent. Latin America's population, at 70 million in 1900, rose to 166 million in 1950, and 448 million by century's end.

These trends were in large part the result of major breakthroughs in medicine and public health programs. A wide range of new chemicals and drugs came into use, most dramatically DDT, which promised to eliminate the scourge of malaria from the tropical world. In one of the United Nations' most dramatic early accomplishments, the World Health Organization, in conjunction with national agencies, sprayed DDT over vast mosquito breeding grounds in the 1950s. This and other campaigns lowered death and morbidity rates in tropical countries, thus for decades thereafter in most developing nations birth rates and population increase remained at high pre-industrial levels. It proved far more difficult to reduce birth rates and move toward control of the population explosion than eradicate endemic diseases or alleviate infant mortality. The 1960s saw dramatic warnings that global population would outstrip the resources needed to sustain it. Paul Ehrlich's book, *The Population Bomb*, led the way in creating a dark new Malthusian vision of the future, accurately predicting that the world's population would exceed six billion by century's end. The population debate thus provided important underpinnings for the emerging environmental movement, though as yet it did not come to grips with the converse issue, over-consumption in affluent societies.

Postwar demographic pressures in the developing world created megacities like Mexico City, Cairo, and dozens of others that outstripped London and New York in size. Unlike what were formerly the world's largest cities, these new urban conurbations had far less adequate resources to cope with the huge influx of poor people from the countryside. The turbulence of vast urban slums meant danger to political elites, and mounting pressure to increase agricultural productivity. Until at least mid-century, expanding food production had continued to be primarily extensive: expanding arable at the expense of grasslands, wetlands, and forests. By the 1960s, croplands were encroaching on many marginal lands, areas with low fertility or inadequate water, or acreage on slopes with thin, easily eroded soils.

Against this background, a quarter century of intensified agricultural research bore fruit in the Green Revolution. The core research behind this breakthrough led to the creation of hybridized food stocks, especially grains, especially such global staples as wheat, maize (corn), and rice, which produced far greater crop yields in shorter growing cycles than their predecessors. The new wheat varieties, developed in Mexico, produced breakthrough harvests in the rich soils and irrigated lands of Punjab in northwestern India from 1967 onward. India had faced near-famine in the early 1960s, and remained viable only with the import of tens of millions of tons of surplus wheat production from the grain belt of the United States. From the late 1960s, India produced minimally adequate wheat for its own markets, and even began exporting it to the Middle East. But there was a high environmental price to pay for this and similar "miracle" harvests of maize and rice in India and elsewhere in the developing world. The new seeds demanded far higher applications of both agro-chemicals and water. Hence the environmental costs of food production underwent a major shift, from the earlier pattern of loss of non-arable land, to the rapid reduction of water resources and sharp increases in polluting chemical runoffs into groundwater and rivers. And these processes were occurring at a time when fresh water resources were dwindling over much of the globe, especially in areas where water was pumped by a new generation of tube wells from underground aquifers, such as in the western United States, India, and parts of Africa.

By late in the twentieth century, the world's oceans also faced ominous pressures. Oceans are probably the most complex, and certainly the least known, of the planet's ecosystems. And they are a global commons, with no state administration to monitor resources, establish or enforce limits to the catch beyond the limited and internationally recognized coastal waters of each nation.

From the 1950s, mechanized trawlers and seagoing processing plants put accelerating pressures on deep-water fishing stocks. North Atlantic cod fisheries, which had provided a major source of protein for the entire periphery of that ocean for centuries were virtually fished out by the 1980s. Even with severe international restrictions on the annual catch and the industry partially dismantled, stocks of cod are not expected to revive soon. Elsewhere throughout the world's oceans, similar patterns of highly capitalized, ocean-going fleets from industrialized countries such as Japan and Russia marginalized local coastal-zone fishing communities by the 1980s, and tenaciously resisted regulation of the catch. As a result, by the end of the century, stocks of most commercial species were in steep decline, as entire pelagic (deep ocean) food chains were compromised. And there was no end in sight, except that each species whose numbers crash means the collapse of a portion of the fishing industry. In this case, market forces began to suggest that a remnant of a severely depleted species (and along with it, its ecologically related species) might survive, to rebuild slowly—if further disruption of its habitat, including marine pollution, was not so fatally intensive.

THE COLD WAR: MILITARIZATION
AND SURROGATE WARS

Lurking behind all these trends in the post–World War II global economy was the Cold War that polarized the politics and economies of much of the world from 1948 until 1990. Most of what has been written about the Cold War centers on geopolitics of the two blocs, and arms race of the two camps' military machines. But the Cold War had massive environmental implications, as well.

In the aftermath of the Russian Revolution, private property was eliminated from the Russian economy and the administrative apparatus of the state assumed vast power over the priorities of economic development. Industrialization took pride of place, partly for the prestige of out-pacing the industrialized West, and partly to support the Red Army in the face of painfully experienced and imagined threats, such as a resurgent Germany. The forced collectivization of the Russian farm economy in the early 1930s produced massive food shortages, but as yet only limited damage to the land's fertility and the viability of water regimes. Then the staggering losses of Russian people and infrastructure in the first years of World War II reinforced the Soviet planners' conviction that massive industrialization was essential. War's end brought all of eastern Europe under Soviet control, and by the late 1940s, the wide agricultural zones of central Asia were consolidated into the Soviet system as well. From then on, the urban and industrial economy took primacy, and much of the industrialization that occurred was linked to military production.

There was virtually no concern for the buildup of pollution in the air (including the atmosphere), the soil, or the groundwater. Unlike the more open societies of the West, where citizens and a much more independent press could openly expose and protest the effects of pollution, there was little possibility of grassroots dissent in Soviet countries until well into the 1980s.

In general, Soviet industrial technology was even more polluting than its Western counterparts, as its drive to expand energy supplies indicated. Following Marxism's consistent emphasis that human striving, if properly harnessed, could bend Nature to its will, Soviet economic ideology disregarded natural systems even more blatantly than the ideology of free market capitalism. Khrushchev's great drive into central Asia in the 1960s, which was intended to feed the Soviet industrial labor force, became notorious for its disruption of natural systems. Vast irrigation systems on the rivers draining into the Aral Sea led to the classic problems of waterlogging and salinization of the farmland, and deprived the Aral Sea of its inflow, which in turn resulted in the severe shrinkage of that once impressive body of fresh water. By the 1990s, when international access to information about the Soviet bloc became more fully public, this was recognized as one of the greatest ecological follies of human history.

The opposite side of the Cold War divide fared only somewhat better. In central Europe along the Iron Curtain, Warsaw Pact and NATO armies conducted elaborate exercises virtually within sight of each other. For forty years, tanks and armored convoys rumbled through village streets and across former farmlands, their formalized ballets degrading valuable crop producing areas. Across the Atlantic, the vaunted military-industrial complex of the hegemon of the NATO alliance created its own range of environmental stress. By the 1950s, the United States had a global web of hundreds of military installations, each of which placed demands on the environment of the locales in which they were established. To support this, the greatest military establishment in history, large segments of American industry were committed to military production, often with a degree of invisibility to the public that masked severe pollution and radioactive waste.

In locations close to inexpensive power, such as the power plants at Niagara Falls, the concentrated chemical industry was so careless in storing its toxic wastes that the ground water of the entire region was polluted so severely that many local people were felled by various types of cancer. More severe was regional pollution of soil and ground water around major nuclear processing sites, especially where military secrecy prevented public knowledge of troubles for many years. The Rocky Flats arsenal just outside Denver and the spent nuclear fuels at the Hanford installation in Washington State became notorious by the 1970s for vast accumulations of radioactive waste, much of it accumulated in the 1950s. That decade was the worst for nuclear pollution, including both the ground and air where the nuclear powers pursued a race for weapons superiority at Soviet testing grounds in central Asia, British test sites in the Australian desert, and American sites in Nevada. In remote Pacific islands, the British briefly, the Americans aggressively, and the French persistently (until the 1980s) carried out nuclear tests that destroyed coral reefs and their nearby marine ecosystems, infected local communities of humans and other land species with radiation, and sent clouds of fallout drifting across the Pacific.

The Cold War was also hot in some places, especially mainland Southeast Asia, where Washington, Moscow, and Beijing confronted each other in the second Indochina War and other less persisting clashes. A major rationale for American involvement in Indochina under both Presidents Kennedy and Johnson was the determination not to be deprived of access to Southeast Asia's rich resources, as the United States had been by Japan in early 1942. But conventional U.S. forces had severe difficulty coping with insurgency by National Liberation forces operating on their own social and natural terrain, so the Americans quickly turned to the time-tested U.S. strategy of deploying overwhelming technological force. With technocratic hubris, which had characterized Western armies in the Third World for a over a century by then, the White House was sure that saturation bombing by "conventional" weapons and B-52 bombers could bring North Vietnam to its knees, particularly backed by the threat of destroying the dikes that kept the Red River from flooding the rice-rich plains of Vietnam's heartlands. Vast areas of rural Vietnam, and later Laos and Cambodia as well, were pocked by bomb craters, which disrupted food production and provided breeding grounds for malarial mosquitos. Persistent work by local farmers has gradually brought some semblance of order back into these disrupted lands, since the end of the American occupation and victory of the communists in 1972 and 1975, respectively.

When this devastation was not enough to bring the communists to terms, the U.S. Air Force augmented its firepower with massive deployment of chemical defoliants, designed to deprive the National Liberation Front of the vegetative cover in the hill forests of western Vietnam and the Mekong Delta, which proved the most effective zones for their conduct of guerrilla resistance. American chemical giants, led by Dow Chemical, harnessed their production of agricultural pesticides to this effort. This marked the first major use of chemical warfare since World War I, triggering widespread international condemnation of the American military for violating treaties on the conduct of warfare. The long-term ecological disruption to the defoliated forests was unpredictable at the time, since this had been an unprecedented campaign. Indications in recent years are that the forest has revived in many places more vigorously than some had feared. But the public health disruption, in the form of many forms of cancer and severe birth defects for afflicting subsequent generations, is a well documented chapter in human ecology.

In other parts of the world, what have been labeled "resource wars" became a new chapter in ongoing colonial rivalries over access to strategic resources. In Central America, following Fidel Castro's success in eliminating American neo-colonial hegemony in Cuba and allying with Moscow, leftist popular movements began to erode American-allied authoritarian regimes in Guatemala, Nicaragua, and elsewhere. The environmental impact of the local wars that resulted was often paradoxical. In the lowland forests along the Caribbean littoral and especially in the border region of Nicaragua and Costa Rica, the threat to local Miskito Indians by the Contra forces prevented them from carrying on their traditional subsistence hunting for several years. Wildlife populations rebounded, as they often do when the human presence is brutally diminished.

Newly independent countries in Africa experienced a number of resource wars in the Cold War decades that were usually linked to interventions on the part of the leading Cold War adversaries. In Liberia, opposing factions in a brutal civil war used profits from illegal hardwood timber to help finance their military operation, but were careful to avoid the Firestone rubber plantations until the mid-1990s. Each faction hoped to capture the profits from rubber sales, but ultimately chaos and destruction prevailed on the plantations. In Sierra Leone, the illegal export of diamonds as well as timber sales enabled civil war rivals to maintain brutal and endemic violence. In eastern Africa, the genocidal wars in Rwanda and the rain forest of eastern Congo, with their attendant chaotic refugee movements, resulted in widespread damage to forests and wildlife. In drier ecosystems farther north, especially Darfur, the environmental cost of persistent inter-ethnic war has still to be assessed.

Wars and heavy militarization in the Middle East since 1948 had far greater consequences for the strategic balance between East and West, but not all of the conflicts in the region were surrogate confrontations linked to the Great Powers' access to petroleum. Some conflicts have been primarily over water rights, a quintessential source of hostilities over a vital and increasingly scarce resource. Though no overt warfare has recently broken out between upriver and downriver countries on the Euphrates and Jordan rivers, that threat remains ever-present. Other Middle East conflicts clearly involved foreign access to the region's vast petroleum reserves. Underlying the Gulf War was American intervention to turn back Saddam Hussein's occupation of Kuwait, which threatened American access to that tiny nation's substantial petroleum reserves. The role of that strategic interest was certainly one major factor, but the question of the war's ecological impact is a different and more empirical one. Conclusions have to be tentative, since there is still only incomplete data about wartime damage to the fragile ecosystems of the desert and the Persian Gulf waters and coastal zones. As for the massive fires set in the oil fields by the Iraqi Army as it retreated northward, there was ultimately far less regional atmospheric pollution from the vast plume of smoke than observers initially predicted.

In the aftermath of the First U.S.-Iraq War, Saddam's assault on the southern marshes along the Tigris-Euphrates watershed and its Shia population led to the draining [of] three quarters of one of the greatest wetlands in that part of the world, a major resting place on the annual migration routes of millions of Eurasian birds. Since Saddam's fall in 2002, there has been some limited reconstitution of the marshes. Similarly, surrounding the Second U.S.- Iraq War, which was precipitated by an American-British invasion in 2002, was the controversy over whether control of Iraq's massive oil reserves was the dominant strategic concern. Until now, the more important question for environmental history concerns the damage the war has caused, and that remains little explored at this point, due to the ongoing warfare waged for the last half-decade.

In sum, the Cold War and its vast proliferation of armaments in virtually every country left a daunting long-term legacy of ecological damage and distorted resource use. But, at least formally, the Cold War ended in the early 1990s. By century's end, the central question had become whether the overlay of ecological stress from global militarization during the Cold War decades, on top of broader trends of rising population (that had begun to slow) and rising consumption patterns (that showed no signs of abating) made possible any movement toward an ecologically sustainable biosphere. Perhaps only a major international economic slowdown (such as that which began in late 2008), followed by a restructuring of societies along the lines of cleaner energy systems and more efficient, less polluting, and more modest production of consumer goods and military hardware, could begin to slow the movement toward catastrophic climate change.

TOWARD SUSTAINABILITY?

An important counter-current in the environmental history of the twentieth century world emerged in the 1960s: a wide and increasingly sophisticated spectrum of efforts to manage global resources on a more sustainable, hence enduring basis. Only in the late-1980s did widespread public and political recognition of the danger of global warming become prominent. But warnings of severe environmental stress date back at least to the 1920s, when fears of "timber famine" and possibly irreversible soil erosion circulated. Parallel concerns over urban and industrial pollution, which led to and were in turn heightened by Rachel Carson's highly influential 1962 book *Silent Spring* created widespread public concern over the effects of a new generation of chemicals.

By the late 1960s, these concerns began to coalesce with international alarm over the trend in global population. The debate over whether sheer numbers of people or high consumption levels was the greater threat to the biosphere was about to emerge. In the same years, international institutions for monitoring and managing natural resources were strengthened. The United Nations sponsored its first global environment conference in Stockholm in 1972, which led to establishing the United Nations Environmental Program to coordinate the environmentally important aspects of the work of other agencies, such as the United Nations Development Program. Parallel to the United Nations' initiatives was the work of private foundations and inter- and non-governmental organizations. In the area of global forest management, for example, the forestry branch of the UN Food and Agriculture Organization developed links with the far older organizations of professional foresters, IUFRO, the International Union of Forest Research Organizations, and its offshoot, the Society of Tropical Foresters.

Somewhat parallel to the forestry organizations, efforts to preserve wildlife around the world had begun at the dawn of the century, through the international movement to create national parks and wildlife protected areas. Wildlife protection was centered on an international organization of wildlife biologists and parks managers, the International Union for Conservation of Nature (IUCN), which was set up in its mature form in 1948 in close collaboration with the fledgling United Nations. Soon thereafter the World Wildlife Fund was organized to raise funds and publicize global wildlife challenges for the wider public. Until the late 1970s, the broader movement of non-governmental organizations that worked for similar goals was largely found in Europe and North America. After that, a wide variety of local and national environmental organizations proliferated rapidly, led by India, which has remained an international leader in citizen activism and non-governmental research. One of New Delhi's outstanding new organizations was the Centre for Science and Environment, which published detailed annual surveys of the state of India's environment, a model for other countries to follow.

Globally by the 1990s, this movement came to be understood in terms of the rubric of biodiversity and the precipitous loss of species of flora and fauna that has been a fundamental feature of ecological decline in modern times. The scientific core of this movement emerged as the field of conservation biology, which has given greater rigor to international efforts to restore damaged natural systems. All these strands came together in 1992, when the United Nations as well as hundreds of non-governmental groups from many countries marked the twentieth anniversary of the Stockholm conference by converging on Rio de Janeiro for an "Earth Summit." Intensive discussions produced major advances toward defining an international agenda, but with little in the way of enforcement. Not surprisingly, the actual results over the following decade were disappointing.

By the end of the century, many national governments had developed complex environmental laws and agencies, but many of the latter continued to have weak enforcement powers and political support. Two important developing nations, India and Brazil, could show some progress in managing land and water resources more efficiently. But many smaller countries had made little or no headway on these vital issues. International environmental agreements also held significant hope of making a difference, particularly in relation to the rising threat of global warming and atmospheric change. The Montreal Protocol of 1987, which established international standards for reducing the impact of industrial compounds on the ozone layer of the upper atmosphere, was implemented to an impressive extent by industrial countries in the 1990s. More important still was the effort to begin reducing greenhouse gases in both industrial and industrializing countries, which led to the Kyoto Accord of 1997. As a new millennium began, implementation of the Kyoto standards was spotty at best, as support for the accord was severely undermined by the strong opposition of the Bush administration in the United States.

For Americans in particular, and the world in general, fundamental questions concerning how to place limits on consumption and on the generation of toxic wastes remained unanswered as a new century began. But an important debate was gaining momentum around the world among environmental experts, development specialists, policy planners, and even the general public around the issues of over-consumption, whose meaning nonetheless remains highly contentious and poorly defined. The twin forces of overpopulation and over-consumption continue to resist adequate understanding and effective management.

SELECT BIBLIOGRAPHY

Long Historical Perspectives

Burke, Edmund, III, and Kenneth Pomeranz, eds. *The Environment and World History.* Berkeley: University of California Press, 2009.

Christian, David. *Maps of Time: An Introduction to Big History.* Berkeley: University of California Press, 2004.

Crosby, Alfred W. *The Columbian Exchange: Biological and Cultural Consequences of 1492.* Westport, CT: Greenwood Press, 1972.

———. *Ecological Imperialism: The Biological Expansion of Europe, 900–1900.* Cambridge: Cambridge University Press, 1986.

———. *Children of the Sun: A History of Humanity's Unappeasable Appetite for Energy.* New York: Norton, 2006.

Hughes, J. Donald. *An Environmental History of the World: Humankind's Changing Role in the Community of Life.* London: Routledge, 2001.

LaFreniere, Gilbert F. *The Decline of Nature: Environmental History and the Western World-view.* Bethesda, MD: Academica Press, 2007.

Marks, Robert B. *The Origins of the Modern World: A Global and Ecological Narrative.* Lanham, MD: Rowman and Littlefield, 2002.

Radkau, Joachim. *Nature and Power: A Global History of the Environment.* Cambridge: Cambridge University Press, 2008.

Richards, John F. *The Unending Frontier: An Environmental History of the Early Modern World.* Berkeley: University of California Press, 2003.

Simmons, I. G. *Environmental History: A Concise Introduction.* Oxford: Blackwell, 1993.

———. *Global Environmental History.* Chicago: University of Chicago Press, 2008.

Smil, Vaclav. *Energy in World History.* Boulder, CO: Westview, 1994.

Williams, Michael. *Americans and Their Forests: An Historical Geography.* Cambridge: Cambridge University Press, 1989.

———. *Deforesting the Earth: From Prehistory to Global Crisis.* Chicago: University of Chicago Press, 2003.

Regional Environmental Histories
[Each has a major portion on the twentieth century.]

Boomgaard, Peter. *Southeast Asia: An Environmental History*. Santa Barbara, CA: ABC-CLIO, 2007.

D'Arcy, Paul. *The People of the Sea: Environment, Identity and History in Oceania*. Honolulu: University of Hawaii Press, 2006.

Dovers, Stephen, Ruth Edgecombe, and Bill Guest. *South Africa's Environmental History*. Athens: Ohio University Press, 2003.

Elvin, Mark. *The Retreat of the Elephants: An Environmental History of China*. New Haven, CT: Yale University Press, 2004.

Gallini, Stefania, Stuart McCook, and Lise Sedrez. *Latin America and the Caribbean: An Environmental History*. Santa Barbara, CA: ABC-CLIO, forthcoming.

Garden, Donald S. *Australia, New Zealand, and the Pacific: An Environmental History*. Santa Barbara, CA: ABC-CLIO, 2005.

Hill, Christopher. *South Asia: An Environmental History*. Santa Barbara, CA: ABC-CLIO, 2008.

Hughes, J. Donald. *The Mediterranean: An Environmental History*. Santa Barbara, CA: ABC-CLIO, 2005.

Issar, Arie H., and Mattanyah Zohar. *Climate Change: Environment and History in the Near East*. New York: Springer, 2007.

Maddox, Gregory H. *Sub-Saharan Africa: An Environmental History*. Santa Barbara, CA: ABC-CLIO, 2006.

McCann, James. *Green Land, Brown Land, Black Land: An Environmental History of Africa, 1800–1990*. Portsmouth, NH: Heinemann, 1999.

Miller, Shawn William. *An Environmental History of Latin America*. Cambridge: Cambridge University Press, 2007.

Sowards, Adam M. *The United States West Coast: An Environmental History*. Santa Barbara, CA: ABC-CLIO, 2007.

Whited, Tamara L., et al. *Northern Europe: An Environmental History*. Santa Barbara, CA: ABC-CLIO, 2005.

Wynn, Graeme. *Canada and Arctic North America: An Environmental History*. Santa Barbara, CA: ABC-CLIO, 2006.

The Twentieth Century World

Adas, Michael. *Machines as the Measure of* Men. Ithaca, NY: Cornell University Press, 1989.
———. *Dominance by Design*. Cambridge, MA: Harvard University Press, 2006.

Beinart, William, and Lotte Hughes. *Environment and Empire*. Oxford: Oxford University Press, 2007.

Berry, Brian. *Comparative Urbanization: Divergent Paths in the Twentieth Century*. 2nd ed. New York: St. Martin's Press, 1981.

Closmann, Charles E., ed. *War and the Environment: Military Destruction in the Modern Age*. College Station: Texas A&M University Press, forthcoming.

Eckes, Alfred E., Jr. *The United States and the Global Struggle for Minerals*. Austin: University of Texas Press, 1979.

Glantz, Michael H., ed. *Climate Variability, Climate Change, and Fisheries*. Cambridge: Cambridge University Press, 2005.

Gleick, Peter H., ed. *Water in Crisis*. Oxford: Oxford University Press, 1993.
———. *The World's Water, 1998–99*. Washington, DC: Island Press, 1999.

Gorman, Martha. *Environmental Hazards: Marine Pollution*. Santa Barbara, CA: ABC-CLIO, 1993.

Gugler, Josef, ed. *World Cities beyond the West*. Cambridge: Cambridge University Press, 2004.

Heywood, V. H., and R. T. Watson, eds. *Global Biodiversity Assessment*. Cambridge: Cambridge University Press, 1995, chap. 11.

Holdgate, Martin. *The Green Web: A Union for World Conservation*. London: Earthscan, 1999.

Jackson, Kenneth. *Crabgrass Frontier: The Suburbanization of the United States*. New York: Oxford University Press, 1985.

Jacques, Peter. *Globalization and the World Ocean*. Lanham, MD: AltaMira, 2006.

Josephson, Paul R. *Industrialized Nature: Brute Force Technology and the Transformation of the Natural World*. Washington, DC: Island Press, 2002.

Kaufman, Les, and Kenneth Mallory, eds. *The Last Extinction*. Cambridge, MA: MIT Press, 1993.

Markham, Adam. *A Brief History of Pollution*. London: Zed Books, 1994.

McCully, Patrick. *Silenced Rivers: The Ecology and Politics of Large Dams*. 2nd ed. London: Zed Books, 2001.

McNeill, J. R., *Something New under the Sun*. New York: Norton, 2000.

McNeill, J. R., and Corinna Unger, eds. *Environmental History and the Cold War*. Cambridge: Cambridge University Press, forthcoming.

McNeill, J. R., and Verena Winiwarter, eds. *Soils and Societies*. Isle of Harris, UK: Whitehorse Press, 2006.

Melosi, Martin. *Effluent America: Cities, Industry, Energy and the Environment*. Pittsburg, PA: University of Pittsburg Press, 2001.

Meyer, William. *Human Impact on the Earth*. Cambridge: Cambridge University Press, 1996.

Myers, Norman. "Population, Environment, and Development," *Environmental Conservation* 20 (1993): 205–216.

Petulla, Joseph. *American Environmental History*. 2nd ed. Columbus, OH: Merrill, 1988.

Pimentel, David, ed. *World Soil Erosion and Conservation*. Cambridge: Cambridge University Press, 1993.

Postel, Sandra. *Last Oasis: Facing Water Scarcity*. New York: Norton, 1997.

Princen, Thomas, Michael Maniates, and Ken Conca. *Confronting Consumption*. Cambridge, MA: MIT Press, 2002.

Roberts, Callum. *The Unnatural History of the Sea*. Washington, DC: Island Press/Shearwater Books, 2007.

Rudel, Thomas K. *Tropical Forests: Regional Paths of Destruction and Regeneration in the Late Twentieth Century*. New York: Columbia University Press, 2005.

Solbrig, Otto T., and Dorothy J. Solbrig. *So Shall You Reap: Farming and Crops in Human Affairs*. Washington, DC: Island Press/Shearwater Books, 1994.

Soluri, John. *Banana Cultures: Agriculture, Consumption, and Environmental Change in Honduras and the United States*. Austin: University of Texas Press, 2005.

Soule, Michael E., ed. *Conservation Biology: The Science of Scarcity and Diversity*. Sunderland, MA: Sinauer, 1986.

Steinberg, Ted. *Down to Earth: Nature's Role in American History*. Oxford: Oxford University Press, 2002.

Strasser, Susan, et al., eds. *Getting and Spending: American and European Consumer Societies in the Twentieth Century*. Cambridge: Cambridge University Press, 1998.

Tarr, Joel. *The Search for the Ultimate Sink: Urban Pollution in Historical Perspective*. Akron, OH: University of Akron Press, 1996.

Tucker, Richard P. *Insatiable Appetite: The United States and the Ecological Degradation of the Tropical World*. Berkeley: University of California Press, 2000; rev. ed., Lanham, MD: Rowman and Littlefield, 2007.

Turner, B. L., II, et al., eds. *The Earth as Transformed by Human Action: Global and Regional Changes in the Biosphere over the Past 300 Years*. Cambridge: Cambridge University Press, 1990.

Van Driesche, Jason, and Roy Van Driesche, *Nature Out of Place: Biological Invasions in the Global Age*. Washington, DC: Island Press, 2000.

Vitousek, Peter, et al. "Biological Invasions as Global Environmental Change," *American Scientist* 84 (1996), 468–478.

Webb, James L.A., Jr. *Humanity's Burden: A Global History of Malaria.* Cambridge: Cambridge University Press, 2009.

Williams, Michael, ed. *Wetlands: A Threatened Landscape.* Oxford: Blackwell, 1990.

Wilson, Edward O. *The Diversity of Life.* Cambridge, MA: Harvard University Press, 1992.

Yergin, Daniel. *The Prize: The Epic Quest for Oil, Money and Power.* New York: Touchstone, 1991.

ABOUT THE CONTRIBUTORS

Michael Adas is the Abraham E. Voorhees professor at Rutgers University. His books include *Machines as the Measure of Men: Science, Technology, and Ideologies of Western Dominance* (1989, 1991–1993), which won the Dexter Prize, and more recently *Dominance by Design: Technology, Social Engineering and America's Civilizing Mission* (2005, 2009). With Peter Stearns and Stuart Schwartz, Adas has also written several college and Advanced Placement editions of *World Civilizations: The Global Experience and Turbulent Passage: A Global History of the Twentieth Century*.

Paul N. Edwards is associate professor in the School of Information at the University of Michigan and founder of the University of Michigan Science, Technology and Society Program. He is the author of *The Closed World: Computers and the Politics of Discourse in Cold War America* (1996) and more recently coedited a volume on *Changing the Atmosphere: Expert Knowledge and Environmental Governance* (2001).

Carl J. Guarneri is professor of history at Saint Mary's College of California, where he teaches American and world history. His publications include *The Utopian Alternative: Fourierism in Nineteenth-Century America* (1991), *America in the World: United States History in Global Context* (2007), and (with coeditor James Davis) *Teaching American History in a Global Context* (2008).

Gabrielle Hecht is associate professor of history at the University of Michigan. Her first book, *The Radiance of France: Nuclear Power and National Identity after World War II* (1998, 2009), won awards from the American Historical Association and the Society for the History of Technology. Her current book project, entitled *Uranium from Africa and the Power of Nuclear Things*, draws on archival and fieldwork conducted in Africa, Europe, and North America.

Adam McKeown is associate professor of history at Columbia University, where he teaches courses on the history of globalization, world migration, and drugs. He has published *Melancholy Order: Asian Migration and the Globalization of Borders* (2008) and is working on a history of globalization since 1760.

John H. Morrow Jr. is the Franklin professor of history at the University of Georgia. He specializes in the history of modern Europe and of warfare and society. He has written a number of books and articles on early airpower, including *The Great War* *in the Air: Military Aviation from 1909 to 1921* (1993, 2008). His most recent book is *The Great War: An Imperial History* (2004, 2005). He is presently writing a history of the Second World War.

Jose C. Moya is professor emeritus at the University of California, Los Angeles, and professor of history at Barnard College, Columbia University, where he also directs the Forum on Migration. His book *Cousins and Strangers: Spanish Immigrants in Buenos Aires, 1850–1930* (1998) received five awards, and the journal *Historical Methods* devoted a forum to its theoretical contributions to migration studies.

Jean H. Quataert is professor of history at Binghamton University, State University of New York. She has published extensively in German women's history. In the last decade, she has turned to transnational and global history, with a focus on human rights and international law. Her latest book is entitled *Advocating Dignity: Human Rights Mobilizations in Global Politics, 1945–2005* (2007).

Bonnie G. Smith is a Board of Governor's professor at Rutgers University. Her books include *Ladies of the Leisure Class* (1981) and *The Gender of History: Men, Women, and Historical Practice* (2000). Her edited works include *Global Feminisms since 1945* (2000) and, with Beth Hutchinson, *Gendering Disability* (2003). She is also a coauthor of several editions of *The Challenge of the West*.

Howard Spodek is the author of *The World's History* (2010), coeditor (with Doris Srinivasan) of *Urban Form and Meaning in South Asia* (1993), and producer and writer of the documentary film *Ahmedabad: The Life of a City in India* (1983).

Richard P. Tucker is adjunct professor of environmental history in the School of Natural Resources and Environment at the University of Michigan. His recent work includes *Insatiable Appetite: The United States and the Ecological Degradation of the Tropical World* (2000, 2007), and works on the history of the environmental impact of war and environment.